PRODUCTION AND AUTONOMY

Anthropological Studies and Critiques of Development

Monographs in Economic Anthropology, No. 5

Edited by

John W. Bennett

and

John R. Bowen

UNIVERSITY
PRESS OF
AMERICA

Lanham • New York • London

Society for
Economic
Anthropology

SEA

Copyright © 1988 by the

Society for Economic Anthropology

University Press of America,® Inc.

4720 Boston Way
Lanham, MD 20706

3 Henrietta Street
London WC2E 8LU England

Printed in the United States of America

British Cataloging in Publication Information Available

Library of Congress Cataloging-in-Publication Data

Production and autonomy : anthropological studies and critiques of
development / edited by John W. Bennett and John R. Bowen.
p. cm.—(Monographs in economic anthropology : no. 5)
Papers presented to the Fifth Annual Meeting of the Society for
Economic Anthropology, held at Airlie House, Warrenton, Va., April 11–13, 1985.
Includes bibliographies and index.
1. Economic development—Social aspects—Congresses. 2. Economic
anthropology—Congresses. I. Bennett, John William. 1915–
II. Bowen, John R. III. Society for Economic Anthropology. Meeting
(5th : 1985 : Airlie House) IV. Series.
HD73.P763   1988
306'.3—dc 19   88–10779 CIP
ISBN 0–8191–6984–6 (alk. paper)
ISBN 0–8191–6985–4 (pbk. : alk. paper)

Harold Schneider, one of the founders of the Society for Applied Anthropology, and the host of its first meeting in Bloomington, Indiana, died on May 2, 1987, just as this book was in the final editorial stages. Without Hal, the Society probably would never have been. We will all miss him.

CONTENTS

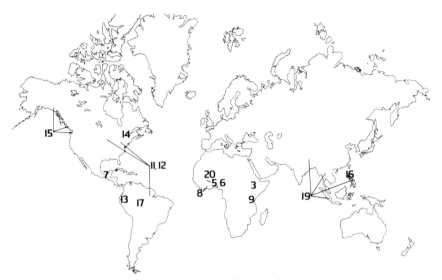

Numbers indicate chapter number in this volume

REGIONS DISCUSSED

EDITORS' PREFACE

Most of the papers in this volume were presented to the fifth annual meeting of the Society for Economic Anthropology, held at Airlie House, Warrenton, Virginia, April 11-13, 1985. John W. Bennett was Program Chairman, and John R. Bowen participated in the conference as a panel organizer. Our editorial effort is strictly collaborative; we both stand behind the various issues discussed in our respective opening and closing essays, although we are obviously not in complete agreement on all matters. The editors agree that anthropological work on international development is significant, and deserves more serious consideration by the discipline. By the same token, we believe that anthropologists working in development need to give more attention to the theoretical contributions of development research to the discipline. However, Bennett is principally interested in anthropology's contribution to development, while Bowen is more concerned with the contribution development research makes to anthropology. These different emphases are reflected in the editors' respective essays.

The title of the Conference featured the term, "the development process." In the course of the conference, it became apparent that so far as anthropologists are concerned, there is no single "process," but diverse emphases and approaches focusing on the dialogues between large social entities and local communities that characterize the modern and emerging world system. These dialogues take place on many levels, implicating individual actors, microsocial formations, state structures, diverse cultural milieux, and specific phenomena: e.g., producer prices, irrigation systems, bureaucracies, and political traditions. The thrust of anthropological work is that no single outcome of development interventions can be predicted easily; development is a continuation of the many avenues of change distinctive for particular societies.

As the book took shape, two major topics emerged: (1) changes in local production systems as initiated either by governments, from the "outside," or by local people themselves, from the "inside"; and (2) the struggle for control over resources needed for production between small-scale or local producers, and government and foreign agencies. Hence our title, "Production and Autonomy." We believe that these two topics represent the principal contribution to date made by anthropologists to the understanding of development, both as a scholarly topic and as a real-world undertaking.

Our emerging objective was to produce something more than a

simple transcript of conference proceedings. Rather, we intended
the book to be a sample of those studies of development which
have significance for the discipline of anthropology. We
therefore selected particular conference papers for publication
that had disciplinary significance and rejected others that
lacked it. We also solicited papers from persons who did not
attend the conference in order to include particular topics for
our general theme: Production and Autonomy. One important topic
in development theory and practice not covered by a separate
paper is the ecology of development, or the issue of "sustainable
development." We regret the omission but regret even more the
fact that research on the ecology of development is simply not
well represented in anthropology. We include some discussion of
the issue in Bennett's introductory chapter.

        We would like to thank a number of people who contributed to
the final product. Nancie Gonzalez and Carolyn McCommon did
yeoman work in the conference arrangements. Karen Lucas
supervised the editing and processing of the manuscript. Sue
Cunningham, Lorien Gray, Bob Jamieson, Mary Kennedy, Kathie
Laird, Jayvarre Little, Joan Lowrey, Stacey Lowrey, and Marcella
Waddell all provided valuable assistance at various stages.
The Washington University Department of Anthropology provided
facilities for completion of the manuscript, and other help,
without stint.

1. INTRODUCTORY ESSAY

ANTHROPOLOGY AND DEVELOPMENT: THE AMBIGUOUS ENGAGEMENT

John W. Bennett

1. The Moral Dilemma

Development is a worldly activity, carried out by people with a stake in its outcome; it is the consequence of public planning and execution, and, to an increasing extent, of private investment. In the First Development Decade of the 1950s, it was an idealistic venture, designed to improve the lot of the common man in the new nations - the former colonies. Emphasis was placed on activities that might increase income and improve social welfare. That many of the means were inappropriate to these ends (in particular, rapid and premature industrialization) became evident in the Second and Third Decades, and development as a scholarly topic has been marked by vigorous theorizing and polemical debate.

There has also been a decisive change in the guidance mechanism of the process. Much of the idealism has given way to disillusion, desperation, and realpolitik-ism - the change in part the result of the failure of benevolent ends, but also of major changes in the world economic system that have made it increasingly necessary for the new nations to find their economic niche - and to pay their debts. National economic health and survival have gradually come to dominate the objectives, and development is seen as a political imperative. To an ever-greater extent, development has been taken over by public and private bureaucracies and removed from the arena of public choice - which creates problems of conscience for people such as anthropologists, whose skills and knowledge clearly have a relation to the process of planned change, but who at the same time may not wish to conform to the dictates of those in charge of the national policy. Scholars and technical people, especially those in the fields of social behavior, may feel they have less and less control over the process, but at the same time, continue to feel the obligation to participate.

Energetic efforts by anthropologists and others have certainly had consequences: although the national imperatives are stronger, experiments in locally planned development initiatives have also increased, as well as emphasis on socially collective solutions, like cooperatives. More awareness of the ecological and social impacts of development have led to attempts to modify them. These and other aspects of the contemporary

1

scene are largely the results of critical research and policy analysis by people such as authors of papers in this volume. Although they have not, perhaps, stemmed the tide of world-systemic domination, they have forced the shapers of development initiatives and policy to consider the consequences of their actions.

Anthropologists have a historic stake in the welfare of local populations. Or more precisely, anthropologists hold to the doctrine of local self-determination to the extent possible: the right of people to make their own decisions about change. Because development has become a historical and national necessity, anthropologists are drawn into participation even as they protest its means and ends; their rationale, as exemplified by Thayer Scudder's paper in this volume, is that by participating critically they may discover ways to do the job with less social and environmental cost. Still, to do so is to facilitate development, and such facilitation may seem to violate the anthropologists's credo of self-determination of local populations. Hence the moral dilemma: by staying out, anthropologists may help to perpetuate the costs and disbenefits; by coming in, anthropologists may ease the burden of rapid change but nevertheless further the loss of cultural integrity.

Consequently the anthropological literature on development has a dual or ambivalent character: there are, on the one hand, the materials represented by the majority of the research papers in this volume: these represent what we call later the "research facilitation role": anthropologists performing analytic-critical tasks focused on particular social groups and communities. Then there are the independent critical statements, represented by the pieces by Richard Adams and Harold Schneider. Another variety of the independent critical literature is not represented in this book: the "victims of the miracle" theme, where development is seen as a destructive force, failing its presumed beneficiaries and destroying their culture. The anthropological literature on development thus has two faces: not a simple positive and negative, but on the one hand, a resigned, skeptical, analytic perspective; and on the other, a negative view - which itself has degrees of rejection and accusation. Hence the dilemma leads to ambivalence, or what I shall call the "disciplined marginality" of the engagement.

Although the moral dilemma is the crux of the matter, there are other facets. A second arises from the traditional anthropological conception of the change process. Development is a conscious effort to change - and change rapidly - the relations of people to society and the world largely by economic means. Anthropology, however, has traditionally viewed change as a natural process, and cautioned its practioners to avoid

2

involvement with the world of social manipulation, "politics,"
and planning. What right has anyone to induce people to change
their ways? The issue is complicated by the growing awareness
among anthropologists that their desire to protect the integrity
and self-determination of human groups can be viewed as simply
another form of paternalism and arrogance - the other side of the
development coin. Again, ambivalence.

Third, anthropologists have generally espoused a gradualist
concept of change that arose mainly out of the objectivist
tradition of anthropology and its desire to scientize humanism.
Culture change was viewed as slow evolutionary transformation,
not a willed revision of the social order - the latter was
"politics." Fourth, the ambivalence toward development is
matched by the reluctant acceptance of "applied anthropology" and
the passive contempt many academic anthropologists exhibit toward
applied practitioners. Some development anthropologists resist
identification with applied anthropology for this reason. There
is also the issue of commitment to specific social goals - a fact
of life that anthropology somehow submerged or avoided in the
long years of "scientific" cultural relativism.

Fourth, development evolved in the 1950s under the stimulus
of colonial revolutions, postwar internationalism, and a version
of the "white man's burden" modernized and purged (one hoped) of
its demeaning and discriminatory overtones. Guilt over the
colonial past and its barbarisms and hypocrisies was a prominent
motive; development was conceived as helping the rest of the
world "catch up" with progress, so long delayed by the desire of
the colonial powers to focus or constrain change and
modernization. Anthropologists had their own source of guilt in
their historic acceptance of colonialism in order to study tribal
peoples in peace and quiet. They also had their resistance to
corrupting influences of modern society on exotic local cultures.
Hence there arose the "ethnographic present" style of
ethnological presentation, offering a pure, largely
unacculturated view of tribal existence even where the population
studied was actually extensively transformed.[1]
Anthropologists resisted the idea of modernizing change even as
they began studying it; the abstract concept of acculturation was
a way of doing the job without getting tarred with the worldly
brush.

Aside from these particularistic studies of local tribal
groups affected by industrial society, anthropologists were drawn
into larger theoretical currents in the social sciences and
historical fields, most of which can be summarized by the term
"modernization theory." This approach developed out of the work
of sociological and universal historians like Max Weber, Arnold
Toynbee, and Karl Polanyi, who were concerned mainly with the

3

rhythms of Western civilization, and the extent to which other cultures succeeded or failed at adhering to the patterns. It was an essentially normative approach: modernization was an inevitable, and presumably desirable process, because in accordance with the doctrine of progress, change toward the modern institutional pattern was considered a good, and isolation and stagnation a bad thing. It was an evolutionary idea as well - probably the last of the nineteenth-century evolutionary social theories, because it was assumed that all societies, sooner or later, would undergo "modernization." All development work in the First Development Decade, the 1950s, and most in the Second, was underlain by modernization theory.

However, as development efforts proceeded through the fifties and sixties, their seamy side became apparent, and the development fraternity's unrealistic expectations of harmonious modernization emerged as a focus of criticism. Anthropologists began their critical effort in the late 1960s and early 1970s, and it emerged mainly as a defense of the rights of local populations to determine their own destiny, or at least to pick and choose among the inducements. This was one underlying theme of Margaret Mead's classic book, Cultural Patterns and Technical Change (1955): based on the acculturation work of the 1940s, the principle of selective or adaptive change was converted into the "right" of people to choose what they wanted or could use without conflict. And hence on to the "victims" theme of the 1970s and '80s: the removal of local food self-subsistence by converting farmers into plantation workers, or even military units. This theme has some echoes in Harold Schneider's piece in this volume. Richard Adams's paper, on the other hand, goes to the very top of the problem: he acknowledges the worldly and historical nature of development, but at the same time criticizes it for attempting conscious, purposive, controlling change for the benefit of the great powers - in its own way, another look back at the anthropological notion of change as a covert, evolutionary process - in preference, perhaps, to planned, short-term transformation. (There are echoes of Social Darwinism here: although anthropologists have rejected the notion that success goes to the strong, there remains the idea that it is risky for outsiders to attempt to direct and control change.) It is better to let people alone and permit them to work out their own accommodations. Human adaptive skills are a great resource.

2. Anthropological Models of Change and Intervention

Although anthropologists have been ambivalent toward developmental change, an engagement with the process of change,

and roles that external experts and specialists may play in the
process, they have been part of the discipline since the late
nineteenth century. Critical views have not prevented
anthropologists from doing research on change, and the effort
produced a series of approaches we may describe as follows:

I. Acculturation theory: 1930s-1940s.

As noted above, acculturation was really the first attempt
by American anthropologists to deal systematically with the
changes resulting from the impact of industrial societies on
tribal peoples. The model featured the idea of two "cultures" in
contact, with change in the weaker, or less-developed (as one
would say today - or as the Wilsons put it in the 1940s, those of
lesser "scale") as the result. Change was viewed as something
that happened to discrete societies, not a general, or worldwide
historical process - although there was some generalized
awareness of this. The model permitted some engagement with the
real-world process of transformation that began with colonialism,
but at the same time avoided intimate participation
-intervention- with the process and its consequences for
indigenous peoples. Acculturation was objectivist, "scientific";
the anthropologist remained aloof, on the whole, from the social
costs and gains associated with the process. In the United
States, acculturation studies became a principal means for
investigating changing status of American Indian societies on
reservations.[2]

II. Technological Change theory: 1940s-1950s.

This model was ushered in following World War II and the
rapid dissolution of colonial empires - and also during the first
stirrings of "development" and was underlain by "modernization
theory," as noted above. The definitive early version appeared
in Margaret Mead's United Nations-sponsored effort,
Cultural Patterns and Technical Change, which appeared about the
same time as teams of anthropologists in the Trust Territories,
India, and Latin America were doing background research on the
consequences of military occupations, early efforts at
self-government, and the first rural community development
projects.[3] The model held that the principal force
engendering change was technology, defined broadly as tools,
techniques, new ways of producing food and material culture, and
accompanying institutional innovations. Change was viewed as
something caused by forces and introductions coming from "outside
the culture." The approach was an advance on the older
acculturation theory insofar as it was tacitly acknowledged that
local instances of change were part of a worldwide process - a

5

new stage in culture history. The technical antecedents of the approach are to be found in the "applied anthropology" movement beginning in the 1940s in the United States, and in the British colonies in the first two decades of the twentieth century.[4] The role of the anthropologist in the process of modernizing technological change was visualized mainly as researcher, but also to some extent, as a constructive participant. The normative view of change was on the whole favorable, consonant with the optimism and paternal high-mindedness typical of the early postwar and post-colonial era, reinforced by modernization theory.

III. Interventionist Microlevel Anthropology: 1950s and early 1960s.

Things moved rapidly in the First Decade, and anthropologists were carried along with the proliferation of development projects created by the expansion of foreign aid. The technological change model began to give way to an interventionist approach in which the "change agent," including the anthropologist, worked directly with the indigenous population in order to help persuade them that change was desirable, and also to assist them in devising ways to accomplish the change with minimal stress.[5] This role, of course, persists in the "development anthropology" of the contemporary period. A well-known domestic version was Sol Tax's "action anthropology" (Tax 1958), in which anthropologists formed teams to help reservation Indians improve their lot and make use of government programs. This approach was voluntary; in other contexts, anthropologists were employed by the development agencies. Both approaches, however, generated considerable controversy in the discipline, for reasons already indicated.

IV. Development Anthropology: 1970s and 1980s.

The coming of age of development planning and projects coincided with a gradual diminishing of academic opportunities for anthropologists, and the consequent search for practical training appropriate to the job openings in the international field. Applied anthropology and development anthropology degree programs emerged in departments across the United States, and a search for ethical and theoretical rationales for such careers went into high gear. A number of books and professional papers on "development anthropology" appeared,[6] but the issue of anthropological participation in development is by no means settled, as the remarks in the first section of this paper imply. By the 1980s, the field may be characterized by a series of roles that anthropologists may choose among, or may be required to

6

accept, depending on the terms of employment:

A. The first is a continuation, with considerable elaboration, of the research facilitation role described earlier for the technological change model. This has become a distinctive function in which the anthropologist is one member of a multidisciplinary team charged with the responsibility of doing background research in order to set the stage for a particular project funded or directed by an international agency or a ministry of development in a Third World country. The majority of such operations concern village communities and rural districts, and agriculture is the principal target - in contrast to the 1950s, when "community development" was the theme. The research team is expected to define the constraints and opportunities present in the indigenous economy and culture with respect to the project objectives. The anthropologist's chief function is, perhaps, to show how the objectives can be met with minimal social damage or disruption.

B. The second role is a continuation of the microlevel interventionist role of the 1950s, which by the 1970s and 1980s had become what we shall call the participant employee role. Essentially an occupational role, the anthropologist is a member of a project administration team, which may do research, but more importantly, has the responsibility of actually putting into effect the project objectives. The anthropologist is not a volunteer observer or researcher, as he or she often was in the earlier period, but is a salaried worker - it is a way of earning a living. In this role, the anthropologist typically has the least amount of self-determination: if he questions the advisability of the project, he has restricted opportunities to state his objections publicly. Change is accepted as a desirable or necessitous "given." Often the anthropologist in one of these jobs may move between the several roles described in this sub-section; e.g., the team may assign the anthropologist a somewhat independent research evaluative function at the same time he must assist in implementing the plan.

C. Research evaluation then follows - this, like the foregoing, can be an occupational role, and the incumbent may be hired to evaluate the results of the project after it has been in operation or is terminated. However, greater opportunity exists for the anthropologist to exercise independent critical sense. In some cases, the researcher can be self-funded, but access to the site usually has to be obtained from the agencies involved, so there are constraints. However, a researcher who can link up with academic institutions and scholars in the host country may attain considerable independence. Even in such cases, the development agency or research institute may fund publication of the results. This has become increasingly common as

7

self-criticism of development activities has become a regular feature of agency work.

The papers in this volume represent work accomplished by anthropologists in all three of these contemporary "development anthropology" roles. The main issue behind these functions is, of course, the degree of critical independence. The emergence of academic development research institutes, like the Land Tenure Center of the University of Wisconsin (see their paper in this volume), and Harvard Institute for International Development, has facilitated the independent function, even though these institutes accept contract work from the government agencies. The Institute for Development Anthropology (see Scudder's paper) is, on the other hand, only loosely affiliated with academic institutions and is essentially a private contract agency in which the "research facilitation" role is perhaps the dominant one.

It should be noted that anthropologists working in the development field generally produce monographs and reports for their employers that are directed toward the practical problems of planning, executing, and evaluating development projects. Some of these monographs are substantial, and do contain theory, but always with reference to practical issues. Academic or purely scholarly anthropologists rarely see these reports and monographs, because the material is not generally released through academic publishing channels. Sometimes the authors produce an article-length version for an anthropological journal, but usually playing down the practical side. Thus, a dual standard of judgment prevails (as it has always, for "applied anthropology"): a practical, or real-world standard that judges the piece on the strength of its contribution to a particular human endeavor; and a scholarly standard, which judges the piece in terms of its contribution to theory. The trick is to write papers that serve both ends. We think that the papers in this volume suggest such possibilities.

In general, the series of related or overlapping roles defined above for development anthropology has engendered the present state of ambiguity concerning the anthropologist's relationship to the development process, with the "moral dilemma" in the background. The "models" of change and intervention described above are to be contrasted with the views of the independent anthropological critics of development, disenchanted with the failure of expectations, and in fundamental disagreement with the methods. These independent critical views have a common element in their emphasis on the need for more local autonomy and self-determination, but this theme can be translated into a variety of perspectives, depending on ideological and disciplinary views. One set is related to the concept of

8

dependency, or the proposition that under world-capitalist systems, the new nations do not really develop, but are simply bound more tightly to the large industrial nations, losing autonomy and economic well-being in the process.[7] A second set is more strictly or narrowly anthropological: these perspectives emphasize the importance of sociocultural and behavioral factors as causative agents in change, over against the purely economic, and we shall now consider this issue.[8]

3. The Significance of Economics

Thus, still another factor in the disciplined marginality of anthropology vis-a-vis development concerns the fact that economics and economists have dominated the field. Before we examine the implications of this, we need to describe the main reason for it. The basis of the economics hegemony is to be found in the fact that the post-colonial world evolved in the strict framework of the nation-state. Not one single former colony elected to accept a different type of political geography. In actuality, the former colonies took over the basic Western historical sequence: from grassroots revolt of subject peoples, to full-scale revolution, to declarations of independence, to negotiated freedom, to proclamation of national identity with a name, flag, government, etc. National self-determination was the banner of the independence movements. Even in East Africa, where a regional confederation with sensible reallocation of unevenly distributed resources in the former territories would have been the most logical framework for subsequent development, the independence movements demanded the separate nation-states of Tanzania and Kenya. The situation was even more irrational in West and Central Africa, where a number of nations, each based on tribal or quasi-tribal territories, or simply old colonial boundaries, emerged to confuse the resource and ethnic map and serve as a constant source of internal and external jockeying for position and economic wherewithal. There were partial exceptions: Indonesia is an example - a nation-state, yes, but a unifying type, combining the many separate tribal and communal identities. However, its permanence is not a foregone conclusion.

The reasons for this statism process were many, and certainly one of the main ones is the ideological dominance of the concept of nation and nationality as the sure route to power and self-sufficiency: the model of Europe since the Middle Ages. But another reason is to be found in institutions: in the modern world, accountability is the key to power, and only nations have full accountability: they have treasuries, credit balances,

9

import-export policies and controls, customs bureaus, ministries charged with responsibilities, taxes, private and parastatal companies, regulated by or in partnership with, the state. Development was assumed from the start, as recompense for the constraints of colonialism, and only national governments, especially in the ambiguous social systems of former colonies, could provide the necessary direction. These are the real instrumentalities of development, and this fact was known by both the powers that be, who were remaking the world, and by the new independence governments, who were the presumed beneficiaries of this remodelling effort.

Hence the economists. Economics as a profession has a social agenda: to develop the Economy, not merely to research economic facts and construct theories. Sociology has something of an agenda, to improve Society, but it is vague and no one quite knows how to do it. Anthropology has no historic agenda: its task was pure research, the construction of cultural portraits. That a kind of agenda has subsequently emerged was implied in the foregoing sections, but this is self-defined: Society does not require anthropologists to defend local self-determination. In contrast, Society requires economists to guide the process of production for survival.

Hence the new nation-states and their powerful patrons asked the economists to do their historic job. The fundamental rhetoric of development - even in the fields of "social development," such as education, migration, and labor - is economic: the costs and gains of proposed changes are measured by monetary values. The logic follows: change the economy, and all the rest follows; fund the project, and the results will emerge; budget the new university, and it will produce valuable social capital. And all this takes place in the frame of the nation-state, not the locality. The Locality is dependent on the State, not the other way around. The other way is, in fact, the "traditional society," and to get rid of the traditional society was precisely what every postwar independence government was attempting to do, as fast as possible. Only national governments can undertake to guarantee the direction, financial probity, and the other accountability dimensions for a plan of action to alter the mode and output of production and its distribution. In a nutshell: the new governments are mainly interested in growth rather than development - because growth serves the national interest.

Therefore, economists came to be ubiquitous in development not merely because there are a lot of them, but because they are the chosen cognitive instrumentality of national-level progress. Granted, of course, that a certain cultural factor was in operation: a Western bias, or in the language of the later

10

world- systems-dependency theorists, <u>capitalism</u>. If one wishes to see development as simply a bid for world control by the capitalists this is one's privilege, and there is no doubt that capitalism, as an economic engine, has accepted opportunities. However, the process is more complex. The choice of the State frame by the former colonies was not the result of a capitalist plot, but a natural evolutionary step, because no fully tested alternative model existed. From Magna Carta to Japanese centralized feudalism, the course of history had been in the direction of the State and its economic responsibility for the Nation. Thus, in broad historical outline, development was simply the continuation of this evolution: from public and private sources, national and international, altruistic and greedy, a move to bring the world into one interdependent frame of productive effort. And in this broad sense, development has been an outstanding success, achieved in a remarkably short time.[9] The world is now, for better or for worse, economically intertwined. Rich or poor, we all depend on each other, and the situation makes the old world of nationalistic wars seem outmoded and futile - and also increasingly dangerous.

The dominance by economists of development planning and execution had several implications, and anthropologists have participated in the criticisms of these implications. In the first place, the agenda of production was implemented by economic theory - it was not merely a practical task, but had to be rationalized by a particular form of social prediction. Development could not just happen: it had to evolve by plan, over a period of time. Therefore, theory had to be used to ensure that the predicted outcomes would in fact occur. This theory was basically behavioral, and it was largely invented by economists, not borrowed from the behavioral sciences (including anthropology). In fact, anthropology's <u>acculturational</u> theory of change - basically one of slow, adaptive, consensual choice, was specifically disavowed by economics theory. The latter held that people constantly seek to enhance their power position, and to gratify their wants. (One does not need to get involved in "profit maximization theory" here, which was widely misunderstood by social scientists).[10] In simpler terms, the theory focused on humans as valuing creatures who have wants that they can articulate and seek to satisfy. This is not wrong, but economists work with limited data: <u>economic</u> wants, and because economics must measure things by quantitative values (usually money), they came to assume that by promising more money, people would perform in predictable ways. Here is where the development issue comes in: by promising economic gains, the participants or "beneficiaries" will automatically work harder, accept the technological innovations, assume the attitudes of commercial agents, etc., and thereby implement the plan.

11

This was a crucial step, because it assumed that other values or motives such as politics, ideology, aesthetics, feelings, religion, and status identity were not especially operative. In fact, most of them were completely ignored in the formal tracts called "project papers" by some development agencies. They had to ignore these things, not only because the authors of the papers were for the most part economists (or technical specialists with economics-type thought processes) but because to attempt to handle such variables would doom the project from the start. By focusing only on a simple, predictable pattern of incentive, the atmosphere of certainty could be achieved. No one has attempted a full count, but I surveyed project papers from USAID and the World Bank for all East African livestock projects in the 1970s (Bennett, et al., 1986), finding that the official evaluations of the project results were all mostly negative, i.e., no project had attained its predicted goals. Why? Because "extraneous" factors such as social organization, authority, status differentials, aspiration levels, educational achievements, cultural customs, and drought all intervened in the supposed economic incentive process. (Incidentally, this evaluative focus on "failure" also meant, for these particular projects, that many real gains in the areas of social experience, community formation, redirection of certain values such as those for land tenure, and so on were ignored, because they were not stated as goals in the original protocols.)[11]

These covert simplicities of the economistic approach to development began to surface in the early 1970s, as another general effect emerged: income inequality. The expected benefits to the supposed beneficiaries were not materializing; instead, the rich were getting richer and the poor poorer. This had been predicted by economic theorists themselves, notably Simon Kuznets in the 1950s (Kuznets 1955), but in the headlong application of economics theory to the planned change process of development, it was - had to be - ignored, because of the operation of the political imperatives already described. The process is in fact elementary: to develop the economy, and in the usual short time period specified in funded programs and projects, one has to rely on those people with the requisite skills and connections, the very people who already occupy the top of the pyramid in the productive system. The effect was felt as well in those new countries that chose a socialist national framework, because they nationalized resources and therefore further centralized access to the factors of production. Only the governments "got rich" in these countries (although there were other social gains).

The result is well known: eventually the target of development was redefined as "basic needs," or as benefits for the poorest classes (e.g., World Bank 1975). Well and good, but economistic thinking once more got the upper hand: needs and poverty were defined in terms of economic values: income, cash surpluses, the possession of "modern" consumer goods, and so on - all of the familiar mensurative development objectives of the preceding period. No real change was made in the basic process of planning development - only some new types of projects, and closer attention to the social consequences of pricing and other factors. Many of these changes had good results - a general philosophy of "helping people to help themselves" began to prevail, and instead of mammoth programs staffed with expensive foreign experts, local elites, and featuring overpowering technology, there appeared smaller, more locally oriented projects aimed at supplying basic instrumentalities such as schools, co-ops, or roads, and allowing for some continuation of subsistence farming. However, the efforts were miniscule compared to the magnitude of deprivation and dislocation created by the narrowly conceived and unrealistically targeted projects of the past. And this fact led to the international outcry over the inequalities of the "rich and the poor nations," the "North and South," and hence the dependency theories. And, from there, on to the urge to get private capital into development and away from the governments and power blocs and elites. And we all know what that led to: the confusing international indebtedness problem, which can be seen either as something leading to world bankruptcy (bad) or as a transfer of Western capital to the Third World (good). Time will tell.

4. Development: Micro and Macro Levels

It is implied in much of the foregoing discussion that development must be viewed as consisting of several social magnitudes, which we can symbolize by the "micro-macro" rhetoric. This is important because anthropologists focus on the lower levels of magnitude, while development specialists tend to be concerned with the macro levels, regardless of the specific targets of development programs. At the most macro level - the world system - the results can be described as a success, as already noted. The former colonies and other marginal societies have indeed been drawn into association with world economic trends and interdependencies.

However, when anthropologists speak of development, they usually mean what the field representatives of the foreign aid agencies mean: particular projects in particular places, affecting particular populations and regions. And it is in such particular "projects" where we so often find "failure." The African livestock projects once again: Schneider refers to the reports that some $600 million in development aid for

13

pastoralists appeared to have little or no effect, at least with reference to the stated project objectives. But this failure was not total - pastoralists were drawn into the development economics of their nations in varying degrees, for better or for worse, as citizens of nations - not as wandering tribalists outside the body politic, as they were in the past. Such people are required by their national governments to play a role in the political economy and ecology of their countries; the only issue is precisely what role, and it is here where the anthropologist can help. This process of national incorporation is and will continue to be painful, but there are alternative strategies of change available. Most important is the need to incorporate the supposed beneficiaries in the planning process.

It seems clear that anthropologists will continue to find difficulty in influencing the macropolitical processes of development on the national scale. This is not their forte; their training as professionals does not include systematic instruction in the way the world is put together on a trans-regional or national basis. Some of us think that more needs to be done in this line, but few anthropological academic training programs have tried it. The anthropologist who works in the development field gains practical knowledge of this process, but is continually beset with doubts about its value and insecurities over his lack of preparation. This is so because the more the anthropologist comes to identify with national goals, the more likely he may come to see local populations as reactionary, and as this happens, his credo and critical sense are damaged. The anthropologist functions best as the spokesperson for the micro level, because by doing so, he forces the attention of the planners on alternative strategies. The dilemma is reinforced by the predominantly rural locus of most of the anthropological work on development - it is rural populations that have been the target of agricultural, community, and resource development programs that have so often gone sour. Although the anthropologists have been aware of the growing problems in the Third World Cities, due to displacement of the rural population, they have only just begun to study these people systematically (i.e., other than as objects of "migration" studies). Leo Despres's and Susan Russell's papers in this volume are among the few anthropological researches on urban populations undergoing development.

A major critical response to the dictatorial-benevolent process of macrodevelopment has taken the form of concepts of "development from below," "participative development," or "local autonomy." Anthropologists were not, in most cases, the sole authors of these concepts, which emerged in various professional groups including dissenting economists, but certainly anthropologists have vigorously espoused them in theory and

14

practice (see Richard Salisbury's case study in this volume); and we should remember Sol Tax's "action anthropology" (e.g., Tax 1958). The movement simply advocates planning in which the direction and rate of change affecting localities should be set, to the extent possible, by the local people themselves. More importantly, the approach advocates much fuller use of local skills and knowledge in any development operation, whoever may set the goals. If there is one field of experience with development that has become a matter of general consensus among all the practitioners it is this one of indigenous knowledge. The heyday of the outside expert who is expected to know all the important facts regardless of his total lack of experience with the social and environmental circumstances is rapidly drawing to a close. Most everywhere the local people are now consulted and their knowledge and opinions valued - although the political forces behind development often do not permit effective use of this local expertise, and as Delores Koenig shows in her paper, the difficulties in incorporating local people in the development process are inherent in the whole conduct of the foreign-aid development operation, and are not really amenable to modification. And language barriers, lifestyle factors, and so on continue to make it difficult to apply. Anthropologists can shine here if they choose to, but this choice is not without doubt and ambiguity. However satisfying it may be for the anthropologist to demonstrate to the outsiders that his clients are in reality people of wisdom and experience, he nevertheless is exposing them to intervention. Some anthropologists have decided that incorporative change is inevitable, and do their best to bring local expertise into contact with the planners, but others hold back, avoiding the double role of agent for the locals and also for the external forces that seek to bring the former into the new era. They reserve the right to disagree with the goals set by the nation.

Thus, development-from-below has not been easy to plan and execute because many development programs and objectives are not really planned for local benefits: it is a matter of seeking local conformity to patterns of action in order to benefit the nation, in order to provide a source of foreign exchange, raise food production, manipulate prices through output control, provide a base for taxation, or to stifle or redirect political unrest. Hence the benefits to the locals are often not really the issue; it is the conformity of the locals to larger plans, bureaucratically conceived, that motivates development planning. Consequently the hidden agenda in such cases is really the judicious use of compulsion and force, rather than one of finding the pathway to local benefits. Benefits, if achieved, are the carrot behind the stick, so to speak. In such situations, which are all too common, there is a limit to the extent to which genuine benefits and local definitions of same can play a

15

significant role. This is the way the State (or quasi-states like trans-national corporations) functions, regardless of cultural style or tradition.

5. The Myth of Planning

Albert Hirschman noted, in what may be the most insightful statement on the development process yet published (Hirschman 1975), that often the most successful (from any criterion) outcomes of projects were the least expected - unanticipated consequences, or what he called the "hiding hand." This rather fanciful term referred to the fact that the uncontrolled variables affecting the project have a way of guiding the course of change regardless of the planned means-end schema. The local people working for the project may have their own loyalties and social strategies which can be used to push the activities in unforeseen directions. The irony and humor of such processes have been the topic of several novels and short stories. That is, quite aside from making the local people formal participants and directors of change, they may take indirect control anyway. This is not only a microsocial level phenomenon, but occurs at the highest levels of the ministries. The foreign aid funds that pour down invisible ratholes do not always line the pockets of the elite, but may be redirected to useful projects for which it may be impossible to secure public aid.

Hence the "myth" of planning. In an essay published many years ago, I noted that most planning in our society seems to wind up as rationalizations for the status quo, not as new departures or changes (Bennett 1959). The example given was street and highway construction: designed to solve traffic and transportation problems, it has tended to make them worse by facilitating movement, hence increasing congestion. The general process was eventually conceptualized by Fred Hirsch, in his Social Limits to Growth (1976). Thus, much agricultural development has tended to reduce production, rather than increase it. (Or the reverse: many of the development initiatives designed to reduce herd size and increase offtake among pastoralists resulted in increased herd size and reduced offtake!)

Planning is expected to bind the future, but although humans certainly bind time, they find it difficult to bind the future to pre-set courses. This is so because in adaptive change the presumed beneficiaries or participants may find ways to sabotage, avoid, or change the plan. Again this presents a peculiar paradox for the anthropologist: must he inform his employers that

16

the locals are "adapting," rather than conforming, or should he conceal their perverse ingenuity? Moreover, there are technical paradoxes: although development presumably means to open things up, to accomplish it requires constraints and controls. Of course the intricacies sometimes work out, but it is a difficult and contradictory process. Planned change rarely works the way it is supposed to; simple drift, or muddle, is the usual course. Anthropologists, of all professionals, should understand that drift is not necessarily unplanned, but is simply change that allows for the redundancies and contradictions of mind-changing and generational rhythm. Plans within plans.

Geoff Wood (1985) calls attention to the "donative rhetoric" in the foreign aid-project mode of development. By this he means the disguised interventionist perspective we have commented on earlier: change is introduced and compelled for the good of the people, whether the people have any say in it or not. Coupled with the economistic theory of incentives, this means that the factors that importantly influence change, or restrain it, are often systematically excluded from the plan. Moreover, the rationale for the plan is created by labeling the beneficiaries as "poor," "deserving," "in need," etc. This puts them all in single categories - "beneficiaries," regardless of their actual positions and aspirations. We mentioned the problem of defining poverty exclusively in terms of income distribution, whereas in fact definitions of the goals and aspirations of the various low-income groups vary greatly by other criteria.

Still, anthropologists need to recognize that in part the "donative" intervention was a matter of simple urgency, at least in the early stages of development, especially in the pre-1950 period of colonial and internal-colonialist history (see Salisbury's history of Canadian Governmental provision for Cree sedentarization in his paper). Structural changes in settlement pattern and subsistence economy created vulnerabilities; responsible national governments, prodded by reformers, had no choice but to provide services and institutional changes.

Even more important, anthropologists have come to recognize that their own proclivities toward paternalism may be part of the problem, and not necessarily the solution. Cases where local participation and direction of development have succeeded are all alike in that the local people simply took political control of their affairs, via mobilization of the growing number of educated persons, and hence the recognition that paternal shepherding is always limited in scope. The State can help people, but only in terms of the State's own values and goals.

17

6. The Temporal Rhythms of Developmental Change

And finally, there is the factor of time. One of the most familiar critiques of the development process is the inadequate sense of time displayed by the aid agencies and the legislatures or treasuries that fund them. Again: accountability - in this case, the belief that if payoff does not appear soon after an investment, it must be adjudged a loss. So long as government remains the dominant donor or manager, projects will have short durations and a built-in proclivity to negative evaluation. Private corporate bureaucracy is somewhat more flexible, but the same rules generally apply: they are made by accountants.[12]

Anthropologists believe that on the whole, significant social change is relative mainly to internal, indigenous criteria. Economics predictive theories of incentive behavior (or political pressures) may hold that five years is enough time to move from half-commercial to full-commercial institutions or orientations, but local societies always have their own rhythms (it may be shorter or longer). The most generalizable or cross-cultural temporal cycle for agrarian societies is generational: you acquaint Father with the necessary changes, but they are not realized until the Sons take over. That is, a minimum two-generational cycle is common. The second anthropological finding concerns the way this generational rhythm is modified by factors of risk and knowledge. If risks and uncertainty are high, even the second generation may be unwilling to change; if uncertainty and risks are low, perhaps even the first generation will jump at the chance. These patterns are so pervasive that on close inspection by the writer of a number of research projects designed to ascertain the influence of such factors as the media, social status, income level, and so on, on the acceptance of innovation in agriculture, it became apparent that the ingenious attempts at correlation or factor analysis could have been dispensed with by a simple analysis of the generational position of the individuals in the sample, crossed with data on the degree of uncertainty of the environment (physical, economic, social). In any case, the influence of generational progression on change is so important that development programs should be phased with it as a matter of course. They rarely are.

Project duration also affects the question of sectorial temporality. Each institutional facet of a program or project may have its own temporal cycle, and this creates almost insuperable problems for bureaucratically defined durations that, as already noted, are hardly the longue duree. In general, the closer one gets to institutional sectors related to human learning and habit formation, the longer it will take to achieve

18

the desired change. Learning is not a single-dimensional behavior, but an effect of several dimensions working together: need, desire, motivation, fear, confidence, literary skills, threats and rewards in the environment, and so on through many others.[13]

In all of the previous contexts, development aid agencies and ministries have become wiser and more tolerant that they were in the 1970s, when the "failures" began to become a heavy burden. The heyday of the large, funded, ambiguous, ambitious, naive development project is over. Anthropologists had something to do with this change, but perhaps not as much as they would like to think. My experience tells me that the best and most perceptive criticisms of development have always been internal; a curious matter, because the agency man who writes a naive public blurb on development "success," privately may give you the most incisive criticism of the program that you can then dress up in your own professional jargon in order to take the credit. Such is bureaucracy, governmental and academic.

7. Anthropological Change

What has contact with the world of development done for anthropological ideas? Three main things (see John Bowen's closing chapter for much more on this topic):

First, although anthropologists have traditionally emphasized the gradual nature of change, their participation in - or at least observation of - development processes required some revisions in this doctrine. As noted earlier, project planners had to assume that change would take place in the period designated in the project plan, and to back up this expectation, they utilized economic incentive theory. According to the theory, people will change their behavior when promises of increased wealth or well-being are made. However, this rarely occurs - usually people demand some material evidence of the promised benefits before they accept the innovation in its entirety. The anthropologist, down into the 1950s, argued that change was gradual and slow, because factors other than gain were influencing behavior.

But it soon became apparent that in some instances the beneficiaries did immediately accept the plan, and behaved accordingly. Thus, the myth of the "irrational peasant" was found to be false, and equally, the "myth" of invariable slow change was also shown to be too simple. Agricultural economists, anthropologists, and institutional economists began looking into the situation in the 1960s, discovering that the whole matter

19

seemed to rest on the way the farmer perceived uncertainty and risk. This led Theodore Schultz toward his well-known treatise on the "rational peasant" (Schultz 1964).

What really collapsed in this episode was the age-old idea about the innate mental backwardness and sheer cussedness of "peasant" behavior, in place for thousands of years in all civilizations with an agrarian base. Anthropologists have played a significant role in this episode, but were by no means the only players in the game. But at least the experience served to increase and deepen anthropological knowledge about agrarian behavior. This is one major professional gain from anthropological participation, however quixotic, in development.

The second gain is change in the romantic egalitarianism that pervaded anthropological theories of tribal existence. It was not that anthropological research on social hierarchy did not exist - it is simply that the hierarchical tendencies in social organization were not fully appreciated: although anthropologists might acknowledge domination and hierarchy as a sociological fact, the existence of this universal pattern seemed to be missing in theories about the "nature of culture."

However, once anthropologists began to contemplate development, and to participate in development research, it became apparent that change in the distribution of rewards, or in the scarcity-abundance ratio, immediately generated social differentiation as individuals and groups sought to control the new allocations. Presumably such social dynamism always characterized human societies, however small, but in the older ethnology, the anthropologist was never on the spot when the change or shift in hierarchy or dominance emerged. However, in instantaneous planned change, the effect appeared before the very eyes of the researcher. It is this realization that human beings are prone to drives toward power and domination that creates tension between the development anthropologists on the one hand, and those who continue to feel that development is anathema: that the resulting changes in social organization and structure awake sinister forces in human nature. But in my view, development has had a desirable impact on anthropological theory because it forces anthropologists to become more realistic about human behavior.

The third consequence is the recognition of adaptation as the key behavioral process in social change. Anthropologists remain more or less committed to "culture" as the master concept, although the older notion that it was the major causative agent in behavior has long since withered (Bennett 1976). If anthropologists have become more 'realistic' about behavior insofar as they now acknowledge its dark side, they are also more realistic in the sense of recognizing the coping-manipulative aspect of behavior - the process that enables humans to deal with change either positively or negatively. The two-sided nature of adaptation is the crucial aspect, because it permits defensive action in the local interest - a mode that anthropologists concerned with the "rights" issue can build upon. Adaptation came to be recognized in many contexts of research, perhaps especially the ecological, but as a practical mode of human response, I believe that development anthropology eventually will be recognized as the principal agent in bringing anthropology into the modern world system.

8. Apocalypse Then

Development is, after all, a human-centered process; and human-centeredness, the environmentalists of the 1970s reminded us, is not the solution, but part of the problem. Apart from its grandiose geopolitical processes and objectives, development basically was designed to raise expectations: a dangerous course of action because it is easier to make promises than to fulfil them. Most development projects are essentially high risk ventures: you promise benefits; thereby increase expectations of consumption and well-being; and then risk the chance that the whole thing may go sour, leaving a disappointed and resentful population. Even worse is the case where people have been persuaded to scrap useful institutions and technologies in the promise of better ones - only to find the innovations don't work due to some fatal flaw, or increasingly, to the scarcity of resources.

And even worse than this is the degradation of resources used in order to meet momentary goals without concern for the future. As populations increase in response to promises of the better life, and traditional curbs on fertility are abandoned, governments lose sight of the need to balance needs, resources, and population, focussing only on the here and now. And in the Western countries whose populations are not increasing, even diminishing, the race for increased consumption benefits continues, and the demand for resources continues to rise.

Putting it all together: Peter Raven, in an address before the American Association for the Advancement of Science in 1987 reminded us that the world population will reach almost 8 billion by 2020 A.D.; that the population of tropical countries would increase from 1.1 billion in 1950, to more than 5 billion by 2020; that 80,000 sq. miles of tropical forest, the habitat of most of the world's species, are destroyed each year, currently

21

about one-fourth of this being used for producing beef "for the sake of keeping the price of a hamburger in the U.S. about a nickel less." The litany continues from all sides: acid rain; atmospheric carbon dioxide increasing from human combustion activities and the loss of plant cover worldwide; a galloping rate of species extinction that will reach 100 species a day in a few years or months. The opposition is vocal and impressive, but it is a prayer on the wind: the institutional processes are at fault, and well-meaning conservation, and sheltered districts like biosphere reserves and gene banks and national parks are no answer to the headlong rush to consume resources.[14]

The process is worldwide, but there are two critical sectors: the tropical countries and the temperate industrial areas. In the tropics, the effects are felt most prominently on soil and water: e.g.: land erosion in Java and the Himalayan foothills due to excessive slope cultivation; groundwater abuse in parts of Africa and the Middle East; range overgrazing in the same regions; the loss of rain forest in the Amazon basin - and others. Such loss of resources feed the steady erosion of agricultural productivity (caused, of course, by many other factors as well) which has resulted in a drop of from 5 percent to 20 percent in food production in many tropical countries in the past two decades - while at the same time the populations of these countries have displayed 2-plus percent growth rates.

In the Western industrial countries the big issue is, in the broadest sense, pollution (in addition to the familiar problems of soil and water abuse). The industrial might of the developed countries has continued to expand, creating the "world system" of multinationals and their various bastions and outliers. The consequences are known in detail for the European and North American countries; the effects in the socialist or "centrally planned" countries are less well known. However, for the Soviet Union, we have reports on the fouling of Lake Baikal, one of the world's largest reservoirs of fresh water, with paper mill discharges; the overdose of chemical effluents in the complex hydraulics of lakes and rivers in the Leningrad area; poisoning of wells in the Urals; fallouts from radioactivity accidents, Chernobyl only the most recent; fish kills in the Crimea - and other situations comparable to those in the capitalist countries. Industrial pollution and resource degradation have no political preferences so long as economic growth remains the main goal.

If central control and planning of the type found in socialist countries cannot change the pattern of resource abuse, any more effectively than democratic means, then we must consider other methods. The basic problem is not so much a matter of control and regulation of industrial and agricultural development, but the modification of cultural expectations and

22

patterns of fertility. The issue is the breakdown of local, institutionally-regulated systems of ecological balance among fertility, resources, and human desires. That is, the problem is basically social and cultural, not technological. And it is here where anthropologists can play a role. What motivates people to have children, or not to have them? How do people establish standards of well-being in adjustment to the resources necessary to sustain them? How best can humans accept limits to consumption? How can populations re-establish control over their own resources in the face of national attempts to seize them?

Anthropologists have produced significant research in these fields, but often the work is not connected to "development." It exists outside the field, related to different disciplines and initiatives: public health, family planning, demography, the nature of values, symbols, and ritual. One recent effort, that concerned with "common property institutions" is closer to the development field insofar as its impetus comes from groups concerned with re-establishing property institutions with greater responsibility for the sustained yield of resources over longer periods of time. If resources are held in common, the collective good is seemingly better observed and served - an argument with considerable merit, but the effect is by no means automatic. Still, it points toward the source of the problems: the need for local groups to recapture responsibility for and control over their resource base. The loss of this control is, in the last analysis, the most serious consequences of "development," whether we are concerned with farmers in Africa or city folks in the industrial north.

The cultural issues are momentous and the most important facing humankind since the invention of writing: how can human needs and wants on a worldwide scale be disciplined? How can we adjust the exceedingly defective methods of social and economic planning to runaway aspirations of personal gratification and national autonomy and power? How can the proliferating and self-reinforcing system of rising expectations be brought under some kind of stable governance? How can we curb the escalating wants of the developed world in order to share our wealth with the developing nations, and thereby achieve a more equitable distribution of the unevenly distributed resources?

Is this development? Yes, but a different side of the problem. Anthropologists, being human-centered, worry mainly about the effects on indigenous populations, and no one faults them for that. But in less than a century all human populations, indigenous or otherwise, will feel the effects of the destruction of the physical resources that foster food production, biological diversity, beneficial climate, and the security and repose necessary for human innovativeness and well-being. Are

23

anthropological priorities misplaced, even futile in the face of the ecological apocalypse? Will it be an apocalypse; or will we find ways to ward off its most serious consequences - biological reserves, gene banks, fertility controls, controlled development, monitored to prevent the worst abuses of resources?

I do not know, but my pessimism is rampant. Things will get much worse before they get better, and the human proclivity to act only in crisis probably will once more characterize the situation. Planning? Doubtful. Humans like to plan, but they do it badly and they cannot find the time - at least not in the current gratification-prone and nationalistic atmosphere of human-centered "development." Clearly population must be brought under control, and the prevalence of greed and gratification as the major human goals of this era will have to be curbed, and things returned to an earlier level of modesty and sacrifice. These things will probably come about, but not through "development"; only through the renunciation of at least some aspects of development. Is this, in reality, religion?

What does all this really come down to? First, the process of resource degradation cannot be stopped so long as most of the world's population exists at a level of dire poverty. Still, the ecological issues - the "sustainability" ethic - also represent an urgent agenda. Where do anthropologists stand? As I have suggested in this essay that a major role is to protect local people against the depredations of the developers. However, this is not sufficient; it is only half of the problem. Development is an urgent agenda; some version of it must be accomplished if global inequalities, and the consequent environmental effects, are to be modified. So anthropologists must participate in development, and continue to seek both social and environmental goals. They must participate in the search for a sustainable route to the well-being of a world population. And let us hope that population can, in some fashion, be brought under some sort of control over the next generation.

Surely there is a task here for cultural anthropology. It transcends the immediate goals of development projects, important though these may be at the microsocial level of the community, the region, and the nation. The problem with "development research" is its narrow focus on the processes that feed resource abuse and demographic instability: a larger objective and frame of inquiry must be found. Anthropology prides itself on the long view; the historical approach to civilization and culture, but with the decline of evolutionary theory this frame of reference has been in eclipse. Anthropology's ambivalence over development is appropriate, but without a renewal of research on the aims and destiny of humanity it does nothing to solve the problem of the future. This issue hovers above the papers in this volume, and we offer no solution, only the hope of a new start.

Notes

[1] A graphic consequence of the "ethnographic present" attitude appears in the case of the photographer Edward Curtis, who posed Indian subjects in stock costumes and performed other manipulations in an effort to present images of pre-contact Indian life. Curtis can be accused of fraud, but as Lyman (1982) suggests, he was engaged in a romantic and nostalgic operation typical of the period when the Indian was viewed as a "vanishing race." Most or all of the distinguished ethnologists of the period - Holmes, Morgan, Grinnell, Lowie, and others - accepted Curtis's pictures as "authentic" and commended him for performing an invaluable service. Curtis did take a few pictures of the acculturated modern existence of the same Indians he dressed up in "aboriginal" settings, but such photos were rarely publicized or sold.

[2] The basic theoretical statement is Herkovits et al., 1938. The best-known collection of acculturation researches is Linton, 1940. Abstracts of the literature of the period are found in Siegel, 1955.

[3] For typical studies of the period, see Goodenough, 1963, and Niehoff 1966.

[4] The classic statement of the British effort is Brown and Hutt, 1935. For an overview of applied anthropology, see Bastide, 1971.

[5] The early interventionist approach is exemplified by the following: Arensberg and Niehoff, 1964, and Barnett 1956.

[6] See Cochrane 1971, and Poggie and Lynch 1974.

[7] A great deal has been written on dependency and dependency theory. The "theory" is principally an ideologically derived critique of the imbalance in nations' wealth, and how "development" is in part, at least, a means for maintaining the former colonial inequalities by economic control and domination. "Dependency," on the other hand, is an empirical condition that varies greatly among nations, and includes cases where the "dependent" nation on the periphery has considerable power over the dominant nation in the "center." For critical discussions of the theory, see Chilcote and Johnson 1983. For an empirical

study of a particular case of relative dependency, see Evans 1979.

[8] See, for example, Halperin, 1977. The term "substantive" refers to the theories of Karl Polanyi, who represents for many anthropologists the most eloquent spokesperson for emphasis on the social, cultural, institutional, and physical aspects of social change; i.e. that economic matters generally follow the social, rather than precede them, in change processes. The point of view is by no means confined to the Polanyi group, however: see Long, 1977. In its most general sense, the view is nothing more than a statement of the topical specialties of anthropology and sociology and an affirmation that they are important in studying and introducing social change.

[9] A study of the annual reports of the World Bank, especially the summary data tables appearing at the rear, provides information on this. Year after year, the purely economic-growth aspects of development show a gain in the majority of countries, but the data on income distribution, social indicators, etc. show lags, gaps, and inequalities.

[10] See J. W. Bennett & D. Kanel 1983, for a presentation of the economists' concept of utility and profit maximization in the context of agricultural development. The concept does not regard "maximization" as a matter of extraordinary effort, but simply as whatever it requires, under prevailing conditions, to sustain a particular business enterprise. The choice of the term "maximization" was of course unfortunate, and obviously economists and utilitarian philosophers over-applied the idea - much as natural selection was stretched to mean survival of the fittest.

[11] The economics issue is not merely one of replacing quantitative measurements with qualitative ones. As noted, the main problem was the predictive ideology of economics thinking, not the measurement of change by material standards. Since the world of development is part of the world of economics, it is inescapable that economics become part of the analysis. Anthropologists need to know economics, not scorn it, and certainly the sponsorship of this volume by the Society for Economic Anthropology implies this. Anthropologists are right to reject the simplistic foisting of industrial economics on agrarian cultures, but they still need to know the economics of quantitative value analysis, because this is the way nations measure status and assign benefits.

[12] For an insightful analysis of how the governmental and bureaucratic organization of foreign aid influences the temporal and other dimensions of development projects, see Tendler, 1975.

[13] Irving Hallowell's (1945) paper on the significance of learning and other behavioral processes in acculturation is my candidate for the most neglected statement in anthropological theory. If it had been taken seriously by the discipline as a whole, the course of research on the nature of change would have shifted away from cultural abstractions to a study of human behavior as an adaptive and creative force. Lacking a behavioral theory of change, anthropologists naturally have had difficulty assimilating developmental change theory.

[14] The most readily available surveys of world environmental conditions and associated survival issues, like population and food, are the annual volumes produced by the Worldwatch Institute, with the generic title, State of the World. Worldwatch also produces a widely used series of pamphlets on all these issues, summarizing current best research in the field. The Population Reference Bureau has a useful pamphlet series on demographic trends and processes; and the United Nations has a variety of publications. Specific reports on the state of the physical environment are issued by many sources, for example OCED. Samples of the above types of reports are found in the list of references to follow.

References

Arensberg, Conrad M. and Arthur H. Niehoff. 1964. Introducing Social Change: A Handbook for Americans Overseas. Chicago: Aldine Publishing Company.

Barnett, H.G. 1956. Anthropology in Administration. Evanston & N.Y.: Row, Peterson & Co.

Bastide, Roger. 1971. Applied Anthropology. New York: Harper & Row.

Bennett, John W. 1959. Planned Change in Perspective. Human Organization 18;2-4.

----- 1976. Anticipation, Adaptation, and the Concept of Culture. Science 192, pp. 847-853.

Bennett, John W. and Don Kanel. 1983. Agricultural Economics and Economic Anthropology: Confrontation and Accommodation. In: Economic Anthropology: Topics and Theories. S. Ortiz, ed. Society for Economic Anthropology, Monograph No. 1. New York: University Press of America.

Bennett, John W., Steven W. Lawry, and James C. Riddell. 1986. Land Tenure and Livestock Development in Sub-Saharan Africa. Washington, D.C., AID Special Evaluation Study No. 39. Agency for International Development.

Brown, G. Gordon and A. McD. Hutt. 1935. Anthropology in Action: An Experiment in the Iringa Province. London: Oxford

University Press.

Brown, Lester R. and Others. 1987. State of the World 1987. N.Y.: Worldwatch Institute and W.W. Norton.

Chilcote, Ronald H. and Dale L. Johnson. 1983. Theories of Development: Mode of Production or Dependency. London: Sage Publications.

Cochrane, Glynn. 1971. Development Anthropology. New York: Oxford University Press.

Evans, Peter. 1979. Dependent Development: The Alliance of Multinational, State, and Local Capital in Brazil. Princeton: Princeton University Press.

Goodenough, Ward H. 1963. Cooperation in Change: An Anthropological Approach to Community Development. New York: Russell Sage.

Hallowell, Irving I. 1945. Sociopsychological Aspects of Acculturation. In: The Science of Man in the World Crisis. R. Linton, ed. New York: Columbia University Press.

Halperin, Rhoda. 1977. A Substantive Approach to Peasant Livelihood. In: Peasant Livelihood, edited by Rhoda Halperin and James Dow. New York: St. Martin's Press.

Herkovits, Melville J. et al. 1938. Acculturation: The Study of Culture Contact. New York: J. J. Augustin.

Hirsch, Fred. 1976. The Social Limits to Growth. New York: The Twentieth Century Fund and Harvard University Press.

Hirschman, Albert O. 1967. Development Projects Observed. Washington, D.C. The Brookings Institution.

Kuznets, Simon. 1955. Economic Growth and Income Inequality. American Economic Review 45; 1-26.

Linton, Ralph. 1940. Acculturation in Seven North American Indian Tribes. New York: Appleton Century.

Long, Norman. 1977. An Introduction to the Sociology of Rural Development. London: Tavistock Publications.

Lyman, Christopher M. 1982. The Vanishing Race and Other Illusions: Photographs of Edward S. Curtis. New York: Pantheon Books and the Smithsonian Institution Press.

Mead, Margaret. 1955. Cultural Patterns and Technical Change. Manual originally prepared for the World Federation of Mental Health, Paris, UNESCO. Reprinted 1955 and subsequent years by Mentor Books.

Merrick, Thomas W. and Staff. 1986. World Population in Transition. Population Bulletin No. 41, No. 2 Washington Population Reference Bureau.

Niehoff, Arthur H. 1966. A Casebook of Social Change. Chicago: Aldine Publishing Co.

Organization for Economic Cooperation and Development (OECD). 1986. The State of the Environment 1985. Paris: OECD.

Poggie, John H., Jr. and Robert N. Lynch. 1974. Rethinking Modernization: Anthropological Perspectives. Westport, Conn.: Greenwood Press.

Raven, Peter. 1987. Killing our World. Keynote Address to the

Annual Meeting of the American Association for the Advancement of Science, Chicago.

Schultz, Theodore. 1964. Transforming Traditional Agriculture. Yale Univ. Press.

Siegel, Bernard J., ed. 1955. Acculturation: Critical Abstracts, No. America. Stanford Anthropological Series, No. 2, Stanford University Press.

Tax, Sol. 1958. The Fox Project. Human Organization 17; 17-19.

Tendler, Judith. 1975. Inside Foreign Aid. Baltimore: Johns Hopkins University Press.

Wilson, Godfrey and Monica Hunter. 1945. The Analysis of Social Change: Based on Observations in Central Africa. Cambridge Univ. Press.

Wood, Geoff ed. 1985. Labelling in Development Policy. London: Sage Publications.

World Bank. 1975. The Assault on World Poverty: Problems of Rural Development, Education, and Health. Washington, D.C.: International Bank for Reconstruction and Development & Johns Hopkins University Press. /inc xerox.endjob

SECTION I. OVERVIEWS AND CONTROVERSIES

The papers in this section present contrasting views of
development. The first two essays were given as plenary
addresses to the 1985 conference. Richard Adams takes a
global-historical perspective, extending the environmental
concerns of Bennett's essay to the study of power and energy.
Adams's evolutionary approach is situated in the line of
anthropological thought running from Lewis Henry Morgan to Leslie
White, Elman Service, and Marshall Sahlins. His specific
contribution is the focus on the growth of the "regulatory
sector" and the energy-based limitations on its growth. Harold
Schneider takes a point of view from the ground up; his
principles of development are in fact admonitions to those who
make facile assumptions about the nature of human motivation,
particularly to those who underestimate the importance of power
in social change. The paper by Robert Bates is a written version
of remarks made at the conference about what kind of a field
"development anthropology" might be. Bates urges anthropologists
to use the particular perspective of development work to study
bureaucracies and the processes of decision making.

2. EVOLUTION AND DEVELOPMENT

Richard N. Adams

The Evolution of Development

The nineteenth-century vision of making the world a better place in which to live was called "progress." It was a coal-fueled ideology for a vast colonial expansion; and it was crushingly discredited by World War I and the subsequent era of stagnation and depression. "Development," in a sense, a petroleum-fueled successor to the vision of progress, accompanied the spread of industrialism in the post-colonial nationalizing that followed World War II. If the illusion of progress was dashed by the First World War, the "development" illusion was cracked and fragmented on the one hand by increasing poverty, social movements and revolts, military interventions and regional wars, and on the other hand, by environmental pollution and degradation. Marshall Wolfe has recently summed up development's failures in five points. First, in spite of some increase in national income, benefits failed to follow. Second, industrialization and modernization destroyed existing identity systems, but provided no coherent new identity. Third, international economy and politics became increasingly unstable, experienced increasing crises of debts and balance-of-payments, transnational penetrations, and the assumption of hegemony by the military; in short, planning fell into discredit. Fourth, the population explosion devastated natural resources and created unbelievable urban agglomerations. Finally, as industrialized countries fell into stagflation they lost their plausability as models (Wolfe, 1984, 158).

In failing to reach these goals, was development a failure? Or were the goals set for it materially unobtainable? Were they, perhaps, working against imperfectly understood larger processes, which even when recognized were largely rejected?

In the early 1950s, Europe and Japan showed evidence of real recovery. The myth was emerging that know-how, capital, and a desire to pull oneself up by the bootstraps were all that were necessary for a nation to achieve the wonderous level of living manifest in the United States. Low income and poverty were synonymous with underdevelopment, and development meant increasing gross national, or domestic, product.[1] It was assumed that the enhanced quality of life enjoyed by industrialized countries, i.e., those with high national product,

33

was due to the high consumption made possible (and necessary) by
increased production.[2] It followed that by expanding markets
in the world's non-industrial and post-colonial populations, not
only would the world's poor enjoy the riches of the West, but the
industrial producers would also reap profits. The goal of
development was, in short, to expand consumption everywhere, but
specifically to bring the rest of the world into an
interdependent network with centers of industrial
production.[3] In these terms, it may be argued that
development has enjoyed considerable success.

Although specialists may differ on the aspects of
development they regard as being most salient, all commonly used
indices, such as GDP or GNP, that correlate highly with, and
directly or indirectly depend upon, increasing the level of
energy consumption.[4] Expanding bureaucracies in the poor
countries and promoters of development in the industrial centers
shared the view that the clearest indicator of developmental
success was the intensification[5] of productive effort through
increased energy inputs; such inputs, of course, increase energy
consumption. Intensification was usually phrased as
productivity, emphasizing an increase of efficiency of human
labor outputs. This was, of course, achieved by supplementing
high amounts of nonhuman energy.

It is interesting that in these years little note was taken
of the fact that energy increase was also the only seriously
proposed objective measure of social evolutionary advance (White
1949, 1959). The lack of interest stemmed from various reasons.
For one, evolution was seen as a long term process, one that
could not be observed in the brief decades after World War II.
Also poor countries were seen as engaging in a catching-up
process that was merely setting things right, and had nothing to
do with more profound processes such as evolution. In the United
States, a politician would never have sold "development" to the
fundamentalists by advertising it to be the same as "evolution."
Moreover, energy was seen as materialistic, cheap and easy to
get, hardly a proper measure for the advance of humankind.

Besides not perceiving that ("development") masked a
profound evolutionary process, social scientists and politicians
shared some dangerously misleading illusions about the nature of
evolution. One was that because efficiency had been the
watchword of industrial success, efficiency in human productivity
was also accepted as a beneficient sign; it was part of
development. In fact, of course, the increase in energy
consumption was accompanied by an accelerating inefficiency of
energy use.

Another stemmed from the success the leaders of the

34

industrial world had in putting Western Europe and Japan back on their industrial feet; it gave the illusion that one could with equal ease set the rest of the world in order. The fact that both Western Europe and Japan had earlier been industrial powers was not seen to place them in a different category than, say, Ghana, Malaysia, Syria, Ecuador, or Guatemala. The importance of history and antecedents as conditions for "development" was depreciated in the enthusiasm for the magic of industrial "know how." But development was, for better or worse, a phase of evolution and it worked in its own ways.

The advent of OPEC controls and skyrocketing energy prices of the mid-1970s sharply drew attention to the fact that the long accepted ballooning of energy consumption not only posed a serious economic problem, but was also phenomenally inefficient (World Bank 1983,28). As energy sources came in short supply, inefficiency suddenly became a serious problem. When this happened, however, the response paralleled earlier history. The new concern did not focus on energy efficiency so much as on conserving specific energy sources. Indeed, although the rate growth of energy consumption declined between 1974 and 1980 (especially in low income countries and in industrial market countries), the decline occurred in only 17 of 121 countries reported on by the World Bank (1983, 162-3). The prevalent philosophy of development did not regard efficiency to be the major issue; rather, it was considered an inconvenience that had to be observed in order to increase the amount of work output in the face of input restrictions.

This lack of concern, however, did not hide the fact that the newly industrializing powers had very little control over the energy consumption processes now set in motion. The demand for consumer and industrial consumption could not be stayed when commercial energy prices exploded. The rising energy costs set in motion by the OPEC policies thus became the major factor in increasing the indebtedness among developing countries, and in locking debtor and creditor nations in an embrace that is increasingly uncomfortable under the current rules of the game.

Another aspect of development also became clearer in this era. Development directed from positions of dominance at the top or outside of a society could have limited success at best, and could be actually counterproductive. People did not always take kindly to being pressed to produce more. Successful development had to be self generating, in a very considerable degree, and excessive outside efforts could even destroy the potential that existed locally. Outsiders showed little genius for getting people to exert themselves to produce more. As a reaction, there emerged a concern with "participation," "endogenous" or "grass roots" development. Although still stimulated from the outside, endogenous development encouraged more local decision making at the risk of generating conflicts with the power structure of the society. It was not received with universal enthusiasm, because it could be perceived as weakening the power of central government. This always raised the potential for construing local action as usurping economic privileges or even promoting political insurgency. Both could lead to governmental repression.

The Development of Social Evolutionary Thought

The vision of social evolution has changed markedly over the past four decades. In 1960 the dominant paradigms were still marked heavily by Spencer, Tylor, Morgan, Marx and Engels, Childe, White, and Steward. In recent years, however, some quite different perspectives have appeared from a number of quarters. These include ecology and ecosystems theory (e.g., Binford 1968), cybernetics, information, and general systems theory (Flannery 1972), neo-marxist interpretations (e.g., Friedman and Rowlands 1978), the "Modern" Darwinian synthesis (Huxley 1943), thermodynamics, and far from equilibrium theory (Prigogine, Herman and Allen 1977).

Although Darwin introduced his evolutionary theory in the middle of the last century, the neo-Darwinian paradigm of reproduction, variation, and natural selection had no visible scientific effect on sociocultural evolutionary thinking for over a hundred years. "Social Darwinism" was a political miscarriage with little scientific impact in this area. The first real Darwinian impact came in the guise of sociobiology, a headlong neo-Darwinian claim that some classical cultural patterns were epigenetic products of genetic predispositions (Wilson 1975, Dawkins 1976, Barash 1976). This leap-frogging reductionism assumed cultural patterning to have been favored by natural selection because these patterns enhanced inclusive fitness of genes that have yet to be discovered.

As both an outgrowth of, and a reaction to, sociobiological excesses, a less flamboyant Darwinian contender has been the "co-evolution" approach (Campbell 1965; Cavelli-Sforza and Feldman 1971; Durham 1982; Rindos 1984). While rejecting sociobiological reductionism, co-evolutionism asserts that neo-Darwinist mechanisms can apply equally to culture traits and biological genes. Although they improve on sociobiology, coevolutionists err in forcing culture into a simplistic genetic mold. Culture lacks any empirically identifiable units that play a role comparable to that played by the gene in biological

36

evolution. Durham has followed Dawkins in proposing some kind of
mental unit--a "meme"--that is supposed to correspond to the
gene. Unfortunately, the meme smells heavily of ether and
flogistine and is even more elusive than the sociobiologist's
gene for altruism. For better or worse, the neo-Darwinian
paradigm describes genetic reproduction. Whatever else it may
be, culture is minimally part of the human phenotype, not the
genotype; and at the most, it can be argued to include all sorts
of material things and mental models that pose serious problems
for a simple reproductive organic model. Equally important,
"co-evolution" refers classically to an evolutionary
interdependence of self-organizing, autonomous, organic entities
-- such as lice and human beings. Culture is not an independent
self-organization, but is epigenetic to the human organism.
Unlike the louse, culture does not reproduce itself; it is
immanent, not parasitic or symbiotic, to human behavior.
Although we cannot expect human beings to survive apart from
culture, they can and do live full and happy lives free of lice.
(cf. Bennett 1980.)

The only parts of this cultural assortment that can readily
be mapped on the neo-Darwinian model are certain subsets,
aggregates of parts, that are themselves self-organizing and self
reproductive. These may be argued for societies, but not for
cultures. Human social organizations are phenotypical
adaptations, but they are close analogues to organisms in that
they reproduce, yield variants, and suffer random change similar
to mutation. They are affected differently by natural selection
because they are Lamarkian rather than Darwinian. External
forces can not only affect their reproduction, but may introduce
variations at any point in the process.

Although Darwinian mechanisms apply analogically to the
self-organization of social systems, socio-cultural processes are
much more open for inspection than is biological evolution. The
reproducing or failing to reproduce of cultural elements, i.e.,
those to which meaning is attached (such as saying "Good Morning"
every day) can affect future events. Social organizational forms
are maintained by reproducing sets of relational events (e.g.,
the domestic unit is constantly maintained through the daily
reproduction of spouse and parent-child behavior). Finally,
social organizations maintain and replicate themselves, both
consciously and unconsciously. Besides maintaining and
reproducing themselves, some social organizations spawn social
forms quite different from themselves. Culture is unique to
human development, there is no satisfactory homology to be found
in other species. It is a kind of chemistry of social
organization, by which the meanings that provide the symbolic
material of human social interaction are given form. Our models
and interpretations are framed in terms of these existing

37

meaning-form associations. Thus, "mutations" in human society appear as changes in the association between meanings and forms; some may be of clear origins; others may be quite unpredictable.

Although reproduction, variation, and mutation find easy analogues in societal processes, natural selection is more complex. All the equipment human beings need for further reproduction pertains to their own organic constitution. In contrast, human society are more than an organization of human beings, because it includes a variety of nonhuman components--material things, speech sounds, etc. -- that are absolutely essential to its nature and reproduction. In order to reproduce human society, human beings piece their own behaviors together with cultural equipment, and integrate the assemblage into some kind of conformance with their mental models.

With respect to human society, natural selection acts not only directly on individual reproduction, but also through an assemblage of human and nonhuman things called culture. Reproduction of a social group that uses fire, bows and arrows, scapulmancy, bark houses, and incipient domestication requires reproducing both the people and the things. Reproduction and survival of human society is more flexible than the reproduction of human beings.

Development in Evolution

If development intensifies energy consumption, then its role in social evolution cannot be explained in neo-Darwinian terms alone. Recourse must be had to two additional bodies of theory: Lotka's principle of energy flux; and the nature of complex systems. Let us first discuss Lotka. The principle states that,

> In every instance considered, natural selection will so operate as to increase the total mass of the organic system, to increase the rate of circulation of matter through the system, and to increase the total energy flux through the system, so long as there is presented an unutilized residue of matter and available energy[1922, 148].

Although formulated originally to apply to biological populations, and rejected by some biologists, Lotka's principle is applicable to society.[7] However, it is peculiar epistemologically in serving as both a tautology and a theory. The principle states that so long as free energy is available, those forms will be favored that consume more energy. Because consuming more energy is tantamount to favorable survival, and

38

unavailable energy cannot be consumed, the statement can be read as a tautology. However, it can also be read as stating that if there is competition among living forms, and if there is free energy available, then the forms that consume greater energy will be favored over those that use less; as such, it is also a theory. Its utility for understanding human society derives from the fact that it permits both human and nonhuman energy forms to be included in a single framework of analysis. It is possible to map calculated energy costs of production on to this tautology, and thereby compare the amount of energy that societies consume in the production process. It is necessary to compare different kinds of energy forms because the extra-somatic energy forms are so diverse in human society.

The evolution of ecosystems also illustrates Lotka's principle. So long as free energy is available, K-strategy systems may emerge. They cannot, however, eliminate r-strategy systems, because they depend upon the latter for their own consumption and reproduction. When the consumption of energy equals the supply of free energy, of course, K-strategy systems cease to expand and the systems levels off into a steady state. (A discussion of r and K strategies will be found in Pianka 1978.)

The utility of complex systems theory lies in the proposition that the complexity[8] of structures increases with energy flow. These structures are taken here as self organizing, dissipative structures. Such structures are far from equilibrium, a value measured by the amount of energy they require to maintain their form. This too can be illustrated by reference to the ecological strategies. An expanding ecosystem increases energy consumption and grows more complex in the process. The specific formal characteristic of complexity is that it appears as hierarchy (Simon 1962; Pattee 1973; Bronowski 1970). In the ecosystem, this is manifest through the consumption of r-strategy forms by K-strategy forms. Human societies are components of ecosystems, and their own expansion necessarily conforms to this pattern. Human social expansion, however, is not simply that of an expansion of K-strategy human beings engaged in consuming r-strategy species because the former also obtain much of the increased energy from extra-somatic, non-living, sources. Additionally, human hierarchies bifurcate and stratify human society so that an r-strategy component (workers) is domesticated by a K-strategy component (rulers). Thus, an analysis of the ecosystem pattern is replicated within human society.[9]

This replication of the ecological process within human society complicates the application of the neo-Darwinian model. Let us, for simplicity's sake, model hierarchical societies as

39

being composed of two self-organizing sectors. One is a lower or work sector, relatively large and fragmented into many small and overlapping self-organizing components. The other, a small upper, ruling or regulatory sector has power over, and thereby makes decisions for, the lower sector. Natural selection is, then, confronted both by the society as a whole, and separately by each sector.

Every complex society has a regulatory sector. It comprises all the people who make the decisions for the society and the people who facilitate and assure that the decisions are carried out. It includes the people in public administration; security forces such as police, armed forces, taxing authorities, regulatory bureaus, the bureaucracy as such. It also includes people in business, commerce and finance (those through whom market decisions are made and are carried out). Finally it includes people involved in education and religion, and other activities that train people's minds how to think, and therefore, what kinds of decisions to make. The regulatory sector is not to be confused with dictatorships, tyrannies, democracies, or any specific governments. Rather they constitute the sector of every state that does these things. They are the central nervous system of a state.

Irrespective of what may motivate the individuals in the regulatory sector, the sector as a whole has two indispensible methods of seeing to the continuity and survival of the society. The first is to assure the continuity and welfare of the work sector of the society. This is usually done by intensifying the energy harnessing and consumption of energy by the work sector. This is necessary both because the society lives off that energy, and because the regulatory sector itself must draw on it for its own welfare, survival and continuity. This may be done by pressing the workers to exert more energy, and to multiply their numbers; or by increasing their consumption of coal, petroleum, and wood in the production of things.

The other is to guarantee its own continuity and survival. Regulatory sectors, which emerge as hierarchies over the work sectors, self-organize themselves to reinforce and improve their controls. In planning for development, a hierarchy will try to reduce threats to its control and seek to enhance its power. The people who are the objects of development, then, become instruments to retain or enhance the hierarchy's base of power. The Lotka thesis is reflected here, as all increases in energy flows or forms give the regulatory sector greater potential power bases. To accomplish its task, the regulatory sector needs the cooperation of the work sector. One way this is done is to identify the interests and goals of both sectors as being one; i.e., that what is good for the regulatory sector is good for the

40

country. Development, therefore, will be pursued by the hierarchy only if it is seen to be in its best interests, whether it is sponsored from the top down or endogenously.

To summarize thus far, this view argues that any self organizing component of a society may attempt self development. However, insofar as such efforts strategically increase energy consumption, the regulatory sector will seek to control them. Moreover, development programs are part of a hierarchy's strategy to enhance its own environment. Because the rest of the society is part of that environment, the welfare of the hierarchy will vary with its ability to increase the flow of energy in the work sector.

The Darwinian Consequences of Development

If we use the Darwinian paradigm to interpret evolutionary consequences of development over the past three to four decades, we would come out with something like the following:

1. Population explosion. The central Darwinian consequence of development has been to enhance human reproduction. No matter how devious may have been the mechanisms, the population explosion seems to be an indisputable developmental consequence of industrialism and it began to make its appearance before the term "development" came into vogue. It has been enhanced directly through simple public health measures; and indirectly because increasing family size is one of the few ways that economically and politically marginalized rural peoples can increase income in the face of declining real wages.

2. Reduction of ecological and species variability. Industrial development reduces ecological and species variability within the biosphere. To the degree that it is guided by high energy processes, agricultural variability declines, and broad spectra of bioforms are destroyed by pollution and toxic substances such as pesticides and herbicides. A specific ecological consequence of intensified exploitation is the spoilage or effective exhaustion of strategic resources. Important among these are atmosphere, top soils, water, forests, petroleum, and the air.

3. Reduction of cultural variability at the world level. Parallel to reducing species variability, development aims to reorganize peoples with diverse life ways into standardized, but presumably more productive, patterns. Training in new techniques, formal education, reorganization of labor, legal

41

constraints, and public health, are used to bring society-wide behavioral conformance. Folk knowledge of local environment is displaced by popularized standard knowledge. Diverse local and ethnic myths are displaced by myths to rationalize the regulatory sector as being part of the natural order. Most devastating has been where failure to conform has been met with genocide, as currently among aboriginal peoples in the Amazon and Guatemala. Of a different genre has been the role of production intensification in exacerbating the Sahalean drought.

4. Increased levels of living differentiation. While destroying earlier cultural variety with one hand, development differentially favors the life chances within populations. It substantially raises the living level among some but marginalizes others along regional, wealth, occupational, and ethnic lines. At the same time, new local groups (which I think of as "survival vehicles") emerge to cope with problems that have been created, or left unattended, by the hierarchy, and thereby evolve new cultures, characterized by Edward Sapir as "spurious" (1924). Their intent is to solve problems, and in so doing they create new cultural material. Because these new forms are built with elements already present, they are only rarely seen as exotic.

5. Increasing energy flow and complexity. In the economic interpretation, development seeks to increase individual productivity. Although this is in part achieved by improving technological efficiency, the major increase in productivity derives from vast increases in nonhuman energy. By standing on the back of these "energy slaves," individual human beings can appear to be more productive. The vast increase of energy consumption thus entailed has helped to expand the hierarchy and to generate new, lower level, self interest groups.

Development, Hierarchy and Societal Self Regulation

Given the apparently destructive and unpleasant consequences just listed one must wonder why development takes place at all. The answer must be given at two levels: that of energy dynamics and that of motivation. In the first, the answer lies in the fact that expansion of population and nonhuman energy flow conform to Lotka's principle. They will continue to offer survival advantages so long as free energy can be harnessed. In terms of human motivation, however, the issue is quite different. It may be possible for some species to survive in a state of universal misery and suffering, but it is not necessarily possible in the human case. Because our mental models can describe suffering, they can also imagine and seek its absence.

42

The human motivational reason for persistent expansion lies in the fact that not everyone is equally miserable. Although development is adverse for some people, it benefits others. Among the beneficiaries are, of course, the members of the society's regulatory sector. Even as some of the poor grow poorer, development also enriches some of the rich and strengthens some of the powerful. Development at the motivational level persists, therefore, because it benefits the very sector of the population that has the strategic capacity to decide whether it should be pursued. Of course, it may favor some parts of the regulatory sector over others, so just how it should be done may be subject to some dispute.

Irrespective of the mechanism that produces it, however, the ultimate measure of development is the increase in per capita energy consumption. Until the advent of industrial uses of fossil fuels, human society depended on human labor supplemented by wild and domesticated plants and animals, wind, and water. All societies dependent on these kinds of energy sources could support a limited number of individuals dedicated to regulating the operation of the society. The transition to fossil fueled industry began an expansion in the dependence on commercial energy resources that has increased in fits and starts ever since. Economists and demographers have observed that this led to a change in the structure of labor in society, with differential changes in the sector of primary production (agriculture and mining), secondary production (manufacturing), and the so-called terciary sector, or services. These structural changes, however, were not of merely economic significance; they also reflected profound changes in the way a society organized and regulated itself.

A modern nation can be conceived of as a self-organizing set of human and nonhuman components that reproduce themselves by (1) transforming material things, i.e., extract resources and fabricate products from the environment for the purpose of (2) reproducing and maintaining the human beings, and (3) specializing the regulation of the society in a social hierarchy, a regulatory sector. Prior to industrialization only some three to five percent of the people in a state would be in the regulatory sector. One result of the growth of commercial energy, however, has been to increase the proportion of people specializing in regulatory activities. Increasing use of commercial energy necessarily removes people from the primary and secondary productive sectors. What the society then does with these people is determined by the manner that it self-organizes and reproduces itself. One measure of this is simply the size, i.e., the proportion of the total population that specializes in regulatory activities. (The method of analysis used here is spelled out in Adams 1982a, 1982b; a book manuscript is in preparation.)

The accompanying figures show the historical trajectory of the regulatory sectors -- the percent of the population engaged in administrative, security, commercial, financial, and educational activities -- of a number of contemporary nations in the era of growing commercial energy comsumption. They show two major processes at work. First (Figure 1) is that in the aggregate the increase in commercial energy is accompanied by an increase in the percentage of the population in the regulatory sector. Second (remaining figures) is that the regulatory sectors of the individual nation-states conform to cultural-historical patterns that reflect propinquity and historical antecedents.

Although aggregate data show that the per capita regulatory sectors increase with per capita commercial energy, the process is complex. It appears that any regulatory sector has the potential of finding ways to increase the energy consumption. However, not all will make a serious attempt. Indeed, some, such as the Chinese Cultural Revolutionaries and Cambodians under Pol Pot, positively reduced it. However, a regulatory sector can apparently only grow so far without an increase in nonhuman energy consumption. For example, it appears impossible to obtain a regulatory sector larger than 7.5 percent if the society's energy consumption is under 500 kg-cal of coal equivalent per capita. Thus the size of a regulatory sector can be constrained by the amount of energy available, but can also inhibit energy consumption expansion.

Given that in the aggregate there is considerable leeway for action, it is not surprising that individual cases show diverse behavior. This diversity, however, is also under some very interesting constraints. Figure 2 shows three North European countries (France, Belgium, and the Netherlands); Figure 3 shows four Anglo-American countries (Great Britain, Canada, Australia, and the United States); and four Scandinavian countries (Denmark, Sweden, Norway, and Finland). Figures 4 and 5 then contrast one northern European country with the Scandinavian and the Anglo-American. It is evident that each set of countries has a very different historical trajectory. Whereas all begin at the same low "preindustrial" level, the northern European set increases more rapidly in the nineteenth century, but then tends to level off early in the twentieth century. The Anglo-American set increases steadily through both centuries. The Scandinavian set does not start its increase until the twentieth century, but then traces an ascent that parallels and catches up with the Anglo-American. The central European set of Germany, Italy, Switzerland, and Austria shows a remarkable conformance until 1960. Figure 6 shows them, but also includes the Netherlands to show how they are distinct from the northern European group.

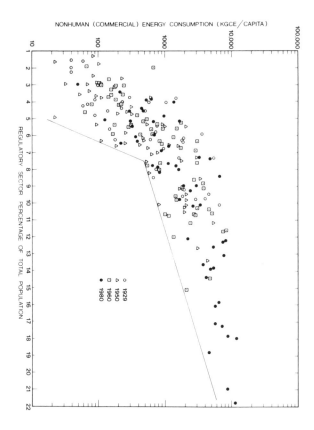

Figure 1. Regulatory sectors of 70 countries compared with
national commercial energy consumption (kg coal equivalent per
capita) for 1929, 1937, 1950, 1970.

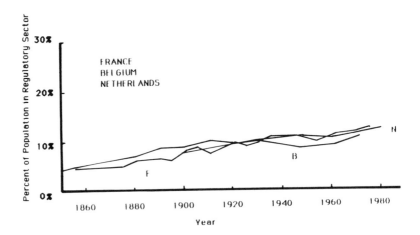

Figure 2. Regulatory sectors of France, Belgium and the Netherlands.

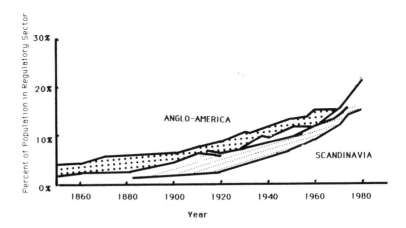

Figure 3. Regulatory sectors of Anglo-America (Australia, Canada, Great Britain, and the U.S.A.) and Scandinavia (Denmark, Finland, Norway, and Sweden).

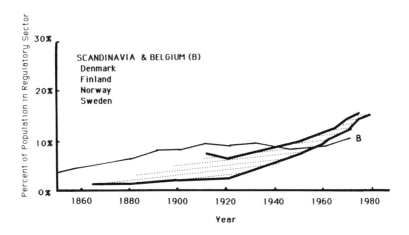

Figure 4.   Regulatory sectors of Scandinavia compared with
Belgium.

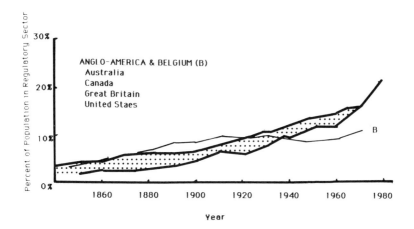

Figure 5.   Regulatory sectors of Anglo-America compared with
Belgium.

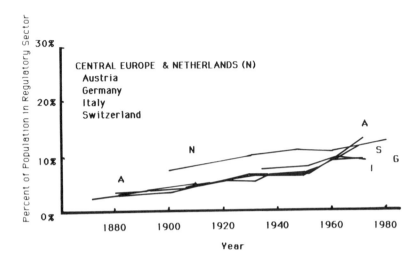

Figure 6. Regulatory sectors of Central Europe (Austria, Germany [West Germany after 1945], Italy, Switzerland) compared with the Netherlands.

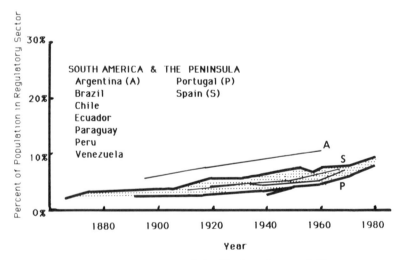

Figure 7. Regulatory sectors of South America and the Penninsula.

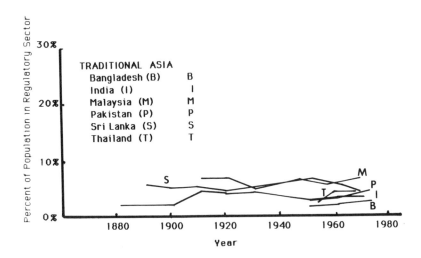

Figure 8.   Regulatory sectors of traditional Asian countries.

49

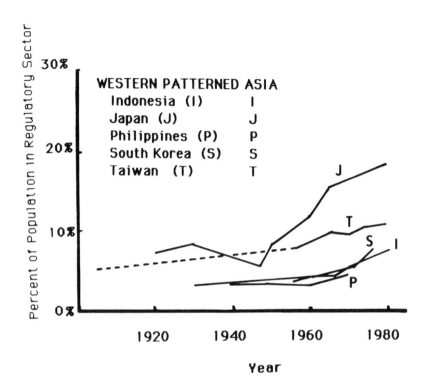

Figure 9. Regulatory sectors of western patterned Asian countries.

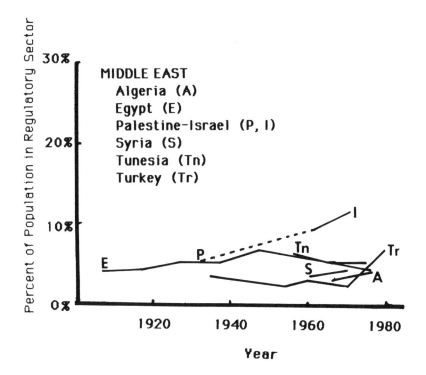

Figure 10. Regulatory sectors of the Middle East.

In Europe, Spain and Portugal show the lowest and slowest expansion of the regulatory sector. What is interesting is that most South American countries follow the same pattern with one major exception. Argentina's regulatory sector was drawn from late nineteenth- and twentieth-century European immigrants, and shows a trajectory more similar to France (Figure 7).

European and Anglo-American countries almost all show an increase in the regulatory sector that accompanies the increase in commercial energy consumption. This is not a universal trait, however, and in Asia and the Mideast patterns can be profoundly different. There is a strong tendency for nations of Asia (Figure 8) and of the Middle East (Figure 10) simply not to increase this sector. Figure 9, however, shows that some countries (most suggestively those with strong, aggressive capitalist export sectors) have taken on the western patterning. These materials suggest a great many things and pose even more questions; there is no space here to examine them as such. Rather, I want merely to suggest certain implications that they may have for understanding development.[10]

1. One of the early hopes of western development enthusiasts was to increase democratic participation in the society. The viability of this notion fell under the dependency arguments that began to appear in the middle 1960s. In contrast, however, if the size of a regulatory sector size induces participation in regulating a society, these figures show some increase in almost all European societies and many less industrialized. Moreover, this was related to the growth of commercial energy consumption. Societies with low energy consumption must anticipate spending considerable time and effort in simply increasing energy consumption before they can expect a pronounced increase in such participation. This suggests that the much discussed "trickle down effect" does not even begin without increasing commercial energy consumption and, in some places, it may not drip at all.

2. Economic development experts have been slow to accept a determinant role for culture, and even slower to understand what such a role might be. The policy shift toward endogenous development was a step toward recognizing the cultural importance of the local level. These data show, further, that every society's hierarchy organizes itself and its society both "horizontally" and "vertically,"[11] in ways similar to immediately neighboring or migrant peoples, and immediately antecedent societies. Regulatory sectors rarely show major leaps, and the kinship with neighbors is patent in the cases shown here. Those who feel that economic processes have a life of their own might be reluctant to label these processes as "culture." However, the way a society regulates itself is wholly non-genetic and is the product of past practices as they are cast against

experience and prejudice. This is, however, self regulation, and much of that is what economists have, correctly or not, seen as "economic."

Apparent discontinuities in extending cultural patterns can be partially explained by known horizontal influences. For example, Argentina exhibits a much higher regulatory sector than the rest of Latin America; but the population of that sector specifically selected itself out of Europe late in the last century, and is not derived from the colonial Spanish and Portuguese antecedents. One can only speculate that migrants to Argentina brought a predisposition to run things differently than those who had been much longer in Latin America.

3. Although the regulatory sectors of Western nations tend to grow with commercial energy increase, few Asian and Middle Eastern countries have shown such tendencies. It is important to understand that there is no proximate determinism here. Merely increasing commercial energy consumption will not automatically yield an immediate increase in the regulatory sector. The most common pattern of performace in Asia and the Middle East shows no consistent increase in the regulatory sector at all. There are important divergencies toward the western pattern, however. Japan and Taiwan are marked, and some other countries (e.g. Turkey, South Korea, the Philippines, and Indonesia) show gradual increase by the 1970s.

4. Let us, for a moment, put aside the stereotypic economic preference to take development as an increase in commercial energy consumption (and GDP) and, instead, see it as the way that the society applies the resulting increases in organizing and reproducing itself. The diversity in regulatory sectors illustrates the importance of culture-historical factors over short-term grafting. While development is inherently an endogamous process, but the manner and rate at which it will take place -- and whether it takes place at all -- is heavily influenced not only by its immediate history, but also by immediate and specific external cultural influences. Although the Marshall Plan did increase GDP, it did not make Italy's regulatory sector act very differently from Austria's or Switzerland's; nor did the "economic miracle" make Brazil's pattern significantly diverge from the rest of South America; and Japan's regulatory expansion after World War II seemed bent upon regaining a direction already in evidence before the war.

In short, if we take development as the increase in per capita energy consumption of a society, then it is clear that it makes a regulatory sector increase possible. It does not, however, determine whether, how, or when a society will in fact change. Preexisting culture can delay regulatory sector growth in some societies as well as hurry it in others. Also, countries wishing to increase participation in regulative activities apparently have no choice but to increase their own commercial energy consumption. Given the cost of energy in recent years, this has posed serious problems for many countries.

5. Finally, there is nothing that suggests a strong correlation between quality of life and the increase of energy consumption (Nader and Beckerman 1978). The classic measure of economic development has been GNP or GDP, figures that generally correlate with the consumption of commercial energy. The behavior of the regulatory sector, however, shows that there is an indeterminism between the presence of energy consumption and whether that consumption improves the quality of life of the people.

Conclusions: Development, Directionality, and Darwinism

In a broad evolutionary perspective, development may be seen as a high energy version of what was first manifest thousands of years ago in efforts to domesticate other living things. The controls people gained over plants and animals to enhance their survival was replicated in the emergence of civilization, as emergent hierarchies centralized power over the larger society, i.e., domesticated people, in order to assure their own survival.

Although neo-Darwinism has emphasized the random nature of evolution, there is a directionality inherent in the emergence of hierarchy, modelled in Bronowski's "stratified stability" (1970), Simon's "architecture of complexity" (1962), and Lotka's principle (1922). The emergence of hierarchy was immensely important, because it established mutually amplifying coevolutionary systems within human society itself -- i.e., the regulatory and working sectors of society. This directionality reflects the selective preference experienced by hierarchical societies over those that failed or preferred not to opt for hierarchical growth. It is a historical trajectory that conforms to Lotka's principle; it is not a cosmic predictor. Dinosaurs also created very large forms, but eventually were replaced by others that individually used less energy. Whether they did this for the reasons proposed in the last phase of Lotka's statement is not currently known.

Domestication established two distinct coevolutionary systems. One was the interdependence that evolved between human behavior and domesticated plants and animals, at first universal but rapidly relegated to a working sector (Rindos 1984). The other was the interdependence that evolved between a domesticated working sector and a specialized regulatory sector. By controlling many things of internal importance to the society's members, this hierarchy became a major natural selector not only of the working sector, but of the society as a whole.

Development extends domestication into the industrial and post industrial eras, an acceleration of the social evolutionary process by simply following Lotka's principle. The intensification of energy consumption in the context of already high energy conditions has not only increased complexity but, of greater moment, has created much greater non-linearity and indeterminancy. Whether this is cause for optimism or pessimism, for hope or threat, depends on one's individual predisposition. Prigogine, who has certainly done as much as anyone to bring a convincing and useful model of how indeterminancy emerges and works, seems to find hope in the argument that "individual activity is not doomed to insignificance" (Prigogine and Stengers 1984, 313).

As against this, the world-wide intensification of energy consumption inexorably continues. The most often voiced concern is that we may run out of energy. This, of course will not happen in the human future. Rather, the problem is both larger and more strategic: it is not where the energy will come from, but where it is leading us. If we were we to obtain -- through control of fusion, magnetism, or what you will -- a reliable and endlessly expandable source of energy, the real problem would be precisely that it would lead to ever greater complexity and indeterminancy, producing nonlinearities beyond the coping ability of the human intelligence. The tip of the iceberg appears in the much discussed "information explosion." It is no accident that the construction of super-computers in one part of the world is accompanied by heightened revolutionary and terrorist action in another. It is naive to see this as uniquely a problem of capitalism; it is one of high energy dissipative structures, hierarchial systems that intensify their energy consumption beyond the capacity of linear controls.

The advantage of Darwinism over Spencerian and Marxist evolutionary models is that it describes abstractly the mechanisms by which evolution operates. The process of development, which in some respects may appear peculiar to our era, is, in Darwinian terms, merely an extension of species expansion. However, the preceding discussion suggests that in applying it to social evolution, Darwinism is not enough.

First, the obvious directionality that has pervaded the past 10,000 years of human history goes undescribed in the Darwinian statement. Second, although "fitness" and reproductive advantage

55

can describe past conditions, they may actually obscure the pending extinction of a population or species confronting environmental change. Third, sociocultural change includes both "Lamarkian" and "Darwinian" processes. Fourth, because human societies incorporate large amounts of nonhuman energy and material into themselves, and because Darwinian statements are primarily formulated to account for life, many important areas are left unaccounted for.

An examination of development in exclusively Darwinian terms would conclude that high energy human societies enjoy some kind of special fitness. In fact, of course, from the relativistic standpoint of biological reproduction, it is the low energy societies that have the highest rates of reproduction. High energy societies imitate the K-strategy, whereas the low energy societies tend to adopt an r-strategy. This would not be a very telling observation if we were comparing, say, dogs and mosquitos, i.e., two different species. But it appears that within this single species the different strategies interact to produce a self-expanding system.

Development, then, is a process as old as civilization, one that began when some human beings first tried to get plants and other human beings to work a little harder for them. The expanding nonhuman energy introduced by industrialization accelerated domestication into "progress" and then into "development." The current emphasis on endogenous development underlines that how this increasing energy is used lies in the nature of the society, in their historically evolving processes of power and distribution. All societies are today under both internal and external influences to expand their uses of energy; but how they decide to do this is expressly an internal, endogenous, matter.

Notes

[1] "From the viewpoint of the economic system as a whole, the central feature of modern economic growth is an immense and continuous rise in the yield from human economic activity" (Easterlin 1968, 396-7). "The fundamental basis for this productivity growth has been technological innovation.... Specifically, the use of methods involving mechanization and high-energy inputs per worker and the associated shift toward a mineral-based economy especially set off many modern techniques. Large and carefully controlled volumes of energy are applied to productive processes, drawing on mineral sources such as coal,

petroleum, and natural gas; in contrast, premodern energy inputs, deriving largely from human animal, wood, wind, and water sources are much smaller and more erratic" (Ibid, 398).

[2] The argument is, of course, discredited. The ample evidence against the notion that quality of life varies with the quantity of energy consumed is throughly reviewed by Nader and Beckerman (1978).

[3] "Foreign trade enables developing countries to specialize in production, exploit economies of scale, and increase foreign exchange earnings needed to pay for imports. A good export record also strengthens creditworthiness and permits greater access to private loans.... The developing countries exports are directly affected by growth in the industrial countries" (World Bank 1983, 29).

[4] Although the energy-GNP ratio is used as a variable in development analysis (Berndt and Wood 1974), the two vary closely. De Janosi et al. (1972) obtain an r of .83 to .98 for 30 nations between 1953 and 1965; Mazur and Rosa (1974) report r of .94 for 47 nations in 1970. As is the case with energy, GNP or GDP fail to measure quality of life.

[5] Discussion of "intensification" began in earnest with the work of Boserup (1965), and has expanded widely in the anthropological literature. See Spooner (1972), Wilkinson (1973), Cohen (1977), and Harris (1977).

[6] Anthropologists who favor endogenous development on moral grounds may be discomforted by my "rationalistic" approach. In the long run, however, it will be the success of endogenous efforts and not their moral attributes that will recommend their continued use. Endogenous development is also seen by some as an overt rejection of an older "applied anthropology," or "top down," approach, which they regard to be synonymous with imperialism; "participation" they argue, is not merely more democratic, but also more humane and categorically good. This may be true, but both are equally sponsored from "above" or "outside." See Adams 1979.

[7] So far as I know, Lotka's principle was introduced into anthropology by Leslie White (1959, 36-7) followed by Sahlins and Service (1960, 7).

[8] "Complexity" here refers to a functional complexity, the number of relations of interdependency within a system or structure; not the statistical measurement of entropy. Complexity may increase with the addition of, or change in, the number of parts (because each new part implies new relations) as

well as without new parts, merely by increasing the relations among existing parts.

[9] Rindos (1984, 185-9) argues that domestication shifted a K-strategy human society in the direction of the r-strategy. I believe he misses an important point, however, because as energy flow increases human population, it reorganizes into hierarchical self-reproducing groups, and is not a simple multiplication of people.

[10] The data on which these figures are based come from national censuses and UN data on national energy consumption. They can be had from the author for the cost of photocopy reproduction and shipping.

[11] Cavelli-Sforza and Feldman refer to "vertical" and "horizontal" transmission (1981).

References

Adams, Richard N. 1975. Energy and Structure: A Theory of Social Power. Austin: University of Texas Press.
----- 1979. The Structure of Participation: A commentary. In: Politics and the Poor, Vol II, Political Participation in Latin America. Mitchell A. Seligson and John A. Booth, eds. pp. 9-17. New York: Holmes & Meier Publishers, Inc.
----- 1982a. Paradoxical Harvest. Cambridge University Press.
----- 1982b. Natural Selection, Energetics, and Cultural Materialism. Current Anthropology 22(6):603-624.
Barash, David P. 1977. Sociobiology and Behavior. New York: Elsevier.
Bateson, Gregory. 1979. Mind and Nature. New York: E.P. Dutton.
Bennett, John W. 1980. Human Ecology as Human Behavior. In: Human Behavior and Environment, Vol 4, Environment and Culture. Irwin Altman, Amos Rapaport and Joachim F. Wohlsill, eds. pp. 243-277. New York: Plenum Press.
Berndt, E.R. and D.O. Wood. 1974. An Economic Interpretation of the Energy-GNP Ratio. In: Energy: Demand, Conservation, and Institutional Problems. M.S. Macrakis, ed. pp. 21-30. Cambridge, Mass.: The MIT Press.
Binford, Lewis R. 1968. Post Pleistocene Adaptations. In: New Perspectives in Archaeology. S.R. Binford and L.R. Binford, eds. pp. 313-341. Chicago: Aldine.
Boserup, Esther. 1965. The Conditions of Agricultural Growth. Chicago: Aldine Pub. Co.
Bronowski, J. 1970. New Concepts in the Evolution of Complexity:

Stratified Stability and Unbounded Planes. Zygon 5:19-35.

Campbell, Donald T. 1965. Variation and Selective Retention in Socio-cultural Evolution. In: Social Change in Developing Areas: A Reinterpretation of Evolutionary Theory. Berringer, H.R., et al., eds. pp. 19-49. Cambridge, Massachusetts: Scheckman.

Cavelli-Sforza, L.L. and M.W. Feldman. 1981. Cultural Transmission and Evolution. Princeton University Press.

Cohen, Mark N. 1977. The Food Crisis in Prehistory. New Haven: Yale University Press.

Cottrell, Fred. 1955. Energy and Society. New York: McGraw Hill Book Company.

Dawkins, Richard. 1976. The Selfish Gene. New York: Oxford University Press.

Durham, William H. 1982. Interactions of Genetic and Cultural Evolution: Models and Examples. Human Ecology 10:3:289-323.

Easterlin, Richard A. 1968. Economic Growth: Overview. In: International Encyclopedia of the Social Sciences, Vol 4. David Sills, ed. pp. 395-408. New York: The Macmillan Company and the Free Press.

Flannery, Kent V. 1972. The Cultural Evolution of Civilizations. Annual Review of Ecology and Systematics 3:399-426.

Friedman, Jonathan and M.J. Rowlands. 1978. Notes Towards an Epigenetic Model of the Evolution of 'Civilization'. In: The Evolution of Social Systems. Jonathan Friedman and M.J. Rowlands, eds. pp. 201-278. The University of Pittsburgh Press.

Harris, Marvin. 1977. Cannibals and Kings: The Origins of Cultures. New York: Random House.

Huxley, Julian. 1943. Evolution, the Modern Synthesis. New York: Harper & Brothers.

de Janosi, P.E. and L.E. Grayson. 1972. Patterns of Energy Consumption and Economic Growth and Structure. Journal of Development Studies 8:241-49.

Lotka, Alfred J. 1922. Contribution to the Energetics of Evolution. Proceedings of the National Academy of Sciences 8:147-151.

Mazur, A. and E. Rosa. 1974. Energy and Lifestyle. Science 186:607-610.

Morgan, Lewis Henry. 1964. Ancient Society. Leslie White, ed. Cambridge, Mass.: The Belknap Press of Harvard University.

Nader, Laura, and Stephen Beckerman. 1978. Energy as it Relates to the Quality and Style of Life. Annual Review of Energy 3:1-28.

Pattee, Howard. 1973. Hierarchy Theory: The Challenge of Complex Systems. New York: George Braziller.

Pianka, Eric R. 1978. Evolutionary Ecology. Second Edition. New York: Harper and Brothers Publishers.

Prigogine, Ilya, Peter Allen, and Robert Herman. 1977. Long Term Trends and the Evolution of Complexity. In: Goals in a Global Community. New York: Pergamon Press. Ervin Laszlo and Judah

Bierman, eds. pp. 1-64. London: Duckworth.

Rindos, David. 1984. The Origins of Agriculture: An Evolutionary Perspective. New York: Academic Press.

Sahlins, Marshall and Elman R. Service. 1960. Evolution and Culture. Ann Arbor: University of Michigan Press.

Sapir, Edward. 1924. Culture, Genuine and Spurious. American Journal of Sociology 29:401-429.

Simon, Herbert. 1962. The Architecture of Complexity. Proceedings of the American Philosophical Society 106:467-482.

Spooner, Brian J., ed. 1972. Population Growth: Anthropological Implications. Cambridge, Mass.: MIT Press.

White, Leslie. 1949. The Science of Culture. New York: Grove Press.

----- 1959. The Evolution of Culture. New York: McGraw Hill Book Company.

Wilkinson, Richard. 1973. Poverty and Progress. New York: Praeger.

Wilson, Edward O. 1975. Sociobiology, the New Synthesis. Cambridge, Mass.: The Belknap Press of Harvard University Press.

Wolfe, Marshall. 1984. Participation: the View from above. CEPAL Review 23:155-180.

World Bank. 1983. World Development Report 1983. Published for the World Bank. New York: Oxford University Press.

3. PRINCIPLES OF DEVELOPMENT: A VIEW FROM ANTHROPOLOGY

Harold K. Schneider

The term "development" is taken so much for granted these days that it is hard to remember that when it first became prominent in the early 1960s it raised the hackles of anthropologists, invoking images of the telic evolution so despised by persons trained in the Boasian tradition. It challenged the then uncontroversial anthropological notion that each society has reached an adjustment to the world that is best for it and that requires no change. I still remember the puzzlement on the face of an economist whom I questioned on this issue, who seemed to feel that the term was quite objective and uncontroversial. Today the term is unblushingly invoked by anthropologists, who, it seems, have acquired a new understanding of exotic societies, one which does not treat social and cultural change as abhorrent. Still, my estimate is that although anthropologists may have accepted the idea, they have done so on different terms than others, terms which may uniquely contribute to the development process.

The purpose of this paper is to demonstrate, through the listing of a series of "principles," the nature of this anthropological understanding as I would, and have, explained them to non-anthropologists interested in development. My reason for enumerating them to a group consisting mainly of anthropologists is to test them against your understanding and to ask for modifications, expansions or even rejections of the principles in order to arrive at a more useful general understanding of the process. In another session of this meeting Dan Aronson argued that anthropologists should not pass themselves off as health, agricultural or other kinds of specialists. My "principles" are meant to contribute to his plea that we stand by what we have to offer. The principles were derived from a close examination of case studies explored by myself and my students in several courses on development in recent years. The title of this presentation could well have been "the process of development." I chose "principles" in the sense of "fundamental truths" to emphasize the focus on the hard realities of the process over ideological pleas.

I want to underscore the fact that this is my view, which will not be shared by all anthropologists. It is a view that derives from my own concern with analytical economics, political economics and the revitalization process. However, I don't expect it to deviate radically from the understandings of other anthropologists. And even if it does, this too will stimulate

61

response that will make plain the variation in anthropological views, which should in itself be a contribution to dealing with development.

When considering these principles you will note that none is discrete. All overlap. Therefore, each may be seen as simply emphasizing some aspect of a general process.

I apologize in this account for the emphasis on Africa. It is difficult to control information on development for the whole world. My specialization in Africa leads me inevitably to take my examples from that area.

There are eleven principles.

1. The people of the Third World, those toward whom development activities are directed, are decision-makers who evaluate options open to them and attempt to move in directions that will improve their well being.

This principle is worded rather awkwardly in order to avoid saying that these people are "rational," with its connotation of human beings as lightning calculators focused single-mindedly on the maximization of utility or profit. When development activities first began those who had the most powerful roles in it - economists, political scientists, managers from donor agencies, and the like - seem to have worked with the assumption (also prevalent in anthropological thought) that Third World people were different from ourselves in this respect. For example, they believed that such people were not price responsive and that getting them to produce more required something more than offering them a better price for their goods. This view seems now to have been abandoned, replaced by the idea that such people are like ourselves, completely susceptible to price.

I believe, like most of you I am sure, that human beings are responsive to incentives, but I do not believe that the only incentive is price. However that point will be dealt with later. For the moment I will skirt it by saying that generally speaking, Third World people seem to be responsive to incentives that will improve their lives as they define such improvement, and that ideas about improvement in standard of living correspond in great part to our own. Many anthropological studies have demonstrated this point, not the least of which was Polly Hill's classic account (Hill 1961) of the introduction of cocoa farming in Ghana, an event paralleled in its significance for this point by the introduction of coffee growing among the Chagga of Tanzania, cotton growing among the Teso of Uganda, and fur trading among the Indians of North America in the last century.

62

Illustrating this shift in point of view, up to very recently development theorists in Africa assumed that pastoral people would not sell off cattle in large numbers because of some peculiar even irrational attachments to the beasts, but now they seem convinced that they will sell if the price is right although the response is complex, and often seemingly contradictory, depending on circumstances. It is an irony of this situation that having made this reorientation in thought (prompted by economic anthropologists, among others), that pastoralists are responsive to incentives, developmentalists must be further challenged on the grounds that the price is not the only incentive. The truly valuable anthropological contribution to this problem is the recognition on the one hand that people like this are responsive to incentives, combined with the understanding that responsiveness rests on evaluation of the utility of various courses of action, and that the favored utility may be different from the one held by development theorists.

2. Development is a combination of two elements, one well understood and the other not: thus, development consists of both an increase in the production and consumption of goods but also, and inseparably, change in consumption attitudes to value those goods valued by people of the industrial world.

This point is easily illustrated. The Somali people produce in prodigious amounts a good highly valued by them, camels. If we were to understand development to mean only an increase in production of goods it would stand to reason that we could accomplish development by increasing Somali production of camels. The very idea is ludicrous. Besides their own demand, the international market for camels is very limited. The Somalis seem to have only one important market, Saudi Arabia, and they sell more than enough camels to satisfy that market. The point of view of development specialists about this Somali situation is manifest in the phrase, repeated ad nauseum, that Somalis (and Third World people in general) are "one of the poorest people in the world", a phrase applied to most Third World people. What this seems to mean is that the Somalis don't produce goods valued by most people in the rest of the world, which makes them "poor." That Somalis consider themselves to be rich (at least when they have lots of camels) seems to carry no weight in development estimates.

As a consequence, development policy for Somalis stresses taking up and exploiting the rich agricultural region in southern Somalia, and developing a fishing industry, proposals in which the Somalis have shown little interest. Similarly, development specialists have proposed a fishing industry for the pastoral Turkana and an expanded cotton industry for the agropastoral

63

Teso. I once knew an agricultural officer in West Pokot who seriously advocated that the Pokot produce kapok, presumably for the life jacket market. (The Pokot destroyed his agricultural plots.)

I do not mean to suggest by my tone that Third World people should not be encouraged to abandon traditional values. In fact, I believe many of them are quite willing to do so. I merely suggest that development people have assumed that what they value will also be valued by Third World people. If the latter do not respond, for example, to the opportunity to sell cattle, it is because they allegedly don't understand the proposal. On the other hand, some modern development planners, realizing that Third World people may have good reason to reject suggested changes, such as increasing livestock sales, have come up with explanations that depend on their imaginations more than any ethnographic investigations. For example, in the case of the Somalis again, Konczacki (1967), a development economist, has argued that the reason they won't give up camel pastoralism is that maintaining large herds (i.e., not selling off many animals) is a hedge against drought and famine. Many of you know that I have argued that people like the Somalis use livestock as stores of value and media of exchange and that their refusal to sell more camels, or to turn to other means of production are affected by this view of camels at least as much as any considerations relating to potential drought and famine.

The point can be illustrated another way. When I worked with the Turu people in 1959-60 I often came across men described to me as wealthy who wore dirty old clothes suggesting that they were impoverished. And Indian storekeepers used to complain that the Turu would seldom buy anything from them that cost more than Shs. 20, implying that they were not price responsive. It turned out that there was a general Turu belief that the wise man put his resources in cattle, sheep and goats and that people who spent money on clothes and other store bought goods were impecunious. In short, the Turu were like many Americans of past generations, who felt that consumption for its own sake was somewhat disreputable. The developer can understand this within our own tradition, where such people invested wisely in land and other goods that had future potential. But they do not seem to understand this among people whose ideas of what constitutes a good investment are invisible to them. Thus, while development theorists may have come to the conclusion that Third World people are "rational" they have difficulty sticking with the conclusion when such people make investment decisions relative to exotic values. There is thus a temptation once again to return to the opinion that such people are in fact irrational or stupid. The grossest example of this process that I have come across lately had to do with the present famine in Ethiopia where two different

64

NBC reporters, speaking from the scene, and apparently dependent for their views on local "experts," explained to viewers that the reason for the famine was that the people overgrazed their land and were ignorant of good agricultural practices. In other words, the people were stupid.

3. While development is importantly an increase in production of material goods and increased consumption of material goods it is also a political process.

The meaning of this point is simply stated. When the development process begins it is inevitably accompanied by a rearrangement of the social structure, specifically relations of power because social structure is a manifestation of exchange relations, and exchange relations are intimately affected by the kinds of goods, relative value of goods, and amount of goods in circulation, all of which are likely to be affected by any important shift in production activities. While not inevitably so, it seems generally to be the case that this production shift manifests itself most prominently in society as a polarization of power in which some people gain in ascendance over others to a degree greater than formerly. A good example of this comes from Salisbury's (1962) pioneering study of the Siane of highland New Guinea. It will be remembered that Salisbury's account focused on the introduction of steel axes in this New Guinea community and its socioeconomic effects. The steel axe, being a more efficient tool, made it possible to accomplish various material production activities in a shorter time, thereby releasing time for reallocation. Among the options before them Siane generally chose to invest the new time in power politics (an increase in certain kinds of exchanges) and in the end Salisbury found that the community was somewhat more polarized than it had been before.

A natural question that arises in this context is why is polarization so general? Why do relations not stay the same or become more equalitarian? I have never seen a satisfactory answer to this question, which in my opinion is one of the most important before social anthropology today. One can think of many good hypotheses. For example, development is the introduction of a new technique for producing valued goods. The process must start somewhere. Those who get in on the ground floor get the major part of the benefits. The first Chagga to grow coffee and sell it must have become wealthy very quickly. But does the polarization persist, or is it a short-term aberration?

4. Third World people are not primarily oriented to production for subsistence.

65

The most perverse idea to pervade development work may be the notion that unlike ourselves people of the Third World are primarily oriented to feeding themselves. Linked to this, for no overtly discernible reason, is the notion that these people are not very skilled at doing so. A clear example of this attitude comes from a story which appeared in the New York Times on March 2, 1983, in which Alan Cowell said, speaking of Rwanda:

> Every square mile of land is virtually under cultivation, and pressure, with 500 people vying for its benefits. Technically, it is among the world's poorest nations, but 19 out of every 20 Rwandese are subsistence farmers, whose husbandry and industry are striking, and who by and large feed themselves - no mean feat in Africa.

Anthropologists, admittedly, were subject to the same prejudice until fairly recently when Sahlins (1974) published his ideas about the original affluent society. Now we are used to thinking that Third World people are perfectly able to feed themselves, a view that, however, must be modified by the fact that traditional methods of production that may have been adequate have been interfered with by modern developments, such as the rise of new governments. My studies of the Turu revealed the interesting fact that the first German commander of the Singida station, Eberhard von Sick, who was an accomplished ethnographer, estimated that Singida was the "bread basket" of the whole area, exporting food to surrounding societies (which, incidentally, were able therefore to feed themselves through "international" trade rather than "subsistence production"). When I worked with the Turu they were still prodigious producers although they were apparently not exporting much food.

This general prejudice among development planners is revealed in many ways, of which the most prominent is emphasis on schemes to increase food production and failure to take into account other motivations for the production of the kind of wealth called "food." To many, if not most, Third World people crops are valued goods, not food, produced with the intent of converting them into other values. This fact is most apparent when we consider the things they produce that have no food value - cocoa, coffee, kola nuts, cocaine, heroin, and the like. The subsistence explanation for production is humorously challenged by the widespread use of grain to make beer, which the Africans I knew considered to be food, like any other, but which developers, to judge by their silence on the subject, do not.

However, there seems to be some contradiction with respect to this view embodied in the current emphasis on the need to "get the prices right" in order to increase agricultural production. But, on the other hand, one wonders whether low pricing policies

66

may not be in some part motivated by the idea that the people being appealed to are only "subsistence farmers" who are driven primarily to feed themselves and who don't need the surplus food for anything else.

5. Third World people are motivated to obtain power.

A famous example of this principle is the account of the abolition of "sister exchange" marriage among the Tiv of Nigeria recounted in Margaret Mead's classic book (1955) on development, Cultural Patterns and Technical Change. In this stunning example we find older Tiv men exercising power over women, children and young men by control of the marriage (for reasons I won't go into). When this form of marriage was abolished and brideprice marriage therefore made the reasonable choice, an opportunity presented itself to young men to evade the power of the older men and accomplish marriage without their help, marriage being the path to independence and power. They leaped at the opportunity, to the surprise of anthropologists at the time, who were persuaded that young men would obey the dictates of their elders. I have always suspected that this account left out an important consideration. At the time this happened new opportunities for making money were presenting themselves to young men as the British built a railroad through the country and they probably began to chaff under the rule of elders whereas in the past they had no opportunity but to do as they were told.

Even today I am not sure that anthropologists, not to say developers, have accepted this fact of desire for power (or freedom). We do not always seem to understand that any human community is characterized by a balance of power susceptible at any time to rapid reformation as avenues to power open to the have-nots. I believe that in most times (I shall discuss the exceptions below) this process operates in such a way that if opportunity presents itself any one person will strive for all the power he or she can get, to the point of establishing himself as lord of all. Human beings are not naturally egalitarian.

6. Most development is accompanied by polarization and equity while desirable must usually be forsaken for increased production and consumption, at least in the short run. This principle directly challenges a policy underlying much development work today, most specifically in the form of the mandate from Congress to the United States Agency for International Development, which states that development must proceed with equity.

Human beings are used to inequitable social conditions. Most have lived with them and probably will live with them in the future, although it can be argued (as in Dumont 1977) that increasing equity, represented by decentralization of power, has

67

Benevolent inequity ≠ western individualist
social obligation   inequity

No

been a concomitant of industrialization. Ironically, the most despised of Third World people seem to be those who are most egalitarian, seeming to suggest again that development theorists believe that equality is a good thing only if accomplished on their terms. And African government policies are anti-pastoral, seeking to drive pastoral people into agricultural production. I spoke of the attempts to turn Somalis into farmers and fishermen, which would undoubtedly insure low incomes to them and make them subservient to the people who control the land, as has been the case in most agricultural societies throughout history.

Egalitarianism is a difficult condition to achieve because human beings are, as I said, seemingly motivated to seek power, manifested in control over other people. It takes a special set of circumstance, in which opportunities to obtain wealth are easy and widespread, to create the kind of dynamics that counters this power-seeking propensity. In pastoral societies these circumstances consist of the volatility of livestock wealth due to a combination of climatic and disease conditions that make wealth insecure as periodic droughts and epidemics decimate herds, combined with the fact that for various reasons individuals have comparatively easy access to the means of production that lead to wealth. Wealth and power rise and fall rapidly, among many African pastoralists, pig producers in the highlands of New Guinea, the pastoral societies of North Africa, the pastoral societies of the Middle East, and the nineteenth-century Indians of the North American plains.

It is an open question whether people refer increased consumption to increased power. Certainly, as among the impecunious Turu, it is possible to be beguiled by consumption. But not all people are so short-sighted. Development policy that seeks to promote equity cannot hope to do so by simply mandating it. The conditions of access to the production of wealth by the individual must be made widely available. In the nineteenth century the individual Tiv was apparently able to do this because the chief store of value and medium of exchange was cloth, which any person could produce even if its production had to be difficult in order not to inflate the supply. In the modern world agricultural production is not usually a path to fortune for small producers, and the production of large-scale valued goods requires capital, which excludes most people in the Third World.

Tanzania chose to mandate equity. It is embedded in its constitution. But that mandate has not produced equity. Developmentalists, it would seem, have ordinarily to choose development without equity or have nothing. Alternately, they could embark on the difficult task of helping to create new production and exchange systems that would allow relatively easy

access to the means of production or wealth that will insure
equity through economic dynamics.

**7. Third World people do not necessarily need direction or even
infusions of capital to accomplish development.** They have shown
abundantly that they are willing and able to undertake new and
profitable enterprises if the opportunity avails and the
incentives are right.

One would think this point needs no stressing, but
development specialists seem to work with the assumption that
Third World people can accomplish little without help. One of
the most famous examples of self-motivated development in African
history is the rise of the cocoa industy in Ghana, as Hill so
well documented (1961). It was Akwapim people in southern Ghana
who in the last part of the last century hit on the idea of
growing cocoa (which they did not even consume themselves) for
foreign markets. They invested in new lands for this purpose,
using the proceeds of their palm oil industry, moved to those new
lands for the sole purpose of producing cocoa and built roads,
bridges and the other infrastructure necessary for the purpose.
Less well known, but documented by Massing (1980), was the growth
of the Kru economy in Liberia and Ivory Coast based on trade with
European coastal shipping, which made the Kru an affluent people
until colonial policies destroyed their system in modern times.
In other places we find the impressive growth of the cotton
industry among the Teso of Ghana (aided, I hasten to add, by a
push from British colonial authorities in the early part of this
century who insisted that they grow cotton, a pressure the Teso
would surely have resisted if cotton production had not proved so
valuable to them).

Other examples are not hard to find. Ironically, in many of
these cases (if not all) one must conclude that these development
successes were brought to a halt either by colonial or modern
government policies. The next principle, when we get to it, will
take up the matter of why this was so.

These examples suggest that development may often be
accomplished by encouraging what some call "bottom up"
development rather than always attempting "top down" programs.
When I worked with the Turu I found government people who spent a
lot of time trying to find new crops the Turu could grow in order
to expand their economy: tobacco, cotton, vegetables, cashews. I
seldom found anyone who tried to understand what the Turu were
thinking and what ideas they had about what to do. Developers
today seem often to be of the same genre. There seems to be
little attempt to get to know the "target" populations. New
programs are developed at a distance and imported into an area
with high hopes and often disastrous results. The best example

69

(or is it worst) is attempts at pastoral development in Africa. At the 1979 Harper's Ferry workshop on pastoral programs in Africa it was pointed out that after 20 years and over $600 million no pastoral program had been a success. Typically such programs involved imposition of ranching schemes on pastoral people. That these were inappropriate was not suspected since no one seems to have tried to find out what the pastoralists thought about this or attempts to find out were superficial. Working at a distance, often with theories influenced by "the tragedy of the commons," decisions are often made hastily. In this case, if one believes, as many public-choice theorists do today, that grazing lands held in common will inevitably be abused due to the fact that the rational individual will grab all he can get reasoning that if he doesn't others will, it makes sense to impose on such people schemes to control grazing. That this theory may not accord with the facts is usually given little consideration.

Could there be indigenously inspired pastoral development? Perhaps. There is one case in Kenya of Kaputiei Masaai who seem to have abandoned the traditional system for beef ranching. They did it on their own. But why they did it is not clear since no one seems to have bothered to talk to them about it.

8. All development programs occur within a national political context and are affected by this fact.

While this principle seems obvious, when we consider how often development programs are designed without taking this principle into consideration one must conclude that something is wrong.

There is practical value in dividing this principle from the earlier one stressing the power-maximizing propensities of people even though this principle says the same thing at a higher level. The modern nations of Africa are made up of people who are no less driven to control others than people at the local level. No matter how desirable a development project may seem at the local level, it must come to terms with national, and even international, politics.

This principle is well exemplified by what is going on presently in the Mbeere district of Kenya, where the government is engaged in a long-term introduction of "individualized land tenure." ILT, as we may call this tongue twister, is a program that was suggested by the Swynnerton plan, which was developed during the British colonial administration and carried forward under the independent government of Kenya. Its rationale was that holding land in common, as the Mbeere and many other Kenya people do or did for the most part, creates a problem of the commons: everybody's business is nobody's business. It was

70

decided that giving individuals title to land would encourage them to utilize it more efficiently. (This, parenthetically, is a good example of "top down" type programs.)

While the rationale for ILT might be defensible (some public-choice theorists would today certainly challenge it on the grounds that the commons does not always have a negative impact) its defensibility turned out in the end to be irrelevant. Today the ILT process is well extablished in Mbeere causing a disruption of production by indigenous people due to the fact that the individually held plots of land are not viable for traditional methods of agricultural and livestock production. Cattle are being sold off in large numbers because of the lack of grazing caused by closing the commons, and land is being sold off to outsiders because in the context this seems to Mbeere the most reasonable thing to do. For example money from land sales can be used to pay for the education of children who have an occupational future.

The disruption caused by the program is surely obvious to people in the Government of Kenya, but there is no attempt to do anything about it, not even reforming the inadequate adjudication system that goes along with the ILT. The reason, one may speculate, is that however badly ILT may serve the Mbeere as a whole, it serves some people in the powerful sector of Kenya society differently.

One could cite many examples of this conflict between national and local interests, including de Garine's (1978) impressive account of the effects on the plains people of Northern Cameroon of government policy to foster the cotton industry. De Garine complains that the adverse effects on the people, including reduction in the quality of nutrition and impoverishment due to the reduction in grazing lands, need to be countered but urges, uniquely, that it does no good for the anthropologist to complain about injustice and expect the government to take heed. He feels that the anthropologist must get into politics and affect policy - wise advice, in my opinion. In this case, the government of Cameroon, for its own reasons, has decided that it wants cotton to earn foreign exchange, even if some people have to suffer to accomplish this goal. All governments make decisions like this and the only ways to affect them are through normal politics - or revolution.

My discussion of the Mbeere and people of northern Cameroon is not meant to suggest that anthropologists should commit themselves to fight "ethnocide." What each of us chooses to do about situations like this is a private matter. I merely want to underscore the point of this principle, that a development program cannot be treated in isolation from the political

71

atmosphere within which it resides.

9. The accomplishment of development involves some degree of luck.

That Somalia is nearly all semi-arid land, fit only for
human beings and camels, or that Tanzania has little in the way
of mineral wealth, are facts in the development equation that
must be kept in mind. Some people will have more trouble
accomplishing growth than others because they are not favored by
nature. To talk always of the failure of government policy in
Tanzania without taking note of the mineral poverty and
horrendous climate of the country is to place too much weight on
the power of development intervention.

This is not to say that such conditions cannot be overcome.
After all, Japan is also an environmentally impoverished country
but has been able to transcend this fact by various means.
African countries could do the same. But it is also possible
that some countries may never develop. It is well to keep in
mind that the history of development in the industrial world
depended importantly on luck. One would be hard put to claim
dogmatically that all the important mechanical, or even
organizational, components of industrial countries - plows,
engines, military structures - appeared inevitably.

10. Development policy is often doctrinaire.

I state this principle conservatively, reserving the
possibility that like the long-sought honest man, there may
actually be such a thing as a truly objective man in this world.
One suspects that in evaluating a situation, the average human
being brings to the evaluation 9/10ths ideology and 1/10th
objective evaluation of the facts. This principle applies no
less to development theorists and anthropologists than other
humans, although I hope that each of these groups, as an
outgrowth of their training, are able to attain a better than
average level of objectivity.

Like principle 8, this principle can be abundantly
documented. Some of the examples are bizarre. For example,
there is some suspicion in my mind that the promotion of
individualized land tenure is at least in part due to the belief
held by Americans and Europeans, and internalized by African
leaders, that private ownership of land is a Good Thing, no
matter what else may be the case. My own research experience has
made it clear to me that people who hold these views have found
it very difficult to believe that anything can be money that is
not rectangular paper or round metal in form. Or, conversely, I
sometimes suspect that policy with respect to pastoral people

72

rests on the hidden, ideological notion that raising cattle for other than beef or dairy products is perverse.

The point can be illustrated differently, and perhaps more telling, by reference to the "stimulant" industry. Africans are great producers of alcoholic drink, which they make from a great variety of things, including grain, palm oil, and bananas. Since the development process encompasses in large part the encouragement of production that will fulfill consumer demand, thereby leading to rise in income, leading to further expansion of production - the familiar dynamic economic growth cycle - one wonders why beer, for example, has not been given more attention. In Burkina Faso studies by Saul (1981) in the southwestern part of the country have shown that the production and sale of beer made from red sorghum is an important source of income and engine of production, benefitting especially the women. Furthermore, the export of red sorghum mash earns more foreign exchange than other crops, such as cotton. Nevertheless, the government of Burkina Faso has not supported this industry, giving subsidies instead to cotton. The export of red sorghum, in fact, is illegal. And the government has apparently given support to European brewers, whose operations in the country require the import of ingredients, thus using up foreign exchange. (I should add that something I read recently suggests a change in government policy in Burkina Faso.)

One suspects that the failure to support the liquor industry, and perhaps a kola nut industry, rests in part on moral grounds, the idea that these are disreputable products. The negative attitude toward such crops as heroin in other parts of the world is induced in part by international politics, the pressure brought on grower countries by the United States and other industrial nations.

This should not be taken as a criticism of those who turn their backs on such products, any more than many East Africans, or Moslems, can be faulted for refusing to have anything to do with pigs. But it seems to me that being aware of such biases is salutary in working out development policy. After all, Ghanaians have made a good thing of producing cocoa, which they don't use themselves. Admittedly, there are no moral prejudices against cocoa. But what of African grains, like finger millet (eleusine), which seems to be considered an inferior grain? Africans are experts at producing eleusine, pennesitum and sorghum. Why not give attention to promoting them for beer production? The answer seems to reside in a point made earlier. Development demands not only increased production of valuable goods, but the right goods.

11. Under certain fairly well defined circumstances human

beings will shift to a revitalization mode.

Cults, as revitalization movements are usually called, are frequent among human beings, a fact usually not acknowledged, apparently because they are considered to be abnormal. For example, they arose frequently during the colonial period in many parts of the world - New Guinea, Africa, North America. The Mau Mau movement in Kenya is a case in point. Such movements are often thought of as a result almost exclusively of colonialism. But such an interpretation is narrow indeed. There are revialization movements all over Africa today, under nationalist governments. The Matsitsine movement in northern Nigeria became prominent in the news just recently. A prophet called Matsitsine arose among the Moslems and became a magnet for young men, according to the newspaper accounts. Whatever the cause or the dynamics of the movement, it led to riots and the intervention of the Nigerian police and army. Matsitsine was killed and his followers declared that he was the true chief prophet of Allah, not Mohammed. Further riots caused further clashes, in the course of which thousands of Matsitsinites have been killed (as well as some police and soldiers).

The accounts of the movement that I have read refer to it as a "Moslem fundamentalist movement," a description that Moslems must find outrageous considering that the claim that Matsitsine is the true prophet would constitute the most fundamental kind of heresy in Islam. But this example does suggest the depths of our misunderstanding of movements of this type.

While development has probably not caused as much disruption as colonialism perhaps because it is not carried out with such a heavy hand, it has had this effect often enough, and the implementation of development programs has the potential for generating revitalization movements, where it has not already caused them.

It seems to me that people involved in development would do well to obtain some understanding of the revitalization process and develop methods of dealing with it other than simply reacting to what appears to be mass paranoia. It is difficult to speak accurately of such movements because we seldom learn much about them except the sensational reports we read in the newspapers but it is necessary to try. For example, in the case of Iran what appears to have happened is that it was undergoing rapid development when Khomeini rose to power. I have the impression that nobody in the U.S. government really understood what was happening or how to deal with it. But a diagnostic feature of such movements is that one cannot deal with their members on what is normally considered to be a rational level. They feel they know what is right, they are totally committed to destruction of

74

the evil that they perceive as the cause of all their troubles, and the evil they perceive is often those who originated the development process.

The best policy to employ with such movements is not clear. One policy, used by such diverse groups as the Germans when they set up their colonial regime in Tanganyika, or the Nigerian government in dealing with Matsitsinists, is simply to come down hard on the cults. Cults, despite their doctrines that they are impervious to the weapons of the enemy, are ultimately responsive to brute force. This approach, I think most developers would agree, is not humane and so some other tactic is necessary. Certainly, one acceptable approach would be to try to diagnose the source of discontent and remedy it, the way the psychiatrist seeks the cause of paranoia in his patient and tries to alleviate it. Whatever is done, understanding the dynamics of such groups and the root causes of rebellion seems to be a good first step toward dealing with the problem.

In Africa today the revitalization process seems underway in a number of places other than northern Nigeria. So-called Moslem fundamentalism appears rampant in northern Sudan. Whether this is the case or not makes all the difference in the way the development planner must respond to the situation. A Moslem "fundamentalist" movement might be little different from what we think of as normal politics and so subject to reason and compromise. A true fundamentalist cult could not be approached through compromise and reason.

In much of old French Equatorial Africa the Bwiti movement is operating, as is Kimbanguism in Zaire. And in southern Zaire such movements seem to be endemic.

Complicating matters further, there is a sense in which all of us are revitalized to one degree or another. In this aspect of our beings we are idealistic, certain of the truth of our convictions, sharply focused in our goals and cooperative with others of like mind in pursuit of our convictions. For achieving material ends based on rational assessment of a situation this is a serious impediment because seen from the other perspective no truths are certain and compromise of principles is necessary. Development itself may be seen sometimes as a kind of movement to help the materially less fortunate, and as a revitalization process, it shares all the virtues and faults of any such movement.

Do the principles I have listed make a truly original contribution to the understanding of developing, unique to anthropology? I would like to suggest that they do by referring to the widely acclaimed works by Robert Bates (notably Bates

1981) on understanding what has gone wrong with development in Africa. Bates has described himself as a political scientist, but he also knows a lot about anthropology. Has anthropology anything left to suggest to Bates?

Bates's thesis can be condensed to the following propositions:

a. Individual rationality does not equal social rationality. It is a mistake to conclude that because the resources of a society are being "misused" individual decision-makers are therefore irrational, as in the case of the pastoralist who increases the size of his herd on the common to the point where destruction of grass cover causes erosion.

b. A general rise in income does not equal an increase in individual welfare. A rise in income may represent a rise for a few and no rise, or a decline, for others.

c. The values of a government do not necessarily equal the values of the people as a whole. What the people who control the government want does not necessarily coincide with what people outside the government want.

d. Social equilibria are not necessarily equal to economic equilibria. In other words, while a market may conform to the economic conditions that define it as efficient this condition is not necessarily a good thing for society in general. African governments are not agencies for maximizing social welfare, even if they say they are, but political coalitions designed to obtain and hold power. In most cases this means interfering in efficient markets and holding down agricultural prices in order to placate urban elites with cheap food because they are the main support of the government. The result is that such governments are locked into the position of keeping prices to farmers low because to raise prices would be to create discontent among the urban elites and possible overthrow of the government.

Bates's ideas represent a view complementary to mine. A comparison of the two points of view shows that they are substantially in agreement. They both accept the idea that rural people are decision-makers who seek to maximize well-being, and both perceive well-being as determined by more than just the price of material goods exchanged in the market. The good life includes power as well as material wealth. Both points of view also see development as occurring within a national system involving the rural producers and the urban elites and government, whose actions affect each other. Bates is not concerned with the question of whether rural people would undertake development on their own or whether such actions would be beneficial. He has nothing to say about the role of chance in development. And he has no reason to take up the question of whether development policy is doctrinaire.

However, it seems to me that there are certain areas of Bates's thesis that would benefit from attention to some of the principles I elucidated. In the first place, attention should be given to the matter of the difference between culture change and economic development. An important implication is that Africans would not necessarily be mollified if the prices were right. When economists talk about the growth of an African economy they are talking about the sector that they consider "developed," or modern, and ignore what I call the indigenous sector. Thus, they do not measure the growth of livestock herds indigenously managed; they might describe the Somalis, for example, as experiencing no growth when in fact their herds grew and the Somalis themselves considered their economy to be growing. To the Somalis the problem is not so much that the government is not paying the "right" prices for livestock but is interfering in the indigenous economy and stalling herd growth. This problem is at least as serious as getting the prices to rural producers right.

Next, there seems to be a bias against nationalist government in Bates's analysis. The government is represented as doing an injustice to rural producers by paying them unfairly. There is no reason to believe that these same farmers would not act exactly as the government if they were in the same position. As Bates must be aware, a social system is a system of competition for power as well as goods. If we combine this point with another point I made, that the economic conditions are such that they may preclude political economic equality, the situation we have in Africa may be inevitable. Put another way, we should separate in our thinking the notions of increased production and equity, focusing on the question of what we really want from these African countries. There are probably ways to bring about increased production without a substantial, and perhaps impossible, restructuring of the economy so that there is more opportunity for everybody. That is also another way of saying that it seems unlikely that rural people can be expected to gain economic and political power through the production of agricultural goods.

If what I say about the pervasiveness of revitalization or idealistic thinking is true, another way of putting what I just said is to suggest that insofar as it is possible, the achievement of development requires the clear specification of rationally achievable goals, the development of methods of accomplishing them and a forsaking of moralistic approaches that divide the world into good and bad. I realize that this may be impossible. Insofar as it is impossible so is reaching development goals.

Finally, the balance of forces in the countries represented by Bates, in which an urban elite poses a constant threat to the government if its aspirations are thwarted, is a classic situation in which to expect revitalization. The scenario would be that a movement, lead by a prophet, would arise among the elite when their feelings of deprivation reached the breaking point and this would manifest itself as an attack on the government or whatever body is perceived as the cause (e.g., donor countries like the United States) and the rise of what Turner (1969) called **communitas**, a communalistic movement dominated by a revitalization ideology, which in Moslem countries these days often takes the form of "Moslem fundamentalism" or even African nativism (as occurred in the Mau Mau movement, where the ideology eschewed the drinking of Coca-cola and the use of European utensils for eating). It seems to me that understanding politics in many countries in Africa today requires that we realize that leaders (such as Mugabe in Zimbabwe) are themselves experiencing revitalization and that they resort to "socialism" or "marxism" as the ideological vehicle for expressing this process, the way many small cults in southern Zaire use Christianity as a matrix for their essentially non-Christian system of beliefs and rituals (cf. Ranger 1972).

If this suggestion is true, the way to understand such countries is not as having fallen into the Communist orbit, but as undergoing social upheaval as a result of the disruption of a mazeway (Wallace 1955) or, as I would rather put it, as attempting to reconstitute social relations in such a way as to make a playable game.

The reader will have to decide whether the differences between Bates and myself are radical or merely matters of emphasis. The reader will also have to decide whether either or both of us are experiencing revitalization in our views of development, and then the reader will have to decide whether he or she is also experiencing revitalization. We end up, then, in a world of Through The Looking Glass, a world that tends to emerge when one, like Lewis Carroll, the author of <u>Alice</u> <u>in</u> <u>Wonderland</u>, spends too much time on mathematics.

References

Bates, R.H. 1981. Markets and States in Tropical Africa.
Berkeley: University of California.

Dumont, L. 1977. From Mandeville to Marx. Chicago: U. of Chicago
Press.

Garine, I. de. 1978. Population, Production, and Culture in the
Plains Societies of Northern Cameroon and Chad: The
Anthropologist in Development Projects. Current Anthropology
19:42-57.

Hill, Polly. 1961. The Migrant Cocoa Farmers of Southern Ghana.
Africa. July 31(3):209-230.

Konczacki, Z.A. 1967. Nomadism and Economic Development of
Somalia. Canadian Journal of African Studies. pp. 163-175.

Massing, A. 1980. The Economic Anthropology of the Kru
(West-Africa). Wiesbaden: Franz Steiner Verlag.

Mead, M., ed. 1955. Cultural Patterns and Technical Change.
Mentor Books.

Ranger, T. 1972. Connections Between "Primary Resistance"
Movements and Modern Mass Nationalism in East and Central
Africa. In: Perspectives on the African Past. M.A. Klein and
G.W. Johnson, eds. pp. 547-576. Little, Brown Co.

Sahlins, M. 1974. Stone Age Economics. Chicago: Aldine.

Salisbury, R.F. 1962. From Stone to Steel. Melbourne: Melbourne
U. Press.

Saul, M. 1981. Beer, Sorghum and Women: Production for the Market
in Rural Upper Volta. Africa 51(3):746-764.

Turner, V.W. 1969. The Ritual Process. Chicago: Aldine.

Wallace, A.F.C. 1955. Revitalization Movements. American
Anthropologist.

4. ANTHROPOLOGY AND DEVELOPMENT: A NOTE ON THE STRUCTURE OF THE FIELD

Robert H. Bates

Anthropology is an academic discipline. To become an anthropologist, one must undergo academic training in a university, studying the books and papers written by one's predecessors. As in any academic discipline, the ultimate justification for work in the field is that it contributes to knowledge: that the books and papers written by those who come after us will be different--and, one hopes, better--than those written before we did our work.

Anthropology is an academic discipline. To most people, academicians look like drones. We don't lift anything heavy; we work, by and large, in clean and well lighted places; we tend to enjoy our work, to sleep well, and to get exercise, if we want it. The ultimate justification for the good life of academicians is that, all appearances to the contrary, their work is in fact socially useful--that it will, in short, make the world a better place.

Development anthropology appears to differ from most other fields of anthropology in that its center lodges to a greater degree outside the academy. An ironic result is that, on first appearances, it seems to make a stronger case for being socially useful than it does for being academically significant. In the long run, of course, this is not healthy, either for the practitioners of this subdiscipline nor for anthropology as a whole. For unless development anthropologists can make an impact on the intellectual foundations of their discipline, graduate programs will not invest in that field. Development anthropology will then suffer the fate of any isolate; it will fail to reproduce itself and face extinction. Equally as important, those portions of anthropology that rest more firmly in the academy will have failed to have drawn upon the experiences and learning of an extraordinarily active portion of the discipline.

The claim that development anthropology has proven socially useful rests on obvious grounds. Development agencies and government programs have an impact upon the lives of people, many of whom are unable to give voice to their interests or to exercise political power in defense of them. The world being what it is, roads will be built, dams constructed, and "slums" "renewed," despite anyone's attempts to prevent them. One of the special contributions of development anthropology has been to reshape and reconfigure such interventions, out of a regard for

81

the interests of the powerless.

The defense of the intellectual significance of development anthropology rests on several grounds, some of which are controversial. One ground for such a defense is, of course, that more knowledge is always to be preferred. Knowledge in anthropology comes from fieldwork. And development anthropologists tend to spend more time in the field than the rest of us. The problem with this defense, however, is the quality of the data that are generated. As the farming system controversies have shown, the optimal strategy for collecting data for purposes of policy intervention may well not be the optimal strategy for collecting data for academic research. Those of us who have taken leave from university positions to serve on consultancy missions can vividly recall the tension between academics and policy makers--a tension often spawned simply by differences concerning what one regards as relevant data and the price, often in terms of time alone, that one is willing to pay to acquire them.

If the contribution of development anthropology to the academy does not lie in the quality of the information it collects, it must lie in the ideas it generates from these data or the interpretative framework it brings to them. I detect several major themes that may help to define this contribution.

One theme is that of challenge: Development anthropology repeatedly challenges academicians to look at people and institutions in real world settings. More than most academicians, development anthropologists live and work in the world that other anthropologists purport to write about. Development anthropologists therefore constitute a useful and relevant audience for academic musings. For if the theorizing of academicians does not ring true to them, then it could be that the academic writings are simply not addressing the world as it actually is. When that condition is revealed, then it is in the interests of all of us to take corrective measures.[1]

A second major contribution of development anthropology is surely to point out once and for all the futility of developing partial models of human societies. Theories can simply no longer be built on the notion that there exist self-contained, autonomous, bounded communities. Such a model may have possessed validity at one time, but even then perhaps only for island cultures. As development anthropology repeatedly demonstrates, it certainly lacks validity in the present era.

A third major contribution of development anthropology is to enlarge the scope of anthropological inquiry. Some development anthropologists pursue classical policy analysis: they take the preferences and initiatives of public agencies as given and show how their programs could be improved. But others have gone beyond the role of policy analysts by taking the agencies themselves as objects of study. An important contribution of development anthropology may therefore be to strengthen the tendency of anthropologists to expand their field of study to include elites, managers, bureaucracies, and public institutions, as well as local communities.

A fourth major contribution of development anthropology is related to the last: The building of bridges to other disciplines. It is states and markets that most frequently intervene from the outside world. The reasons why they intervene in the ways they do tend best to be comprehended by people in political science and economics. Although anthropology has traditionally interacted with sociology and psychology, under the impact of development anthropology, it may well alter its conception of what other disciplines are most relevant, and bring anthropology into closer contact with economics and political science.

As a member of one of these neighboring disciplines, these are what I perceive to be the major contributions of development anthroplogy to its own, parent discipline. A deeper assessment of its impact must come from a card carrying anthropologist. I, for one, anxiously await such an accounting. In the meantime, it may be fun and rewarding to sketch out what a "great work" in development anthropology might look like.

Its subject would probably be variation--variation in forms of intervention and variation in patterns of local response. It would draw more heavily than most anthropological studies on political science, in attempting to account for variations in the forms of state intervention; "development," as we understand it, tends to be an activity of governments. It would also draw heavily upon economics; the form of intervention has a lot to do with the relative costs and benefits of different ways of attempting to secure public objectives. And this portion of the book would contain a marvelously rich analysis--an account of the internal life of the bureaucracy such as only an anthropologist could provide. What would make the book different from political science or economics or organizational behavior would be the emphasis given to the second major portion: the analysis of the impact of the intervention upon the institutions and behavior of the local community.

The book would take advantage of the implicit experimental design offered by the series of development interventions. That is, it would show how variations in the institutions or their properties affected the way in which people respond to

"exogenous" shocks. It would also go beyond the limits implicit
in such an experimental design to show the way in which
variations in the characteristics of local communities fed into
and conditioned the forms of public intervention. In so doing,
it might just celebrate, a bit, the role of the development
anthropologist in helping to liberate people -- to transform them
from subjects of fate (or bureaucracies) into shapers of their
fate in a world in which political and economic forces transcend
local communities.

Notes

[1] A colleague unkindly suggests that a rough translation of
these comments would be: Put short, a lot of recent faddism, much
of the French persuasion, would not have taken hold, had it been
put to this test. And the world would have been a better place. I
leave it to the reader to judge whether this was my intention.

SECTION II: THE SOCIOCULTURAL MEDIATIONS OF PRODUCTION

The essays in this section examine how small-scale producers perceive and react to changing opportunities for and constraints on their activities. Each of the authors considers both the local contexts of production (including cultural, ecological, and political factors), and the supra-local networks, institutions, and sources of change. The papers by Mahir Saul, Constance McCorkle, and Sara Berry present three perspectives on changing West African agriculture. Saul addresses the issue of relative efficiencies in private and public marketing channels, and concludes that private traders have their inefficiencies, too. McCorkle's analysis is more concerned with the economic and cultural trade-offs between cotton and cereal cultivation. Berry analyzes how gender roles shape economic behavior, and, in particular, how social and political relations hinder women in the cultivation of tree crops.

The other papers examine different aspects of the problem. Sara Scherr show how the methods of economists and anthropologists can complement each other in the study of economic change. Her essay is also a profile of local producer types in Mexico. John Galaty also is concerned with how differences in socioeconomic structure lead to different responses to large-scale changes. His case is the reaction of Tanzanian pastoralists and agro-pastoralists to political and ecological constraints. Ricardo Godoy considers how ecological differences in Indonesia have limited the effectiveness of government production policies. Gregory Truex describes a different kind of "production," namely crime as a response to the new opportunities provided by economic development. Finally, Emilio Moran and Stephen Gudeman analyze the incentive structure of frontier communities as a special case of development.

85

5. THE EFFICIENCY OF PRIVATE CHANNELS IN THE DISTRIBUTION OF CEREALS IN BURKINA FASO

Mahir Saul

The West African grain marketing literature usually implies a contrast between the performance of national grain distribution organizations established by governments and that of private traders, a comparison generally favorable to the latter. The operational inefficiencies of public structures have been scrutinized in great detail (CILSS 1977; Wilcock 1978; Ouedraogo 1983), and this type of evidence is sometimes used to exhort African governments to confine their economic activities to functions that the market can't or won't perform, that is, providing public goods and controlling the level of aggregate demand (Berry 1984:65). Berg notes for Mali, for example, that traders use resources more efficiently as the supply of their services is highly elastic, that they make decisions with greater speed and more flexibility, that they lower transport costs by such things as carrying two-way cargoes, and that there is a stronger urge for material incentives in their case (1979:158-159).

The purpose of this article is to qualify these conclusions by pointing to some other factors that might be relevant in this comparison. I also suggest that the dichotomy, government organization/private traders, does not exhaust all organizational possibilities in Burkina Faso. I wish to address two specific issues. The first one is whether private trade channels are efficient in distributing grain, and whether they can be relied on as the exclusive mechanism where there are large production variations from year to year resulting in unexpected local food deficits. The second issue is whether the activity of merchants is efficient in terms of transportation costs, when one also takes into consideration social costs and alternative modes of storage and grain distribution. I show that capital limitations and the personalized nature of trade links lead merchants from different centers to operate in the same producing zones in the post-harvest period and then redistribute the grain geographically through transactions among themselves, thus causing technically unnecessary transportation for the grain.

Burkina Faso shares with the other countries of the Sudano-Sahelian zone of West Africa a precarious food grain situation. Its grain imports compared to domestic production are lower than those for most other countries in the region (Wilcock 1978:101, Europa Yearbook 1984), but they are growing. A major set of problems, however, are related not to the total amount of

87

production but to the uneven distribution of production in different regions of the country. The problems of distribution discussed here follow from this situation.

Major food crops in Burkina Faso are white sorghums and millet (Pennisetum). Red sorghum, the major ingredient in the production of local beer, is often grown for sale or for rituals. Cereals are mostly grown in family farms ranging between three and six hectares, but there is a growing minority of large farmers who till much wider areas. Most farmers grow a variety of food crops and some export crops (cotton, sesame, peanuts) using hoe technology. The use of animal traction and plow technology, however, is also spreading with the help of many extension and credit programs. The majority of farmers reserve most of their producton for their own consumption. The total cereal production of the country is estimated to average around 1.2 million tons, and 15 to 20 percent of this amount is assumed to reach the market. This marketed grain needs to cover the demand in major cities (Ouagadougou, Bobo-Dioulasso, Koudougou) and in provinces that regularly have a poor harvest (Figure 1). The major pattern in the flow of grain is determined by the location of surplus and deficit zones. One sharp contrast exists between the north of the country, with a yearly average rainfall around 500 mm and with chronic grain deficits, and the south, which includes areas receiving more than 1100 mm of rainfall. The heavily populated central plateau shifts between good and bad crop years and because it includes large cities is also dependent on surpluses coming from the east, south and especially western part of the country. In addition to that there are significant intraregional flows. Even in surplus regions poor or poorly distributed rains lead to pockets of grain shortage, and even in overall surplus conditions not all households are assured of an abundant harvest. Therefore, in many rural areas there is a strong demand for cereals, which is created partly by households that cannot produce all the grain they need, and partly by grain using rural industries such as brewing and market cooking. Furthermore, this demand is not evenly distributed throughout the year. In many localities farmers sell heavily in the post-harvest period and most of the grain deriving from such sales is taken out of the area. In contrast rural demand is concentrated in the rainy season and often must be fulfilled by local imports through urban centers. Another characteristic of the Sudano-Sahelian grain markets that follows partly from this sales pattern is the existence of very strong inter-seasonal variations in the price of grain. Grain prices reach their lowest point at the time of harvest and usually more than double in the rainy season, before the next harvest.

Like most neighboring countries, the government of Burkina Faso (formerly Upper Volta) has created public institutions to

Figure 1.   Map of Burkina Faso.

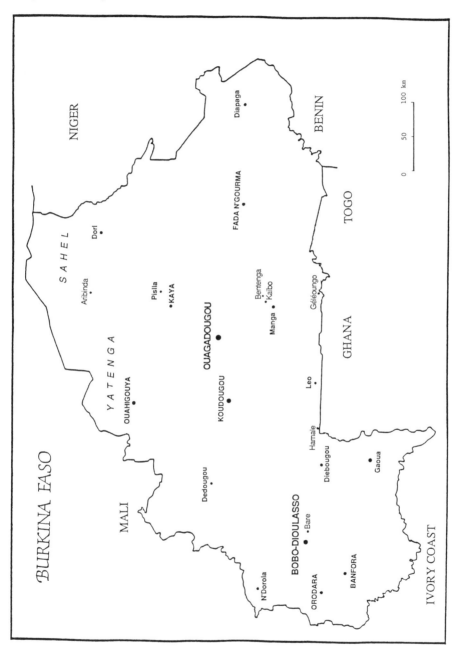

participate in the marketing of grain, originally to face problems primarily related to the distribution of imported and donated cereals during the drought period between 1968 and 1972. The organization that came to dominate public participation in the market is the National Cereals Office (OF.NA.CER.), created in 1971 with a mandate to stabilize producer and consumer prices by grain purchases in surplus areas and sales in deficit areas.[1] In its first few years OF.NA.CER's role was largely limited to managing the storage and distribution of food aid. In time, however, it took a more active role, building national stocks, trying to contribute to the stabilization of prices by grain purchases, and sales of these and food aid at officially announced prices. OF.NA.CER's activity has not supplanted the private traders who are still responsible for moving most of the marketed grain throughout the country; neither did it manage to reduce urban grain prices close to the level of official prices in the rainy season. Nevertheless it has an important role in supplying grain in the deficit regions of the north, and some impact on prices through its buying campaigns and through its sales in urban areas. It is also thought to occupy an important role in government plans for food security, hence the discussion among donor agencies on the nature of its role, its performance, and the virtues of having an unhampered private system.

The collection and distribution of grain in Burkina Faso is largely achieved by a chain of different types of intermediaries. At the lowest end one finds primary handlers who may start bulking at very small units (such as the enameled bowls holding 2 to 2.5 kg of grain popular among the Mossi). The chain includes independent traders, commission agents, wholesalers, brokers, major merchants, and often ends with retailers who operate in the stalls of city markets. But these functions are not clearly separated and most individuals combine several of them. The system includes some other unusual features. For example, the units commonly used in retailing (in cities very often a 100 kg sack) may be larger than those at which bulking starts. Also bulking does not always proceed toward increasingly larger volumes; a merchant can break bulk to sell to another merchant from a distant city who continues to bulk, a practice that creates successive loops of bulking and debulking as the grain is moved toward the consumer.

Major city merchants who control large funds are instrumental in the establishment of collection networks and grain flow patterns. These large merchants are usually also involved in the export of oil crops, the import and distribution of staple consumer goods, and truck transport. A grain merchant may travel widely in the post-harvest period and spend a long time in producing zones to coordinate buying activity. Success largely depends, however, especially for the larger merchants who operate in a wide geographic area, on a system of collecting agents (for more information on the operation of the grain market in Burkina Faso see Ouedraogo 1983, Sherman 1984, Saul n.d.).

There are various types of grain collecting agents employed by merchants. Some may be residents who receive large funds from the merchant during the post-harvest period to acquire grain in the area in which they live. Usually the resident buyer is a village notable, for example an ambitious farmer, a village trader who operates a small shop to supply basic consumer goods, a village chief, or a civil servant stationed in the village. Because in rural markets grain is most abundantly supplied in the post-harvest period, this is the time when resident buyers are active. In this period they receive frequent visits from the merchant or from one of his representatives who monitors the collection, evacuates the product in big lots, and brings additional funds when the money is exhausted. As the dry season advances grain becomes scarcer, its price rises, and most buying agents become less active or stop working for their merchant altogether.

In Bentenga, for example (a large Mossi and Bisa village in south central Burkina, now the province of Zoundweogo), there were two resident buyers in 1979. One of them, the operator of one of the two village mills, bought for the owner of the mill, who was a wealthy merchant and herd owner in the nearby town of Kaibo. This very merchant was selling most of his grain to merchants from the capital city of Ouagadougou and it is possible that he was himself operating partially on the basis of credits or advances provided by them. The second resident buyer was the instructor of the village school who was collaborating with a major merchant from Ouagadougou. A third merchant stationed in the subprefecture capital of Manga worked with major merchants of the capital but also had managed to obtain formal credit from the National Bank of Development; he collected grain with his truck in the region but could not get much from this village. The two resident buyers collected more than 25 tons of white sorghum and large quantities of other grains in the first two weeks of January alone. In the month of April they were not active anymore. A little grain continued to trickle into the village market, and an upsurge in red sorghum sales occurred in late July when a good harvest was in sight and the maize started to be harvested.

Such a bimodal sales pattern was common in this region. It had the first peak in the post-harvest period, a time when farmers were selling primarily food grains to the resident buyers of major merchants, and a much smaller second peak in the pre-harvest period, when the new crops were almost mature and some of the larger farmers would sell the red sorghum that they

91

kept in storage in the marketplace to take advantage of the higher price (for a discussion of this pattern see Harriss 1979 a and b).

One important point for our discussion is that resident buyers are involved only in the collection of grain; they don't take any part in its sale. In the buying period they usually keep the grain in their home or in an attached room until a bulk large enough for the merchant to evacuate is achieved. They do not store the grain for long periods of time. Consequently the grain is not available on the spot for future needs.

There is a second type of agent on whom merchants rely even more importantly for the collection of grain. These are usually young people residing in large cities, very often living with the merchant himself. They travel widely in rural areas and purchase grain for their employer in rural markets, from farmers and from independent small traders, and may also coordinate the resident buyers who work for their master. They are rewarded with a commission on the volume they collect, but sometimes they are related to the merchant by a kinship or quasi-kinship tie, in which case the relationship is based less on immediate rewards and more on long-term obligations. Ethnic ties are sometimes important in establishing such links, but collaboration across ethnic lines is also widespread. The association between merchant and especially agents linked by kinship often continues for several years and sometimes results in the merchant setting up his former employee as an independent trader by providing him with capital and even a wife. As in the case of resident buyers, these agents are active in the purchase of grain during the post-harvest period.

Another type of intermediary one encounters in village markets are independent traders who buy grain with their own personal funds. There is a large variety of individuals who engage in such activity. Many of them come from large cities to attend periodic markets and return home at the end of the day. They use commercial vehicles (frequently also owned by major urban or regional merchants) to send their purchases to the city and to commute, but sometimes they may possess a bicycle or a moped for travelling around the country. Usually they operate on very limited funds, so that they have to turn over their money as fast as possible to remain in business. The most common pattern is for them to act simply as bulkers and sell their purchases at the end of the day to major merchants or their agent. Sometimes this transaction takes place in the same marketplace, before leaving for town.

In the post-harvest period many independent traders take at least part of the products they collect to the city to retail it

themselves, and thus retain the full margin. In Bobo-Dioulasso
many small traders, especially women, sell this grain in urban
markets in open stalls. They attend rural markets only on
certain days of the week, selling what they have collected on the
following days and recuperating their capital before returning to
buy more grain. Some of them bring back only red sorghum, which
they supply to the beer brewers in the city, while they sell the
other grains and shea (karite) nuts that they have collected to
merchants' agents on the spot. Others may have a neighborhood
clientele. For example, Salam Sawadogo attends three or four
markets within a distance of twenty kilometers to the city and
collects both cereals and export crops. In the post-harvest
season he is able to bulk two to three sacks (of about a hundred
kilograms) each market day. He retains the grain for sale to
consumers in his neighborhood, while he sells the shea nuts and
other oil crops to major export merchants. In the rainy season
his village purchases drop and for a few months in the year he
may run out of grain to sell. When this happens he buys grain
from major merchants in the city to supply his customers. He
operates with a capital under 500,000 F CFA (or about $1250). In
Ouagadougou and Bobo-Dioulasso, many small traders like him stop
their trade in the rainy season altogether and go to farm
somewhere in the country.

In addition to traders, many urban consumers and women who
brew or have small market restaurants give money to an
acquaintance in a village to buy some grain directly in the
period following the harvest and thus take advantage of price
differences, which are at the peak in this period. One can even
see in village markets occasional visitors who take advantage of
their presence there to purchase grain for their regular use.

It is clear from this description that in Burkina Faso the
links between grain producing areas and consumption centers
change in intensity throughout the year. The relationship is
very strong in the post-harvest period when all kinds of
intermediaries rush to rural areas to collect the grain offered
for sale. Besides the major merchants who send their agents and
reestablish their relationship with resident village buyers, a
large number of small independent traders are active in rural
markets, some of whom are involved in the trade only seasonally.

The situation starts to change toward the month of April
when grain becomes scarcer and prices begin to rise quickly.
Less grain is now offered for sale in rural markets and the
potential seller is a different type of farmer. Most of the
small farmers who sell occasionally do not have any more grain to
market. Most grain now comes from middle range and large farmers
who were able to store part of their marketable crop in order to
take advantage of higher prices. These farmers usually also have

contacts and often personalized long-term relations with large merchants' agents. For small traders, it becomes less profitable to wait in marketplaces and bulk by buying in small quantities. Furthermore, high grain prices increase the logistical problems of those traders who operate efficiently. Together, these two factors result in many of the small independent traders withdrawing from the grain market or operating at a much smaller scale.

For large merchants the buying period can extend a little longer. As the market glut comes to an end they discontinue their relationship with resident buyers. Increasingly their aim becomes to identify large farmers who possess important quantities of marketable grain and then convince them to part with their grain. Because this mode of operation requires an acquaintance with the region and long-established personal trade relationships, merchants who have been active for a long time have an advantage over those who try to compete in unfamiliar territory. When rains start in the month of May, many roads become waterlogged and transportation costs increase. Merchants stop buying in rural areas and urban centers and villages are almost disjoined. Transportation of supplies to large northern consumer centers such as Ouahigouya or Kaya from major cities where the stocks are located becomes very difficult, but the flow continues intermittently, owing to the efforts of some major merchants established in those centers and to the National Cereals Office, which obtains grain through food aid and through its own participation in the market. The cities themselves, however, have largely to rely on previously purchased grain for urban consumption and for sale to those northern merchants.

An important facet of the grain market in Burkina Faso is that merchants operate in such a way as to collect grain in a very large area, but store and sell it in the urban centers where they are based. The available trade capital is concentrated in the major or secondary urban centers and this is where most of the cereals to be consumed in the rainy season are stored. Producer villages have the grain that households have stored for their own needs. However, because not all households can store sufficient grain for their own needs, either because of insufficient production coupled with the inability to buy in the post-harvest period, or because they have marketed more than their available surplus under pressing cash needs, many villages develop an unsatisfied consumer demand in the rainy season. This demand may be for consumption in the household, or in order to sponsor work parties on the fields (often financed by selling animals in the farming season). An additional demand is created by women who buy grain for their processing activities. This shortage can be acute depending on the size of the previous harvest, and on the distribution of production potential among

94

different households.

If the community is divided into large farmers who have important marketable surpluses and many others oscillating around subsistence level, the former sell most of their surplus to urban merchants before the rainy season comes and there is greater likelihood that on the aggregate village stocks will fall below the level needed to meet local demand after the rains start. Part of this demand can be met through sales by small village speculators who store grain to sell later for a profit. For example, some successful farmers may use their savings to keep a few sacks of sorghum or maize to sell to fellow villagers in the farming season. Usually there are also small women traders who accumulate stocks by buying grain or exchanging it against condiments in the post-harvest period. In the farming season there is also some house trade that occurs between needy farmers and more successful fellow villagers who have stocks. Some redistribution of meals and uncooked food takes place between households as part of kinship obligations, friendship, or general solidarity links, especially in years of shortage. All these mechanisms, however, frequently fail to assure an adequate supply and the village may face a crisis. A few examples will illustrate this possibility.

In the village of Bentenga in southern Mossi country, where I conducted research in 1979, there was no trader who had stored grain in the rainy season, despite the fact that in the preceding dry season this village had sold more than 100 tons of sorghum and millet to two resident buyers and to traders who attended the market. In the rainy season the periodic village market was not properly operating and one could very rarely find grain in it. A villager could buy grain only in Kaibo, a regional center 7 km. away and on an all-season highway to the capital; in large market centers in Bisa country to the east where many people had family relations; or in Manga, the regional capital that was 20 km away. Some farmers did have to go and buy grain in those places.[2]

In Bare, another village in the western part of the country where I conducted research in 1983-84, some shortages did appear despite the fact that this village is also located in a highly productive area and not very far from the city. They were due to the fact that the 1983 harvest was considerably below average. The few traders who regularly attended the marketplace managed to obtain almost all the available grain after the harvest and evacuated it to the city. One important village trader, a woman, managed to buy important quantities of millet (about fifty tons), but she refused to sell it until very late in the rainy season when prices were near their highest point. Other small farmer speculators did not have the possibility of purchasing grain. This village has also an active Village Group, one of the

95

voluntary cooperative organizations stimulated by the Regional Development Organization (ORD). The Village Group had established a Cereal Bank the previous year, but could not do so this year because of financing problems. As a result, early in the rainy season several farmers who needed to buy grain could not do so in the village; they had to go to the city of Bobo-Dioulasso, 25 km away, and transport the grain to the village by their own means.

In the rainy season one commonly sees villagers traveling to regional centers, or major cities, to buy grain, because it is not available where they live. Ironically, most merchants in Bobo-Dioulasso and Ouagadougou mentioned that these farmers were one of the major sources of information they used to follow the development of the current farming season in different parts of the country so that they could plan their buying campaign for the coming harvest. Merchants are not interested in directly supplying these rural areas because the demand is relatively thin and transportation in bulk costly.

In years when a large region falls short of its average production, rainy season shortages may be disastrous. When the small merchants in regional centers run out of grain and face a large demand it is up to them to go to the major city and buy cereal to supply their customers. They encounter several problems there: transportation may be difficult, their restricted networks may make grain hard to find (hence an important role for brokers in city markets), and also their capital may not allow them to buy sufficiently large quantities. Finally the low purchasing power of rural consumers may make it impossible for them to buy this highly priced grain. These problems create delays and dangerous breaks in the availability of grain in rural centers. Interestingly, this type of crisis often occurs in regions that normally produce a surplus. For example, Wilcock describes such a crisis in the productive area close to the Ghana border (1978:211), and according to Ouedraogo who conducted his research in the east, the lack of a backflow of grain to producing areas is one of the major shortcomings of the private trading system (1983). This is so because in areas where high consumer needs in the rainy season are regularly anticipated there are local powerful merchants who store enough grain to satisfy local needs, and OF.NA.CER and international relief organizations are also active there.

An apparent solution to prevent such acute shortages of grain in rural areas is to achieve greater local-level commercial storage. This step is difficult because only a negligible amount of trade capital can be found in villages and small regional centers, because little capital is accumulated and the capital that does accumulate is drained off--together with its

96

accumulators--to places with more interesting business opportunities. A policy encouraging a development in this direction should take into consideration not only these realities, but also another possibility that may emerge if local storage is exclusively in the hands of traders. Because in rural areas the number of resident traders is inevitably small, the local supply of grain may be highly concentrated in the rainy season. In villages one can frequently encounter monopolistic structures, as illustrated by the example of the trader in Bare who refused to sell her grain until prices reached a certain level. Similar situations exist in many other parts of the country. They can perhaps partly explain the paradoxical observation that in the later part of the year the relation between rural and urban grain prices is reversed, regional centers reaching prices higher than those in major cities (this trend is evident in six graphs given by CILSS [1977:101-3]).

Another possible way to remedy rural shortages is the intervention of public institutions. In fact, in many parts of Burkina Faso, the National Cereals Office and some international relief organizations are the main agents taking action to relieve acute local grain scarcities. In some instances this operation cannot be effective by itself, because of difficulties in information collection and insufficient means for quick response, and many observers have pointed out the desirability of encouraging other supportive mechanisms.

Naturally, a major improvement in the system would be to help farming households achieve higher incomes and higher productivity so that a larger proportion of them could store enough grain for their own needs. Paradoxically the accomplishment of such an objective may lead in the short run to a greater degree of farmer self-sufficiency in food grains and less involvement in the market. To help farmers achieve greater strength is the avowed purpose of many development programs carried out in the country, but this issue is a complex one that probably will not be completely resolved in the near future, hence the usefulness of some additional measures in the domain of marketing itself. What is suggested here is the development and strengthening of Village Cereal Banks managed and controlled by the farmers themselves, an institution that constitutes one of the elements of the current national rural development agenda. These organizations could have the potential to improve the prevention of localized rainy season shortages, especially if they are backed up with capital and logistical support. One danger in an overly atomistic organization, however, is that unnecessary stocks may be tied up in certain regions in years in which other regions develop a more urgent need for them, so that a coordination at the national level is unavoidable for such a structure to provide a useful contribution.

97

The second theme I wish to discuss here is that of social cost implications of the collection and storage practices discussed above with particular reference to the distances involved in the physical movement of grain. Because of the personalized nature of collection networks each merchant operates mainly in areas where he or she has an advantage in getting at the grain, thanks to familiarity and contacts. The share of the merchant's involvement depends on these links and on the amount of capital he or she controls. Usually these two are related as the wealthier merchants are also the ones that possess the widest set of personal links. Merchants based in one major city have joint interests in trying to obtain low farmgate prices and keeping transportation costs as low as possible. Usually they try to make formal or implicit agreements among themselves in order not to compete with each other in such a way as to raise prices. Merchants of different regions, however, may have opposing interests when they try to increase their market share in each other's territory or in some neutral territory. Their primary purpose is to collect as much grain as their funds allow during the low-price, post-harvest glut.[3] When rains start and the buying campaign in producing areas is over for most of them, merchants of large consumer centers are dependent for their supply on those merchants who were able to achieve higher stocks, that is, those with whom they were often competing in the same producing areas earlier in the year. For the sake of illustration I will consider here the case of three major groups of merchants that were active in the western part of the country in 1984: the merchants of Ouagadougou, those of Bobo-Dioulasso, and those of Ouahigouya.

The capital city of Ouagadougou is the largest consumption center in the country. Originally the city was supplied by its own hinterland, but now receives a large percentage of its needs from the surplus regions of the western and the eastern part of the country (Saul 1986). It also acts as a major transit and bulking point for the grain deficit regions of the north including Ouahigouya. Ouahigouya is the base for some of the wealthiest national merchants who, besides cattle trade and many other occupations, are also involved in the regional import of sorghum and millet. In years of drought they go as far south as around the city of Bobo-Dioulasso to buy directly from producers, but later in the season they are supplied by the major merchants of this city and Ouagadougou. Bobo-Dioulasso is the center for the most productive grain producing region of the country. Interviews with merchants reveal that the largest stocks in the nation are amassed there, and most grain going ultimately to the capital and to northern regions originates from these stocks. This national pattern results in intricate movements of grain as the following examples show.

Lamina and his brother are among the most important grain merchants of Bobo-Dioulasso. They have an extensive system of agents and buyers that they established in the past two decades to collect grain and export crops. They have five main assemblers who specialize in different regions. Their trade activity extends to a large area to the north, south, and west of Bobo-Dioulasso; and like many other major merchants of the city they collect most of their grain in the two provinces to the north of the city, Kossi and Moun-Houn. Dedougou, which is at a distance of 180 km to the city and connected to it by a very bad road, is an important bulking and transit point for this activity. The important amount of grain they collect there is thus shipped south, and is stored in the city for a longer or shorter period of time. Part of this grain reaches the consumers of the city through the intermediary of retailers who own stalls in the central market. But an equally large and perhaps even larger part of it is purchased by merchants of Ouagadougou and Ouahigouya (360 km and 385 km away respectively) and ultimately reaches consumers in these distant places.

But Dedougou is also a grain-collection area for many traders coming from the capital. For example, Koanda Halidou, one of the larger grain dealers in the Sankaryare market of Ouagadougou, has a brother who is stationed in Dedougou and who buys grain for him covering an area of about ten villages. The direct distance from Dedougou to the capital is only 245 km and the state of the road not as bad as the one connecting Dedougou to Bobo-Dioulasso. Grain originating in Dedougou that reaches Ouagadougou via Bobo-Dioulasso travels a distance more than twice as long in all as the direct route between the two centers. When Dedougou grain is taken to Ouahigouya after storage in Bobo-Dioulasso, it is transported over a distance almost three times as long as the direct distance.

Because the extra travel distance is reflected in transportation costs, one would think that merchants from Ouagadougou and Ouahigouya have a cost advantage in receiving the grain directly, either by collecting it themselves or from local assemblers. This advantage, however, is not driving, for the moment, the Bobo-Dioulasso merchants out of the market. Two reasons can be identified for their continuing importance: first, the intruding merchants from the central plateau and the north probably do not have enough capital to clear all the grain supplied; secondly Bobo-Dioulasso merchants started to operate in this area a long time ago and established links that -- in the absence of local capital owners -- give them primacy. Concurrently, transportation cost differences are also easily absorbed by them, thanks to the large margins they achieve when grain is stored and sold for high prices later in the season.

To pursue the above example, the Ouagadougou merchant in question, Koanda Halidou, is not particularly successful in collecting grain in the Dedougou region; he told me that even in the post-harvest period he receives from this town only about ten tons of grain every other week. In 1984 the center of his operation had shifted to Hamale, a previously insignificant town at the Ghanaian border that acquired importance when a record maize harvest in northern Ghana corresponded to a drought in the Sahel and its market became one of the important points of entry for Ghanaian maize. Many Ouagadougou merchants such as Halidou started to tap this source before the 1984 sorghum and millet crop appeared on the market in Burkina Faso. Many were going as far as Wa in northern Ghana to buy truckloads of maize from assemblers there. The gross profits achieved from the operation were considerable.

Hamale is connected to the capital through Leo, by a road of 275 km, part of which is very bad. In Hamale some Bobo-Dioulasso merchants were also active, however. For example, Ousman Ouedraogo from Bobo-Dioulasso was buying there and taking the grain by an equally bad road to his city, 207 km west. Ousman has the reputation of being one of the largest suppliers of Ouagadougou and Ouahigouya merchants. He is wealthy but he is especially known for achieving very large volumes of transactions through quick turnover. Thus most of the grain he collects in Hamale is transferred in about a week or ten days to another merchant form Ouagadougou or the Yatenga, and in the case where it goes to Ouagadougou it reaches its destination after having travelled 290 km more than if it were taken directly.

These examples could be multiplied. Gaoua and Diebougou are also areas where both Bobo-Dioulasso and Ouagadougou merchants are active, and a large part of the cereals purchased there by the former finally reaches Ouagadougou after a few more transactions and an additional 285 km. In the westernmost section of the country, Orodara merchants purchase grain in N'Dorola, while Bobo-Dioulasso merchants purchase both in N'Dorola and in Orodara during the same time. Finally Ouahigouya merchants are competing with Bobo-Dioulasso merchants all over the provinces of Kossi and Moun-Houn in locations halfway between the two cities, but an important portion of what Bobo-Dioulasso merchants collect there ultimately reaches Ouahigouya too, either going all the way back north, or taking an even longer detour, first to the east to Ouagadougou, and then north-west to Ouahigouya.

It must be recognized that in certain instances bad road conditions may explain the convoluted track that grain follows. Trade between two centers may pass through a third center that acts as a transit point, rather than flowing directly, because the longer track consists of better roads. This is commonly the case with small rural centers where one sees farmers sell their surplus to merchants of regional centers, and later when they need grain travel to buy it again from them. Roads are better between villages and these centers than among the villages themselves, and farmers have difficulties in attending other rural markets and transporting their purchases. The patterns illustrated above, however, cannot be explained by such factors. Sometimes a longer road is taken by a trader because there are other economies in increasing the number of stops. For example, Bougoumpiga Mahamadi, a small trader in Ouagadougou travels to Gaoua to buy shea nuts and locust beans (nere). Then he goes to Bobo-Dioulasso where he sells the karite nuts to an exporting merchant, buys cereals in their stead, and transports this cereal and the locust beans collected in Gaoua to his base city. This, however, is an unusual pattern; most often the grain changes hands each time it reaches a major city. The excess transport cost that we are taking into consideration here is a social cost, not one that is materialized or calculated by one merchant. Its reasons are partly in capital limitations of individual merchants, and partly in the nature of the collection networks, which push merchants and traders to collect grain in regions where they have an organizational advantage but not necessarily the ones where grain can reach the final consumer with lowest transportation costs.

The fact that the patterns in the movement of grain are more often due to the way the merchants organize their trade rather than road conditions or other physical factors can most clearly be seen in the case of some northern merchants who in years of good harvest may in the post-harvest period buy grain from farmers in their own region and take it to Ouagadougou to sell, while later in the year they do the reverse and bring grain purchased outside. One example is a large trader from Pisila who in the early 1960s started as a buying agent, collecting first shea nuts and later cereals for Ouagadougou merchants. Now he owns bars and trucks, distributes beer, and has many other occupations including, most importantly, provisioning his town (which is located in an area that finds itself short of grain in many years) with cereals purchased in the west and in the capital. But he told me that in the post-harvest season he may still bring grain that he has collected in his native region to sell to Ouagadougou merchants. His decisions are based on a number of business factors including liquidity needs and repayment of bank credits, but it is certain that, especially in this grain deficit region, it would make sense from the point of view of social costs if marketed grain were stored on the spot rather than being shipped away and later replaced by regional imports.

Problems involving unnecessary transportation costs have been pointed out in the operation of the National Cereals Office also. In the case of this organization, such costs are due to the inability to predict local needs, to insufficient local storage capacity, or to miscalculation. Because decisions are made within one organizational structure, the inefficiency and its causes can be more easily identified. In the case of private traders, similar patterns lead to transportation costs that are equally high or even higher from a social point of view, but these costs are not internalized by traders, and the fact that cereals change hands several times during their journey makes it more difficult to identify the inefficiencies and estimate their magnitude.

It may be interesting to note that the crosscurrents occur even in the circulation of grain across international borders. Researchers have commented that officially unrecognized flows of grain from one West African country to another occur, depending on local supply conditions and prices (Wilcock 1978, Ouedraogo 1983). Such movements, however, continue even without large production shortfalls on either side. Ousman Ouedraogo, the large Bobo-Dioulasso merchant mentioned above, regularly purchases grain in the eastern regions of Mali, where he has connections. In years in which these regions have an abundant harvest a larger amount of grain is taken to Burkina and vice versa. But the flows continue when neither side has an exceptional harvest. Furthermore, in most normal years grain flows in both directions. This is facilitated by the fact that merchants in western Burkina and eastern Mali are connected by many historical, ethnic, and family ties. Such exchanges contribute to a more balanced distribution of grain throughout the wider region and it is desirable that they be recognized officially and not discouraged. Yet one can see little cost effectiveness in physical flows that negate each other.

What is true for grain is also true for export crops such as shea nuts. Merchants collect these crops in surrounding countries as well, and thus part of the exports of Burkina Faso originate outside of its own territory, including northern Ivory Coast, which is in the direction through which the product is ultimately evacuated for export. The fluctuations seen from year to year in the export of these crops by individual countries are partly due to this non-official trade. Differences in export regimes and the level of taxation adopted by different governments explain part of this movement, but again it should be emphasized that in most years the trade goes in both directions to cancel each other partially. As in the case of food grains, it is the organization of private trade channels that partially explains these flows.

In summary, then, it should be realized that private trade channels, despite the axiomatic arguments that they are driven by high motivation and creativity, are not free of inefficiencies. They do not have the flexibility to respond to localized, but acute and serious shortages. They also do not necessarily achieve minimum costs in the distribution of grain when one considers the social cost of transportation. In addition to private trade and the centralized government grain distribution system, schemes that help farmers play a greater role in the interseasonal storage of marketed grain by building stocks sufficiently large to meet local demand may contribute to remedy both shortcomings.

Notes

*Research for this paper was conducted in 1978-79, in 1983-84, and in 1985 with the support of National Science Foundation, Wenner-Gren Foundation, University of Illinois Research Board, and USAID consultancies with Purdue University West Africa Projects, and University of Michigan Center for Research on Economic Development. I owe thanks to many individuals and especially to the farmers and merchants of Burkina Faso who patiently educated me in matters concerning them. I am solely responsible for the opinions expressed here.

[1] There were two other institutions established in Burkina for similar purposes and that operated at the same time as OF.NA.CER. The Sous-Comite de Lutte Contre les Effets de la Secheresse concerned itself with the distribution of food aid grain and used the logistical capacities of the military who were active in its organization. The Comite National pour la Constitution et la Gestion des Stocks de Cereales de Reserve was created in 1976 as a precondition for the receipt of FAO-coordinated multi-donor aid in creating a national system of emergency stocks.

[2] No shortages developed in that year because the harvest was good, enough farmers had red sorghum, which they had stored until the new harvest.

[3] For more information on these and other characteristics of the organization of the grain market in Burkina Faso, see Saul n.d.

References

Berg, Elliot 1979. Reforming Grain Marketing Systems in West
    Africa: A Case Study of Mali. In: International Workshop on
    Socioeconomic Constraints to Development of Semi-Arid Tropical
    Agriculture, Proceedings, pp. 147-172. Patancheru, A.P.,
    India: ICRISAT,

Berry, Sara 1984. The Food Crisis and Agrarian Change in Africa:
    A Review Essay. African Studies Review 27(2):59-112.

CILSS(Comite Interetat de Lutte contre la Secheresse dans le
    Sahel) 1977. Marketing Price Policy and Storage of Food Grains
    in the Sahel: A Survey. 2 vols. Ann Arbor: CRED, University of
    Michigan.

Harriss, Barbara 1979a. There is Method in my Madness: Or is it
    Vice Versa? Measuring Agricultural Market Performance. Food
    Research Institute Studies 17(2):197-218.

------- 1979b. Going Against the Grain. In: International
    Workshop on Socioeconomic Constraints to Development of
    Semi-Arid Tropical Agriculture, Proceedings. pp. 265-288.
    Patancheru, A.P., India: ICRISAT,

Ouedraogo, Ismael 1983. A Socioeconomic Analysis of Farmers: Food
    Grain Marketing Linkages and Behavior in Eastern Upper Volta.
    Ph.D, dissertation. Michigan State University.

Saul, Mahir 1986. Development of the Grain Market and Merchants
    in Burkina Faso. The Journal of African Studies 24(1): n.d. The
    Organization of a West African Grain Market. Forthcoming.

Sherman, Jacqueline 1984. Grain Markets and the Marketing
    Behavior of Farmers: A Case Study of Manga, Upper Volta. Ph.D.
    Dissertation, University of Michigan.

Wilcock, David C. 1978. The Political Economy of Grain Marketing
    and Storage in the Sahel. Ph.D. Dissertation, Michigan State
    University.

6. "YOU CAN'T EAT COTTON": CASH CROPS AND THE CEREAL CODE OF HONOR IN BURKINA FASO

Constance M. McCorkle

"... a German agriculturalist ... was ... in charge of a project to encourage the cultivation of cotton for export. Cotton is sold through a government monopoly and earns much-needed foreign exchange, so its production is heavily supported by central government. Had he been successful? Wildly so; in fact the people had spent so much time growing cotton that they had grown no food, prices had rocketed and a famine had only been averted by the intervention of the church relief projects. Strangely, he seemed in no way depressed by this outcome" (Barley 1983:25).

Across the last two-and-a-half decades throughout French West Africa, postcolonial government and private enterprise in the form of the French transnational cotton company or CFDT[1] have jointly promoted large-scale cultivation of cotton as a major cash and export crop. In many regions, farmers have responded enthusiastically--some authors say "wildly" (Barley ibid.)--to the many enticing incentives to grow cotton. Sometimes, they have done so even to the neglect of staple food-grain production. Certainly this has been increasingly the case in the Sahelian nation of Burkina Faso, formerly Upper Volta. As cotton production has risen, cereal production and marketing in Burkina have stagnated or declined (Haggblade 1984, 1986). In consequence, the country's traditional "bread basket," the Volta Noire region, threatens to become a "cotton bowl" instead.

This forms the crux of what I have termed the cotton/cereal equation (McCorkle 1985). Under current farming-system and other constraints, there is a direct trade-off between cotton and cereal as farm managers proportionally allocate their finite supplies of land, labor, capital, and technological knowledge and inputs to one crop or the other. More investment in cotton seems to mean less cereal, and vice versa. Here I examine this formula in one representative Volta Noire farming community, highlighting how cultural and social considerations in the form of a "cereal code of honor" interact with economic impulses to cash-crop cotton.

The study village, Dankui, lies some 25 km east of the Volta Noire River and 46 km southwest of Dedougou, the capital of the Volta Noire ORD (Organisation Regionale de Developpement). The village is inhabited in nearly equal proportions by Bwaba, Mossi, and semi-sedentary Fulani. Research was carried out with a 30 percent random sample of village compounds. The research mandate was to study farm managers' grain marketing decision-making. However, it quickly became apparent that this could be understood only vis-a-vis their cash-cropping of cotton and their nonmarketing of grain, which averages more than 90 percent of compound cereal disposals.[2]

Cotton and Cereal in Village History

The staple food grains in the Volta Noire are sorghum, millet, and maize. Although these cereals are not grown solely or primarily for commercial aims, both in the past and today Volta Noire farmers typically sell some portion of their production. In Dankui, only sorghum is marketed in any quantity by most compounds. It therefore constitutes the major grain in the equation discussed here. Until 1960 cotton apparently occupied an economic niche similar to that of gourds today. That is, most Dankui families cultivated a bit of a traditional variety of cotton for their own consumption; and a few also raised an extra share for sale or exchange.

In the early 1960s, the CFDT initiated a massive program to introduce commercial cropping of Allen cotton, an improved variety. Working through the government ORD structure, the company acted as both a production enterprise and an agricultural credit and extension service. CFDT's introduction of cotton in Burkina paralleled that described by Campbell (1984) for the Ivory Coast. The company controlled all distribution of seeds, fertilizers, herbicides, and pesticides; strictly supervised agricultural techniques and timetables; was uniquely responsible for collecting, purchasing, ginning, transporting, stocking, and marketing all of the new crop; and shared subsidies, operations costs, and revenues with national government in a variety of financial schemes. Now operating in Burkina under the name of SOFITEX (Societe Voltaique des Fibres Textiles), the company retains this vertically integrated, parastatal structure.

In Dankui, so successful was the CFDT campaign that by 1962 nearly every village compound cash-cropped at least some cotton. In 1964, a full-time cotton extension agent was installed in the community. By 1966, overall production reportedly had increased dramatically. Thereafter, say villagers, cotton production has continued its steady rise. Cotton now constitutes the cash-getting "king" for most Bwa and Mossi compounds in Dankui. This is evidenced in the results of a controlled ranking task in which farmers named cotton their number-one cash-getter. In contrast, the primary food grain, sorghum, ranked only eighteenth out of 20 possibilities.[3]

Both the diachronic shifts and the synchronic alternatives in Dankui farm managers' cotton/cereal production and marketing strategies are schematically represented in Figure 1. Strategy I represents the traditional organization of production, with only a little or (today) no cultivation of cotton. Some 10 percent of Dankui farmers still adhere to this pattern. The "mixed conservative" strategy II incorporates both crops, but retains the emphasis on cereal production. It is no accident that a majority of villagers (63 percent) opt for this formula. For reasons outlined below, it is usually a dependable cash/food crop combination in this drought-prone area.

Strategy III reverses II's relative emphasis on cotton and cereal. Farmers following this production plan represent the avant-garde of commercialized agriculture in Dankui, comprising approximately a fourth of community compounds in 1983. Under normal political-economic conditions, III's cotton/cereal mix is a viable option, and one that can earn a substantial cash income. However, as we shall see, this can be a "risky" strategy insofar as it forces producers to rely more heavily upon market purchases for critical supplies of food grain.

In their own view, what motivated 90 percent of the Dankui sample to move from strategy I to strategy II or even III in the space of only some two decades? Farmers' stated decision-making rationales expectedly centered on the multiplicity of economic, technical, and even social incentives to produce cash-crop cotton, and the corresponding lack of such incentives to market cereal commercially. But informants also described a code of cultural constraints on grain disposals generally, and on sales in particular, which figured in their adoption of commercial cotton-growing.

Cotton Incentives and Cereal Disincentives

Dankui farmers cited a veritable host of SOFITEX/ORD incentives to cash-crop cotton. Equally important, they contraposed these incentives to the lack of equivalent mechanisms for cereal production and marketing.

For example, nearly all informants mentioned the thorough-going technical extension package for cotton, as well as generous credit arrangements requiring no immediate cash outlays for agricultural inputs like fertilizer, insecticides, herbicides, plows, cultivators, and carts. Coupled with the greater drought resistance of the improved cotton, respondents averred that these technical and financial supports make cotton a "safer" crop than cereal, which enjoys no such advantages.

Farmers also appreciated SOFITEX's extremely convenient system of input-delivery directly to, and cotton-pickup within, the village. This was contrasted with the time and labor shortages, transport costs, uncertain demand, and fatigue that often make selling cereal in marketplaces unattractive and inefficient for farmers. Of course, an alternative is to sell to grain merchants. But villagers felt that most such dealings are characterized by extreme negative reciprocity; and in the case of ill-advised advance sales (see below) or credit defaults, they can lead to disgrace or imprisonment for farmers.

With regard to grain traders, the most common complaint was that they constantly endeavor to cheat farmers on cereal weights and measures. Or as one village wit quipped, "If a trader can't make a deal dishonestly, he won't make it at all." Just the opposite is said to characterize cotton transactions. Informants described the fairness and accuracy (or in their words, the "preciseness") of SOFITEX's weighing, grading, credit, and payment operations. Villagers also expressed confidence in their cotton transactions because, along with company employees, trusted community officials and locally known ORD authorities oversee most of these operations.

Interviewees further commented on SOFITEX's guaranteed purchase and pricing policies. Most frequently cited was the cotton company's announcement of a firm annual price just before planting time each year. In contrast, real-market grain prices are impossible to predict at planting. Farmers also expressed great satisfaction with the "high price" of cotton and with SOFITEX's lump-sum, on-the-spot, cash payment plan.

Finally, nearly all respondents cited the timeliness of SOFITEX payment as an important factor in their decision to cash-crop cotton. Normally, the "cotton money" arrives just when a family's annual cash needs are greatest. These include the yearly head and livestock taxes, school fees, loan repayments, reimbursement of agricultural labor, and two sets of holiday expenses. All these cash outlays fall in the immediate post-harvest months of December and January, precisely when cereal prices are lowest.

The Cereal Code of Honor

The many incentives to cash-crop cotton and the corresponding disincentives to market cereal commercially are further reinforced by a complex and pervasive array of sociocultural norms and concerns pertaining to cereal disposals. This tradition arises from the tremendous importance of staple food grains in assuring the Burkinabe farm family a secure and satisfying life. Cereal must always be on hand to meet myriad needs. Moreover, a portion of these needs must be met with grain derived from compound production--not from market or other channels.

Table 1's grain budgets suggest something of the multiplex roles of sorghum in village life. Predictably, everyday consumption constitutes the compound's major disposal category and, indeed, the overriding aim of cereal production in Dankui. Also included in this "line item" are the many meals daily fed to visitors and distributed to other compounds in token of kinship, friendship, and community spirit. These prestations create, reaffirm, and invigorate village social and economic relations.

Grain-for-milk exchanges take place between Bwaba and Fulani; the extra milk is an important supplement in Bwa children's diet. Grain-for-beer exchange among Bwaba represents a culturally significant expenditure because beer is imperative for the proper fulfillment of many religious and social obligations. The native sorghum beer, dolo, is de rigueur for certain ceremonies (notably agricultural rites); manufactured beer or other beverages cannot be substituted. Across all ethnic groups, substantial amounts of cereal are required for the hearty meals and urns of grain-based beverages entailed by extraordinary ceremonial events like marriages and funerals.

Adequate cereal supplies must also be on hand for the food and drink with which to host the numerous work parties that are a near-universal part of crop production in Dankui, and for in-kind reimbursement of certain other types of assistance in agriculture. The need for seed is self-evident. Grain is also needed for feeding livestock (particularly fowl) and sometimes for securing care for cattle through herding contracts with Fulani.

Furthermore, sorghum is the coin in which Bwaba and Mossi must pay annual tribute to the village chief, in recognition of his authority. Much of this grain is redistributed in the fulfillment of chiefly duties--entertaining visiting officials and pesky anthropologists, holding rituals and feasts to maintain good relations with the ancestors and thus ensure village well-being; distributing gifts of food to the old, handicapped, and destitute; and so forth. Indeed, grain gifts and charitable donations are a regular feature of Burkinabe rural life--as part of kin, community, caste, tenant, and trading-partner obligations; in thanks for special aid; or in return for

Table 1

TABLE 1

ANNUAL COMPOUND GRAIN BUDGETS: PERCENTAGE
OF COMPOUND PRODUCTION (SORGHUMS) BY DISPOSAL CATEGORY

	Bwaba	Mossi
"Everyday" consumption	73%	82%
Sales	8%	8%
Animal feed	3%	3%
Grain for work-party consumption	3%	2%
Payments-in-kind for agricultural labor	3%	1%
Gifts, tithes, and charitable donations	2%	2%
Grain-for-milk exchange	2%	0%
Tribute to village chief	1%	1%
Seed	1%	1%
Grain-for-beer exchange	1%	0%
Ritual reserves	1%	0%
Grain payments for herding	1%	0%
Special social and ceremonial consumption[a]	?	?
	99%[b]	100%

[a]This line item appears as a question mark because funerals, marriages, special propitiatory rites, longterm visits from distant relatives, and etc. are uncertain events in any given year.

[b]Sums to 99 due to rounding.

recipients' "blessings and prayers" (see McCorkle 1986).

In addition, the Moslem Mossi are expected to tithe a tenth of annual compound cereal production in Zakat as thanks to Allah for the harvest, and to give alms of grain on the last day of Ramadan. These tithes and alms are to be distributed to Koranic students and teachers, marabouts (holy men), mosque personnel, beggars, and the needy in general. Animist Bwaba must maintain ritual reserves of cereal from year to year to forestall magically future crop failures, in accordance with the belief that a once-empty granary can become an always-empty granary.

It should be emphasized that tribute (Zakat) and ritual reserves must derive from a compound's own production. Purchased or gift grain cannot be used to meet these obligations. Put another way, there are two kinds of cereal in Dankui: one that can be obtained through market or other exchanges, and one that cannot.

In a compound's total grain budget, sales clearly constitute only one among more than a dozen disposal options, most of which take nutritional, social, ideological, or production priority. Yet just as clearly, sales form the second largest disposal category for the average Dankui compound (see again Table 1). Farm managers must exercise care in both their production planning and their disposal decisioning to see that sales do not "eat into" other, more critical cereal needs. Because staple food grain is fundamental to the actualization of every aspect of family and community existence in Dankui, when supplies run short, life quality is profoundly affected.

Small wonder, then, that cereal disposals are hedged about by an array of cultural proscriptions and prescriptions, exhorting farm managers to prudent, self-rewarding, and community-minded stewardship of compound cereal stocks. Together, I have termed these sanctions a "cereal code of honor," in accordance with sample members' repeated references to the "honor" and "pride" or the "shame" (translated respectively from the French honneur, orgueil, honte)[4] attaching to different instances of cereal disposal. Neither is it any accident that this code is particularly explicit with regard to sales.

Briefly, cereal sales can be effected in essentially two ways. First is of course direct sales--whether in the marketplace, at home, to cereal merchants at the farmgate or their place of business, or to the Groupement Villageois (GV), the community agricultural cooperative. The GV buys only during the immediate post-harvest period, in order to resell cereal during the May-August soudure, "hungry season" (lit. "joint" or "seam"). The aim is to earn operating capital for the GV and at

the same time keep a security stock of grain in the community to
bridge the hungry-season gap between diminishing supplies of
sorghum and millet and the first maize harvest in September.
With the exception of the GV, direct sales can be made throughout
the year.

Second is advance sales to merchants and the GV. These most
often occur in the hungry season, when family cereal stocks may
be depleted, and all other means of obtaining grain (or cash with
which to purchase grain) may be exhausted. Advance sales can be
contracted in return for immediate supplies of emergency food
grain, or for cash. In either case, they are repaid in kind at
harvest at a hefty rate of interest.

Now, selling cereal from compound production can constitute
a disgraceful act, to be conducted on the sly and then dissembled
from relatives and neighbors; or it can be an honorable act, even
a civic service, which wins status and prestige. When and why is
it which?

In the cereal code of honor, advance sales uniformly carry a
distinct social stigma. They are viewed as an admission of inept
planning on the part of compound management. Such sales are said
to be most common among younger compound heads, who are more
susceptible to the lure of modern consumer goods and lifeways.
According to their elders, these foolish young men are always
wanting money in order to buy gas to gad about on their mopeds,
to go out drinking or _faire le weekend_, and in the case of some
unfortunates, to cater to frivolous wives' clamors for finery.
But when--for whatever unhappy constellation of reasons--
compound cereal reserves are exhausted early in the year and no
other solution seems possible, even established compound elders
will turn to advance sales as a desperate way of bridging the
hungry-season food gap. This is a dangerous ploy. If the
harvest contracted for is poor, farmers can become trapped in an
ever-tightening downward spiral of advance sales, emergency
repurchases of cereal, and constant indebtedness and
disgrace.[4]

Large sales of grain at harvest-time are likewise generally
frowned upon. The feeling is that, ceteris paribus, this is
tantamount to unlicensed gambling with corporate property. As
one elder sagely admonished, "It is impossible to know the
future." Another added, "People who sell grain at harvest-time
have forgotten how they suffered during the hungry season."
Through ill-considered sales of grain, a man reveals himself an
irresponsible steward of his corporate trust. As such, he
becomes a threat not only to his own compound's economic, social,
and ideological existence, but also to that of his kith and kin
insofar as he looks to their sometimes-also-slim cereal stocks to

cover his losses.

In consequence, there are strong, community-wide sentiments against risky grain sales that may later prove to have been "too much, too soon." A man making such a sale often tries to hide the fact in hopes of escaping the social and economic sanctions on his folly should he come up short of cereal later in the year. These sanctions take the form of institutionalized gossip and outright refusals of food or cash assistance from his social network. As one informant eloquently explained, "The whole village will talk about me if I sell my cereal. And later, if I need to buy or borrow grain, they will refuse to help me, saying 'You just go and buy back your grain from the person you so foolishly sold it to!'" If a man persists in his mismanagement, eventually his wives and children wll abandon him. He will be left to his solitary fate or, at best, reabsorbed as a dependent member of a related compound.

However, there are several conditions under which harvest-time sales are acceptable. One is the case of bumper crops that leave a clear surplus even after all foreseeable family grain needs for the year are taken into account. This surplus can be marketed to merchants and others without "shame." Even so, large sales at this time create the lingering suspicion that the seller is "vain" and that, in one man's words, "He wants to show off his success as a farmer." But one can escape any breath of social opprobrium and even earn "honor" from harvest-time sales if these are made to the village cooperative. Such transactions are favorably viewed as community-minded. "And anyway," confided informants, "we can always buy back the grain if we need to."

Another instance in which large harvest-time sales are socially acceptable is a sort of subcase of the surplus situation. A few farmers elect not to cash-crop cotton (Figure 1's strategy I). For these men, grain sales move to the fore as a major source of agricultural income when harvests are good.

Also, any compound head can make smallish harvest-time sales as a stopgap measure to meet the most pressing December-January expenses. Such transactions may be indicated when cash from shea nut sales (October-November) is exhausted, earnings from sesame (December) are poor, and concomitantly SOFITEX is delayed in its purchasing program. Modest sales of food grain then offer an acceptable last-minute cash-getting option when it becomes clear that one's "cotton money" will arrive late.

After the first few months following the cereal harvest, sales generally become less stigmatized as the year advances. Unanticipated grain drains stemming from surprise visitors, deaths, or other emergencies have (or have not) been safely weathered. Remaining stocks can therefore be more accurately evaluated vis-a-vis known compound needs. Also, as newly planted fields begin to sprout in June-July, farmers can start to assess their upcoming cereal harvests. And grain prices progressively rise, peaking in August. By the May-August hungry season, men who decide they have a surplus may begin to sell to those less fortunate.

In the logic of the cereal code of honor, hungry-season purchases of staple food grain are seen as "shameful" indications of poor compund management. On the other hand, sales at this time are viewed as "honorable." This view is linked to a pervasive moral obligation to offer any hungry-season cereal surpluses for sale first to relatives, then to friends and neighbors, next to co-villagers generally, and only lastly to outsiders and merchants. Moreover, kith and kin ideally receive "special deals" on grain. In contrast, strangers are almost always charged the going market rate, no matter what the season.

In any case, there is 100 percent agreement among sample members that one is morally obligated to sell or give grain to one's social relations so long as own-compound consumption is not thereby prejudiced. Interviewees elaborated this point with comments like: "When I have sorghum and they [relatives and friends] have none, I cannot leave them in hunger"; "One must come to the aid of those who are suffering"; and "You never know but what a day will come when you will find yourself in the same situation."

Hungry-season sellers in Dankui are farm managers who--in addition to generating a surplus above all their compound's nutritional, social, ceremonial, etc. needs for food grain--have also astutely manipulated their other resources so as to stave off cereal sales until they coincide with maximum profit advantage. These actions reflect sound farm management and wise portfolio administration. Such men earn village-wide reputations as competent corporate planners.

Furthermore, given the ethical dicta outlined above, a man who is able to sell grain during the hungry season is seen as something of a community benefactor. Surplus producers in a sense purvey a community security stock that they release just when it is most needed. Their co-villagers appreciate this service, and they reward such men with respect and prestige. Unlike irresponsible corporate managers--who not only imperil their own compound's well-being, but also impose a burden upon broader kin and village resources--good managers who generate surplus cereal prove an asset to the community at large.

Finally, it should be noted that traditionally the ultimate ideal of the code is to make no grain sales of any sort. Cash needs should instead be met from other sources--primarily sales of livestock (cattle, sheep, goats, pigs, poultry), shea nuts, sesame, gourds, and, today, cotton. Moreover, one should strive not only to be fully self-sufficient in cereals but also to have healthy hungry-season or end-of-year surpluses to dispense gratis to needy relatives, the elderly and the handicapped, holy men, and so forth. A few compound managers have been able to achieve this philanthropic ideal consistently, at least in the past. Predictably, they are among the wealthiest inhabitants of Dankui. These paragons naturally earn the highest "honor" of all.

In summary, cereal is far more than just one among many items that can be sold or eaten. Of course, it is the "staff of life" in the diet. But it is also the coin in which much of social, political, and ideological, as well as economic, exchange is conducted. And the astute and civic-minded management of cereal stocks is one of the principal measures of a man's worth. This coin is far too valuable for it to be lightly expended on what might be labeled "asocial" sales. Aside from entailing considerable time and trouble, often-uncertain profit advantage, and sometimes even personal risk, such sales lead to no social reward or mutual economic obligation. All they earn is money. In the final analysis, staple food grain was not, and is not, a preferred market commodity in Dankui.[5] Or in one elder's definitive formulation of the cereal code of honor, "Cereal is a thing a man should not sell."

Cotton and Cereal, Markets and Politics

In addition to the multiple cotton incentives and cereal disincentives discussed earlier, the cultural code described above lent extra impetus to Dankui's adoption of commercial cotton cultivation. Among other considerations, farmers viewed cash-cropping cotton as an opportunity to approximate cultural ideals more closely and to achieve greater "honor" thereby. That is, cotton money could be substituted for onerous cereal sales (most notably in the immediate post-harvest period) as a way of earning critical cash. Unlike cereal, cotton carried no baggage of cultural meaning to impede its marketing. Or as one man succinctly put it, "You can't eat cotton. Cotton is just for selling. You can't do anything else with it."

However, in the rush to adopt cotton, cereal production suffered. Not only was less land planted to food grain but, equally important, cotton and cereal directly competed for scarce human labor at key points in the agricultural timetable.[6] As Haggblade (1984:19,20) has documented for Burkina as a whole, in Dankui, too, "... the rapid rise of cotton production ... has been diverting agricultural resources from food to non-food production."

The net result in Dankui predictably was a dwindling of both compound and community food reserves, and concomitantly a growing reliance upon market purchases of grain to make up for production shortfalls. In other words, in precise counterpoint to farmers' expectations, the cereal code of honor was weakened rather than strengthened. The shift in cotton/cereal production strategies among some 90 percent of Dankui compounds left farm families "exposed to the cold winds of a market that they barely understand," to borrow Hart's (1982:145) expressive phrasing. In the intense heat of the West African savannah, these winds blow especially cold through the fickle grain market of Burkina. Having cast their fate to these winds, in 1983-84 Dankui cotton growers discovered just how desperately human well-being is impacted by market vagaries.

For one thing, 1983 was a drought year, so cereal harvests were poorer than expected. Whether because of failed fields, ill-advised advance sales of grain, over-investment in cotton to the neglect of cereal, or (most typically) a combination of these, 90 percent of the farmers in the sample found themselves lacking the cereal to meet even everyday consumption minima until the next harvest--much less all the other items in their annual grain budgets. For a number of these men, this was the first such experience in their farming lives. Across the sample as a whole, a mean 1983-84 shortfall of more than three months was expected in compound cereal stocks, in comparison to the previous year's reported mean of only half a month.

Normally, this would not have constituted an insuperable situation. Farm managers with foreseeable shortfalls would simply have used their cotton money to purchase additional cereal supplies at cheap post-harvest prices. These could be obtained from local merchants or from other villagers who had paid more heed to the cereal code of honor in their production and marketing decisioning. In the hungry season, further supplies could be sought from the same sources or from kin and the GV. But 1983 revealed a critical error in many managers' cotton/cereal calculus. Although they could indeed count on a stable cotton market to generate cash, they had not fully reckoned on potential instabilities in the nation's grain market --to which now, more than ever before, they were subject.

Even at its best, the Burkina grain market is notoriously unstable. Quantities and prices vary widely both inter- and intra-annually according to rainfall and other production parameters, marketing costs, the quality and price of grain in adjacent countries, and still other factors (Moussie 1985).

In addition to these more or less expectable fluxes, however, 1983-84 witnessed acute disruptions in the grain market due to political upheavals. After a series of coups and counter-coups, a new revolutionary government took power and promptly issued a string of edicts aimed at tight control of grain markets, prices, and merchants.[7] The government also created a nationwide youth brigade--the Comites de Defense de la Revolution or CDR--to enforce these edicts. These muscular measures halted or drove underground much of Burkina's private-sector grain trade for a period of months. A corollory was the illegal channelling of a good deal of Burkinabe cereal to neighboring countries where it could be marketed more easily and profitably.

At the local level, normal trading among grain merchants and in village marketplaces was severely handicapped by a number of events related to these moves at the national level. For example, the National Cereals Offices (OFNACER) conducted an especially aggressive purchasing campaign in the Dankui region, either directly or through GVs and the CDR. All such purchases were trucked out of the region. Moreover, in some marketplaces --including the area's largest--OFNACER operated under an exclusionary rule that forbade cereal merchants to buy in bulk while government purchasing was on-going. The CDR kept zealous vigilance over traders to ensure that this rule was not broken and, later, to check that they complied with official prices -- which were set at artificially low levels. Additionally, the new government imposed strict limits on the quantity and distance of grain shipments by individuals; and local merchants were threatened with confiscation of cereal stocks if the CDR believed they were hoarding.

One important outcome of such events was that many local-level merchants withdrew from the grain trade. In consequence, local grain markets were disrupted and depleted, and normal cereal backflows were interrupted. Many Dankui farm managers were caught short by this "double whammy" of drought and political disorganization of local grain markets. Despite pockets full of cotton money, people could find little cereal for sale anywhere. The results for family and community well-being were devastating, affecting every line item in Table 1's grain budgets.

To illustrate briefly, in 1983-84 several sample members found themselves obliged to consume their carefully selected seed grain -- some for the first time in their farming lives. Many

117

others feared they would soon be forced to the same extreme. Farm managers worried about where they would find not only seed for next year's planting, but also grain for food and drink with which to host critical agricultural work parties. At the same time, many Bwaba were faced with the prospect of eating their ritual reserves, thus imperiling future harvests supernaturally as well as naturally.

Predictably, most compounds cut back sharply on the quantity of grain fed to livestock, or suspended such feedings altogether. Livestock health and productivity accordingly began to deteriorate. When grain-for-milk exchanges were halted among all but one Bwa family in the sample, Bwa children's diet presumably also suffered. And herding contracts with Fulani were cancelled or re-negotiated. As one compound head summarized, "It is simply not possible to give out grain in these ways now."

Similarly, the normal flow of beer exchanges and grain gifts was drastically reduced. For example, across the sample as a whole, gifts, tithes, and other charitable donations from the 1983 harvest reportedly dropped by roughly half, in comparison to 1982. Indeed, among the Moslem Mossi, more than twice as many families as in the preceding year were unable to tithe at all. With regard to tribute, a number of compounds made only half their annual grain payment to the chief; others paid nothing. Ensuing arguments over failure to render tribute began to fray the fabric of village political organization.

Taken together, reduced gifts, tithes, and tribute made for less food assistance for the poor, handicapped, devout, et al. just when it was most needed; weakened socioeconomic and political integration due to people's lessened ability to ratify and reinforce important kin and non-kin links materially through generous meals, beverages, and prestations of grain; imperfect relations between humans and their gods, insofar as rituals were performed cheaply and tithes were minimal or absent; and relatedly, psychological stresses stemming from loss of self-concept or fear of supernatural reprisals because of the inability to meet normal socioeconomic obligations or to maintain even a pretense of living up to ideological canons.

Finally, thefts of stored grain began to occur. These entailed additional worry with extra outlays of cash and foodstuffs for special protective rites for granaries. As a participant at one such rite sorrowfully remarked, "Before, there were no robbers [of grain]." This sudden spate of thefts in turn led to acrimonious charges and countercharges between ethnic groups, thus further straining community relations.

In summary, the 1983-84 cereal shortage directly imperiled

118

the well-being of the farm family, their relatives and ancestors, their livestock, their future harvests, the social and political integrity of their community, and more. (For a complete analysis, see McCorkle 1986.)

In these circumstances, not surprisingly Dankui farmers began to reevaluate their cropping strategies--particularly those following Figure 1's strategy III. This formula was now seen as risky--not in terms of ecological, technical, or financial success in cotton cultivation but rather in terms of an uncritical reliance upon cotton money in the context of a shaky grain market. In one man's summary of the situation, "Too many people went 'cotton crazy.'" By the next planting season, most had decided to ease back on cotton production and pay more attention to cereal.

Conclusion

These Volta Noire farmers are representative of the kind of third-world rural populations on whom agricultural development efforts focus. One of the oft-stated aims of such efforts is to increase farmers' income from agriculture. From this perspective, the success of cotton cash-cropping throughout much of West Africa might be viewed as a development coup--one in which cooperation between private enterprise and government has brought "improved" agricultural technology to the countryside; introduced a valuable and hardy new crop; and created fair, convenient, and relatively stable outlets for it.

But increased income does not per se imply increased human well-being and security in third-world milieux. As so many authors have pointed out, the move from a traditional, subsistence-oriented farming system to more "developed" farming practices and new cash crops is highly problematic. The new farming system may be adapted to short-term supply and demand trends and to profit maximization in average years, but not to long-term ecological and economic forces and to survival in bad years (after Barlett 1980:5-6). Moreover, as illustrated here, from the rural producer's perspective, "bad" years must be defined not only meteorologically but also politically.

As Hart (1982:134) observes, most West African farmers have learned these lessons the hard way. A shift to commercialized agriculture (particularly of non-foodstuffs) has led to subsistence shortfalls and the rundown of food reserves, with the erosion or elimination of collective mechanisms of social distribution and insurance against hardship--like the cereal code of honor described above. The repercussions of such a shift are profound, affecting the entire sociocultural system.

119

Figure 1

FIGURE 1

COTTON/CEREAL PRODUCTION STRATEGIES

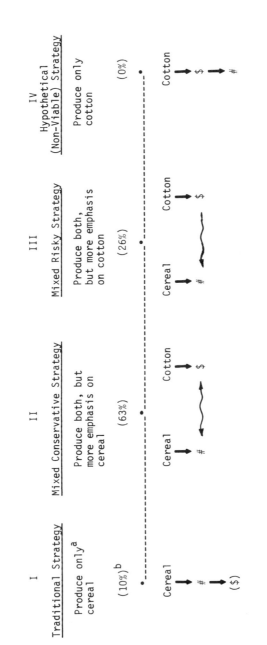

$ = Product sold for cash.

= Cereal consumed to meet compound needs. Surpluses can also be sold for cash, as indicated by arrows.

aBut traditionally, along with small plots of local cotton.

bPercent of sample in each category (excluding Fulani and griots) for whom SOFITEX payment figures were available. II and III are respectively defined by 1983 gross cotton earnings of less or greater than the mean of 127,917 CFA. Median earnings were an exact 100,000 CFA with a range of 24,000-370,000 CFA. During the period of research, the CFA fluctuated around 400 to U.S. $1.00. Percents sum to 99 due to rounding.

120

In planning for agricultural development, it is time that policy makers, too, learn these lessons.

Acknowledgments

My thanks to Drs. J. Eric Reynolds and Mahir Saul and to the editors of this volume for many helpful comments on earlier drafts of this article.

Notes

[1] CFDT stands for Compagnie Francaise pour le Developpement des Fibres Textiles. The many links between the CFDT and postcolonial governments have already been documented for several areas -- e.g., Achterstratt 1983 for Senegal; de Wilde 1957 for Mali; and an especially insightful study, Campbell 1984 for the Ivory Coast. It is not my intent to describe and analyze these phenomena in their national and global political-economic contexts. Instead, I wish to examine how they interact with family and community life.

[2] I conducted the research in 1983-84, while serving as Project Anthropologist on the Burkina Faso Grain Marketing Development Research Project (USAID Contract No. AFR-0243-C-00-2063-00), directed by the Center for Research on Economic Development at the University of Michigan, Ann Arbor. For specifics of sampling procedures, the farming system, community life, economic transactions, etc., see McCorkle 1986. Fulani are not discussed here because they neither grow cotton nor market cereal.

[3] For details on the structure, rationale, and statistical outcomes of this ranking scale and on the iterative battery of intensive interviews that accompanied it, as well as the calculations behind Table 1's grain budgets, see McCorkle 1986.

[4] Significantly, Jean Capron, a leading anthropological authority on the Volta Noire region, also remarks this deep-seated sense of honor and shame. For example, in discussing attitudes toward indebtedness, he writes:

> The notion of honor holds, at the level of individual behaviors, a privileged place; social reputation and position are still today, in the eyes of Bwa farmers, as important as economic success; their pursuit serves as an incentive in all daily activities, both private

and public. Awareness of the dishonor that attaches
to transgressions of group values can even ... lead to
suicide; thus, even when he does not always reach this
extreme, a farmer's inability to repay a debt is
experienced by him as a burning social failure"
(Capron 1973:308; translation mine).

[5] Nor, apparently, anywhere in Burkina. As Dejou et al. (cited
in McCorkle 1986:100) report from their "rapid rural
reconaissance" of grain markets throughout the nation: "Even in
surplus areas, the unanimous answer to the question, "Why are you
selling your grain?" is "Because we have to." It seems that
nobody chooses to sell grain. They do so only out of necessity.
They would very much prefer to keep their grain, even if they
think they have enough to last them through the next
harvest...always sales are made because people need money."

[6] As both Dankui farmers and Western researchers have observed,
one of the most serious such conflicts arises in weeding
schedules. Villagers also emphasize harvest bottlenecks, when
they are sometimes obliged to host costly extra labor parties in
order to get in both cotton and cereal crops on time. In a very
real sense, therefore, it takes grain to make grain, and to
cash-crop cotton, as well.

[7] In a personal communication, Mahir Saul notes that these
moves were consistent with national grain policies in Upper Volta
since the mid-1970s. However, the Sankara government added fresh
controls and--at least initially--pursued their enforcement
vigorously. As Saul observes, the ultimate effect of these
attempts at centralized control upon national-level marketing
structures is debatable. But their impact in the Dankui region
between the 1983 and 1984 harvests is not.

References

Achterstraat, Alexandre. 1983. Agriculture d'Autosubsistance ou
    Agriculture de Rente? Amsterdam and Dakar: Free University
    Institute of Cultural Anthropology/Non-Western Sociology.
Barlett, Peggy F. 1980. Introduction: Development Issues and
    Economic Anthropology. In: Agricultural Decision Making:
    Anthropological Contributions to Rural Development. Peggy F.
    Barlett, ed. pp. 1-16. New York: Academic Press.
Barley, Nigel. 1983. The Innocent Anthropologist: Notes from a
    Mud Hut. London: British Museum Publications, Ltd.
Campbell, Bonnie K. 1984. Inside the Miracle: Cotton in the Ivory

Coast. In: The Politics of Agriculture in Tropical Africa. Johnathan Barker, ed. pp. 142-171. Beverly Hills: Sage Publications, Inc.

Capron, Jean. 1973. Communautes Villageoises Bwa: Mali, Haute-Volta. Memoire de l'Institut d'Ethnologie IX. Paris: Musee National d'Histoire Naturelle, Institut d'Ethnologie, Musee de l'Homme.

de Wilde, John C. 1967. Mali: The Development of Peasant Cotton Production by the CFDT. In: Experiences with Agricultural Development in Tropical Africa, Vol. III, The Case Studies. John C. de Wilde, ed. pp. 301-336. Baltimore: The Johns Hopkins Press.

Haggblade, Steve. 1984. An Overview of Food Security in Upper Volta: A Report Prepared for USAID/Upper Volta. Ouagadougou: USAID.

----- 1986. Making Sense of Food Security Statistics: Pointers from Burkina. Paper presented at the Seminar on Agricultural Policy and Food Security, Center for African Studies and Office of International Agriculture, Univ. of Illinois, Champaign.

Hart, Keith. 1982. The Political Economy of West African Agriculture. Cambridge: Cambridge University Press.

McCorkle, Constance M. 1986(1984). Pride, Preference, and Practice: Farmers' Grain Disposal Decisions in a Voltaic Community. Final Report (Anthropology) for the USAID Burkina Faso Grain Marketing Research Development Project. In: The Dynamics of Grain Marketing in Burkina Faso, Vol. III, Research Report No. 1 (134 pp.). Ouagadougou and Ann Arbor, MI: Center for Research on Economic Development.

----- 1985. The Context of the Cotton/Cereal Equation in Burkina Faso. Paper presented to the American Anthropological Association, Washington DC.

Moussie, Menwouyellet. 1985. An Assessment of Grain Marketing in the Sahel: The Case of Burkina Faso. Jefferson City, MO: Lincoln University Department of Agriculture and Office of International Programs.

123

7. INCORPORATING MACROECONOMIC VARIABLES IN ANTHROPOLOGICAL RESEARCH[1]: EXAMPLES FROM A DEVELOPING PETROLEUM REGION

Sara J. Scherr

As research into developing country farming systems and rural organization has matured, we have seen growing collaboration between microeconomists and farm management specialists on the one hand, and anthropologists on the other. The field of economic anthropology has blossomed, and more anthropologists have been trained in basic microeconomic theory and field methods. Similarly, field economists have become increasingly appreciative of, and concerned with quantifying, concepts that were originally derived from anthropological research. Household decision-making, risk analysis, and systems of access to rural factors of production are but a few of the areas in which there has been a fruitful exchange of skills from the two disciplines.[2]

As an economist with some training in economic anthropology, I believe that anthropologists can contribute much more than they currently do to the policy and practice of economic development. We can move beyond the obvious benefits provided by a mutual focus on microeconomic/local-level behavior, to explore the possibilities for interdisciplinary research on macro-level economic development policy. This will require methodological changes by practitioners of both professions. Economists, particularly macroeconomists and sector economists, need to recognize the limitations of aggregate analysis, and the critical importance of understanding heterogeneous economic response patterns, which can often better be explored by trained anthropologists.[3] Economic anthropologists need to be able to design their own research to address macro-policy questions directly.

In true interdisciplinary research, we cannot have different professions working at different "levels," an approach that begs the important issues of multi-level linkages. In this paper, I illustrate the benefits of integrated micro-macro research with an example from my own work on aggregate agricultural supply and labor market response to the recent petroleum boom in Tabasco state, Mexico.[4] From this experience, I draw a set of general guidelines for using local-level studies to analyze aggregate economic behavior.

Even for the many economic anthropologists whose work is not policy-oriented, greater understanding of macroeconomic variables may help interpret observed behavior in communities, households, and local organizations.[5] This article will be useful to both those who work with economists on development policy research and those who wish to borrow from macroeconomic analysis for their own purposes.

Agricultural Production and the Petroleum Boom in Tabasco

Tabasco is a small agricultural state on the southern Gulf Coast of Mexico, with just over a million inhabitants, and a hot, wet climate. In 1973/74, the national oil company (PEMEX) discovered in the region[6] what proved to be one of the world's largest petroleum deposits. The subsequent decade brought enormous economic changes to the state.

In 1970, the basis of the Tabasco state economy was agriculture, giving the majority of the population their principal occupation. The most important products were cacao, bananas, coconut, and livestock for export both internationally and to the rest of Mexico, and subsistence maize. The densely populated, more fertile, and less flood-prone areas of central Tabasco were dominated by smallholder campesinos; the seasonally flooded regions to the east and other parts of the state were dominated by largeholder ranchers. Map 1 shows that the principal locus of the 1970s petroleum boom occurred precisely in the densely populated area.

It was widely expected that the agricultural economy of Tabasco would suffer serious disruptions as a result of the petroleum boom. The international experience of agricultural production under petroleum boom conditions has been, with few exceptions, pretty dismal.[7] Indeed, the proportion of Tabasco's economically active population whose principal occupation was in agriculture, declined dramatically from 62 percent in 1970 to 43 percent in 1980. The implications for Tabasco's agricultural economy, which was exceptionally labor-intensive (in part because labor-replacing technology was unavailable), seemed ominous.

But, contrary to the expectations of macroeconomists, Tabasco experienced a remarkable agricultural boom. Between 1970 and 1983, banana and sugar cane production tripled; cacao production doubled; coconut production increased by 50 percent. The number of beef cattle in the state rose 70 percent, and the number slaughtered quadrupled (Instituto II, pp. 1067-1068). My research objective was to explain this astonishing performance in the midst of very high wages, inflation, high returns to non-farm

126

Map 1.

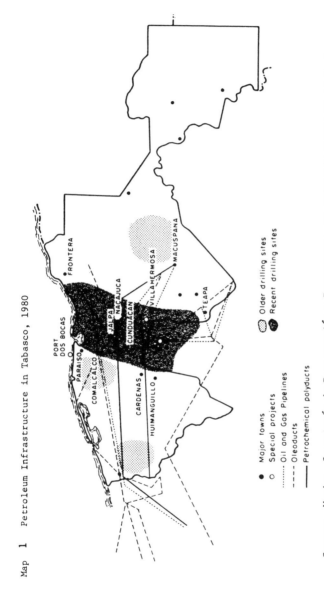

Map 1   Petroleum Infrastructure in Tabasco, 1980

● Major towns
○ Special projects
⋯⋯ Oil and Gas Pipelines
--- Oleoducts
—— Petrochemical polyducts

◉ Older drilling sites
● Recent drilling sites

Source: Mexico, Secretaría de Programación y Presupuesto, *La Industria Petrolera en Mexico,* 1979, pp. 353-55.

127

Map 2.

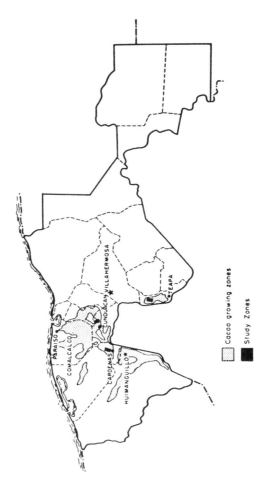

Map 2   Cacao-Growing Zones of Tabasco

128

investments, and participation by agricultural workers in the petroleum economy.

The principal apparent reason for success was unusually high commodity prices for Tabasco's major products in the mid-1970s. Nonetheless, wages had risen more rapidly than had prices. The state government claimed responsibility, through their greatly expanded agricultural investment and technical assistance programs. Most investment projects, however, were still in an early stage, and official technical programs called for enormous increases in agricultural labor use.

I thus chose to look at how the rural labor market had adapted to the petroleum economy. I wanted to develop a state-level "model" of agricultural supply response that would enable policy-makers to estimate how the sector would continue to respond to changes in key macro and policy variables (changing prices, wage levels, mechanization, agricultural investments, etc.), and how these would affect state-level employment patterns.

Agricultural Supply Analysis in Tabasco

This was essentially a problem of aggregate sectoral supply response. Standard economic analysis utilizes a supply response model with a few key variables -- crop price, agricultural wages, non-agricultural wages, fertilizer prices, weather, etc. -- to explain variations in output. Time series data are used to develop "coefficients" for these models. It was not possible to develop such a model for Tabasco on the basis of available data, which were highly aggregated when they existed at all. There were clear methodological problems, anyway, in estimating coefficients for a model based on historical data during a period of major structural change in the economy.[8]

Furthermore, in order to develop a macroeconomic model that would reliably explain and predict aggregate agricultural production and employment, it was necessary to introduce other variables. Exploratory field research suggested that the agricultural sector was highly heterogeneous. Informal surveys showed that some kinds of farmers had reduced, and others had increased, production. Local-level research was needed to determine which groups of farmers were responsible for rising production, and what characteristics enabled those groups to evade the negative economic repercussions of the petroleum boom. The linkage between the micro- and macro-levels of analysis was the central methodological problem for field research, which was

129

resolved in the following way.

Macro-Level Review

After reviewing available macro-data on the economy, and making rough estimates of the relative numbers and types of farmers, and the composition of the landless labor force, I decided to focus my field-level research on cacao farmers, who represented the state's most important agricultural sector. Although cacao production was very labor intensive, and there was a sharp increase in labor costs caused in part by the oil boom, cacao production had doubled. Production had intensified, though wages were rising faster than cacao prices. Good information was available on the history of cacao production in Tabasco, and the organization of production and marketing.

Regional Heterogeneity

The next stage was to determine what relevant heterogeneity needed to be studied to answer the questions on production supply response. For the Tabasco cacao study, there were two key ranges of variability: by socioeconomic region, reflecting differences in regional labor markets and cacao production regimes; and by farm family type, reflecting household relations to the changing state economy.

Socioeconomic regions were differentiated on the basis of differences in wage rates, settlement patterns, proximity to petroleum areas, cacao ecology, and political organization, which could have affected agricultural response patterns. The state government, PEMEX, and the cacao producer associations provided the necessary information.

After determining the six major cacao sub-regions of the state, I chose three communities for study (shown in Map 2): eastern Cunduacan municipio, in the heart of both the cacao and petroleum-producing region; central Teapa municipio, a somewhat marginal cacao area, from which migration to petroleum employment required a substantial commute; and the collective cacao-producing ejidos of the well-known Chontalpa Plan, whose members were institutionally separated from the new off-farm labor markets.[9] The community studies permitted not only the incorporation of regional factors, but provided a framework for analyzing interactions between different types of producers and workers, and between producers and the local economy and policy. This is difficult to do with the pure cross-sectional research approach of most microeconomic surveys.

Household Heterogeneity

130

Aggregate economic and demographic statistics provided an initial overview of farm household distribution. For the cacao-producing municipios (counties), some Census data could be used to differentiate producers. In 1978, a Cacao Census had been taken of over 80 percent of state producers, which provided a distributional profile of input use, condition of cacao plantations, and so on. In 1980, a stratified random sample survey was taken of state households, covering current and historical employment, migration, family structure, and farm holding size and use; of these, 408 families were either currently or previously involved in cacao production.

None of these surveys provided information on farm management, detailed family and farm labor use, or household decision-making patterns. These macro data sources did provide a useful description of the cacao-producing population, and a mechanism for extrapolating micro-level research results. Community and household studies were designed to conform as much as possible with categories found in the macro-statistics.

Exploratory surveys suggested that the most important variable affecting agricultural production was rising wages. Thus the key factor I used to differentiate farmer groups was the household's relation to the labor market, which could be measured by the ratio of land in cacao and family labor. I distinguished households with over six hectares planted to cacao, who were dependent upon hired labor; households with 2 to 6 hectares of cacao, who both hired in and hired out labor; minifundia with under two hectares, who hired in no labor, but who were dependent on hiring out; and collective producers, using family labor for the household plot, and hiring labor for the collective plot.

Family Economy Analysis

But the price and employment response differences were dependent upon much more than the cacao plot size. The farm size characteristics were created by and themselves created a host of very different circumstances for family decision-making. In terms of model-building, this meant that use of a single coefficient to express the relations between cacao plot size and key variables such as labor demand and supply would be quite misleading.

Extensive farmer interviewing in the three communities suggested very marked differences in production and employment behavior by the four types of producers, which was corroborated by stratified analyses of statistics from the Cacao Census and Sociodemographic Survey. Hired-labor-based producers had cut back production, due to rising labor costs and better returns to capital off-farm. Those who continued working off-farm were

131

commonly employed in commercial or professional occupations. Farm employment in this sub-sector declined.

Family-labor-based producers, more concerned with returns to family labor than to capital, were responsible for most of the increase in production. To take advantage of high cacao prices, heads of households no longer worked off-farm; their sons continued to perform key operations on the farm, despite high participation rates in new off-farm jobs. Family members who still worked off-farm were commonly employed in agricultural work. Families with few working members increased their use of hired labor.

Minifundia producers saw both their off-farm income-earning potential and returns from cacao production rise. But though they increased cacao production slightly, off-farm work to meet critical cash needs had priority, and was often in skilled trades, with large numbers substituting own-plot work or non-farm occupations for agricultural day work. Only those with full-time work off the farm hired any outside labor.

Collective cacao production, and particularly new cacao plantings, on the Chontalpa ejidos rose substantially, although there was only limited technical intensification due to serious labor constraints on the ejidos. Other crops, particularly sugar cane, competed sharply with labor availability for cacao. Very few collective producers participated in any off-farm employment, and the role of non-ejidatario workers in total ejidal labor use had risen substantially. Chart 1 summarizes some of the key characteristics of landholding, employment, demography, and production for the four producer groups.

But for purposes of dynamic aggregate analysis, it was not sufficient to document levels of production, migration, employment, and input use for the four different groups; it was necessary to understand patterns of household decision-making. This stage included open-ended farmer interviews, supplemented by detailed farm management and labor studies for a small number of farm households representing each "type" of household.

It was particularly important to understand the principles upon which labor and cash inputs were put into either cacao production, off-farm employment, or other activities. The study established that there were sharply different premises for decision-making about production and employment for the four different types of producers.

Hired-labor-based producers were concerned with maximizing profits, minimizing labor supervision, and providing high status occupations for family workers, and were in a position to move assets freely from one enterprise to another (on- and off-farm) in response to economic incentives. Family-labor-based producers attempted to maximize the returns to family labor, and to manage risk; key concerns were improving living standards and providing some form of inheritance for all children. The farm, and especially cacao production, was central to the family economy.

Minifundistas were more preoccupied with ensuring subsistence, by stabilizing off-farm employment and maintaining multiple sources of income. Land was often more important as residence and security than as the economic foundation of the family. Collective producers were also concerned with maximizing returns to family labor, but in a complex context of balancing the family and collective economies.

These differences in objectives and patterns of response required the development of separate sub-models within the aggregate supply model for cacao production and labor use. Coefficients for household response to agricultural and non-agricultural wages, prices, etc. were all significantly different, and in some cases even had different signs.

For formal modeling and prediction, a larger field survey, stratified by farmer type, would have been needed to develop statistically reliable coefficients (once basic strategies had been determined). But because the field studies were designed for the extrapolation of results through existing aggregate data sources, I was able to make rough estimates of the effect of changing cacao prices, input prices, and wages on each group of households, and then on total state cacao production, farm labor demand, and farm household labor supply. My earlier survey of the characteristics of production for other major state agricultural products enabled me to assess the extent to which the cacao sector experience was shared by other producer groups.

Key Findings

The micro-level research led to four findings of particular importance for aggregate state employment and agricultural production policy. Dependence on aggregate economic analyses would have failed entirely to capture the essence of rural labor market changes.

1) The recorded increase in aggregate cacao production masked a situation in which production was stagnating or declining on perhaps as much as a third of the land planted to cacao (that belonging to hired-labor-based producers);

2) The low levels of permanent internal migration officially registered in Tabasco during the 1970s masked extremely high

133

Chart 1.

CHART 1. A Typology of Tabasco Cacao Producers

Characteristic	Hired-Labor Based	Family-Labor Based	Minifundia	Collective
Size of cacao plot	Over 6 ha	2-6 ha	Under 2 ha	Under 2 ha family plot; variable collective
Percentage of households	10	26	50	14
Percent cacao produced in 1978	30	32	30	8
Value of assets (US $)	Over 50,000	20-50,000	Under 20,000	Under 20,000
Average size holding (has)	14	6	1+	
Median age, head of household	55	49	47	40
% Family EAP in agricultural work as principal occupation	84	80	73	97
Proportion of households with high dependency ratio	moderate	mod. high	high	very high
Migration - % individuals with residence change after 1976	7	11	3	4
Principal type of off-farm employment	commerce, prof.	agricultural work, off-farm	skilled trades	very little
Hired labor as percentage of whole farm labor	essential	supplementary: dependent on demographic stage of family	little needed, unless full-time work off-farm	essential, because competes with cane production
% head of household, primary occupation in cacao farming	76	76	75	48
Principal strategies of household decision-making	Profit max. Asset mobility Minimize labor supervision Upward mobility for family workers	Improve living standard Maximize return to fam. labor Equitable inheritance Manage risk	Ensure subsist. Land as social base Off-farm employ. stability Multiple income sources	Maximize return to family labor Maximize use of private plot Maintain ejidal rights Protect family from econ. risks of collective production
Cacao production in the '70s	Declining	Increasing (Mainly through yield increases)	Stable	Increasing (Mainly through area increases)
Employment in the '70s	Reduced use of hired labor	Increased use of hired labor by small families Decreased hiring out by sons Major decrease hiring-out by head of hshld.	Substituted non-ag'l off-farm employment for ag'l off-farm employment	Declining under-employment of ejidatarios Increased hiring in of non-ejid-atarios

134

Chart 2.

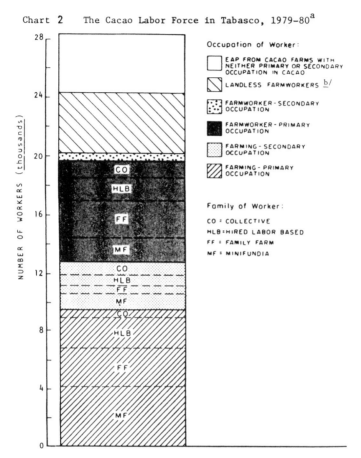

Chart 2   The Cacao Labor Force in Tabasco, 1979-80[a]

[a]The total EAP in agriculture in 1970 was 116,147. Thus, cacao work accounted for 20 percent of agricultural jobs. If only cacao municipios are included (Comalcalco, Cárdenas, Cunduacán, Jalpa, Huimanguillo, Paraíso), the agricultural EAP was 53,630, and cacao accounted for nearly half of all workers.

[b]This figure actually ranges between 3,700 and 4,900, depending upon SST sampling interpretation.

Source: COPRODET and CONAPO, Encuesta Sociodemográfica del Estado de Tabasco, Villahermosa, Tabasco, January 1980; extrapolations from Cacao Subsample.

135

levels of temporary internal migration and non-farm employment;

3) Official aggregate employment statistics, documenting "principal occupation," greatly underestimated native Tabascan participation in petroleum-related activities during the 1970s, and underestimated their participation in agricultural activities. Analysis of the cacao labor market alone showed that a quarter of all those operating farms did so as a secondary occupation; a tenth of all cacao farmworkers worked principally in the non-farm sector. Because nearly all the petroleum sector employment open to unskilled workers was intermittent and of very short duration, most such workers necessarily worked principally in other sectors.

4) A large proportion of the state's farm families--the family-labor-based producers--was in fact structurally capable of increasing agricultural production despite a high-wage economy. Yet this was the farm sector receiving least attention and support from official agricultural development programs.

Using Local-Level Studies to Analyze Aggregate Economic Behavior

This study suggests some guidelines for carrying out local-level studies that can readily be incorporated into analysis of aggregate economic policy. They should certainly be construed as an adjunct to, not a substitute for, standard anthropological field techniques and analysis, which will provide the anthropologists' main substantive contributions to development analysis.

1. Be familiar with material from all analytical levels that has a critical relation to your research question.

Chart 2 presents a stylized representation of a methodology that helps to link macroeconomic problems and micro-level field research.[10] Beginning with the research problem, one moves step by step from general macroeconomic review, to systematic choice of sub-regions and communities for in-depth study, to household case studies and random sample surveys designed to answer specific questions. The results are then linked with macro-statistics showing the distribution within the population of behaviors relevant to aggregate policy analysis.

Where one starts in the pyramid depends on the nature of the research question, and the available data at each level; it should not be determined a priori by the researcher's particular specialty. This approach requires collaboration between macroeconomists and anthropologists, and a continual interaction among the different levels of analysis: household, community, regional, national, and international. Multi-level linkages are likely to be lost if research is organized into independent projects at each level.

At the same time, it is important to recognize that not all projects will require thorough review at each level. One is interested only in collecting the minimum information needed to answer specific research or policy questions.

2. Understand the nature of the explanations being offered (explicitly or implicitly) by economists for particular behaviors.

Devise your own research to test these explanations directly. Find out from the economists what sorts of findings would be inconsistent with their models. A major potential contribution of anthropological field work is to identify significant behavior differences in populations that require disaggregation in sector, regional, and macroeconomic models, e.g., the cacao farmer supply response typology.

An excellent resource for reviewing the macreoeconomic issues relevant to agricultural communities and policies is Timmer, Falcon, and Pearson's Food Policy Analysis (1983), particularly Chapter 5. The authors trace through the linkages among macroeconomic policies; fiscal, monetary, and macro price policies; their effects on inflation, exchange rates, interest rates, wage rates; and in turn the effects of those variables on food prices, rural incomes, rural-urban terms of trade, and public food and agricultural policies.

One can use these concepts to help organize the initial exploratory survey and statistical review of the regional economy as a whole, before choosing communities for in-depth study. In the field, one can then examine historical trends in key variables to see how they should have affected (or in fact did affect) your study population, and the range of local responses to those impacts.[11]

3. Be able to reduce the richness of anthropological field conclusions to a few key variables that are likely to make a significant difference in aggregate analysis.

Applied economic development theory has become increasingly sophisticated; many of the simplistic models that you may have seen in introductory economics courses are repudiated in practice. However, economic models do try to explain outcomes with the fewest possible variables--this is a big philosophical and practical difference between economic and anthropological research. It is important for the anthropologist working in an interdisciplinary project to remember that macro-policy analysts can incorporate into their models only certain types of information. For technical reasons, these must be quantifiable or amenable to ranking.

4. Determine how widespread are the particular behaviors you observe and analyze.

Map out where the people are who are _like_ those you studied. Try to include some analysis of the numbers of individuals in different types of behavioral response regimes, through linking identifying characteristics to existing census or large-scale survey data. The local-level response patterns (spot-checked for validation and variation in other producing regions) can then be used to characterize group dynamic behavioral response.

5. Focus your research -- and present your findings -- in terms that suggest relationships.

Ask yourself (and your informants) how their behavior would change with major changes in those macroeconomic variables you have found important.

Macro-policy models are concerned not only with describing the behavior of individuals and groups, but with the dynamic changes in economic variables that stem from simultaneous decision-making. For example, to find out how rising off-farm wages affect the total level of off-farm employment by farm households, one must know the feedback effect that changing global availability of farm labor will have on actual rural wage levels.

Macro-models can integrate these variables, but their reliability is critically dependent on accurate component data on the sensitivity of farmer response to particular variables (elasticities, in economic jargon).[12] In the case of Tabasco cacao supply analysis, the key variables were farmer response to the price of cacao, the price of labor, the price of purchased inputs, and urban wage levels. Even where one cannot come up with historical elasticities and coefficients, the basic relations among variables can be established. Findings of unusual or unexpected elasticities are particularly useful.

6. Draw policy conclusions from your research.

Policy research is by definition applied; policy-makers want to know how what they do or do not do will affect the problem. Anthropologists have tended to be reticent about drawing such conclusions. One reason why economists have dominated many policy debates is that, whether reliable or not, they have developed a methodology for analyzing problems in the form of "if this happens, then that will happen."

Anthropologists have an enormous and critically needed contribution to make to many of these debates. But this will often require a systematic effort to extrapolate the particularistic insights of local-level field research into a general policy context. Most of the important macroeconomic concepts can be learned well enough by anthropologists to test their mechanisms and measure their impact in the field. I hope that many more will be inspired to take the plunge and do so.

Notes

[1] I would like to thank John Bowen and John Lynam for their suggestions and criticisms of the material in this paper.

[2] See, for example, new anthropological techniques described in Barlett (1980), Merrill (1984), and Greenwood (1978); extensive appendices on social and cultural concomitants of agricultural systems in Shaner, Philipp, and Schmehl (1981); the role of anthropologists in agricultural research in Rhoades (1983).

[3] I argue, in a paper addressed to economists (Scherr 1984), for greater disaggregation of actors in economic models and research, and for incorporation of more community-level field analysis.

[4] My field research on agricultural response to the petroleum boom in Tabasco, Mexico was carried out 1978-81. The research was funded by the Tinker Foundation, and facilitated by the Tabasco State Development Commission (now COPLADET) and the Department of Agricultural Economics of Cornell University.

[5] There is a good deal of fuzziness in the definitions of macroeconomic and microeconomic spheres of analysis. Microeconomics is the study of the basic units of economic activity--households, businesses, farms. Macroeconomics is the study of aggregates in the general economy, and the relations among aggregate variables, for example, the national money supply; total government, investment, and consumer spending; currency exchange rates, etc. Between the micro and macro levels of analysis, there are few clearly and successfully defined

linkages. The "middle" layer of analysis of economic phenomena ranges the gamut from sectorial analysis, economic class analysis in Marxist schools of economics, study of producer and consumer organizations and their behavior, structural analysis, and input-output analysis.

Strictly speaking, descriptive analysis of aggregate variables -- the anthropologists' understanding of the term "macro-level"--is not considered by economists to be "macroeconomic analysis," which implies a particular set of theoretical constructs about aggregate economic behavior. Thus the term "macro-micro linkages" may mean different things to anthropologists and economists; anthropologists in interdisciplinary projects need to make clear which "macro" they are referring to.

[6] Extensive petroleum and natural gas deposits have been found from the Reforma area in northern Chiapas, to the central west area of Tabasco state, to the Gulf of Mexico off-shore Tabasco and neighboring Campeche states.

[7] The forces that lead to agricultural decline are discussed in Scherr (1985a) and Scherr (1985b). Key issues are detrimental changes in relative prices within the general economy and labor emigration from the agricultural sector, and the insecurities of farming in regions subject to serious problems of congestion, shortages, high living and production costs, and land expropriation and pollution from oil development projects.

[8] Appendix A of Scherr (1985b) discusses the problems of applying this and other standard analytical techniques in this case.

[9] The Chontalpa Plan was a program set up in Tabasco as a model for intensive tropical agricultural development in the early 1960s, on newly drained land. The infrastructure was completed by 1970, and 6,000 families were settled there, organized into collective production units in the early 1970s. Each family was entitled to 15 hectares of land. Two hectares were used as a private family plot; the rest was under collective management.

[10] Greenwood (1978) provided the seminal material for multi-level research methods in anthropology, and is still one of the most useful references. Berry (1984) also argues for enlarging the focus of rural household analysis to incorporate issues of political economy.

[11] In her study of peasant beekeeping in Yucatan, Mexico, Merrill (1984) provides an outstanding example of how to

140

incorporate national and international economic history in
anthropological analysis of farm household decision-making
strategies.

[12] Norton and Solis (1983) review in detail the uses of a
linear programming model of the Mexican agricultural sector;
several of the articles in the book discuss the critical data
requirements that can only be met through detailed field-level
research.

References

Barlett, Peggy F. 1980. Agricultural Decision Making. New York:
  Academic Press.
Berry, Sara. 1984. Households, Decision Making, and Rural
  Development: Do We Need to Know More? Development Discussion
  Paper No. 167. Harvard Institute for International Development,
  May. Cambridge, Massacusetts: Harvard University.
Ewell, Peter. 1984. The Intensification of Peasant Agriculture in
  Yucatan. Cornell International Agricultural Economics Study,
  A.E. Research 84-4. May. Ithaca, New York: Cornell University.
Greenwood, Davydd. 1978. Community-Level Research,
  Local-Regional-Governmental Interactions and Development
  Planning: A Strategy for Baseline Studies. Paper for USAID.
  May. Cornell University Department of Anthropology.
Instituto Nacional de Estadistica, Geografia, e Informatica and
  Comite de Planeacion para el Desarrollo del Estado de Tabasco.
  1984. Anuario, Estadistico de Tabasco 1984. Volumes I and II.
  Mexico D.F.: Direccion General de Estadistica.
Merrill Sands, Deborah. 1984. The Mixed Subsistence-Commercial
  Production System in the Peasant Economy of Yucatan, Mexico: An
  Anthropological Study of Commercial Beekeeping. Ph.D.
  dissertation. Ithaca, New York: Cornell University.
Norton, Roger D. and Leopoldo Solis M., eds. 1983. The Book of
  CHAC. Baltimore: The Johns Hopkins University Press.
Rhoades, R. 1983. Breaking new ground? Anthropology in
  agricultural research. The case of the International Potato
  Center. A report to the Rockefeller Foundation. Lima, Peru:
  International Potato Center.
Scherr, Sara J. 1984. A Field Research Methodology for Regional
  Agricultural Analysis in Developing Countries: Coordinating
  Macroeconomic and Microeconomic Data Collection and Use. (Draft
  September).
------ 1985a. Agriculture and the Oil Syndrome: The Role of
  Public Policy in Developing Petroleum Economies. Paper
  presented to the International Association of Agricultural
  Economists Meeting. August 26-31. Malaga, Spain.
------ 1985b. The Oil Syndrome and Agricultural Development: The

Case of Tabasco, Mexico. New York: Praeger Publishers.
Shaner, W.W., P.F. Philipp, and W.R. Schmehl. 1981. Farming
Systems Research and Development: Guidelines for Developing
Countries. Boulder, Colorado: Westview Press.
Timmer, C. Peter, Walter P. Falcon, and Scott R. Pearson. 1983.
Food Policy Analysis. Baltimore: Johns Hopkins University
Press.

8. PROPERTY RIGHTS AND RURAL RESOURCE MANAGEMENT: THE CASE OF TREE CROPS IN WEST AFRICA

Sara Berry

The spread of tree crop production in West Africa introduced a potentially significant force for privatization of rural rights in land. Tree crops are generally considered to be the personal property of the individual who plants them. Planters control output of tree crop farms and may also alienate the trees--by lease, gift, mortgage, or sale. In principle rights in trees do not extend to the land on which they are planted, but in practice transfers of trees by sale or pledge have come to be treated as transfers of rights in land as well (Berry 1975; Gastellu 1980; Hill 1963; Lloyd 1962). Since tree crops were developed for their commercial value, increased planting led to the growth of a market in trees themselves. The resulting commercialization of rural assets, together with individual ownership of trees, have been taken to mean that the spread of tree crop cultivation has acted as an impetus towards privatization of rural land rights (Kobben 1963; Biebuyck 1963).

At the same time, there are several mechanisms of acquiring rights in tree crops that do not extinguish previously existing rights and that therefore lead to the multiplication of rights (and right-holders) in individual farms. Inheritance, tenancy and some labor arrangements often create multiple rights in tree crop farms and, in so doing, work against privatization. Over time, the actual pattern of control over tree crops and their proceeds has depended not so much on the formal rules of access and transfer as on interactions among potential right holders. Individuals' access to tree crop farms has depended more on their ability to exercise their claims vis-a-vis those of other rightholders, than on the way in which they acquired their rights in the first place (cf. Hill 1963:112).

Both in acquiring rights over trees, and in exercising and defending them vis-a-vis other claimants, West Africans have drawn on a variety of multi-stranded social relationships, including descent, marriage, ethnicity, and patron-client ties. The development of tree crop cultivation promoted rural commercialization and created a category of individually owned assets, but did not lead unambiguously to privatization or the emergence of a class of capitalist farmers. Instead, both the definition and enforcement of property rights in tree crop economies, and associated patterns of rural accumulation and differentiation, have been mediated through pre-existing social relations that have shaped, as well as reflected, changing

143

patterns of access to and control over productive resources.

In the following pages I develop this argument as follows. First I describe and illustrate processes whereby rights in farms have proliferated over time. Then I trace changing patterns of rights in tree crop farms for two socially defined categories of people--viz., women and sharecroppers--in order to illustrate the ways in which social relations have influenced the construction of property rights and patterns of differential access to rural assets. I conclude with some comments on the implications of changing rights in tree crop farms for the conceptualization of rural property rights and their influence on patterns of agricultural development and rural differentiation in West Africa.

The Proliferation of Rights in Farms

The principle that trees belong exclusively to the individual who plants them suggests that, other things being equal, tree crops are private property. However, other things are not equal. For one thing, most planters have employed other people's labor at some stage in the life cycle of their farms, and labor has often been recruited through pre-existing, multi-stranded social relations. Also, because economic trees (cocoa, coffee and kola especially) usually live and bear fruit for a number of years, most tree crop farms are eventually inherited--a process that often adds new claimants to the roster of persons with interests in a given farm. Both labor arrangements and inheritance practices have worked to create multiple, overlapping rights in particular farms, and to multiply the number of rightholders who have potential claims to the proceeds of a farm or the power to transfer rights therein to other people. This proliferation of rights in farms has also been reinforced by migration and by the transmission of information concerning farm histories in the settlement of disputed claims.

Inheritance

Throughout the humid zone of West Africa, inheritance rules and practices involve the devolution of property to groups of people creating "a drift towards lineage property" (Hill 1963:115). In patrilineal descent systems, a man's property is often inherited jointly by his children, or the children of each wife. In matrilineal Akan communities, a man's property passes to a single heir, but the heir is chosen by the decedent's

144

matrilineal kin (abusua) and is supposed to administer the property for the benefit of the abusua, not "failing to pay due regard to the needs of the sons (and widows) of the deceased" (Hill 1963:113). As farms become the property of groups of heirs, transfers from one individual to another (through mortgage, gift, or sale) may be challenged on the grounds that the person who alienated the farm did not exercise exclusive rights over it to begin with (Okali 1983; Berry 1975; Gastellu 1980). Thus, even outright sales of tree crop farms do not necessarily create private property: "toute partie du terrain vendue a son tour par le detenteur du titre foncier sera reclamee par les heritiers a son deces..." (Weber, 1977:132).

Labor

The principle that trees belong to the person who plants them has been extended to include persons other than the original planter who have worked on the farm. By "investing" their labor in a farm, it is argued, people may build up an interest in it over time--especially if they were not fully compensated for their labor at the time it was performed (Berry 1975, 1985; Okali 1983; Robertson 1983). Such arguments are most likely to be advanced with respect to persons who have worked on a particular farm over a period of years--such as wives, junior kin, or sharecroppers. In principle, claims based on labor do not supercede those of the planter or his or her heirs, but coexist with them; hence, they serve to multiply interests in and claimants to individual farms.

Oral History

Another mechanism through which claims on a farm may multiply over time is the actual transmission and interpretation of information about past transactions. In the past, written records of transfers of rights in farms were scarce, and documents recording the act of planting itself virtually non-existent. Thus, when disputes arose, settlements were likely to be based more on the reputations of available witnesses than on the "facts" of prior transactions (cf., Parkin 1972). Moreover, as the claims acquired through the investment of labor or inheritance were rarely spelled out (in terms of amount or timing), they have been subject to multiple and conflicting interpretations.

Migration

Reinterpretation of rights to tree crops has been common in

145

areas with large numbers of migrant farmers, where disputes often arose over the respective rights of indigenous land holders and immigrant planters. The importance of migration in the development of tree crop production was first demonstrated for southern Ghana by Polly Hill (1963), and subsequently documented in other areas as well (Berry 1975; Chauveau and Richard 1977; Dupire 1960; Kobben 1956; Olusanya et al., 1978). Migrant farmers usually obtained rights to cultivate tree crops in exchange for annual payments that attest to the landowners' continuing interest in the land itself. The resulting overlap of rights to tree crops and the land they stand on has, in turn, given rise to conflicting claims to the income from tree crop farms, or the right to alienate the trees themselves. For example, sales of land have sometimes been reinterpreted as customary tenancies, and the ownership of farms has been disputed by the descendants of both landowners and tree crop planters (Berry 1975; Dupire 1960; Gastellu 1981/2; Kobben 1963; Okali 1983; Weber 1977). In other words, the presence of large numbers of migrant farmers in the tree crop zone has reinforced the tendency for tree farms to "accumulate" claims over time.

The proliferation of rights and interests in tree crop farms means not only that access to and control over tree crop farms is often contested, but also that the outcome of such contests depend on processes of negotiation, adjudication, or conflict among the interested parties. Because particular rights are usually not precisely specified, disputes are rarely settled on legal grounds alone, but also according to the abilities of rival claimants to influence the settlement process. This ability rests, in turn, on social relations and processes not directly tied to tree crop production per se. In the following sections, I will illustrate this point by discussing changing rights in tree crop farms for two categories of people: women and sharecroppers.

Women's "Under-Investment" in Tree Crop Farms

For the most part, rural women in West Africa have participated in tree crop cultivation by working on farms owned or managed by men, rather than by planting and acquiring farms of their own. In Ivory Coast, Nigeria, and Cameroon, both the proportion of rural women who own tree crops, and the proportion of tree-crop farmers who are women are relatively low (Berry 1975; Chauveau 1979; Chauveau & Richard 1977; Galletti et al. 1956; Gastellu 1984; Guyer 1984b; Weber 1977). The chief exception is in areas of Ghana where descent is reckoned matrilineally, and tree crops were grown primarily by local, as

146

opposed to migrant farmers. In some communities, fifty percent or more of the resident women own tree crops (Beckett 1944; Hill 1963; Okali 1983; Mikell 1984; Vellenga 1977). In surveys of two villages--one in Asante and one in Ahafo--Okali (1983:58) found that 44% of the cocoa farmers were women, many of them locally born, who had planted cocoa for themselves on land belonging to their own descent group. Indeed, male strangers to Ahafo sometimes gained access to land by marrying local women. Since a male stranger's access to land is contingent on good relations with their affines--who also stand to inherit his farms--"it is presumed that he cultivates for the benefit of his children" (Okali 1983:62). Even among the matrilineal Akan, however, men own over half the acreage under tree crops, and women's holdings are smaller, on the average, than men's (Hill 1975; Mikell 1984; Okali 1983).

Moreover, in Akan communities where large numbers of women have established or acquired tree crop farms in the past, there is evidence that the incidence of female ownership has declined over time. In the Sunyani district of Ghana, Mikell (1984:206) found that women had stopped acquiring farms after the 1940s; that the proportion of total cocoa output and income produced on women's farms had declined over time; and that--despite many women's expressed desire to bequeath their farms to their daughters--when female farm owners died, their farms usually passed to the control of men. In Akokoaso, rates of female farm ownership were somewhat lower in the 1970s than those recorded by Beckett (1944) forty years earlier (Okali 1983).

The low or declining rate of women's ownership of tree crop farms is not the inevitable consequence of jural discrimination against women with respect to property rights. West African women participate extensively in rural production and exchange throughout the region. Even if, in some societies, marriage and kinship rules have made it difficult for women to acquire the right to plant permanent crops on land controlled by descent groups or communities, a great many rural women have opportunities to earn cash income which they control independently of their husbands or male kin. Because tree crops have become one of the principal income-generating assets available to rural people with modest incomes, one would expect a substantial number of women to have invested part of their savings in bearing trees. That they have apparently not done so is the result of several factors that have combined to restrict women's ability to commute jurally recognized claims to tree crop farms into effective control of the trees or their fruit. These factors include explicit restrictions on women's access to the right to plant permanent crops; limitations on women's ability to mobilize labor (both other people's and their own) for tree crop farming; and women's inability to assert their claims vis-a-vis those of men in cases of disputed rights to particular farms.

In the early stages of tree crop development, many women found it difficult to obtain rights to plant permanent crops on land controlled by the male members of their own or their husbands' descent groups. In an Ewe comunity in eastern Ghana, for example, Bukh (1979) found that women who farmed on their fathers' land were not allowed to plant tree crops because these would be inherited by their children and thus lost to the woman's lineage. Elsewhere, women have sometimes been explicitly prohibited brom planting tree crops (Weber 1977; cf. Galletti, et al. 1956:127; Gastellu 1984).

More often, women were precluded from planting tree crops for themselves by the terms on which they participated in the rural economy as a whole. Also, women have rarely migrated to new farming areas on their own, but tend to follow their husbands and assist on the husbands' farms. In Brong Ahafo, migrant women found that "as strangers their cultivation rights were restricted, [and] they were unable to establish themselves even as subsistence producers on their own since in this capacity they would be unable to pay for the land. They therefore continued in the only way possible, on their husbands' farms" (Okali 1983:97). Hill (1963:116) reported that "it is unusual for a woman to be a member of a company in her own right...," although women were sometimes left in charge of their husbands' farms while the men "were travelling about managing the work on their various lands" (ibid.:117).

Thousands of Yoruba women also "followed their husbands" in migrating to the forest belt to plant cocoa, assisting on their husbands' farms until the young trees were mature enough to support the cost of hired laborers. Like Akan wives, Yoruba women frequently assumed responsibility for managing mature farms when their husbands established new farms or other enterprises elsewhere (Berry 1985; Olusanya et al. 1978; cf. Boutillier et al. 1977; Chauveau, 1979).

In general, women found it difficult to mobilize labor-- their own as well as other people's--for tree crop cultivation. Often they were simply too busy with food crop production and other domestic and productive chores to have time for tree crop planting. In female food farming systems, women are often responsible for providing most or all of the foodstuffs consumed by members of their immediate households, and cannot abandon food crop cultivation to plant and tend tree crops unless they have access to alternative sources of income to buy food (Guyer 1984b). In addition, women do most of the domestic work, devoting several hours each day to fetching wood and water, cooking, and child care--and are often expected to work on their

148

husbands' farms as well. In principle, they could hire in labor to cultivate food crops or help with other income-generating activities (food processing, trade, crafts), and some women do this although those with sufficient working capital to hire in labor can just as well hire labor to cultivate tree crops on their behalf as hire in labor to release their own time to work on tree crop farms (Galletti et al. 1956; Berry 1975).

The majority of West African farmers--male and female--do not have sufficient working capital to establish tree crop farms solely with hired-in labor. Increased labor hiring has been a consequence of, rather than a condition for, the spread of tree crop cultivation, with income from early maturing farms a principal source of working capital for paying hired workers (Berry 1975; Chauveau 1979; Galletti, et al. 1956; Hill 1956, 1963).f For both men and women, it has usually been necessary to establish or acquire mature tree crops in order to be able to substitute hired for unpaid labor. The difference is that men have found it easier to mobilize unpaid labor--usually from subordinate family members, including their wives--to establish tree crop farms in the first place.[1] Husbands' rights to the labor of their wives (and fathers of their unmarried daughters as well as sons) have meant that women are far more likely to work on their husbands' farms than vice versa (Berry 1975:172ff; Dozon 1977:479; Galletti et al. 1956:77; Oppong et al. 1975:72).

In some areas, this problem was exacerbated as men withdrew their labor from food crop production in order to specialize in the more remunerative cultivation of cocoa and coffee (Bukh 1979; Guyer 1984b; Weber 1977). When this occurred, the burden of feeding the household was relegated increasingly to women, tying up more of their labor in food crop cultivation and prolonging their inability to move into tree crop production on their own account.

Also, in farming systems where both men and women participated in food crop production, tree crops proved easier to integrate into men's than into women's fields or farming tasks. Tree crops grow best on newly cleared forest land. Since heavy clearing is usually men's work, men were often able to plant tree crops in direct conjunction with their on-going farming activities (Cleave, 1974). This technical advantage was especially marked in areas where men took full responsibility for initial cultivation of newly cleared forest plots. In Cameroon, for example, "the cultivation of cocoa ... fit into Beti ideas about the division of labor like a hand into a glove. It was grown in field types which had always been associated with male labor.... In terms of labor organization, establishing a young cocoa farm was almost identical to melon-seed cultivation,.. and,

149

like melon-seed, cocoa is a constituent of male wealth" (Guyer 1984b:52).

Restrictions on women's ability to mobilize labor for tree crop cultivation were partly the result of custom and partly a matter of financial exigency. Because their access to the labor of relatives (other than that of their unmarried daughters and young sons) was limited and their responsibilities for the daily provisioning of their households substantial, most women could not afford to invest in assets, such as tree crops, with a long gestation period. They were simply not in a position--socially or economically--to forego current income generating activities in order to invest in income streams that would only materialize after several years (cf. Guyer, 1980; Spiro 1980).

Because of the conditions under which women could mobilize others' labor, and demands on their own time associated with the division of labor by gender in domestic and local farming systems, in the early stages of tree crop cultivation, men planted farms for themselves while women worked on the young farms of their husbands or senior agnates. However, this does not explain why women with accumulated savings from other occupations did not invest more extensively in established tree crops, or why female farm ownership tended to decline over time in places such as Sunyani and Akokoaso. To understand the low and declining rate of women's investment in tree crops, we must also take account of the ways claims on farms were exercised over time.

Throughout the humid zone of West Africa, the division of agricultural and domestic labor is embedded in conjugal and domestic relations. The specific division of responsibility for household expenditures varied among local areas and even households within one locality. Tree crops created new employment opportunities, new demands on people's time and resources, and new flows of cash income in rural economies of the humid zone, but people's responses to these changes were played out in the context of conjugal and domestic relations.

Wives' labor on their husbands' farms and the "returns" they expected, were rarely expressed as an explicit, single-stranded contract, but tended rather to merge with conjugal rights and responsibilities in general. Wives were usually not paid for helping on their husbands' farms. Service on their husbands' tree crop farms often originated as an extension of wives' conjugal obligations to contribute to household consumption and assist in husbands' farming activities. It was expected that husbands, in turn, would contribute to the household budget and provide their wives with additional goods or services from time to time, but what specific additional claims a wife could make in

150

return for her labor on a tree crop farm was rarely articulated.

Accordingly, the rearrangement of domestic rights and responsibilities that followed the spread of tree crop cultivation occurred unevenly, and patterns of control over assets and income varied among localities. In western Nigeria, for example, wives' claims appear to have been directed towards the husband, rather than the farm. I never encountered a court case in which a woman claimed a share of her husband's farm because she had worked on it in the past. Rather, when the husband's farm matured, wives expected to be released from their obligations to help him, leaving them free to develop their own, independent sources of income (Berry, 1975, 1985).[2]

In Akan communities in Ghana, wives' expectations were focussed more directly on the farm. In the Ahafo village studied by Okali, "none of the wives assumed that they had established a joint concern with their husbands in [the sense] that both had equal rights to it, although they did expect some compensation other than the food crops, possibly even a fraction of the established farm" (Okali, 1983:103). Okali also cites a number of court cases in which a woman advanced claims to all or part of an established tree farm on the grounds that she had invested her labor in the farm during her husband's lifetime. Although she does not present a large number of decisions handed down in such cases, her evidence does not suggest that women amassed much property in this way.

In short, even in societies in which women have been able to invest in tree crop farms--through access to planting rights or the means to establish or acquire bearing trees--it has been difficult for them to maintain control over their farms in the long run, or to assert their claims to farms vis-a-vis those of men in the context of open-ended, overlapping, and proliferating rights to rural property.

Sharecroppers

Much of the labor on tree crop farms in West Africa is performed by men, under a wide variety of contractual arrangements. Farmers have often relied heavily on the labor of junior or subordinate kinsmen--especially during the early years when immature trees do not yield enough to cover the cost of hiring in labor to work them, or to release the farmer's time from other tasks for tree crop cultivation. Like Yoruba wives, junior men in Yoruba, Baule, Beti, and other societies worked for their seniors in exchange for future protection and assistance.

151

Often, this assistance took the form of support while the junior kinsman established a farm or other enterprise of his own (Berry 1975, 1985; Chauveau 1979; Weber 1977).

In some areas, male laborers may consider that they have acquired an interest in the farm itself by investing their labor in it. (Okali 1983:99). Sometimes, laborers expect (or are considered) to have acquired an interest in the farm, even when they were remunerated for their labor at the time it was performed. For example, Robertson (1983) argues that in Ghana this was sometimes the case with sharecroppers, especially those who have worked on particular farms for a number of years.

Sharecropping is widespread in Ghana and Ivory Coast, where it takes several forms. In general, sharecropping derives from the Akan custom of presenting a chief or stool-holder with one third (abusa) of any game, minerals, or forest produce collected from the territory under their jurisdiction (Dupire 1960; Gastellu 1980, 1981/2; Hill 1956; Kobben 1956). As people began to migrate into forested areas to plant tree crops, Akan chiefs sometimes granted cultivation rights to stranger farmers in exchange for one third of the farm when the trees were established.[3] Also, some strangers obtained cultivation rights in exchange for one third of the annual cocoa crop. (Hill 1956:14) Such farmers were, in effect, tenants; their position in the cocoa economy was similar to that of Yoruba or Baule tenants who paid a fixed annual amount of cocoa (or cash) in exchange for long-term cultivation rights. Like other tenant farmers, abusa or share tenants owned the trees they planted and could dispose of them--by sale, mortgage, or bequest (Dupire 1960:67; Hill 1956:14). Landowning lineages or chiefs sometimes sought to exploit the possibilities of such tenancies, arguing that land sales to companies of migrant farmers really involved only sales of long-term cultivation rights, and that as continuing "owners" of the land, chiefs were entitled to one third of its fruits (Gastellu 1981/2). Gastellu (1980) also describes cases of Agni chiefs-turned-planters who in effect "leased" stool lands to themselves, claiming one third of the crop as their traditional chiefly prerogative and an additional third as their owner's share of the proceeds of the farm (cf. Kobben 1956, on the Bete; Weber 1977, on the Beti).

Abusa laborers, who weeded and harvested other people's farms in exchange for one third of the crop, were not farm owners. Often referred to in the literature and by English-speaking West Africans as "caretakers," they performed a variety of tasks. In the 1950s, abusa laborers working for Agni farmers in Ivory Coast were expected to spend one day a week helping their employer establish a new plot of cocoa and also to clear a plot for food crop cultivation at the end of the farming season (Kobben 1956:87-88). Sometimes abusa men supplied their own tools; frequently they were given plots of land on which to grow their own food crops while they were attached to a particular tree crop farm (Robertson 1983:467). Like sharecroppers in other areas (and farmers' wives in the tree crop economies of Nigeria and Ghana), abusa laborers frequently served as farm managers, assuming sole charge of a farm while the owner managed additional farms or pursued other occupations elsewhere (Hill 1956, 1963). They sometimes hired in additional labor, or drew on the assistance of their wives and children to enable them to sharecrop more or larger farms (Hill 1963:189; Robertson 1983:467).

Robertson suggests that sharecropping contracts created a basis for laborers to develop rights in land. "In southern Ghana, it is probable that in the many instances where the 'caretaker' is a nephew, abusa is a preliminary step towards inheritance of the farm.... Much the same process may be taking place in the many instances where the 'caretaker' is a son. Abusa may provide a gradual and unostentatious strategy for patrilateral deposition inter vivos" (Robertson 1983:468). Similarly, abusa contracts between non-kin may lead to laborers' acquiring rights in farms over time. Migrants often gained access to land in tree-crop growing areas by working as abusa laborers. In Ghana, Mossi and other migrants entered into abusa contracts with Akan farmers, who also gave them land for cultivating food crops. Eventually they managed to settle their families in the forest belt and some acquired tree crops of their own (Robertson 1983). In western Nigeria, migrant laborers from the Middle Belt rarely planted tree crops, but some established themselves as commercial food crop growers in cocoa farming areas, producing for the local market and even founding their own villages (Berry 1975).

During the rapid colonization of new lands in southwestern Ivory Coast after 1960, competition for agricultural labor was intense and farmers recruited workers (including non-Ivorians) by promising them assistance in establishing tree crop farms of their own (Boutillier et al. 1977; Chauveau 1979; Schwartz 1979). Dupire observed in the late 1950s that abusa laborers stood a better chance than daily or task workers of becoming tenant farmers. In old cocoa growing areas of Ghana, where farm productivity had declined, farmers sometimes gave up their own shares of farm output or granted proprietary rights directly to their abusa laborers in order to retain their services in the face of declining returns to tree crop cultivation itself (Okali 1983). In some areas of Ghana, an abusa man's tenure could be regarded as heritable or even saleable. Some abusa laborers actually received compensation for trees destroyed in the colonial governments's campaign against swollen shoot disease in

153

the late 1940s (Hill 1956).

Sharecroppers are more likely to develop rights in farms if they have worked on them for a number of years. However, abusa contracts do not invariably mature towards full proprietary rights in farms in the long run. In Ghana, as farms planted in the late nineteenth or early twentieth centuries matured, the share of the crop allocated to laborers sometimes declined or abusa laborers were replaced altogether by cheaper nkotokuano laborers (Hill 1963). In general, "it is impossible to estimate the proportion of people who 'graduate' through an abusa contract to full proprietary interest in the farm" (Robertson 1983:469).

Whether or not former laborers assert claims to tree crop farms often appears to depend more on changing economic and political conditions than on the original terms of the labor contract. For example, increases in the proportion of farms worked by sharecroppers have occurred in periods of labor scarcity, which were brought about either by rapid expansion of tree crop planting, as in Ivory Coast in the 1960s, or by declining returns to cocoa production and high rates of rural outmigration, as in eastern Ghana in the same period. Like long-term labor-credit arrangements among agnates or between spouses, abusa contracts have been used to recruit and finance farm labor by farmers without ready access to working capital. Similarly, sharecroppers may expect future assistance from the farm owner in acquiring farms of their own. However, these expectations are not formalized: like labor-credit arrangements among kin, they resemble the generalized expectations of future support that clients hold of their patrons, rather than a futures contract in which amounts and dates of future transactions are clearly specified. The ambiguities of such arrangements leave them open to re-interpretation as economic conditions change, or social and political relations between share tenants and farm owners shift over time. Sometimes the ambiguous nature of contractual relations is reflected in local terminology. In the cocoa farming areas of southwestern Nigeria, the Yoruba term olori oko (lit., owner of the farm) is used to refer both to landholders and to tenant farmers (Berry 1975:95).

The ambiguity of abusa and other long-term labor-credit arrangements is central to understanding differential access to tree crop farms. Robertson (1983:471-472) concludes that, in Ghana,

> usufruct is very durable, may be bought and sold, bequeathed or used as collateral; it cannot however, be resolved into black-and-white categories as distinct as 'ownership' and 'non-ownership'. As Polly Hill has cogently argued, any attempt to define proprietary

154

interest in such terms in fruitless: 'it is the degree
of individual control which must be considered.'
(1963:112). It is therefore unhelpful to think of
abusa as necessarily maturing to outright ownership of
the land....

However, if contractual arrangements are subject to multiple
interpretations--either because of the way they are defined (or
left vague), or because of the conditions under which they are
negotiated and carried out--then contracts are at most only
partial determinants of social outcomes. Robertson's conclusion
that abusa contracts have militated "against the polarization of
southern Ghanaian society into distinct classes" (1983:473) may
overstate the case. The indeterminacy of labor contracts means
not that they have prevented differentiation, but that the
long-term implications of labor-credit arrangments for patterns
of control over rural property are subject to change over time as
economic conditions change and differentiation occurs. The
property rights exercised by particular categories of
people--e.g., women or sharecroppers--depend on their
socio-political position and relations with other groups in the
rural economy, as well as on their command over income or their
access to the means of production per se.

Property Rights and Resource Management: Implications
for Rural Development

So far, I have argued that across the West African forest
zone, rights in tree crop farms tended to multiply over time.
Because of their longevity, most tree crops are inherited, and
inheritance practices usually foster or create multiple claims on
property. Further, the ease with which strangers have acquired
cultivation rights, and labor has been mobilized through
non-market mechanisms, has also contributed to the proliferation
of rights in cultivable land and tree crop farms. Taken
together, these processes created overlapping rights, which have
frequently given rise to tension, litigation, and sometimes
outright conflict.

The issues arising in such conflicts are complex, in part
because the individuals involved are often engaged in multiple
relations of exchange and obligation. As Okali (1983:99) points
out, what participants in a given farming enterprise expect of
one another may depend on several factors:

Persons who assist in farm development are likely to
consider that...they will get some return for their

155

investment.... Returns may be visible in the form of
cash, food crops,... land or other assistance with the
establishment of separate properties and include
ultimately the transfer of ownership of the farm
itself.... Since returns may not reflect inputs in
farms but may rather be related to other services
received or other obligations of the farmers involved,
[resource allocation in] cocoa farming [must be] placed
within the context of total rights and obligations of
the actors involved....

In other words, if a farm owner engages his or her sibling or
nephew as an abusa or family laborer, it may be difficult to
distinguish the farmer's obligations to those persons as laborers
from his obligations to them as junior kin. Similarly, a wife's
interest in her husband's farm, which arises from the labor she
has invested in it over time, may become conflated with her
conjugal rights.

In addition to the ambiguities that surround property rights
that are embedded in multi-stranded social relationships, the
terms of specific contractual exchanges are often imprecise.
Comaroff's (1980) observation that marriage transactions serve to
define spheres of ambiguity within which people negotiate rights
and responsibilities over long periods of time may also be
applied to the delineation of property rights through inheritance
or labor-credit relations. An abusa contract, for example, may
specify clearly what tasks a laborer is to perform in exchange
for a specific share of the crop, while at the same time the
terms of a worker's maturing interest in the farm are left vague,
subject to change with changing economic conditions or shifts in
relations of authority and obligation between the farmer and farm
worker.

The proliferation of overlapping and open-ended rights in
tree crop farms has affected patterns of rural investment and
rural differentiation in the humid zone of West Africa in several
ways. First, if social status (gender, marriage, seniority)
affects a person's ability to acquire or exercise property
rights, the rate of return to investment in a given type of asset
will vary among social groups within a given community. Women
may have "under-invested" in tree crops partly because experience
has taught them that they are likely to receive lower returns
from tree farms than men do.

Similarly, in a tight rural labor market, sharecroppers may
find that farm owners are willing to yield them a higher
proportion of farm output--or an interest in the farm itself--to
ensure access to their labor. This has occurred both in periods
of rural decline and in contexts of rural expansion. In older

cocoa areas of eastern Ghana, declining yields and rural
outmigration in the 1950s and 1960s made it difficult for farm
owners to recruit laborers. To secure labor, many farmers ceded
two thirds or even the entire crop to the abusa laborer who
weeded and harvested the farm (Okali 1983).[4] In the 1960s and
early 1970s, a similar problem of excess demand for farm labor
faced planters in the rapidly expanding tree crop economy of
southwestern Ivory Coast. Farmers recruited sharecroppers by
promising them land (or even farms) of their own--a practice that
enabled some non-Ivorians to acquire farms in defiance of
national law (Chauveau 1979; Schwartz 1979).

Second, because social status and social relations help to
determine people's access to and returns from rural assets, many
rural people devote part of their savings to establishing or
strengthening their social positions, rather than investing
everything in productive capital. In these circumstances,
investment in social status is clearly directed toward future
profit as well as security--contrary to the conventional
microeconomic assumption that profit and security are mutually
exclusive goals (see, e.g., Lipton 1968; Berry 1980). Investment
in social status as a means to strengthen property rights may
help to explain a wide array of rural expenditures, from weddings
to palaces (Berry 1985; Parkin 1972). It may also help to
account for West Africans' widespread preference for relatively
liquid forms of rural assets and income-generating activities.
West African women tend to specialize in trade, processing, or
food crops--rather than investing in tree crops, houses, or other
assets with long gestation or payoff periods.[5]

Finally, the open-ended and overlapping nature of rights in
tree crop farms means that rural differentiation in tree crop
economies arises as much from relations of power as from
relations of production. As we have seen, multiple, open-ended
claims to rural property have created spheres within which actual
patterns of access and control are subject to on-going
re-negotiation or dispute. Redistribution of income or control
over assets themselves can be touched off not only by changing
economic conditions, but also by political processes originating
independently of the rural economy. Chiefs have sometimes taken
advantage of changing political conditions to revive dormant
rights over land and land users, or to re-define the terms of
present land-using arrangements. In Nigeria, as cocoa prices
rose and pressures for local self-government mounted after 1945,
the chiefs of Ife insisted successfully that all "non-Ifes"
growing cocoa on Ife land must pay an annual fee (isakole) to
their Ife "landlords"--regardless of how long they had lived on
Ife soil, or whether they had ever paid isakole before (Berry
1975). This coup affected the division of proceeds from hundreds
of cocoa farms in Ife, and underscored the non-Ifes' status as

"strangers" in the Ife area. This served, in turn, to undermine their role in local political affairs, and helped to protect the dominance of Ife interests in the emerging regional political party system (Berry 1985; Clarke 1980; Oyediran 1973; Peel 1983).

Similarly, in Brong Ahafo, cocoa farming provided not only a source of revenue for various levels of local and national government, but also an arena wherein local political factions struggled for potential advantage at the national level by manipulating the terms of control over rural property, produce, and the loyalties of rural producers (Dunn and Robertson 1973). In Ivory Coast, the government's effort to simplify land tenure and reward agricultural enterprise by abolishing customary tenures and declaring a policy of "land to the tiller" left open the question of allocating cultivation rights in unoccupied areas. As rising prices for cocoa and coffee touched off a scramble for uncultivated land in the southwest, strangers sometimes constituted themselves "chiefs," allocating use rights to latecomers (often in exchange for labor) on land that they themselves had occupied only shortly before (Schwartz 1979:99).

Across the humid zone of West Africa, then, the spread of tree crop cultivation led to the commercialization of various rights in rural property, but not to their consolidation into forms of exclusive control over land or trees. What Polly Hill so aptly denominated "the degree of individual control" over tree crop farms remained subject to redefinition--among kin, through the courts, and through local and national political processes. In all these arenas, the outcome of conflict over rights in tree crop farms depended on the political as well as the economic resources of the contestants, and on their relative successes in deploying these resources to acquire and defend rights in rural property.

Notes

[1] The same is true of food crop production (Guyer 1980).

[2] Some Yoruba women also received gifts of money to help them start a trade, but among my informants, farmers' wives usually obtained such gifts from their agnates rather than their husbands (Berry 1985:95). In Ivory Coast, Baule farmers "employed" their wives (and junior kinsmen) in exchange for expectations of future support or assistance in establishing independent occupations of their own (Dupire 1960:128-9; Chauveau 1979).

[3] In such cases the stranger often sold his portion of the farm, moving on to establish another farm somewhere else with the proceeds (Hill 1963:15-16).

[4] Robertson (1983:469) alludes to this, but does not point out that increases in tenants' share of the output may reflect changes in rural economic conditions rather than an inherent tendency for abusa tenancies to "mature" towards ownership of farms.

[5] Indeed, one wonders whether they also eschew land-augmenting investments (such as fences, wells, alley crops) --for fear of losing control of the assets before they pay off or can be sold. If so, this could contribute to low yields and agricultural stagnation.

References

Beckett, W.H. 1944. Akokoaso: A Survey of a Gold Coast Village. London School of Economics Monographs on Social Anthropology No. 10.
Berry, S.S. 1975. Cocoa, Custom and Socioeconomic Change in Rural Western Nigeria. Oxford: Clarendon Press.
Berry, S.S. 1985. Fathers work for their sons: Accumulation, Mobility and Class Formation in an Extended Yoruba Community. Berkeley and Los Angeles: University of Califormia Press.
Biebuyck, D. ed. 1963. African Agrarian Systems. London: Oxford University Press.
Boutillier, J.-L. et al. 1977. "Systemes Socio-Economiques Mossi et Migrations," Cahiers ORSTOM, XIV, 4:361-81.
Bukh, J. 1979. The Village Woman in Ghana. Uppsala: Scandinavian Institute of African Studies.
Chauveau, J.-P. 1979. "Economie de Plantation et 'Nouveaux Milieux Sociaux,'" Cahiers ORSTOM, XVI, 1-2.
Chauveau, J.-P. and J. Richard. 1977. "Une Peripheree Recentree," Cahiers d'Etudes Africaines, XVII, 4:485-523.
Clarke, J. 1980. "Peasantization and Landholding: A Nigerian Case Study." In: M.A. Klein, ed. Peasants in Africa. Beverly Hills, CA:Sage.
Cleave, J. 1974. African Farmers. New York: Praeger.
Comaroff, J.L., ed. 1980. The Meaning of Marriage Payments. London and New York: Academic Press.
Dozon, J.-P. 1977. "Economie Marchande et Structures Sociales: le cas des Bete de Cote d'Ivoire," Cahiers d'Etudes Africaines, XVII, 4:463-83.
Dunn, J. and A. Robertson. 1973. Dependence and Opportunity: Political Change in Brong Ahafo. Cambridge: Cambridge

University Press.

Dupire, M. 1960. "Planteurs Autochtones et Etrangeres en bas Cote d'Ivoire Orientale," Etudes Eburneennes, VIII:7-238.

Galletti, R., et al. 1956. Nigerian Cocoa Farmers. Oxford: Oxford University Press.

Gastellu, J.-M. 1980. "L'arbre ne Cache pas le Foret: Usus, Fructus et Abusus," Cahiers ORSTROM, XVII, 3-4:279-82.

----- 1981/2. "Les Plantations de Cacao au Ghana," Cahiers ORSTOM, XVIII, 2:225-54.

----- 1984. Une Economie du Tresor: les Grands Planteurs du Moronou. 4 Vols. ORSTOM Bundy.

Guyer, J. 1980. "Food, Cocoa, and the Division of Labor by Sex in Two West African Societies," Comparative Studies in Society and History, 22, 3:355-73.

----- 1984a. "Anthropological Models of African Production: The Naturalization Problem." Man.

----- 1984b. Family and Farm in Southern Cameroon. Boston: Boston University African Studies Center.

Hay, M.J. and S. Stichter, eds. 1984. African Women South of the Sahara. London: Longman.

Henn, J. 1983. "Feeding the Cities and Feeding the Peasants: What Role for Africa's Women Farmers?" World Development, 11, 12:1043-55.

Hill, P. 1956. The Gold Coast Cocoa Farmer. Oxford: Oxford University Press.

-----. 1963. Migrant Cocoa Farmers of Southern Ghana. Cambridge: Cambridge University Press.

Kobben, A.J.F. 1956. "Le Planteur Noir," Etudes Eburneennes, V:7-190.

-----. 1963. "Land as an Object of Gain in a Non-Literate Society," in Biebuyck, ed.

Kotey, R.A., C. Okali, and B.E. Rourke, eds. The Economics of Cocoa Production and Marketing. Legon: Institute of Statistical, Social and Economic Research.

Lipton, M. 1968. "The Theory of the Optimizing Peasant," Journal of Development Studies, 3:327-52.

Lloyd, P.C. 1962. Yoruba Land Law. London: Oxford University Press.

Mikell, G. 1984. "Filiation, Economic Crisis and the Status of Women in Ghana," Canadian Journal of African Studies.

Okali, C. 1983. Cocoa and Kinship in Ghana: The Matrilineal Akan. London: Routledge and Kegan Paul.

Olusanya, P.O., et al. 1978. Migrant Farmers of the Eastern Cocoa Zone of Southwestern Nigeria. Ile-Ife: Department of Demography, University of Ife.

Oppong, C., et al. 1975. "Woman Power: Retrograde Steps in Ghana," African Studies Review, XVIII, 3:71-84.

Oyediran, O. 1973. "The Position of the Ooni in the Changing Political System of Ile-Ife," Journal of the Historical Society of Nigeria, 6,4.

----- 1974. "Modakeke in Ife," Odu, ns 10.
Parkin, D.J. 1972. Palms, Wine and Witnesses. San Francisco: Chandler.
Peel, J.D.Y. 1983. Ijeshas and Nigerians. Cambridge: Cambridge University Press.
Robertson, A.F. 1983. "Abusa: The Structural History of an Economic Contract," Journal of Development Studies, 18, 4:447-8.
Schwartz, A. 1979. "Colonization Agricole Spontanee et Emergence de Nouveaux Milieux Sociaux dans le Sud-Ouest Ivoirien," Cahiers ORSTOM, XVI, 1-2:83-102.
Spiro, H. 1980. "The Role of Women Farmers in Oyo State, Nigeria," Ibadan: International Institute of Tropical Africa.
Vellenga, D. 1977. "Differentiation Among Women Farmers in Two Rural Areas of Ghana," Labor and Society, 2, 2:197-208.
Weber, J. 1977. "Structures Agraires et Evolution des Milieux Ruraux: le cas de la Region Cacaoyere du Centre-Sud Cameroun," Cahiers ORSTOM, XIV, 4:361-81.

9. PASTORAL AND AGRO-PASTORAL MIGRATION IN TANZANIA: FACTORS OF ECONOMY, ECOLOGY AND DEMOGRAPHY IN CULTURAL PERSPECTIVE

John G. Galaty

During the last twenty years, Sukuma agro-pastoralists and Parakuiyo Maasai pastoralists,[1] among others, have moved southward in Tanzania, a migration that has accelerated over the last decade. This migration has had significant social and economic impact on regions lacking any previous notable pastoral tradition, due to prevalence of tsetse. Although the migration has been stimulated by conditions prevalent in the northern rangelands, Sukuma have moved in great numbers while Kisongo Maasai have not. I assess here the influence of various economic, ecological, and demographic factors on this "new" pastoral migration; how they differentially affect pastoral and agro-pastoral communities, given the quite distinct social and cultural matrices within which similar factors are interpreted and work; and finally explore how this contemporary process of migration can help us understand the pastoral expansions that so influenced the history of East Africa.

The Migration Process

It is clear that current migrations, as many in the past, are largely motivated by the search for pasture, and thus are "pastoral" migrations. The political process of pastoral migration is shaped by ecological and economic factors through the stimulus of pasture needs in interaction with climate, environment, and population. Two forms of expansion carried out by pastoralists can be identified. Brandstrom (1985:18) calls the first "continuous" expansion, the movement of pastoralists into neighboring regions, either through incremental drift or definitive occupation. The second involves "leapfrog" expansion (Brandstrom), whereby pastoralists bypass communities in more or less long-distance and discontinuous movements, which we may call "treks."[2] Continuous expansion may be most common to movement by an entire group or community into neighboring regions with appropriate resources, whereas discontinous expansion may be appropriate to later stages of expansion, where prior occupation or environmental differences render neighboring regions less accessible, thus stimulating longer distance "frontier" migrations by individuals, families, or communities. Although the process of pastoralist expansion in African history has most often been thought of as continous, the current Tanzanian experience of leapfrog expansion perhaps should lead us to reconsider the role of the trek in the movement of pastoral peoples in the past.

Pastoral Expansion in Eastern African History

The origin of Eastern Sudanic pastoralism between 3500-4500 B.C. was probably associated with an arid episode in African history, however the first major pastoral movement into East Africa (presumably by ancestral Southern Cushites), which reached the Kenyan Highlands between 1,000-2,000 B.C., may have been associated with somewhat less arid conditions (Ambrose 1984; David 1982). In the second major pastoral movement into East Africa around 1,000 B.C., ancestral Southern Nilotes proceeded down the Rift Valley, probably displacing their pastoral predecessors, who in turn dispersed the Click-speaking hunter-gatherers of Northern Tanzania by the turn of the present epoch (Ambrose 1984; Ehret 1982). The coming to East Africa of (Bantu-speaking) iron-age farmers at that time may have made possible the emergence of both more specialized pastoralism in the Rift Valley vicinity by Southern Nilotes, who could engage in trade for grain (Robertshaw and Collett 1983), and modified agro-pastoralism by Bantu communities. The third great pastoral movement into East Africa by (Maa-speaking) Eastern Nilotes during the first millenium A.D., probably associated with the acquisition of early iron technology, stimulated the further southward movement of Southern Nilotes into Northern Tanzania, bringing them into close contact with earlier agro-pastoral southern Cushitic migrants. The later dramatic expansion of Maa-speaking pastoralists probably arose from the development of a "new pastoralism," with improved iron-technology, new breeds of heat-resistant zebu cattle, and novel forms of social organization (Lamphear 1985; Galaty in press). The Iloogolala represented the "frontier" Maa, who in the sixteenth century pushed the Southern Nilotes out of Southern Kenya (Jacobs 1972), only to be dispersed by the later expansion of confederations of "Central" Maasai-proper, after which they regrouped in North-Central Tanzania as Parakuiyo (Galaty in press).

We can come to some tentative conclusions from this brief sketch of pastoralist expansion in East Africa. A succession of pastoral groups was involved, and although we can trace the cultural and linguistic continuity between present-day communities and the past stages of expansion, today's societies in Northern Tanzania represent complex syntheses out of past encounters and long periods of coexistence and social interaction among groups. The social and economic conditions of today result as much from regional systems of technology exchange, trade, and sociopolitical discourse as from a given cultural and linguistic heritage. The Southern Cushitic Iraqw practice a form of agro-pastoralism in the Mbulu Highlands west of the Rift Valley in Northern Tanzania, while the Southern Nilotic Tatog, including the Barabaig and Taturu, practice more specialized pastoralism with some grain production to the southwest of the Rift Valley. The Rift Valley, its southward extension onto the Maasai Plains, and the Ngorongoro-Serengeti plains and Crater Highlands are occupied by the specialized pastoral Maasai-proper (primarily Kisongo). Parakuiyo Maasai were dispersed throughout districts at the southern periphery of the Maasai plains, coexisting with Bantu-speaking highland cultivators (Beidelman 1960; Rigby 1985). The Bantu-speaking Sukuma occupy the flatlands eastward and southward of Lake Victoria, practicing extensive dry-land cultivation combined with animal husbandry. The patterns and timing of expansion of livestock-keeping pastoral and agro-pastoral communities were shaped by the cultural and political conditions of the given time and place, including the quality of available technology of production and combat. But these processes occurred within set environmental conditions and population dynamics, which were certainly influential both as back-drop for and as a proximate cause, subject to perception and reason, of decisions to move.

The Ecology of Pastoral Migration

Tanzania's semi-arid zone--defined by mean rainfall from 400-600 mm per year (minimum 10 percent probability)--lies like a long, curved knife, stretching with the broad hilt along the broad northern rangelands and the point penetrating the south at the Usangu Plains east of Lake Rukwa (see map). Rain-fed cultivation is precarious here, so one finds a combination of specialized pastoralism, primarily among ethnic Maasai, and pockets of irrigated agriculture. To the west lies a transitional zone receiving an average of 600-800 mm of annual rainfall, where intensive animal husbandry is combined with dry-land cultivation by such groups as the agro-pastoral Sukuma. Beyond, on either side, lie wetter regions receiving between 800-1,000 mm of annual precipitation. This vast expanse of deciduous "miombo" woodland is tsetse-infested, the fly serving as a vector for trypanosomiasis, which renders 60 percent of Tanzania inimical to animal husbandry or substantial human settlement.

But the north/south semi-arid wedge is tsetse-free, providing, as it were, a "corridor" down which waves of pastoral migration have historically passed. Indeed, the existence of two distinct Morsitans sub-species (G. morsitans centralis, north and west; G. morsitans morsitans, south and east, among seven distinct species of tsetse found in Tanzania) on either side

165

attests to the longevity of this corridor slicing through the great tsetse belt that stretches across the African continent (A. Jordan, pers. comm.; Ford & Katongo 1973). But where the wedge narrows live the agro-pastoral Gogo and Hehe, heavily involved both in rain-fed agriculture and animal husbandry, whose population density is higher and per capita livestock holdings much lower than the Maasai living to the north, whose further southward migration they have historically blocked (Fosbrooke 1956; Rigby 1979).

Despite the tsetse-free corridor, livestock have traditionally been contained in the northern rangelands. Of the 12 million cattle in Tanzania in 1978, the third largest herd (after Sudan and Ethiopia) in Africa (Grindle 1980:1), 77 percent are found in the three regions of the north. This proportion is evenly distributed across the Lake Region inhabited by the Sukuma (25.7 percent), the Northern Region by the Maasai (26.6 percent), and the Central Region by the Gogo and Tatog (24.5 percent) (Gov. of Tanzania 1984). The least inhabited regions of the country are the extensive tsetse-infested miombo woodlands, with soils of low fertility, found in huge expanses of west-central and south-eastern Tanzania (see map). For millenia, the tsetse zones have essentially inhibited the further spread of livestock-keeping peoples further southward who inhabit that huge arc of grasslands from the eastern Sahel through East Africa.

Factors of disease and pasture should be balanced against the availability of water in interpreting the distribution of human and animal populations in Tanzania. Permanent water sources are relatively rare, making permanent habitation of many regions quite difficult. Large areas in the northern rangelands are used only in the wet season when standing pools and seasonal streams are available, with settlements and livestock retreating to perennial streams, swamps, and highland areas as the dry season progresses. Deep wells probably dug millenia ago when pastoralists first inhabited the Maasai plains are critical to making it available for human and pastoral exploitation. Struggles between pastoral groups do not appear to have been over pasture as much as control over water sources, such as wells, swamps, and streams (Galaty in press).

Pastoral migration, yesterday as well as today, was constrained by the availability of pasture and water resources, the prevalence of disease, and the political ecology of prior human occupation. These factors combined to inhibit significant southward movement of livestock-keeping peoples. During the Colonial period, the movement of peoples out of their assigned districts was discouraged, although Parakuiyo Maasai continued slow incremental movements adjacent to cultivating groups at the periphery of Maasailand. Current migrations are thus not simply

Map

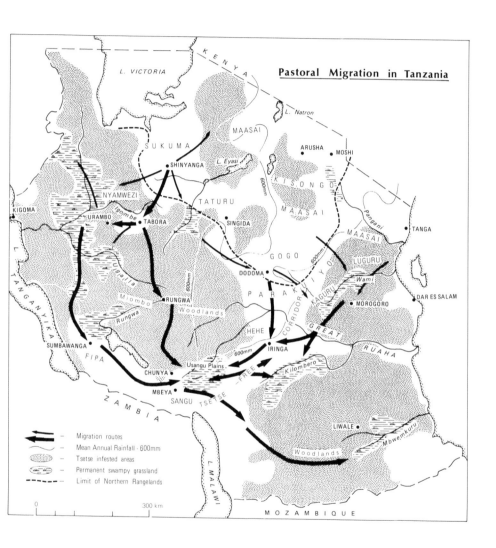

Pastoral Migration in Tanzania

L. VICTORIA

KENYA

L. Natron

MAASAI

SUKUMA

ARUSHA   MOSHI

SHINYANGA   L. Eyasi

KISONGO

600mm

NYAMWEZI

TATURU

MAASAI

KIGOMA

Ipombe

URAMBO   TABORA   SINGIDA

Pangani

TANGA

MAASAI

Ugalla

GOGO

DODOMA

LUGURU

600mm

Wami

DAR ES SALAM

Miombo   RUNGWA

Woodlands

PARAKUIYO

KAGURU

MOROGORO

600mm

Rungwa

HEHE

GREAT

CORRIDOR

SUMBAWANGA

FIPA

600mm   IRINGA

RUAHA

Usangu Plains

Kilombero

CHUNYA

FREE

MBEYA

SANGU   TSETSE

ZAMBIA

LIWALE

Mbwemkuru

Woodlands

L. MALAWI

— Migration routes
— Mean Annual Rainfall - 600mm
— Tsetse infested areas
— Permanent swampy grassland
------- Limit of Northern Rangelands

0   300 km

MOZAMBIQUE

167

a continuation of nineteenth-century processes but represent a new phenomenon, brought about by different degrees of density and land pressure and by a different set of technological possibilities and political factors.

Pastoral Migration Today

In significant numbers, pastoralists are currently moving from the northern rangelands southward, into and through regions previously inaccessible to them due to the prevalence of tsetse and the threat of losing their animals to disease, and the distance from the security of home territory. Moving into and through the sparsely watered woodland, herders essentially "swamp hop," trekking from home areas or transitional zones to regions of seepage and flow, where both pasture and water can be found. Lying within woodland, having only localized grazing, and being infested with tsetse, these areas have been little utilized in the past. Today, herders experience greater pressure for grazing in home areas, so are willing to accept greater risks than before; at the same time technology and infrastructure--in particular veterinary drugs and roads--are available that make those risks less unacceptable.

Cattle are often treated with prophylactic drugs against the threat of trypanosomiasis, in particular samarine, before herders attempt to penetrate the forests. Relatively rapid movement through tsetse zones is possible because of roads that allow Sukuma, for instance, to slice directly southward to the tsetse-free zone of the south proximal to Lake Rukwa, rather than diverting eastward to the tsetse-free corridor from Iringa to Mbeya, where they are less politically welcome. Movements are also facilitated by better communications between regions, because word is more easily passed back by previous migrants, indicating the best routes and preferable destinations. Scouts may go ahead by bus or train, returning for livestock when plans are made. In some cases, pastoralists are known to have sent their livestock from region to region by train, decreasing the losses inevitable in trekking. Thus pastoralists use the technological opportunities of today to effect their migrations, overcoming their inhibitions regarding a political ecology dominated by Miombo forests and groups well-entrenched along the narrow tsetse-free corridor.

Sukuma have long been expanding throughout the northern zone into relatively uninhabited areas of Maswa, Shinyanga, and Geita (Brandstrom 1985: 20-21) and into areas occupied by Nyamwezi, who speak essentially the same language but who practice forms of

168

forest agriculture seldom combined with animal husbandry. Sukuma herders live at the periphery of such villages as Moto Moto, primarily occupied by cotton-producing Nyamwezi who own few livestock of their own. Herders here are resented and play no role in long-term regional plans, although they exploit grazing land little used by others and provide milk and meat through exchange with villagers. Other Sukuma migrants elude village control altogether, moving directly into the forest to settle in glades and clearings, near swamps that provide dry season grazing and regions of lower tsetse challenge. Their animals develop a sort of "premunity" to trypanosomiasis, resistant to fresh infection but liable to recrudescence under stress (Birley 1982: 11):

> Cattle mortality is then often highest at the end of the dry season when nutrition is poor and the herd is stressed. It was the custom in Sukumaland to graze the cattle in woodland at that time, for the threat of further infection in the premunized herd would be smaller than the threat of recrudescence due to nutritional stress (Ibid.: 11-12).

These forest dwellers are viewed with awe and scorn by villagers, who see them as living like animals, outside of normal society. Such migrants utilize the Mbugas northwest in the Ulyankulu Forest Reserve, southwest in the Ugalla Forest Reserve, southeast in the Sikonge Forest Reserve, and east along the Mwembere River and swamp (ODA 1982). By occupying the deep tsetse-infested forests, these migrants are penetrating some of the last internal frontiers of Africa, as technical "trespassers" of Forest Reserves, the legal classification of most of the unused woodlands.

Many Sukuma use Tabora Region as a way-station on their way southward. Sukuma are channeled southward through Tabora because of difficulties in their moving eastward through regions occupied by Maasai, Taturu, Barabaig, and Gogo, who fully use existing range resources. Although Sukuma exercise a certain power of social intimidation over Nyamwezi to their south, even where they are in a minority, they are insecure themselves in the face of pastoralists to their east. On the long trek southward from Tabora to Rukwa, they may stop along the road in the forest to graze for several days or weeks.

After being ejected by the Kisongo Maasai in the nineteenth century. Parakuiyo occupied the neighboring districts of Handeni, Bagamoyo, Kilosa, and Dodoma, from which some have migrated to Morogoro Region since at least the 1950s. The swamp region of the upper Wami River, which lies northwestward of Morogoro town, has proven to be attractive dry season grazing because it is a relatively tsetse-free zone, unoccupied by any other livestock keepers. From Morogoro, Parakuiyo have moved southwestward to the great upland Kilombero swamps, to which Sukuma also migrate. From there, Sukuma have been known to penetrate directly into the most distant and tsetse-ridden forest to reach the Mbwemkuru swamps near Liwale in Lindi Region, where no livestock were traditionally maintained. Movement also occurs from Morogoro and Kilombero further down the main road/rail line to Mbeya Region, where lie the Usangu Plains, a locus of seasonal swamps at the upper reaches of a tributary of the Great Ruaha, which represent the far southern reaches of the great East African semi-arid grasslands.

The complex short and long-distance movements of individual herdowners in Tanzania to localized dry season grazing near the tsetse-ridden forests actually represent a single general pattern of southward migration, with convergence of Sukuma from the northern zone and Parakuiyo Maasai from the central zone in the Usangu Plains in Mbeya, completing a process of north/south pastoral migration begun thousands of years ago but halted until the present by the great Miombo forests of Tanzania.[3]

Comparative Factors in Pastoral and Agro-Pastoral Migration

The most prominent participants in the "new" migrations in Tanzania are the Sukuma and the Parakuiyo Maasai, the former agro-pastoralists, the latter specialized pastoralists in a complementary relationship with neighboring cultivators.[4] Comparable movement does not appear to be carried out by the (Kisongo) Maasai-proper, who inhabit the semi-arid Arusha Region in the northern rangelands. Herders invariably point to the search for better quality pasture as the material reason for migration, but lack of pasture--seasonally and periodically common across all herding regions--is not a sufficient explanation in itself, without an account of the processes by which the human community produces given environmental conditions and under certain circumstances perceives them as inadequate. In Tanzania today, specialized and agro-pastoralists are both engaged in significant long-distance migration (Parakuiyo and Sukuma) and are not (Kisongo Maasai), while paradoxically most movement is occuring from the less arid rather than more arid regions by Sukuma rather than Kisongo. The question is how, for the pastoral and agro-pastoralists concerned, material factors of human and animal demography and the quality and management of the rangelands bear on decisions by herders to migrate, within the larger social and cultural context of the values and functions of livestock, the aims of animal husbandry, the nature and

170

availability of labor, relations between stock-raising and agriculture and between pastoralists and farmers, and the political ecology within which groups are situated.

Pastoral and Agro-Pastoral Holdings: A Contrast

Although in 1984 Arusha and Shinyanga Regions both contained slightly less than 2 million cattle (Arusha, 1,864,410; Shinyanga, 1,810,600), per capita livestock holdings were significantly different given the much higher population densities in Shinyanga, with 2.5 per person in Arusha and 1.5 in Shinyanga. Actually, the majority of cattle in Arusha Region are held by the Maasai of only three districts, in which average holding are close to 10. At selected Parakuiyo villages, average holdings were significantly higher, at approximately 24 per person in Kambala Village and 21 per person in Twatwatwa Village in Morogoro Region, compared with Sukuma cattle holdings of approximately 1.4 per person in Bupandagila Village and 1.8 per person in Mwamashela Village in Shinyanga Region. But average holdings often mask significant disparities in the actual distribution of livestock among herding families or among herders and farmers in a regional setting. For instance, livestock tends to be concentrated in the hands of approximately half the Sukuma population, only 49 percent of households of the Mara Region owning any cattle at all, while 12 percent own 60 percent of the total, nearly 40 percent of cattle being owned by 13 percent of households, nearly 60 percent by 27 percent of households, in Mwamashela Village in Shinyanga Region.[5]

It almost goes without saying that the functions of livestock differ significantly among communities and families, in which animal wealth varies from 1.5 to over 20 cattle per person, leaving aside ubiquitous small stock. Sukuma with far greater interest and investment in animal husbandry than others do not necessarily have less involvement and interest in cultivation. Indeed, herd ownership is often positively correlated with acreage farmed and crops sold, in part because access to animals provides a farming advantage and successful farming provides access to funds to invest in animals (see below). In general, wealthier Sukuma herd owners seem to be more involved in outmigration, not only due to the search for resources but also in response to village pressure, because one herd of several hundred can easily graze an area that would otherwise support the modest herds of perhaps 20 other families. Almost by definition, the herds of more specialized pastoralists are more evenly distributed, due to the subsistence role they play, though the wealthy also represent an important category of migrants among Parakuiyo.

171

The Value and Function of Livestock: A Comparison

Despite similarities in animal care and milk production, livestock functions differ significantly between agro-pastoralists and more specialized pastoralists, as do their respective systems of economic and symbolic valuations of animals. The relative domestic value of livestock tends to be higher among agro-pastoralists, perhaps due in part to the strictly formal determinant of supply, given their relatively smaller herds and per capita holdings. Cattle also provide traction and manure, which increases their "generalized" value. Livestock also represents a medium in which returns on agricultural produce can be invested, thus clearly serving as stores of value and means of capital accumulation for Sukuma, a fact consciously recognized by Sukuma, who call domestic livestock their "banks" (cf. Schneider 1979). Like any form of wealth, livestock inevitably signifies "prestige" and serves as a means of exchange and a token of social relations, as in bridewealth. But this dimension does not contradict but rather reinforces that in the presence of cash crop production in a semi-commercialized rural economy, lacking adequate banking and credit facilities and faced with continuous monetary inflation, the use of livestock for essentially "financial" purposes is both attractive and rational. In Tanzania, government officials and urban dwellers increasingly invest in livestock. This investment function represents a linkage between the two sectors of the agro-pastoral domestic economy and through it the subsistence and commercial sectors of the national economy, which significantly increases potential for herd growth by the household through making available capital from the farming sector with which animals can be procured.

In more specialized pastoral economies, exemplified by the Maasai, livestock tend to serve fewer economic functions, with the subsistence factor becoming paramount. Milk forms the basis for the family diet, rather than a supplement; meat may be regularly consumed, especially through the slaughter of small stock, though of course not so much as to diminish the herd's breeding potential. Because greater time and attention are dedicated to animal care and relatively greater range resources are available, the growth of herds through reproduction is relatively higher and of greater importance, representing as it does the major form of domestic economic growth. But the relative value of any one animal may tend to be lower, so animals tend to be used more freely in exchange. Bridewealth, however, tends to be a much lower "ritualized" number in Maasai communities (5-6 animals), whereas it tends to be a much higher variable number among Sukuma (17-25 are common figures), varying with the wealth, status, and age of participants; in 1975-1976, the average bridewealth given in Mwanza was 13, in Shinyanga 23

(Texas A & M 1976, cited in Grindle 1980:8). Although pastoralists are involved in livestock markets and reinvest returns from livestock trading or cash incomes in livestock, there is little evidence that livestock are seen as "investments" as such, perhaps because of their primary subsistence importance and the fact that in general Maasai have no alternative productive sector from which surplus can be extracted.

The Commercialization of Livestock

Despite the belief of Tanzanians that herders have little commercial activity, in fact Maasai and Sukuma--who together may hold over half the entire national herd-- contribute significantly to the national livestock market. In fact, the commercial productivity of traditional grazing areas is higher than that of state-run commercial (Naco) ranches, and only in percentage offtake, around 12 percent do the NACO ranches appear to surpass the traditional small-scale herder, with 6-7 percent annual offtake (Birley 1982:9). Under normal circumstances, commercial offtake varies within limits defined by a minimum representing the cash needs of the family and a maximum representing the breeding requirements of the herd. In Tanzania, pastoral Maasai appear to be relatively more involved in cattle sales than the agro-pastoral Sukuma, which may be attributed primarily to the difference between pastoral and agro-pastoral systems.

First, cash crops such as cotton provide for many cash needs of agro-pastoralists, who also may have fewer needs for purchased foodstuffs than specialized pastoralists, given the more varied nature of their production and subsistence. So the dependence of the agro-pastoralist on the marketing and exchange of livestock paradoxically may be much less than that of the pastoralist, due to lower limits on offtake (due to lesser need to buy grain and a smaller breeding herd) and the availability of alternative sources of cash. Second, while livestock keepers do respond to differentials in prices offered for their livestock, these responses are also shaped by the generalized value of livestock within each system. For instance, some herd owners in Shinyanga are reluctant to sell in local markets because of awareness of higher prices being offered in the national capital. And in Arusha Region, official livestock markets have virtually disappeared, given higher prices being offered for livestock in Kenya and the black market between the two countries. Livestock keepers often experience difficulties in gaining access to markets, because infrastructure is often absent and the number of traders at auctions fewer and their demand less than the supply of animals provided by herd owners. But independent of price offered, the domestic value of cattle in the smaller herd common

to agro-pastoralists will be higher, which -- despite a
relatively free market that now exists through local livestock
markets in Tanzania -- explains why Sukuma often refuse to sell,
while richer Maasai stockowners sell huge numbers of animals,
seeking higher prices over the border. Thus agro-pastoralists
are able to use their alternative sources of subsistence and cash
returns both to secure greater autonomy from the market and to
accumulate value in livestock, through a dynamic of herd growth.

Animal Husbandry and Range Use: A Comparison

Between 1928 and 1978, Tanzania's national cattle herd
increased from 4.4 to 12 million. Although increase occurred in
all regions, the Sukuma-dominated Lake Zone experienced a
remarkable 3.5-fold rise, with its proportion of the national
total increasing from 25 percent to over 35 percent, whereas the
Maasai-dominated Northern range zone experienced only a 1.5-fold
increase, its overall proportion dropping from nearly 27 percent
to 20 percent (Government of Tanzania 1978). More recently, from
1978 to 1984, Arusha Region (Maasai) actually experienced a
decline in cattle numbers of over 7 percent, with Shinyanga
Region (Sukuma) witnessed an increase of 10 percent. The
contrast between relative stability in Maasai regions and the
dynamic growth in Sukuma regions illustrates different processes
at work over the last half century.[6]

With increased Sukuma human and herd populations, acreage
given over to cultivation has also consistently expanded,
primarily through growth in cotton production stimulated by
higher commodity prices. As a result, less grazing has been
available for an increasing herd, exacerbating a tendency toward
overgrazing that began in Shinyanga during the mid-Colonial
period, decades ago. It has been suggested that

... increased cotton production appears to have
introduced new and accelerating problems of soil
erosion and exhaustion. More cotton is today being
grown on more land at the expense of grazing land and
fallow (Birley 1982:7).

Less efficient use of range resources also has resulted from
the villagization process of the 1970s, in which a relatively
dispersed peasantry was concentrated in residential centers where
administrative, health, and social services were to be provided.
A smaller radius of effective village grazing and cultivation
inevitably resulted, with more distant areas left underutilized.
At the same time, due to labor shortages, with more children
attending schools and greater incentives for adult labor for cash
cropping, time dedicated to herding diminished, with shorter

174

temporal and spatial cycles of grazing (herds in Shinyanga often being kept in their kraals until 11 a.m.) resulting in heavier use of pasture near the homestead. Although Sukuma population growth, village settlement patterns, dispersed labor allocation, and increased cash cropping have led to less efficient range use and thus land degradation, agro-pastoral range use is generally less efficient than that in specialized pastoralism, given sedentarism, competing demands for labor, and less specialized knowledge of and interest in herding (Brandstrom et.al. 1979; 1985).

Despite lower levels of herd growth in the northern districts of Arusha Region inhabited by Maasai (Kiteto, Monduli, and Ngorongoro Districts), localized overgrazing is paradoxically combined with underutilized pasture. Critical high potential dry-season grazing land has been lost to agricultural encroachment, the gazetting of national parks, game reserves, and conservation areas, and the development of large-scale commercial ranches and irrigated farms, increasing pressure on remaining pastureland. Specialized Maasai herders may be more vulnerable than Sukuma to the depredations of drought due to their lack of alternative sources of subsistence or production of crop residues to use as dry-season fodder. Despite increasing loss of rangeland to alternative uses, bush encroachment, and tsetse infestation, followed by pastoralist retreat to the vicinity of localized well systems and increased grazing pressure, little Maasai migration appears to have occurred out of the northern rangelands, perhaps in part due to the significant herd losses recently experienced that decreased pressure on grazing resources.

In contrast, many Parakuiyo Maasai living beyond the northern rangelands as minorities among agricultural majorities are today migrating, continuing a pattern established since the 1950s. In Morogoro Region, several designated "pastoral villages" have been formed for Parakuiyo in an attempt to limit their movement. In each case, pressure on pastoral village resources has been increased by loss of land to state NACO ranches formed next to or within pastoral villages and by competition with rice growers for access to land and water. Parakuiyo pastoral villages are heavily stocked compared with northern Maasai districts. However, grazing appears to be evenly used, with theoretically irrational stocking rates made possible through utilization of grazing resources outside allotted pastoral villages during the dry season, in neighboring villages, forest reserves, or even state ranches. Grazing cycles include full use of daylight hours with both child and adult labor more available for careful husbandry than is true in the agro-pastoral Sukuma case, due to lower levels of educational participation and fewer competing economic demands.

175

Pastoral/Farming Relations

Despite a huge national herd, per capita cattle holdings in Tanzania remain relatively low, at 0.7 cattle per person in 1978 (Grindle 1980:1). A few groups in the north hold the majority of the country's livestock, while in many other areas such as Morogoro, Parakuiyo Maasai tend to raise animals, with other groups such as Luguru or Kaguru primarily cultivating, in an ethnic division of labor illustrated by cattle holdings in Morogoro Region in 1978. Although average holdings were a quite low .32 per person in the tsetse-infested region, in designated "livestock villages" average Parakuiyo Maasai holdings were over 20 cattle per person. Although among Sukuma agro-pastoralists, competition between pastoral and farming specialists occurs within the same ethnic group and community, for the Parakuiyo, pastoral/farming competition involves ethnic as well as economic politics.[7]

In the Sukuma case, pasture tends to have no formal village status and the use of grazing land tends not to involve recognized usufruct rights as is so with land cleared and cultivated. Areas for grazing do tend, however, to be informally or "customarily" regulated, as in Mwamashele Village in Shinyanga where dry season pastures are reserved, herders being fined 500 shillings for using them before the agreed date. Crop residues in Bupandagil are allocated to collective use except in fields immediately adjacent to a farmer's homestead. Large herd owners, nevertheless, are forced to move outside village boundaries to use neutral dry season pastures along with members of other villages, including the Maswa Game Reserve (illegally or with special permission) and the great Mwembere Swamps. Smaller "Mbuga" swamps provide regional sources of dry season grazing and water. These dry season resources may ease competition between large herd owners and home villagers, but not without cost and danger. Maswa Game Reserve is prohibited grazing and also links Sukuma with the Maasai of Ngorongoro and the Serengeti, who raid through the Reserve (as do Sukuma), thus use of the reserve pins Sukuma between the government and pastoral competitors. Similarly, Sukuma use the Mwembere Swamp only with trepidation, because it joins them with the Taturu pastoralists in the east who raid them. The existence of regional dry-season resources thus does not necessarily remove internal pressures on large herd owners for long-distance outmigration.

Seasonal division of wet and dry season pastures is also found among Parakuiyo Maasai pastoralists of Morogoro Region. But due to lack of labor commitments outside of pastoralism, there is probably less tendency to keep herds within village boundaries when grazing quality declines. Herders from Kambala Village tend to use grazing in nearby agricultural villages, where conflicts arise over trampled crops. However, access to water and riverine grazing within their own village is limited by the presence of outside farmers, who cultivate rice during a few critical months in the year. During the dry season, animals from Twatwatwa Village are taken illegally into a nearby forest or onto a neighboring parastatal ranch, technically prohibited but understocked, which was formed on land claimed by the pastoralists. Shortage of grazing, local resentment of herders, and the ambivalence of government toward providing tenurial rights to pastoralists increases pressure on Parakuiyo and exacerbates their political and economic insecurity. Migration is not an option acted upon by the rich alone, but by herd owners at all levels of wealth, who seek interstices of grazing and water among cultivators, forests, and tsetse.

Maasai in the north do not come into such direct contact and conflict with farmers, although the extent of their grazing areas has been eroded by the establishment of large-scale commercial ranches and irrigated farms and by encroachment of Arusha agro-pastoralists. The advantages are clearly less for Maasai in migrating to areas they would share with others, when they exclusively control northern rangelands, the pastoral heartland of Tanzania. The intrinsic value of the northern rangelands for pastoralism, the relative political strength of pastoralists, and the lack of pastoral/agricultural conflict there, makes migration a less attractive option for Kisongo, even during periods of drought and grazing scarcity. Indeed, there is no reason to believe that Parakuiyo would have left the Maasai plains voluntarily, to disperse themselves among farming peoples, if they had not been essentially expelled by the southward expansion of the Kisongo in the nineteenth century.

Conclusion

Patterns of Maasai pastoralist and Sukuma agro-pastoralist range use thus differ, with important implications for herd growth, range degradation, and subsequent migration. Although agro-pastoralists have smaller family and per capita livestock holdings, their animals serve a wider range of social and economic functions than those of more specialized pastoralists, with larger subsistence herds. Agro-pastoral settlement patterns, especially under villagization, lead to less efficient use of range resources and heavier localized overgrazing, with the more dispersed settlements of pastoralists--even under villagization--involving more even use of range resources and less overgrazing, except where movement is highly circumscribed. Dependence on and involvement in livestock marketing tends to be

177

lower among Sukuma, due to their greater domestic economic autonomy, and somewhat higher among Maasai, due to their narrower range of production activities and greater current reliance on the market for subsistence. Parakuiyo Maasai inhabit checkered regions of sporadic pasture, more similar to the Sukuma than the Maasai, who predominate in their own districts. Grazing pressures are of course exacerbated by low rainfall, such as has been experienced twice in the last decade, in 1974-1975 and 1983-1984. Thus drought, demography, and range use conspire in stimulating different responses by Sukuma and Maasai in the north and dispersed Parakuiyo.

The current pastoral migration is both old and new, being both a continuation of millenia of north/south migrations along the East African corridor and a contemporary response to the predicaments and possibilities of the twentieth century, the artifacts of statehood and technology proper to that elusive "modernization." Veterinary drugs, roads, railways, and relative freedom of peaceful movement make possible penetration and traversing of the tsetse-infested Miombo forests, rendering accessible localized grazing resources previously beyond the reach of northern herders.

Current Sukuma and Parakuiyo migrations involve both "continuous" short-distance moves to local and neighboring areas and long-distance "treks" through Miombo woodlands to remote destinations. Such treks are motivated by current demographic, ecological, and political conditions, and are made possible by long-distance communications and social networks, which must have been much more difficult to establish and maintain in the past. Treks are usually by individuals, families, or small groups rather than by communities or pastoral sections, and involve tentative "scouts," "frontier" experiments, followed by a larger number of "colonists," whose travel is made more secure by reports and plans that pass back and forth between new and home areas.

The picture of societal and cultural dynamics involved in current Tanzanian migrations may hold for past periods of transition and movement in East Africa. Recent work on pastoral and agro-pastoral relations in East Africa demonstrates the intermingling of groups in complex regional social and economic systems, involving bilingualism, inter-group marriage and exchange, and relatively long-distance movement made possible by the maintenance of social ties over space and time (Sobania 1979; Lamphear 1985; Waller 1985). Today in the Usangu Plains we find an admixture of pastoral groups from the north together with local farmers in various relations of conflict and cooperation, perhaps not so dissimilar to conditions that existed in the past in the Kilimanjaro/Meru/Sanga Plains region of Northern Tanzania, or the Nakuru/Mau/Kinangop region of Central Kenya (Galaty in press). Many of the pastoral goups we now take for granted are complex amalgams of previous groups that melded together in areas of common migration, experiencing both complementary and competitive forms of resource use and both solidary and conflictual types of social interaction and exchange.

The new pastoral migrations rise out of constraints livestock keepers experience in their home areas. To risk generalization out of a complex process, it appears that migration involves the strong rather than the weak, the relatively well-endowed rather than the poor, and the younger rather than the older. Migrants have experienced frustration and conflict in their home areas, intrinsic to population growth, economic intensification, pastoral/agricultural competition, stratification of herd owners, and local power struggles. In this context, demographic and environmental pressures find specific social and cultural forms of expression, including household movement. Migration is one outcome of current conditions and opportunities, which challenges the constraints of ecology and disease that for so long cut off the avenue of southward movement in Tanzania. The pastoral migrations of today are aggressive, ambitious, and risky responses equivalent to those of past herders, who in moving southward influenced the shape of East African history and society.

Acknowledgments

Material for this paper largely derives from my participation in the 1985 FAO Tanzania Livestock Programming Mission as a sociological consultant. For shared insights and background knowledge, I am indebted to the other members of the mission, W. Ferguson, R. J. Grindle, A. Jordan, and I. Lane, for indispensable assistance to members of the FAO livestock development team in Tanzania, J. Davis, C. I. Beale, and R. McConnell, for help and facilitation to officers in the Tanzanian Ministry of Agriculture and Livestock Development, and for collegiality to Reuben Ole Kune. The paper was originally presented at the session on Culture and Demography at the 1985 Arid Lands Research and Development Conference in Tucson, Arizona, my participation being made possible by a travel grant from the Faculty of Graduate Studies and Research of McGill University. I appreciate comments on an early draft or presentation of the paper by Dan Aronson, Per Brandstrom, Gudrun Dahl, Peter Little, and Eric Worby. The paper benefits from research in East Africa among Maassai communities supported by a Reseearch Grant and Leave Fellowship from the Social Science and

Humanities Research Council of Canada, a Team Grant from the
Fonds FCAR of Quebec, and a Cooperative Grant from the
International Development Research Centre.

Notes

[1] During the colonial period, Il-Parakuiyo were pejoratively
called "Wakwavi" to distinguish them from the (Central)
Maasai-proper, but today are increasingly called by the more
prestigious term "Maasai," which is gaining general currency for
Maa-speakers. There is no standard orthography for the name
"Parakuiyo," variants being "Baraguyu" (Beidelman 1960) and
"Parakuyo" (Rigby 1985); the term likely derives from the Maasai
term "Il-Parakuo," signifying "wealthy or successful
pastoralists." The form "Il-Parakuiyo" was suggested to me by
Mtari Ole Moreto from Kambala Village in Morogoro District.

[2] Issues regarding pastoral migration are raised in Waller
(1985) and Dyson-Hudson and McCabe (1985). After hearing a
presentation of this paper, Per Brandstrom kindly made available
to me his paper on "The Agro-Pastoral Dilemma" (1985), based on
years of experience among the Sukuma, which largely anticipated
the discussion of the dynamics of Sukuma migration put forward
here.

[3] Factors in migration are discussed for Tabora Region in Hendy
(1980) and ODA (1982), for Mbeya Region in FAO (1983) and
Hiemstra (1981), and for the Usangu Plains specifically in Rufiji
Basin Development Authority (1981), Tanzania (1985c), and
Hazlewood and Livingstone (1978). These references have also
been drawn on for other discussion of Tabora, Mbeya, and Usangu
in the paper.

[4] Government and development agency reports relevant to
Tanzania as a whole have been drawn on for the comparisons in
this section, including Akilimali (1983), FAO (1984), and the
Government of Tanzania (1983; 1984; 1985b).

[5] Treatment of livestock holdings, distribution, and sale has
drawn on FAO (1984) and Government of Tanzania (1978; 1983;
1985b).

[6] Information relevant to range use by Sukuma agro-pastoralists
and Maasai specialized pastoralists has been drawn from
literature on Shinyanga Region (Ecosystems 1982; FAO 1972; De
Wilde 1967; Malcolm 1953; Birley 1984), the Lake Zone (Tanzania

180

1982) and Arusha Region (FAO 1972; Galaty 1986; Bennett 1984).
This material has been drawn on for treatment of the northern
rangelands elsewhere in the paper.

[7] Treatment of pastoralist/agriculturalist relations has drawn
from Government of Tanzania (1985a) for Parakuiyo of Morogoro
Region, references cited above for Usangu Plains, and from Galaty
and Aronson (1981) and Sandford (1983) for more general issues.

References

Akilimali, B. M. 1983. Desk Study for Preparatory Assistance
    Mission to Tanzania. Programme for the Control of African
    Trypanosomiasis and Related Developments in Tanzania. Rome:
    FAO.
Ambrose, S. 1984. The Introduction of Pastoral Adaptations to the
    Highlands of East Africa. In: J. Clark and S. Brandt, eds.,
    From Hunters to Farmers. Berkeley: University of California
    Press.
Beidelman, T. 1960. The Baraguyu. Tanganyika Notes and Records
    No. 55.
Bennett, John W. 1984. Political Ecology and Development Projects
    Affecting Pastoralist Peoples in East Africa. Research Paper
    No. 80, Madison, Wisconsin: Land Tenure Center.
Birley, M. H. 1982. Resource Management in Sukumaland, Tanzania.
    Africa 52 (2).
Brandstrom, P. 1985. The Agro-Pastoral Dilemma: Underutilization
    of Overexploitation of Land among the Sukuma of Tanzania.
    Working Papers in African Studies No. 8. University of Uppsala:
    African Studies Programme.
Brandstrom, P., J. Hultin and J. Lindstrom. 1979. Aspects of
    Agro-Pastoralism in East Africa. Research Report No. 51,
    Uppsala: The Scandinavian Institute of African Studies.
David, K. 1982. The BIEA Southern Sudan Expedition of 1979:
    interpretation of the archaeological data. In: J. Mack & P.
    Robertshaw, eds., Culture History in the Southern Sudan.
    Memoir No. 8, Nairobi: British Institute in East Africa.
De Wilde, J. C. 1967. Experiences with Agricultural Development
    in Tropical Africa, Vol. II. The Case Studies. Baltimore: John
    Hopkins Univ. Press.
Dyson-Hudson, R. and T. McCabe. 1985. South Turkana Nomadism:
    Coping with an Unpredictably Varying Environment. New Haven:
    Human Relations Area Files, Inc. HRAFlex Books, FL17-001,
    Ethnography Series.
Ecosystems, Ltd. 1982. Southeast Shinyanga Land Use Study.
    Shinyanga Rural Integrated Development Programme.

Ehret, C. 1982. Population movement and culture contact in the Southern Sudan, c. 3000 BC to ADX 1000. In: J. Mack and P. Robertshaw, eds., Culture History in the Southern Sudan. Nairobi: BIEA.

Food and Agriculture Organization of the United Nations (FAO). 1972. Livestock Development in Masailand, Gogoland and Sukumaland. Interim Report. Rome: FAO (for UNDP).

----- 1983. Proposals for an Indicative Development Strategy for Mbeya Region, 1982-2000. Regional Integrated Development Plan and Rural Development Project, Mbeya Region, Tanzania. Rome: FAO.

----- 1984. Report of the Preparatory Assistance Mission to the United Republic of Tanzania. FAO Programme for the Control of African Animal Trypanosomiasis and Related Development. Rome: FAO.

Ford, J. 1971. The Role of Trypanosomiasis in African Ecology. Oxford: Clarendon Press.

Ford, J. and K. M. Katondo. 1973. The Distribution of TseTse Flies in Africa 1973. Organization of African Unity. Nairobi: Interafrican Bureau of Animal Resources (Map Series).

Fosbrooke, H. A. 1956. The Masai Age-Group System as a Guide to Tribal Chronology. African Studies, Vol. 15.

Galaty, J. G. 1987. Scale, Politics and Cooperation in Organizations of East African Pastoralist Development, In: D. W. Atwood and B. S. Baviskar, eds., Cooperatives and Rural Development, Delhi: Oxford University Press.

----- In Press. People and Pasture, Politics and Prayer: History and Dialectics in Maasai Pastoral Specialization and Expansion. In J. Galaty and P. Bonte, eds., Herders, Warriors and Traders: The Political Economy of African Pastoralism.

Galaty, J. G. and D. Aronson. 1981. Research Priorities and Pastoralist Development: What is to be done?, Introduction to J. Galaty, et. al. eds., The Future of Pastoral Peoples. Ottawa: International Development Research Centre, pp. 15-26.

Grindle, R. J. 1980. Economic Losses from East Coast Fever in Sukumaland, Tanzania. m.n. Centre for Tropical Veterinary Medicine, University of Edinburgh.

Hazlewood, A. and I. Livingstone. 1978. The Development Potential of the Usangu Plains of Tanzania. Commonwealth Fund for Technical Cooperation.

Hendy, C. R. C. 1980. Livestock Production in Tabora Region. Tabora Rural Integrated Development Programme, Tanzania. Overseas Development Administration. Surrey: Land Resources Development Centre.

Hiemstra, Y. G., A. S. Lamosai, and K. W. Mchau. 1981. A Livestock Reconnaissance Survey of Mbeya Region. Mbeya RIDEP. Dar es Salaam: Ministry of Livestock Development, United Republic of Tanzania.

Jacobs, A. 1972. The Discovery and Oral History of Narosura. Azania 7.

Lamphear, J. 1985. The Persistence of Hunting and Gathering in a 'Pastoral' World. International Symposium: African Hunters-Gatherers. University of Cologne: Institut fur Afrikanistik.

Malcolm, D. W. 1953. Sukumaland: an African Peoples and Their Country. London: Oxford Univ. Press.

Overseas Development Administration. 1982. Land Evaluation and Land use Planning in Tabora Region, Final Report. Tabora RIDEP, Tanzania. ODA, Surrey: Land Resources Development Centre.

Sandford, S. 1983. Management of Pastoral Development in the Third World. (ODI) Chicester & N.Y.: John Wiley & Sons.

Rigby, P. 1979. Cattle and Kinship among the Gogo - a Semi-pastoral Society of Central Tanzania. Ithaca and London: Cornell Univ. Press.

----- 1985. Persistent Pastoralists: Nomadic Societies in Transition. London: Zed Books.

Robertshaw, P. and D. Collett. 1983. The identification of pastoral peoples in the archaelolgical record: an example from East Africa. World Archaeology, Vol. 15, No. 1.

Rufiji Basin Development Authority. 1981. Conflicting Interests in the Usangu Plains. Dar es Salaam.

Schneider, H. K. 1979. Livestock and Equality in East Africa. Bloomington: Indiana University Press.

Sobania, N. 1979. The Historical Tradition of the Peoples of the Eastern Lake Turkana Basin. c. 1840-1925. Ph.D. dissertation, School of Oriental and African Studies, University of London.

Tanzania, United Republic of. 1978. The 1978 Livestock Count in Mainland Tanzania and Beef Demand and Supply Study. Ministry of Africulture.

----- 1982. Lake Zone Regional Physical Plan, Main Report. Ministry for Lands, Housing and Urban Development/Tanzanian-Finnish Planning Team/UPD. Ministry for Foreign Affairs of Finland.

----- 1983. The Livestock Policy of Tanzania. Ministry of Livestock Development. Dar es Salaam: Government Printer.

----- 1984. Tanzania National Food Strategy: a framework for action, Vol. 2. Ministry of Africulture and Livestock Development.

----- 1985a. Range Development Programme of the Traditional Livestock Sector: Arusha, Kilimanjaro, Tanga and Morogoro Regions. Rome: ASCON Associated Consultants.

----- 1985b. Provisional 1984 Livestock Census Cattle Results. Ministry of Agriculture and Livestock Development.

----- 1985c. Problems Affecting Livestock Development in Usangu Plains: in Mbeya District - Mbeya Region. Ministry of Agriculture and Livestock Development, Mbeya District Livestock Development Office.

Waller, Richard. 1985. Ecology, Migration, and Expansion in East Africa. African Affairs.

10. CRIME IN THE DEVELOPMENT PROCESS

Gregory F. Truex

The sociology of crime has been a mainstay of European and American academic study for well over a century, but comparative and cross-national research has remained surprisingly underdeveloped. The reasons put forth to explain this revolve around: (1) methodological difficulties with and underreporting of different indicators of crime; and (2) lack of longitudinal, cross-national statistics on crime incidences (Archer and Gartner 1984). However, the lack of robust comparative research reflects not just informational and methodological inadequacies, but also the lack of crime-related issues that will generate interest and resources for the task.

Thus, although there have been recent government-sponsored research programs on international drug trafficking, political violence, terrorism, and hijacking, there has not been a sustained concern with cross-national aspects of "crime behavior" in general. The prospects for such a sustained concern are not good: the linkage of crime behavior to other issues remains anecdotal even when the linkage enjoys scandalous infamy (as in the case of bribery of public officials by multinational firms).

Yet, in some key instances, this linkage is direct, obvious, and widely recognized. Critics (e.g., Bayley 1970; Lopez-Ray 1970; Myrdal 1970) commonly tie apparent defalcations in development schemes in Third World countries, as well as the more common corruptions of government officials through bribery, payoffs, and kickbacks, to the processes of modernization and development. More recently, economic anthropologists and others have described "illegitimate" and criminal behavior as integral to the economic processes of the urban informal sector of developing countries.

The theme of these descriptions is that illegitimate and illegal economic activities are part of a subsistence strategy imposed on participants in the urban informal economy by social, economic, and political forces that exclude them from the benefits of the formal sector. In these descriptions, the members of the urban subproletariat are both passive victims of the wider economic system and, at the same time, rational, active economizers.

This view of the economic basis of crime interestingly links both micro- and macroeconomic explanations while subtly appealing to a widely held view of distributional justice (Cook and

Hegtvedt 1983; Greenberg and Cohen 1982). The abjectly poor of the Third World become their own Robin Hoods--in this case, robbing from the "haves" and giving themselves the opportunity for capital accumulation otherwise almost totally nonexistent.

This view is, however, somewhat at odds with current criminological descriptions and interpretations of crime behavior in developing countries. Although containing references to both illegitimate and illegal economic activities, the literature on the informal sector recognizes no particular connection between these activities and other, more violent, aspects of urban crime in developing nations. Focusing entirely on the productive and transfer effects of crime behavior simply dismisses social consequences that may, themselves, imply important economic relations.

The Concept of Opportunity

The concept of opportunity plays a central role in economic theory. The concept of opportunity also plays an important role in certain structural theories of crime, particularly of juvenile delinquency. However, the meanings of opportunity evoked by these uses differ in important ways.

Opportunity, in the sense of an economic alternative, is fundamental to the entire choice-theoretic foundation of marginalist economics. Costs, for example, are opportunities foresaken within this framework. The demand schedule facing a seller is the opportunity set for that seller. In the theory of consumer's choice under perfect competition, the opportunity set or curve would be the budget plane. One implicit aspect of the economic usage is that opportunity always represents attainable alternatives (Arrow 1963:73 and passim).

In crime theory, however, thwarted opportunity, the unattainable alternative, has been used as a cornerstone for theorizing. Merton (1957) argued that the discrepancy between cultural success norms and actual opportunities could lead to various adaptations, including criminal ones. Merton's original formulation has had a dominating impact in developing an "opportunity" theory of criminality. Cloward and Ohlin (1960), for example, developed the theory that lower-class male juvenile delinquency reflects development of neighborhood subcultures of personally able youths denied opportunities for illegitimate reasons. The concept of relative deprivation reflects this same orientation toward opportunities.

In general, one goal of development is to increase the aggregate of opportunities available in a society. The course of economic development may add new opportunities. It may also delete accustomed alternatives (driving peasants from the land, for example). Development may also increase the sensitivity of actors to relative cost, itself, by making comparison of opportunities possible through monetization and interruption of customary practice (cf. Neale 1971:28). Certainly, the impact of the new opportunities is differentially distributed among individuals and classes in developing countries.

Crime in Developing Countries

Although cross-national comparative crime research is poorly developed, it is not altogether lacking. Using admittedly inadequate statistics and largely unsystematic studies, Shelley summarized the general conclusions of current research (to 1981) concerning crime and modernization:

> Societies characterized by a predominance of violent crimes come to be dominated by crimes against poverty. The critical period of industrialization and mass migration to urban centers is the most disruptive of traditional family and other institutional patterns. Violence rises, but then declines as new institutional controls are formed. The rising standard of living accompanying modernization is then followed by increasing property crime. The latter results from relative, rather than absolute deprivation. . . (Short 1981:ix-x).

Although both violent and property crimes increase with modernization, the availability of goods and the proximity and impersonality of city life lead to a relative increase in property crime (Shelley 1981:44). However, the development process has also produced violent property offenders and gangs (Clinard and Abbott 1973; Lopez-Ray 1964; Mangin 1975; Tschoungui and Zumbach 1962) who have acquired new norms of consumption (beyond material needs) that lead to greater violence (Shelley 1981:44).

Nonetheless, property crime, without violence, "may still be the more prolific aspect of development" (Clinard and Abbott 1973:20). From the point of view of criminologists, this proliferation is not as significant as it may first appear. Although the (self-)reported rate of victimization from petty theft may be quite high--for example, over 30 percent for the poor of Kampala during a one-year period (Clinard and Abbott 1973:20)--"most of the property crime . . . does not involve large-scale loss of property" (Shelley 1981:44).

The high rate of small-scale property crime reflects the

187

limited mobility of recent urban migrants, where the very poor tend to commit crimes near their residence, often against a "victim not much different from the criminal" (Pierre et al. 1962; Shelley 1981:44; Tschoungui and Zumbach 1962:37). Thus, most informal sector property crime is a transfer from one very poor person to another. For the criminologist/sociologist, crime is a preceding condition to be influenced and modified by social processes such as urbanization and industrialization, as the subtitle of Shelley's book, The Impact of Urbanization and Industrialization on Crime, reveals. Crime is considered a particular example of the more general processes of the breakdown of social control.

From an economic point of view, however, property crimes are reasonably described as opportunities that society chooses to regulate closely. Of course, criminologists are perfectly aware of the economic implications of criminal activities. Shelley (1981:51) pointed out that the high crime rates for the developing nations of the Caribbean reflect the presence of many tourists and the peculiar geographic relation of the islands between the South American producers and the North American consumers of drugs. Nonetheless, there is a significant difference in the basic approach of the two academic orientations.

Economics of Informal Sector Crimes

Hypothesizing that more goods flow into the informal sector of the urban economy of Accra than flow out of it, Keith Hart argued that "urban crime may then be seen as a redistribution of wealth with income effects throughout the informal economy" (Hart 1973:86). The implications of Hart's formulation of an input-output model for the intersectorial flows of the urban economy are quite provocative:

> "Loot"--or static wealth lying idle in the homes of the bourgeoisie--is a stock, independent of current income flows, which is mobilised through theft into direct and indirect income for sub-proletarians (Hart 1973:86).

Within his framework, theft and burglary, as well as prostitution, embezzlement, and confidence games, are examples of service exporting activities and transfers that yield a net income flow, in money and goods, to the informal sector. Hustlers, money-lenders, drug-pushers, and gamblers do not yield such a flow because their "customers" are generally from the informal sector themselves (Hart 1973:86). Illegitimate economic activities create a net income flow to the participants in the informal sector, which gives the migrant, for example, a prospect

188

for accumulation of wealth that he or she would otherwise not obtain (Hart 1973:88 and passim). This net flow and prospect for accumulation depends, ultimately, on the validity of Hart's assertion that "illegitimate transfers are borne predominantly by the urban middle classes" (Hart 1973:86). Hart's viewpoint amounts to the claim that crime is economically rewarding to the urban poor--that is, crime pays.

Opportunity for Crime

Hart's formulation is a limited model of criminal behavior compared to the more general choice-theoretic (microeconomic) framework advocated by Becker (1968), Ehrlich (1973), Sjoquist (1973), and Stigler (1970). The Becker-Ehrlich-Sjoquist-Stigler (hence, BESS) models treat criminal behavior in an unrelentingly economic way: those personal and social facts about individuals that sociologists treat as determinants are taken as given. Social and class background, cultural predispositions to violence, risk preference, and all such behavioral characteristics are not modeled. Rather, BESS models handle the crime behavior problem in a most procrustean way:

In a sentence, the models of economic choice theory, of which the criminal choice is a special case, hypothesize that all individuals, criminal and non-criminal alike, respond to incentives; and if the costs and benefits associated with an action change, the agent's choices are also likely to change . . . the decision to commit an illegal act is reached via an egocentric cost-benefit analysis (Heineke 1978b:2).

Both Hart and BESS models deal with opportunities as the central issue. The BESS models implicitly and explicitly assume that benefits and costs associated with a given illegal or illegitimate act can be either monetary or psychic (although, in practice, psychic elements get expressed in monetary equivalents wherever possible) and that people fill their "portfolio" with illegitimate activities only if they have a rational expectation of greater gain from them. Hart linked his model directly to actual material goods ("loot"), whereas Ehrlich's theory (1973), for example, rests on the assumption that each individual tries to maximize a utility function for income that includes "psychic well-being" as well as money and material goods (1973:70).

Somewhat paradoxically, Ehrlich, the "classical economist," explicitly includes psychological and (implicitly) social variables, whereas Hart, the anthropologist, includes only money and material goods. Ehrlich's inclusion of non-monetary forms of reward, however, is a bit of a sham: he actually takes them as

189

"given"--that is, not subject to investigation.

The sociology of crime discounts the role of economic opportunity, but BESS models, to the contrary, emphasize such opportunities, utterly discounting social and cultural factors. In fact, BESS modelers allege that their results explain away such factors:

. . . many crimes against property, not unlike legitimate market activities, pay in the particular sense that their expected gains exceed their expected costs at the margin. This approach may be useful in explaining . . . a variety of specific characteristics associated with individual offenders. . . (Ehrlich 1973:111-112).

BESS models imply that inequalities in legitimate income play a major role in crime activities, because foregoing legitimate income is a cost (to be born if caught) affecting the portfolio of assets at risk. Empirical investigations of such inequalities, however, do not seem to support such an interpretation.

Stack (1984) investigated the inequality-property crime linkage with data from sixty-two nations. Multiple regression analysis indicated that inequality failed to generate crime at the cross-national level:

While research using American samples has demonstrated an inequality-property crime relationship . . . on the whole, this does not seem to be the case in other nations. Inequality may lead to alternative forms of deviant behavior that channel aggression inwardly. . . (Stack 1984:251).

Although the BESS approach places rational decision-making far ahead of any social or cultural effects, it does this at the expense of ethnographically substantiated, cross-culturally testable models. Similarly, although Hart's suggestive input-output model is provocatively appealing in terms of the relation it suggests between inequality of income and property crime, there is little evidence that his substantive assertions are generally characteristic of informal sector subproletarians.

Of course, Hart's thesis is not choice-theoretic and is not exactly reducible to the claim that crime pays for any particular individuals in the informal sector. He claims only that there is a net flow to the urban poor sector from such activities. Thus, Hart's thesis would remain valid, in the face of evidence that most urban poor criminals have a net loss from illegitimate activities, that poor criminals are under the influence of drugs when engaging in these activities, or, more tellingly, that most of their victims are as poor as they. BESS models are not indifferent to these microeconomic factors, although, in the main, they do not deal directly with them.

Nonetheless, these models are economic precisely because they place emphasis on the relative costs and benefits to economic participants, rather than attempting to explain crime through other social facts. Thus,

> by treating the individual's "taste for crime" as a datum, one may build a theory of criminal behavior based upon the opportunities confronting the potential offender. . .
> (Heineke 1978b:2; emphasis added).

The treatment of some categories of criminal activities as functions of the opportunities presented to their perpetrators is not entirely new. Sutherland's "white collar crime" (Sutherland, 1940; 1949) is certainly one such treatment. Other sociologists have attempted to delimit a range of nonviolent economic crimes to be treated in terms of the opportunities presented to their perpetrators (Edelhertz 1970, 1974; Geis 1968; Tappan 1947, 1960).

Horoszowski has uniquely developed his interest in "kinds of conducts related to economic motives . . . in which opportunity plays a dominant, highly provocative, role" (1980:55). This sense of "opportunity" borders on "enticement" because it refers to "convenient situational, timely, spatial and other circumstances favorable for certain advantageous occurrences or behavior" (1980:45). In fact, most such opportunities do not necessarily imply crimes in the normative sense, at all (1980:55-61). Rather, special economic opportunity conduct may be legal, or illegal, or legal but illegitimate (cf. Hart 1973), and so forth.

When presented with a special economic opportunity, one must make a decision: to take advantage of it or not (Horoszowski 1980:63). Of course, special economic opportunities do not only just present themselves, sometimes they are created. In any case, the special economic opportunity approach does not assume clear normative consensus about criminal conduct (as do BESS and Hart models). In the economic development context, the issues might be phrased in terms of questions such as "what special opportunities are presented to the urban poor?" and "given their economically precarious position, how do the urban poor avoid becoming such an opportunity to others (including the non-poor)?" The "special economic opportunity conduct" approach is fundamentally ethnographic. Coming to recognize and deal with the ubiquitous schemes and ploys of everyday economic life is a culture-laden enterprise (Horoszowski 1980:164-165).

Ethnography of Opportunity

For Velez-Ibanez, the ethnographic context of economic activity is primary (Velez-Ibanez 1983:95-111); he uses a method of exposition strongly suggestive of Lewis's (Lewis 1959, 1961) intense ethnographic accounts of the "culture of poverty" (which have fallen into some disrepute, see, for example, McGee 1979:59-62, and Rusque-Alcaino and Bromley 1979:187).

Velez-Ibanez does not use the term, but he does present very enlightening analyses of special economic opportunity conduct. Just as Lewis explored the psychological fragility of interfamilial relations with renowned ethnographic vividness, Velez-Ibanez illustrates the extraordinary difficulties faced by the urban poor in constructing relations of mutual trust in order to meet the social and economic demands of their marginal existence.

In the context of the widespread rotating credit associations he studied in Mexico and the American Southwest, Velez-Ibanez outlines the risks of default and fraud faced by participants:

> Yet there are other uncertainties against which
> safeguards, fixed relations and cultural boundaries are
> useless. Unexpected acts of men, women, and gods occur
> frequently enough to shatter confidence in the most well
> developed systems that are invented . . . the sudden and
> unexpected appearance of inflation, the death of a relative,
> a lost or misplaced wallet, a sudden illness, an immigration
> raid, or unemployment-- all mock intentions, and the
> safeguards against uncertainty melt away. . . . It is at
> such times that an abuse of mutual trust can occur
> (Velez-Ibanez 1983:85-94).

Velez-Ibanez's book describes how such mutual trust is built up, used and, alas, abused.

Among informal sector participants, the newly arrived rural migrant is the most susceptible to being a victim of special economic opportunity conduct (whether legal or illegal). Although they usually represent the slimmest pickings, the newly arrived are also the most vulnerable. To the "Bottle Buyer" of Cali (Rusque-Alcaino and Bromley 1979:194), rural migrants, "rubes," were always there for the picking. From preying on these, the bottle buyer moved on and up by pursuing better opportunities, that is, victims who were better off.

This occupational "mobility" presents an important insight into the special economic opportunities of the informal sector:

192

these opportunities are part of the process of adapting to the urban environment. That is, just as there is a range of occupational opportunities, from self-employment to quasi-wage labor in the informal sector (merging into wage labor of the formal sector), there is a range of subproletarians prepared to take advantage of special economic opportunities in the informal sector.

The most obvious and common special economic opportunity presented in the informal sector must be pilferage, that is, stealing items of low value that are (therefore) not well protected. Because the opportunity is more or less randomly presented, and because by definition no great planning and organizing is required, pilferage might be an example of special economic opportunity conduct that can be participated in by even the most naive newcomer. Other common opportunities such as drug dealing require both greater levels of planning and also, because they produce more, require vigilance to avoid losing one's (ill-gotten) gain. Information, knowledge, and skill requirements are central in the economics of crime as in all economics.

Crime is surprisingly opportunistic, even in developed countries. Los Angeles, by far the national capital for bank robberies, presents peculiar opportunities to drug addicts who produce eighty-five percent of the robbery attempts (Los Angeles Times, March 21, 1985, p. 1). The city is sprawling with many small bank branches, which are connected by a highly developed freeway system, making getaway easier. Other cities, whose drug addiction problem is as great, simply do not present the same opportunities. For subproletarians in Third World cities, the opportunities presented to them will reflect the special social and cultural conditions of their locale, along with their knowledge and skills.

Undoubtedly, there are subproletarians who do prey upon the middle class more than they prey upon other subproletarians. They are most likely not recent migrants, for example, but rather represent the "old hands" at surviving in the urban informal sector. In fact, three dimensions seem to make important distinctions among such subproletarians and their respective special economic opportunities.

Firstly, young males with relatively little schooling produce a surprising amount of crime behavior in both developed and developing economies. From a microeconomic point of view, they have the poorest "portfolios" and the least prospects for legitimate work. Thus, their predominance in illegitimate work is not surprising (cf. Ehrlich 1973:112). In the Third World, young male offspring of recent migrants account for a notably disproportionate amount of crime (Shelley 1981:53-54). Shelley attributes this fact to the "instability of their parents' existence" (1981:54); an equally appealing explanation would be to point out that they (1) have the time and motivation to seek and take advantage of special economic opportunities and (2) they have been raised (and thus have a greater degree of skill and knowledge necessary for success) in the environment in which those opportunities occur.

Secondly, there is a substantive literature on the "journey" effects on crime in urban places (cf. Georges-Abeyie and Harries 1980). For property crimes, in particular, there is a marked distance-decay pattern (Phillips 1980). Although the actual patterns are themselves complex, the idea that poor people have access difficulties in perpetrating crimes against the middle class is not.

What has not been thoroughly explored, in the context of the economics of crime, is the effect of types of urban subproletarian locales. Lomnitz (1977:15-25) differentiates the principal types of subproletarian locales in Mexico City: (1) older, urban vecindades (described by Oscar Lewis); (2) the sprawling, rapidly growing, suburban colonias populares (of which Ciudad Netzahualcoyotl Izcalli is the famous example); and (3) the ciudades perdidas with extremely low housing standards. Opportunities presented by each of these differ substantially.

Thirdly, Lourdes Arizpe (1975, 1977, 1982) has documented the economic impact of migration on the lives of ethnic migrants, particularly women, to Mexico City. One characteristic kind of migration she describes is the "relay migration" of rural peasants where a migrant returns home when replaced by a kinsman in the city (Arizpe 1982:45). These relays limit the urban experiences of the members of the peasant household, thus limiting their access to special economic opportunities.

Even those ethnic migrants not participating in "relay migration" view their sojourn as temporary. They do not try to get technical skills, for example, to climb the ladder of occupations in the city. Rather, they go directly to work, trying to get the most money in the least time in order to return to their natal villages (Arizpe 1975:74). On the one hand, although highly motivated to make money, these indigenes lack the skills and experience to take advantage of the special economic opportunities of the city. On the other hand, they are highly susceptible to being the special economic opportunity of others.

Although the bourgeoisie finds them picturesque, because of their ethnic costumes, the petit bourgeoisie and their economically compatriot, non-indigene, subproletarians are

antagonistic. Small shopkeepers and market vendors find them
often competing with their business and are often behind attempts
to move them off the street. Other marginals are often openly
hostile and rob and exploit them (Arizpe 1975:131-132).

These three dimensions, taken together, place the special
economic opportunity conduct in a more salient ethnographic
context. Each dimension bears on specific aspects of the social
and economic environment in which informal sector subproletarians
must take advantage of the income-generating opportunities they
find.

Conclusion

Hart and BESS models point to the economic "opportunity"
aspect of crime behavior. The approach proposed here emphasizes
this economic opportunity, as against the sociological
"normative" view, in explaining both legal and illegal special
economic opportunity conduct. Crime, particularly property crime
is here seen not as a product of "modernization" but, rather, as
a product of the knowledge and skills available to
subproletarians in their economic context.

However, this context is critical. Taking advantage of
special economic opportunity requires skills and knowledge not
homogeneously distributed among subproletarians in the urban,
informal sector. The ability to take full advantage of the
capital accumulation prospects of the urban environment is itself
one characteristic of development.

Although the "special economic opportunity" approach is
fundamentally choice-theoretic, this approach is also concerned
with the culture-laden enterprises of daily economic life--the
ploys and schemes by which the urban poor eke out a living. The
approach assumes that the subproletarian responds to overt
incentives, that costs and benefits are calculated, but these are
calculated within a social and cultural setting. In this sense,
there is no "taste for crime" as the BESS models imply.

The principal effect of economic development is to present a
wider range of special economic opportunities to the urban poor.
However, most of these opportunities are subject to "close
regulation" by the agents of government and are, thus, illegal or
illegitimate. Although the "relay migration" described by Arizpe
(Arizpe 1982) may be an exception, the economic activities of the
urban poor do not create important net inter-sectorial flows from
the formal to the informal sector.

Of course, there are some "subproletarians" who do make a

195

good living from preying on the formal sector. But these are only part of the range of subproletarians prepared to take advantage of special economic opportunities in the formal (and informal) sector.

Crime is culture-laden, then, in two principal senses not effectively treated by either criminologists or economists. In the first sense, crime is a classification problem. Rossi et al. (1974) discovered that black males with less than high school education viewed "beating up an acquaintance" as much less serious than other groups in their study. As Rossi et al. put it, "the line between manly sport and crime can be thin indeed" (1974:231). That line, of course, is the line of cultural demarcation.

In the second sense, crime reflects particular cultural knowledge for its successful completion. As Velez-Ibanez and Rusque-Alcaino and Bromley eloquently point out, successful special economic opportunity conduct reflects knowledge and skills acquired through membership in a social group. That is, of course, the fundamental definition of culture.

References

Archer, Dane and Rosemary Gartner. 1984. Violence and Crime in Cross-National Perspective. New Haven: Yale University Press.
Arizpe S., Lourdes. 1975. Indigenas en la ciudad de Mexico: El caso de las "Marias." Mexico, D.F.: Secretaria de Educacion Publica.
------- 1977. Women in the Informal Labor Sector: The Case of Mexico City. In: Women and National Development, edited by Wellesley Editorial Committee, pp. 25-37. Chicago: University of Chicago Press.
------- 1982. Relay Migration and the Survival of the Peasant Household. In: Towards a Political Economy of Urbanization in Third World Countries, edited by Helen I. Safa, pp. 19-46. New Delhi: Oxford University Press.
Arrow, Kenneth J. 1963. Social Choice and Individual Values. New Haven: Yale University Press.
Bayley, David H. 1970. The Effects of Corruption in a Developing Nation. In: Political Corruption, edited by Arnold Heidenheimer, pp. 521-533. New York: Holt, Rinehart & Winston.
Becker, Gary. 1968. Crime and Punishment: An Economic Approach. Journal of Political Economy 78:169-217.
Clinard, Marshall B. and Daniel J. Abbott. 1973. Crime in Developing Countries: A Comparative Perspective. New York: John Wiley and Sons.

Cloward, Richard and Lloyd Ohlin. 1960. Delinquency and
Opportunity. Glencoe, Illinois: Free Press.
Cook, Karen S. and Karen A. Hegtvedt. 1983. Distributive Justice,
Equity, and Equality. Annual Review of Sociology 9:217-241.
Edelhertz, Herbert. 1970. The Nature, Impact and Prosecution of
White-Collar Crime. Washington, D.C.: U.S. Government Printing
Office.
------- 1974. A Handbook on White Collar Crime. Washington, D.C.:
Chamber of Commerce.
Ehrlich, Isaac. 1973. Participation in Illegitimate Activities: A
Theoretical and Empirical Investigation. Journal of Political
Economy 81:521-565.
Geis, Gilbert, ed. 1968. White-Collar Criminal, The Offender in
Business and the Professions. New York: Atherton Press.
Georges-Abeyie, Daniel E. and Keith D. Harries, eds. 1980. Crime:
A Spatial Perspective. New York: Columbia University Press.
Hart, Keith. 1973. Informal Income Opportunities and Urban
Employment in Ghana. The Journal of Modern African Studies
11:61-89.
Heineke, J. M. 1978. Economic Models of Criminal Behavior: An
Overview. In: Economic Models of Criminal Behavior, edited by J.
M. Heineke, pp. 1-34. Amsterdam: North-Holland Publishing Co.
Horoszowski, Pawel. 1980. Economic Special-Opportunity Conduct
and Crime. Lexington, Mass.: Lexington Books.
Lewis, Oscar. 1959. Five Families: Mexican Case Studies in the
Culture of Poverty. New York: Basic Books.
------- 1961. The Children of Sanchez: Autobiography of a Mexican
Family. New York: Random House.
Lomnitz, Larissa Adler. 1977. Networks and Marginality: Life in a
Mexican Shantytown. New York: Academic Press.
Lopez-Ray, Manuel. 1964. Economic Conditions and Crime with
Special Reference to Less Developed Countries. Annales
Internationales de Criminologie 1:33-40.
Mangin, G. 1975. La delinquance juvenile en Afrique noire
Francophone. Archives de Politique Criminelle 1:225-240.
McGee, T. G. 1979. The Poverty Syndrome: Making Out in the
Southeast Asian City. In: Casual Work and Poverty in Third World
Cities, edited by Ray Bromley and Chris Gerry, pp.45-68.
Chichester, England: John Wiley and Sons.
Merton, Robert K. 1957. Social Theory and Social Structure. New
York: Free Press.
Myrdal, Gunnar. 1970. Corruption: Its Causes and Effects. In:
Political Corruption, edited by Arnold Heidenheimer. New York:
Holt, Rinehart and Winston.
Neale, Walter C. 1971. Monetization, Commercialization, Market
Orientation, and Market Dependence. In: Studies in Economic
Anthropology, edited by George Dalton, pp. 25-29. Washington,
D.C.: American Anthropological Association.
Phillips, Phillip D. 1980. Characteristics and Typology of the
Journey to Crime. In: Crime: A Spatial Perspective, edited by

Daniel E. Georges-Abeyie and Keith D. Harries, pp.167-180. New York: Columbia University Press.

Pierre, Evelyne, Flamand, J. P. and H. Collomb. 1962. La delinquance juvenile a Dakar. International Review of Criminal Policy 20:27-33.

Rossi, P. H., E. Waite, C. E. Bose and R. E. Berk. 1974. The Seriousness of Crimes. American Sociological Review 39:224-237.

Rusque-Alcaino, Juan and Ray Bromley. 1979. The Bottle Buyer: An Occupational Autobiography. In: Casual Work and Poverty in Third World Cities, edited by Ray Bromley and Chris Gerry, pp. 185-216. Chichester, England: John Wiley and Sons.

Shelley, Louise I. 1981. Crime and Modernization. Carbondale, Ill.: Southern Illinois University Press.

Short, James F., Jr. 1981. Foreword. In: Crime and Modernization, Louise I. Shelley, pp. ix-x. Carbondale, Ill.: Southern Illinois University Press.

Sjoquist, D. L. 1973. Property Crime and Economic Behavior: Some Empirical Results. American Economic Review 63:439-446.

Stack, Steven. 1984. Income Inequality and Property Crime: A Cross-National Analysis of Relative Deprivation Theory. Criminology 22:229- 257.

Stigler, George J. 1970. The Optimum Enforcement of Laws. The Journal of Political Economy 78:526-536.

Sutherland, Edwin H. 1940. White Collar Criminality. American Sociological Review 5:1-12.

------- 1949. White Collar Crime. New York: Dryden Press.

Tappan, Paul W. 1947. Who Is the Criminal? American Sociological Review 12:96-103.

------- 1960. Crime, Justice, and Correction. New York: McGraw-Hill.

Tschoungui, S. P. and P. Zumbach. 1962. Diagnostic de la delinquance au Cameroun. International Review of Criminal Policy 20:35-44.

Velez-Ibanez, Carlos G. 1983. Bonds of Mutual Trust: The Cultural Systems of Rotating Credit Associations among Urban Mexicans and Chicanos. New Brunswick, N. J.: Rutgers University Press.

11. SOCIAL REPRODUCTION IN AGRICULTURAL FRONTIERS

Emilio F. Moran

Introduction

This paper uses a historico-comparative approach to the analysis of production and reproduction. The analysis of production and reproduction is at the heart of the study of social stratification but rarely do analyses feature societies where the process of social reproduction can be empirically studied. Frontiers afford one of the few contexts in which it becomes possible to study the way individuals and households negotiate to form social groups and eventually reproduce the social formations that will become dominant in emergent communities (Blau 1977).

Frontiers have not attracted students of stratification or economics because they appear to be systems that are disorganized and classless. Frederick Jackson Turner, in his influential article on the significance of the frontier in American history asserted that frontier social structures were neither complex nor highly differentiated and organized (1920:212). Frontier studies have been dominated by historians who have either been recorders of the folk life of the frontier, or who have taken a loyalist or revisionist position vis-a-vis the Turner hypothesis. It is particularly the revisionists who have begun to produce the economic knowledge that permits comparative analysis, such as that undertaken in this paper.

The Turner hypothesis suggested that the frontier, with its absence of social controls, cultural traditions, and rigid class formations, permitted the development of the democratic and individualistic traits of Americans. The frontier provided an ideal environment for innovation and for creating a society of yeoman farmers (Turner 1920). This rosy view of the American frontier was later attacked by historians. Led by the superb scholarship of Paul Gates, study after study showed that the American frontier public land policies were better described as ill-conceived and poorly administered--resulting in much of the land falling in the hands of speculators who thereby frustrated the dreams of a democracy based on small farmers (Gates 1954, 1973, 1974). Thus, frontiers constitute a crucible for testing how social systems reproduce themselves. Clarification of how such reproduction is effected is relevant to the understanding of stratification, agricultural change and development, and the behavior of individuals within social and ecological systems. Although these are not the basic questions that Turner and Gates

199

sought to answer, their influence on explanations for the behavior of frontiersmen continues to color the interpretation of currently developing frontiers.

If we are to contribute to the development of a general theory of the frontier, particularly as it bears upon social reproduction, it becomes fundamental to provide a range of cases that provide different conditions under which to examine the generalizations that will be developed. This paper does not attempt to explain social process in all frontiers. My concern is with the first decade of settlement in forested frontiers with no apparent commercial mission evident at the time it begins to be settled yet connected to a barter capitalist economy. I compare primarily four frontier communities that meet the above definition: two in the United States and two in the Brazilian Amazon. The two U.S. communities are widely separated in time and space and in their functional relations to the larger society. Lancaster county, Pennsylvania was first settled in the seventeenth century by a predominantly Quaker-Mennonite population. By contrast, Trempealeau County, Wisconsin was settled in the 1850s by a more mixed population of both American and foreign-born members. The two Amazonian communities included here have been sites of my own research in the past decade. They contrast in a variety of ways: one was part of a government-directed scheme; the other one is privately directed. The former was directed at landless farmers from the least developed regions; the latter was geared at selling land to smallholders from the most developed parts of the country. They are both alike in that they were studied in the first three years of settlement. Other frontier cases will be used when appropriate.

Who Comes to the Early Frontier?

It is common wisdom that most frontiersmen are small farmers seeking to obtain land for themselves and their children--land too dear in their areas of origin. There is a growing body of evidence that contradicts this assumption. In all four communities analyzed in this paper, and all the other ones that provide adequate data, one finds a small number of landed aristocrats and a few successful merchants. Most of the population, by contrast, might be characterized as lower middle class or upper lower class within their communities of origin (Eder 1982:43)--rather than as the lower lower class, which is often too poor to undertake a long-distance move. Turner thought that the differences between migrants were differences in "the stages of occupation." For example, the early frontier was characterized by fur trappers, later by subsistence farmers and merchants, and later still by large-scale farmers with commercial

200

goals for their agricultural production. Although historians have been careful in noting class differences among frontiersmen in the United States, a number of sociologists and anthropologists examining Latin American frontiers have tended to lump most settlers in frontier areas in the category of an undifferentiated peasantry or yeomanry struggling to maintain a peasant mode of production in the face of the penetration of capitalism (Foweraker 1982; Wood and Schmink 1984).

A look at the tax records of Lancaster County in the seventeenth century shows that wealth differentials and probably stratification were present from the beginning of settlement and that such differentials increased over time (see Table 1)--although this should not lead one to overlook that there was a great deal of movement across classes throughout this dynamic period of settlement. Whereas in 1690 the top 10 percent of the population held less than 24 percent of the wealth, by 1800 the top 10 percent held 38 percent of it. Thus, although there was abundant "free land" at this time, one sees marked social and economic stratification and a great variety of origins. Nearly one-third had been craftsmen, one-third laborers or professionals of various sorts, and the other third farmers. Although one must be careful in treating professions as indicators of status, given that many of these people probably occupied many different professional positions in their lifetime, profession or job at the previous location can be used to approximate the most recent socioeconomic status of frontiersmen.

The population of Trempealeau County, Wisconsin in the mid-1800s was also characterized by notable ethnic and economic differences. In the first census of Trempealeau in 1860, one notes that the lowest decile of property holders hold not 10 percent but 1.5 percent of all property, whereas the top decile holds not 10 but 39 percent of all property. It should be noted that this is not the same measure as that used for Lancaster County. The evidence presented in Curti and Lemon do not permit the use of a common and consistent measure for comparative analysis. Curti (1959) showed that the structure of Trempealeau county resembles that of counties in Vermont settled a century before. Thus, it does not appear that the frontier, despite the availability of land, leads to a more "democratic" and less stratified society. Whether this stratification is the same as in areas of origin or whether the distance between strata narrows is an empirical question rarely addressed in studies so far. It can be hypothesized that in the early stages of occupation the distance between households is relatively narrow, as measured by the Gini coefficient, and may narrow even further, due to the limited role of capital in production (Stone et al. 1984). Over time and with capitalist development those

201

Table 1.

Table 1

Vertical Distribution of Economic Status: Percentage of Taxes
Paid by Taxpayers Ranked by Amount of Taxes Paid,
Chester and Lancaster Counties, 1693-1802

| County | Taxpayer Group | | | | Number of |
and Year	Lowest 30%	Lower middle 30%	Upper middle 30%	Upper 10%	Taxpayers[a]
Chester					
1693	17.4	21.1	37.7	23.8	257
1715	13.1	22.9	38.1	25.9	670
1730	9.8	21.7	39.8	28.6	1,791
1748	13.1	21.7	36.4	28.7	2,998
Lancaster					
1758-59	4.2	16.9	45.0	33.9	3,459[b]
Chester					
1760	6.3	20.5	43.3	29.9	4,290
1782	4.7	17.3	44.5	33.6	5,291
1800-2[c]	3.9	13.7	44.2	38.3	7,247

Source: MSS Tax assessments: 1693, Chester Co. Miscellaneous
Papers, Hist. Soc. Pa.; 1715, 1730, 1748, 1760, 1782, 1800, Chester
Co. Hist. Soc.; 1758-50, Lanc. Co. Hist. Soc.; 1802, Delaware Co.
Court House, Media.   See nn. 19, 26, chap. 1.

Note: some columns do not add to 100 because of rounding.

[a]Single freemen excluded from calculations.
[b]Present-day Lancaster Co. only; Lebanon Valley excluded.   Data
for Little Britain Tp. lacking.
[c]1800--Present-day Chester; 1802--Delaware Co. tps. that
separated from Chester in 1789.

Source: J. Lemon, The Best Poor Man's Country, 1972, p. 11.

differences will rapidly increase and lead to the reproduction of comparable degrees of stratification.

What we find in the Brazilian Amazon is no different. Settlers in government-directed communities included past small holders wishing to expand the scale of their farm operations, past sharecroppers and wage laborers, and past urban laborers and craftsmen. Even in the privately run project geared to small farmers in the intensively cultivated region of Rio Grande do Sul, the frontiersmen profile was characterized by rarely over 30 percent small holders, the rest being made up of laborers, craftsmen, low-level professionals, and others with only marginal background in farming. Educational levels were highly variable ranging from 20 percent with post-secondary education, 20 percent with secondary, 30 percent with primary, and the rest with no education at all. Initial capital varied a great deal in both projects with some arriving with the equivalent of the sale of a couple of hogs and a few tools, while others arrived with the proceeds of a well-developed farm. Table 2 provides a comparison of a variety of parameters in the two areas. Indicators of differential past experience noted in Table 2 are: differences in the rate of previous residential mobility, previous credit experience, previous land ownership, and perception of class status. Although in the aggregate the better off population settling in Tucuma did no better in net terms than the capital poor and socioeconomically disadvantaged population of the Transamazon, in both populations one finds remarkable differences in outcome that can be explained by particular circumstances such as experience, education, location, and subsistence strategy.

In short, whether we are talking of seventeenth-century Pennsylvania, nineteenth-century Wisconsin, or twentieth-century Amazonia, one finds in the first decade of frontier occupation a population made up of previous small farmers, previous agricultural laborers, previous urban laborers, and professionals with considerable educational attainments and expertise in management. Most settlers would indicate that their goal is to improve their lot in life, and that of their children, but they vary in their ability to cope with a different physical environment, with frontier isolation, with lack of social supports, and with the problems of applying scarce capital and labor on a land resource whose response to one's inputs is scarcely known.

The Reproduction of Production

The differences between frontiersmen in past experience, in

Table 2.

Table 2

Background and Performance in Two Amazon Frontier Communities

Basic Indicators

Tucuma		Transamazon
US $4,000	Begin. Capital	US $275
1.87	Previous Mobil.	4.6
73%	Previous Credit	21%
57%	Previous Title	20%
6 yrs.	Previous Education	3.2 yrs.
75%	Urban Exper.	30%
87% "middle"	Previous Soc. Class	96% "lower"
80% S; 20% CW	Area of Origin	30%N; 31% NE; 23% S; 14% C

New Location Performance

12 days	Sick days/yr.	11 days
5.4	Cattle	2.3
6.9	Pigs	2.7
42.5	Chickens	21.6
US $2,000	Farm Income	US $ 720
US $2,500	N Farm Income	US $2,000
US $1,500	Yr. Profit	US $1,700
900 kg/ha	Yield/hectare	950 kg/ha

Source: Moran field notes 1973-74 and 1984 respectively.

occupation, and in class have considerable impact upon the patterns of labor allocation, land use, and capital investment that emerge in a frontier area. It is unclear from the literature what proportion of settlers seriously use soil quality as a criteria for location, Lemon (1972:63) in his study of Lancaster county notes that "settlers were probably more concerned with an accessible water supply than with the exact quality of the soil." In all four sites studied here settlers attempted to locate as close as possible to markets and town. Lemon notes that the most predictive criteria for a settler's choice of land were his date of arrival and the location of the nearest available unoccupied land (1972:70). In an area of generally good soils such as southeastern Pennsylvania, reliance on land location as the primary criterion for settlement may prove effective. However, in areas such as the Amazon with a high statistical frequency of acid, low-nutrient soils, disregard for soil quality may very well spell future economic failure if farming is the goal. A potentially important dimension of the reproduction of modes of production becomes the fit between past cultural knowledge and current environmental conditions.

In agricultural frontiers where capital is available for productive purposes, early frontiersmen are characterized by an emphasis on subsistence production, marketing of small amounts of surplus, and considerable involvement in off-farm work. The absence of capital in some frontiers (e.g. Jos Plateau of Nigeria, cf. Stone et al. 1984) seems to delay the emergence of distinctions among farmers and to a temporary period of reduced inequality. This ideal trajectory of frontier development may have been more common in the past than it is at present given the lesser role played by the State in older frontiers, the lower levels of capital investment in some frontiers, and the scarcity of capital in some historic periods. Thus the Jos Plateau material is important to the understanding of what happens in the absence of capital.

Settlers begin their settlement of a frontier by attempting to implant the forms of agriculture that they already know, even when in light of significant environmental differences such practices may be inappropriate (Miller and Thompson 1980; Moran 1982). If the new environment is relatively similar to the old (as was the case with several of the frontiers settled by Europeans arriving in the United States), many of those past practices and crops may work and will be maintained. This was the case with the settlers of Lancaster County. Even so, in Lancaster County yields were only half of then-current average wheat yields (4 or 5 vis-a-vis 8 bushels per acre) and there was a 30 percent minimum turnover in population each decade. These turnover rates, which would elicit cries of failure among contemporary Third World government planners, were common in the

205

U.S. frontier (cf. Curti 1959; Fite 1966) and call for an explanation. The first decade of capitalized forested agricultural frontiers is dominated by a lack of labor to carry out the tasks of town building, road construction, and deforestation. Because of the absence of labor the returns on labor are high, and productive efforts are directed at earning wages, converting cheap or free land into valuable farmland, or at services.

For the government-directed project in the Transamazon Highway, I have shown elsewhere how the 70 percent of non-Amazonians among the settlers ignored the adaptive practices used by the local peasantry, and chose to plant according to schedules from areas of origin as distant and inappropriate as the arid Northeast of Brazil (Moran 1981). Only a small proportion of the frontiersmen dedicated most of their labor and capital to their farm operations. Instead, most chose to disperse their labor into off-farm work, and their capital into the service sector rather than into farm buildings and machinery. To some extent this is not surprising. Wages tend to be 30 to 100 percent higher in the frontier than in areas of origin because of the scarcity of labor (Lemon 1972; Curti 1959; Moran 1981). Document after document blames this scarcity of labor for the low levels of labor investment in farming in the U.S. frontier (Bogue 1963; Gates 1973). As a result, in all of the four frontiers under discussion, while some farmers obtained respectable yields from their farms, the majority obtained very poor results. For the two Amazonian sites, those with excellent yields had an unusually high supply of household labor, with most of it dedicated to the farm operation, and had selected good soils. Even these households, however, devoted a portion of their labor to off-farm labor. In fact, no household with a positive balance between returns on production and expenses was without at least one or two household members working for wages.

The Production of Reproduction

One of the thorniest elements in the whole frontier literature is the assessment of the objectives of settlers. On the one hand, we have the view of Turner and many of the contemporary Amazonian scholars who view the settler as an individual escaping from a stratified society to an open one where he can hew with his family a homestead by his own efforts and contribute to the development of a society more egalitarian than the one left behind. This view is evident in the references to the "aristocratic traditions of the East" in Turner, and in the allusions among some Amazonian scholars to the peasant mode of production seeking to reproduce itself in the frontier and to escape from the oppression of the capitalist mode of production.

What is the evidence that the economic activity of frontiersmen represents a departure from the pattern of economic activity in the larger society?

The evidence presented by many to argue that early frontier settlers represent a peasant mode of production is based on the dominance of subsistence farming during the early period. However, the dominance of subsistence production is more related to lack of infrastructure, lack of labor, and lack of capital than to an ideological preference for a subsistence mode of production. Lemon notes, in referring to seventeenth-century Pennsylvania, that "despite complex commercial connections . . . communications and transport facilities were inadequate, processing operations were unsophisticated, and agricultural tools were primitive. These deficiencies contributed to a continuation of the subsistence aspect of the economy, and to the existence of the family farm as the chief unit of production" (1972:29). It is a common experience of early settlers that roads, markets, and storage facilities are wholly inadequate and substantial surplus production cannot be profitably marketed. In addition, the common experience of low yields following forest clearing militates against too heavy an investment of labor and capital on farming itself.

The research of Paul Gates and his students points to high levels of speculation in the early frontier (cf. also Swierenga 1970; Bogue 1963). This phenomenon may be the result of the predominant role of a land market during the early stages of frontier occupation, to be followed only much later by a commodities market. Speculative activity in land appears to have been carried out in the United States not just by Eastern large-scale speculators but by virtually all elements of frontier society (Cochrane 1979). Allan Bogue (1963) found evidence that large-scale speculators made continuous efforts to extend the time when mortgages were due because they were more interested in the interest than in the land itself. Bogue found evidence that the largest volume of land speculation was carried out by petty speculators. The Iowa Claims Clubs, which earlier had been portrayed as squatters' responses to resist the heavy hand of speculators, were in reality special interest groups formed to defend the speculative activities of their members. Margaret Bogue (1979) showed, further, that three-quarters of the mortgages entered into by farmers in east central Illinois were to buy more real estate, rather than to deal with economic distress or to improve farm management.

The cheap price of land, combined with the high price of labor and the uncertainty of returns on capital given the lack of developed markets, poorly developed infrastructure and lack of experience with local microecological conditions, led most of these early settlers to strategies that emphasize minimum, subsistence-level investment in farming. Subsistence production reduces capital outlays for food and basic necessities and assures legitimate claim to the land. The lower investment of labor in farming also means that the household can allocate a greater portion of available labor to off-farm employment to capitalize on the relatively high wages paid in the labor-scarce frontier. The income from this labor can then be used to buy more land or pay for expensive consumer goods. The dependence on wages is more related to the settlers' proximity to a town or to a major employer than it is to household preference for farm work. In most cases, the wage labor will be in someone else's farm, to build houses or other basic facilities, or for the government in today's frontiers where greater government intervention in population resettlement is common. In both Amazonian communities studied, at least two-thirds of settlers earned at least twice as much from off-farm labor as from farming. The choice to invest most of available labor in wage-earning activities rather than in farm-making represents a short-term strategy in which farming takes a secondary role to capital accumulation.

One could best summarize the strategies of early settlers by saying that what they do reflects an effort to increase the market value of land, rather than its productivity. Thus, in a forested frontier the effort is focused on clearing forest since the market value of land is usually determined by the area that has been "improved," i.e. deforested. In my study of a privately operated Amazonian settlement, there was a strong correlation (r=0.70, p=0.0001) between amount of bank financing and area cleared. Thus, available capital was being used almost solely to maximize the area cleared of forest, rather than to allocate the credit for other farm-making activities. Nor were farm-making activities such as providing for sheds to store tools and equipment, fencing, animal pens or dairying facilities carried out in any more than 15 percent of farms. Additional evidence for the speculative intent of most of these settlers can be seen in the burst of sales of land when the price of land goes up suddenly, as happened in the 1774-1785 decade in southeastern Pennsylvania, in 1860-1870 in Trempealeau county, Wisconsin and in 1981 in the Transamazon region. For example, a $100 lot bought in July 1851 was sold for $1260 in April 1852--and this was before the major increases in land value after 1860! (Curti 1959:18).

In the Amazon, as in seventeenth-century Pennsylvania, the most prosperous farmers had moved the least before going to the frontier and were the least inclined to move again, either to another frontier or to an urban area. They had converted their relatively modest capital into profitable farm operations. Curti notes that they had higher yields per acre than those who left and had attained a relatively high position in the frontier communities. Those in the lowest positions were most likely to remain because the costs of migrating again were too high. It was the lower middle group that, after a generation in the frontier, was most likely to engage in further migration(s) because they had fallen behind in their relative share of income and social rank as compared with the upper ranked group (see Table 1). This finding seems to be supported by the work of Cancian (1965,1981) in non-frontier communities that notes that it is the lower middle class that is most likely to be risk-taking and willing to be innovative.

A further index of whether early settlers really intend to settle down to farming or are simply engaged in speculation is to be found in their investment in local social and political institutions. Though not extensively documented, the few studies that allude to this dimension agree: the better off farmers spend more time visiting others and are more likely to seek social and political offices than do other settlers (Loomis 1938; Sanderson 1938; Curti 1959). It is, in fact, the more able and stable settlers who tend to own general grocery stores and be active in churches--institutions that usually grow to become the heart of local communities' social and political life (Moran 1981). By contrast, the great majority of early settlers are relatively isolated from other settlers and move on eventually. The importance of early arrival in the frontier for those aspiring to local leadership has been rarely studied except for the careful analysis by Curti (1959). Although it was possible to achieve major leadership position if one was under 30 and with total property of under $1,000 in Trempealeau county before 1860, it becomes nearly impossible thereafter. Moreover, early leaders who stayed in the community remained in leadership positions, while only six who arrived after 1860, despite the greater wealth of those who arrived later, were able to occupy leadership positions. Thus, social and political leadership was largely monopolized by the early settlers and even those who arrived later with greater wealth were unable to displace them.

Social Reproduction in the Frontier

This schematic analysis of the process of social reproduction in the frontier suggests that most early settlers go there because of the high-risk/high-gain potential that such areas represent. A minority strategy tends to be to look for good land near roads and markets, to invest most household labor in clearing small areas that can be managed with that labor, to invest net income in farm equipment and buildings, and to help build social and political institutions through participation.

209

The majority strategy contrasts with this one. It is characterized by acquiring and clearing more land than can be worked with household labor, to allocate substantial portions of household labor in salaried occupations to capitalize on the high wages available in the frontier, to invest net income in either consumption or more real estate, and to be little involved in building of social and political institutions. This majority strategy explains why there are such high dropout rates in the early frontier, why subsistence production is dominant, and why the increase in land value is the dominant factor in the early development of frontiers. The increase in land value, in turn, results from national policies toward the particular areas (for example, whether roads and canals are built and maintained), the involvement of local settlers and entrepreneurs in encouraging further settlement and building of basic infrastructure and marketing facilities, and the eventual flow of labor and capital into the region so that production matches the development of roads and markets. This stage, however, occurs later in frontier development. By the time this later influx occurs, the social structure of local communities has been reproduced and high rank positions are dominated by early arrivers whose strategies led to superior results.

In summary, frontiers provide nations with an opportunity to expand their economic areas and to reproduce the social class system and institutions of society. It provides individuals from the upper lower and lower middle class with an opportunity to achieve a significant change in relative social rank within their lifetimes. The processes of frontier development are dominated by land speculation, subsistence agriculture, high wages, and great variation in individual background and expertise. Previous assessments that emphasized the similarity of frontiersmen at various stages have overlooked this wide variation, and have misinterpreted the reasons for the reliance on subsistence agriculture and the pervasive presence of land speculation. The early settlers arrive with considerable differentiation and these differences are quickly enhanced by the frontier environment, so that within a decade there are marked degrees of stratification, and the new society resembles the original one in remarkable ways. On a more positive note, early frontier occupation provides one of the few true opportunities to achieve relatively high social rank in a matter of a few years--and the opportunity to preserve such rank by structuring local community social and political institutions in ways that favor those early arrivers' permanence in power and authority.

Acknowledgments

Library and field research leading up to this paper was made possible by a Tinker Foundation Post-Doctoral Fellowship while I was on sabbatical leave from Indiana University in 1984. I benefited a great deal from the agricultural history collections at the North Carolina State University library and from the counsel of colleagues in rural sociology and agronomy at that institution, in particular John Nicholaides III. I wish to thank Steve Gudeman, Harold Schneider, John Bennett, Davydd Greenwood, Thayer Scudder, Sara Scherr, John Lombardi, Irene Neu, Robert Netting, Robert Hunt, and John Bowen for useful comments upon an earlier version of this paper presented at the Society for Economic Anthropology meetings held at Ayrlie House, April 1985. Responsibility for the views expressed herein are entirely mine.

References

Blau, Peter M. 1977. Inequality and Heterogeneity: A Primitive Theory of Social Structure. New York: Free Press.
Bogue, Allan. 1963. From Prairie to Corn Belt. Chicago: Univ. of Chicago Press.
Bogue, Margaret. 1979. Patterns from the Sod: Land Use and Tenure in the Grand Prairie, 1850-1900. New York: Arno Press. Orig. publ. 1959.
Cancian, Frank. 1965. Economics and Prestige in a Maya Community. Stanford: Stanford Univ. Press.
----- 1981. The Innovator's Situation. Stanford: Stanford Univ. Press.
Cochrane, Willard. 1979. The Development of American Agriculture: A Historical Analysis. Minneapolis: Univ. of Minnesota Press.
Curti, Merle. 1959. The Making of an American Community. Stanford: Stanford Univ. Press.
Eder, James. 1982. Who Shall Succeed? Agricultural Development and Social Inequality on a Philippine Frontier. London: Cambridge Univ. Press.
Fite, Gilbert. 1966. The Farmer's Frontier, 1865-1900. New York: Holt, Rinehart and Winston.
Foweraker, Joe. 1982. The Struggle for Land. London: Cambridge Univ. Press.
Gates, Paul. 1974. Research in the History of the Public Lands. Agricultural History 48:31-50.
----- 1973. Landlords and Tenants on the Prairie Frontier. Ithaca, NY: Cornell Univ. Press.
----- 1954. 50 Million Acres: Conflicts Over Kansas Land Policy, 1854-90. Ithaca, NY: Cornell Univ. Press.

Lemon, James. 1972. The Best Poor Man's Country. New York: Norton.
Lockhart, James. 1972. The Men of Cajamarca: A Social and
  Biographical Study of the First Conquerors of Peru. Austin, TX:
  Inst. of Latin American Studies, Univ. of Texas Press.
Loomis, Charles. 1938. The Developing of Planned Rural Communities.
  Rural Sociology 3:385-409.
Miller, S. and S. Thompson, eds. 1980. The Frontier, Vol. II. OK:
  Oklahoma Univ. Press.
Moran, Emilio. 1981. Developing the Amazon. Bloomington: Indiana
  Univ. Press.
----- 1982. Ecological, Anthropological, and Agronomic Research in
  the Amazon Basin. Latin American Research Review 17:3-41.
Sanderson, Dwight. 1938. Criteria of Rural Community Formation.
  Rural Sociology 3:373-384.
Stone, G.D., M.P. Johnson-Stone, and R. Netting. 1984. Household
  Variability and Inequality in Kofyar Subsistence and
  Cash-cropping Economies. Journal of Anthropological Research
  40:90-108.
Swierenga, Robert. 1970. Land Speculation and Frontier Tax
  Assessments. Agricultural History 44:253-266.
Turner, Frederick Jackson. 1920. The Frontier in American History.
  New York: Holt, Rinehart, and Winston.
Wood, Charles and M. Schmink, eds. 1984. Frontier Expansion in
  Amazonia. Gainesville: Univ. Presses of Florida.

12. FRONTIERS AS MARGINAL ECONOMIES

Stephen Gudeman

Frontier societies are created when an economy expands its borders into a new natural environment. Emilio Moran, who has been examining frontiers for some time, provides us with a comparison of four frontier communities, two in the Brazilian Amazon and two in the United States. The purpose of Moran's study is to counter Frederick Jackson Turner's thesis that the frontier-- being classless, relatively disorganized and socially undifferentiated-- provided a haven for individuals who wished to escape a stratified society. According to Turner, the frontier was the forging ground for the American cultural traits of individualism, innovation, and popular democracy. Moran argues, however, that social stratification is reproduced promptly on the frontier.

But let us consider Moran's data from a different perspective. Frontier societies are "at the margin" of society in a double sense. They mark (as Levi-Strauss [1969] once argued for the incest prohibition) the moment of transition when nature is initially shaped by cultural purpose. Frontiers represent the place and time of a culture's first encounter with nature. Frederick Jackson Turner's thesis was, in some respects, that an arrow of determination ran from nature to culture; by contrast, I hold that a culture reveals and remakes itself as it fashions nature to its ends. In all four frontier societies examined by Moran, for example, settlers turned nature into the margin of culture by implanting their existing economic models. From the time of first settlement, known technologies and forms of agriculture were tried, even when the most immediate evidence suggested they would be inappropriate. Land claimed and farmed was often selected for its accessibility to an established town rather than its natural qualities (with the result that initial yields were generally poor). As Moran suggests, existing social differences were also brought to the frontier. In all four areas a cultural scheme-- capitalism-- directed human behavior. But this takes us to the second and more technical sense of the word "margin."

In capitalism, frontier economies straddle the profit margin, where net returns from the land just match net expenditures. Inside the margin ventures are profitable, whereas those that fall outside the margin incur a loss, and - over time - usually disappear. I term this frontier breakeven point the "Ricardian margin," because Ricardo first elaborated a marginal theory of production, applied it to agriculture, and explored

213

some of the interrelations among a growing population, declining profit levels and the furthest limits of agricultural activity (Gudeman 1984; Ricardo 1951 [1815], IV; 1951 [1817], I). In the Ricardian model, land outside the margin yields neither profit nor rent, land directly on the margin provides a profit, while land inside the margin produces both profit and rent. Ricardo assumed that land outside the marginal point is not farmed but that through population growth and market demand it might eventually become profitable and thus tilled. Ricardian land theory, in fact, is about the frontier, where frontier development witnesses the passage of land from the non-marginal or unused to the infra-marginal or regularly used; and his model fits the four cases at hand rather well. For example, Moran's information suggests that frontier land is marginal in that it lacks many features of infrastructure, including roads, storage facilities, markets, equipment, and information about appropriate technologies. His data also show that much frontier land is actually "beyond the margin" in that farming it does not yield a profit; settlers cannot expect to secure a competitive profit rate or even a flow of income from the land. But Moran also demonstrates that people who flock to the frontier, make claims to land, and farm it are drawn from many sectors of an existent market economy; their new activity does not represent a break with their broader background in a capitalist society but is an extension of it. What face of capitalism, then, is found at the frontier? In what respects is the making of a frontier a capitalist activity?

Overall, as a capitalist project, the frontier offers the possibility of a long-term gain. Moran labels the settlers "speculators," and the term is proper, but it needs further explanation. Speculation is a market activity; the speculator buys under conditions of uncertainty and with the hope that as prices change, a sale can be made and a profit secured. The speculator buys to gain a one-time return rather than trap a secure, immediate and annual flow of income. From this perspective frontiers people are speculators, although they make no capital investment of money in agriculture and put no assets at risk, except their own work to clear and claim the land. Their strategy, which combines low risk of loss with high uncertainty of gain, is based on the Ricardian assumption that as the physical boundary of the economy expands, their land will fall within the true margin of the economy. The frontiersperson hopes that his or her terrain can eventually be sold for a long-term gain or ultimately provide an annual return. The frontier offers people the chance of speculating as on the money market, Wall Street, or the bourse, but without committing any marketable assets except the initial labor of making a land claim.

In light of this general purpose, frontier activity appears highly patterned, and the data Moran presents can be fitted together in a package. First, most frontier farms are used to provide subsistence foodstuffs or goods for use rather than for exchange; only the excess or surplus above needs is marketed. This subsistence orientation, however, does not mean that frontier agriculture is non-capitalist; to the contrary, farm returns taken as foodstuffs lower the monetary cost of living by replacing market purchases with home goods. Furthermore, to have time to earn wages in commercial ventures, many frontier folk keep their own farming efforts at a low level. In the Amazonian communities most people could earn twice as much from off-farm labor as they could from their own farms, with the wage work generating the cash flow needed for living costs. In Brazil, due to labor scarcity, frontier wages were 30 to 100 percent higher than in other parts of the country, and Moran notes that "document after document blames this scarcity of labor for the low levels of labor investment in farming in the frontier." But aside from the scarce labor supply, there was little incentive for (and therefore demand by) most farms to employ wage laborers given the truly marginal position of agriculture. Furthermore, when wealth was accumulated on the frontier, whether in the United States or Brazil, it was usually poured into commercial and mercantile ventures. Money invested in land was limited to the cost of claiming, such as felling trees; the emphasis was on making and expanding personal claims rather than improving already held terrain. According to one study of Illinois cited by Moran, three-quarters of the mortgages were used to buy land rather than improve farms or cope with unexpected losses. Moran's own data suggest that although for one Brazilian area "70 percent of the variance in area cleared was explained by the amount of bank credit provided," less than 15 percent of the loans were used to make improvements. The result -- contra Turner's thesis -- is to produce an economically stratified society on the frontier as some have more, and some less, success in obtaining rights to the land and carrying out commercial activities. Eventually, when the short-term becomes the long and land prices escalate, there may be an outburst of sales, but it is also the more prosperous who stay on the land, while those with fewer assets may migrate once again with, perhaps, new speculative hopes in mind.

In many respects, then, frontier behavior does conform to a capitalist pattern. An analogous activity in the current day may be wildcat drilling, which is also a speculation concerning what nature may offer and a culture might desire. From this perspective, the set of notions concerning rugged individualism and human equality are not, as Turner might have claimed, a result of the impact of nature within culture, but part of the model that humans within a certain economy bring to their

215

activities upon nature. But there is another, almost paradoxical, conclusion that may be drawn: using a Ricardian model of farming profit, one can show how a subsistence form of agriculture is generated by capitalism on its frontier. When, under population pressure, the Ricardian land border is reached, the only alternative - other than international trade - is to begin subsistence farming beyond the economic margin, which is precisely what occurred on all four frontiers. According to the prevailing wisdom, however, production for use (or subsistence) and production for exchange (or profit) are not only logically opposed but historically ordered activities. In the traditional view, as exchange develops in society, existing systems of production for use may briefly be perpetuated and exploited, but eventually market behavior displaces production for the home (Bohannan and Dalton 1965; Meillassoux 1972, 1973; Polanyi 1968; Smith 1976 [1776]). By contrast, on the frontier production for use is engendered by, sustained by, and supports production for exchange. Where capitalist culture meets nature, production for use is a short-term practice undertaken within the long-term project of production for exchange. This conclusion must raise the possibility that such inverted, mixed, and liminal processes just off the capitalist margin are not only more general than previously thought but produced by capitalism itself.

References

Bohannan, Paul and George Dalton. 1965. Markets in Africa. Garden City: Anchor.
Gudeman, Stephen. 1984. Ricardo's Representations. Representations 5:92-114.
Levi-Strauss, Claude. 1969. The Elementary Structures of Kinship (trans. J. Bell, J. von Sturmer, R. Needham). London: Eyre and Spottiswoode.
Meillassoux, Claude. 1972. From Reproduction to Production. Economy and Society 1:93-105.
----- 1973. The Social Organization of the Peasantry: the Economic Basis of Kinship. Journal of Peasant Studies 1:81-90.
Polanyi, Karl. 1968. Primitive, Archaic, and Modern Economies (ed. G. Dalton). Garden City: Anchor Books.
Ricardo, David. 1951. The Works and Correspondence of David Ricardo, ed. P. Sraffa, vols I,IV. Cambridge: Cambridge University Press.
Smith, Adam. 1976[1776]. The Wealth of Nations. Chicago: University of Chicago Press.

SECTION III: THE STATE AND THE STRUGGLE FOR CONTROL

Although the essays in this section often deal with issues of production, their focus is on the political implications of development. In particular, these authors examine struggles and programs for the control of productive resources.

Mary Crain, Richard Salisbury, and Evelyn Pinkerton document struggles for control by communities. Crain describes the local debate over the moral and practical implications of land redistribution in an Ecuador community. Salisbury reports the efforts of the Cree of Quebec (and a group of anthropologists, including himself) to secure the economic viability of local hunting by way of an agreement with the state. Salisbury argues that a cultural community can preserve a degree of autonomy within a nation-state. Pinkerton's fishermen's cooperatives are also cases in which groups obtained control over their resources by way of governmental middle-level institutions, but her case also involves the problem of management of a common property. Pinkerton makes the case for common management structures as the most suitable solution for the fishing groups she studied.

Both Leo Despres and Susan Russell address the advantages of remaining outside organized economic institutions. Despres considers the structural implications of economic development activities in the city of Manaus, Brazil, and, in particular, the advantages that accrue to self-employment. Russell's study underlines the flexibililty of a different informal sector: that of food sellers in a poor section of Manila. She underlines the political and economic significance of state-sponsored supermarkets.

David Freeman and Walter Coward analyze the control of water in state-sponsored and local irrigation systems. While Freeman looks at the general issues of knowledge, incentives, and equity in these systems, Coward describes the "underlying propety grid" implicit or explicit in several Asian irrigation systems, a cultural structure that is often violated by state-initiated irrigated programs.

13. PEASANT IDEOLOGICAL PRACTICES AND POLITICAL PROCESS IN THE ECUADOREAN HIGHLANDS: CONFLICT AND CONSENSUS IN AGRARIAN POLITICS

Mary M. Crain

It has been argued that despite considerable research on peasant society, we still know relatively little about peasant notions of justice, or their conceptions of right and wrong (Brow 1985, Rude 1980, Sharpe 1976, Scott 1976, 1977). These are ideas, however, that help shape both peasant acts of political protest and their acts of acquiesence. Information concerning peasant beliefs regarding the legitimacy of a particular agrarian order is also frequently lacking (cf. Brow 1985).

This paper responds to some of these issues. I give an account of peasant political mobilization of several months duration that occurred while I lived in Quimsa, located adjacent to the Hacienda La Miranda, in the northern highlands of Ecuador.[1] The Quimseno peasantry, dominated until recently by political and economic structures that tied them to the local hacienda system, has had little experience with any form of collective organization. Encouraged however by outside support as well as their own successful resolution of a series of earlier community conflicts, peasants decided to organize a Farm Cooperative.

The paper has four parts: first I sketch the beginning of this mobilization, outlining some of the peasantry's objectives; second I focus on the problems the movement encountered; third I examine the process of concientizacion, or the creation of a new political awareness among the Quimseno peasantry; and fourth I analyze why, in the aftermath of the mobilization, this new form of peasant consciousness was overshadowed by a more powerful hierarchical ideology. By analyzing the local idioms of peasant politics and ideology, this study contributes to an understanding of both the problems that beset peasant political movements as well as the beliefs of many peasants about the legitimacy of a particular agrarian order.

Local Level Political Mobilization

During March 1983, Antonio Sandoval, a former president of Quimsa's town council, called a community meeting at the still unfinished Casa Comunal to discuss forming a Peasant Cooperative

Farm. Several hundred community members gathered for their first meeting that night in the dark and damp Casa Comunal, carrying candles, as electricity had yet to be installed. By this date, Pre-Cooperatives had been successfully formed by several neighboring communities. In each case, individual peasants had contributed a small sum of money to indicate their interest in working collectively to acquire a common piece of land from the surrounding haciendas. They had placed their signatures, or in the case of illiterate peasants, their thumbprints, on the Pre-Cooperatives roster, and then had appealed to IERAC (the National Agrarian Reform and Colonization Agency of Ecuador), soliciting its aid to investigate the possibility of securing land. In many cases, peasants cited both demographic pressure on their existing land base as well as hacienda monopolization of land, water, and forests, as sufficient grounds for petitioning IERAC to undertake a government study. In areas in which government officials had concluded that population pressures on the land were exceedingly high, IERAC had worked with campesinos to negotiate the acquisition of portions of private hacienda land.[2] In almost all cases, and in keeping with IERAC's agrarian policy, the land alloted to campesinos was in the form of communal and not individual holdings. IERAC encouraged economies of scale and tried to deter any attempts by Farm Cooperatives to privatize or individualize the entire holding.[3] The agrarian reform agency initiated adjudications for the transfer of land from the hacienda owner to the peasantry and reimbursed the former for the estimated commercial value of his property. Members of the Pre-Cooperative were given a five year period in which to repay IERAC for the land.

At this first community meeting, the situation of Quimsa's landless or land-poor population, its sueltos and jornaleros was discussed. Sueltos are former wage workers at the Hacienda La Miranda without land today; jornaleros are current wage workers there. Many individuals attending this meeting belonged to one of these two groups and they were particularly interested in working with the nascent Pre-Cooperative, as one strategy for acquiring land. The sueltos claimed that their years of labor for the owner of Hacienda La Miranda entitled them today to some portion of the hacienda land. They had not received land at the time of the local agrarian reform in 1962.[4] There were several reasons why a peasant might not have received land. First, the hacienda had awarded title to subsistence plots only to peasants who had served the hacienda for 10 years or more as tenants, and who were still on the payroll in 1962. Many of the present sueltos worked long years for the hacienda, but had either retired before 1962, or had a hiatus in their years of employment, and consequently were ineligible. Some sueltos were apegados (literally attached, stuck on) to plots owned by their relatives who were former tenants. The jornaleros were day laborers who had begun working

220

for wages at the hacienda during the period following agrarian reform. Although some jornaleros came from the ranks of smallholders and had already received title to land, the majority were too young to have been awarded a plot in 1962. However, by 1983, most members of the group were in the 20 to 30 year age bracket and had large families of their own to support. In many cases, individual jornaleros were also apegados to a parent's or other relative's owned plot and 3 generations of the same family might be trying to subsist on 2 to 3 hectares of land.

Many sueltos and jornaleros who were apegados, and thus in a dependent relationship vis a vis their relatives, had little control over the allocation of the plot. Decisions regarding the use of the land were generally made by the titular (title holder) of the plot, who might choose from any of the following options: to work the land collectively by pooling his labor with that of the apegados, let the apegados sharecrop his land, or divide the plot into miniature portions for individual cultivation. Sueltos and jornaleros had to maintain an amiable relationship with the titular of the plot in order to ensure continued access to land. As the amount of land they could work was generally quite small and rights to its use were subject to change at the titular's discretion, many sueltos and jornaleros hoped to procure their own land to alleviate their overall insecurity.

Other issues were also raised at this first community meeting. In conjunction with the decision to consider the formation of a Pre-Cooperative, several individuals also expressed a desire to understand what the national agrarian reform of 1964 actually meant. Some 20 years after agrarian reform legislation was first implemented, an aura of confusion regarding this legislation continued to prevail in Quimsa. Many villagers pondered whether the goals were to increase agricultural productivity or to redistribute land to the peasantry. Many felt that only by obtaining an accurate description and analysis of national agrarian reform legislation would they be able to evaluate whether their "rights to land" had been violated. Peasants of Quimsa decided to ask government officials from IERAC to attend the next meeting in Quimsa and explain some of the implications of agrarian reform to them.

On April 10, 1983, several officials from IERAC came to the community and patiently discussed the special regulations governing land titles and property deeds, taxation, inheritance and the buying and selling of peasant plots. This meeting with IERAC provided a fine opportunity for several peasants to ventilate their resentment toward the local hacienda owner and the latter's private version of agrarian reform.[5] The local agrarian reform in Quimsa occurred in 1962, two years prior to the national agrarian reform, through the private initiative of

Senor Rafael Rodriguez, the owner of Hacienda La Miranda. One elderly Quimseno, a suelto said: "This patron Rafael, since he understands everything about the law, and we -- we understand nothing. He has tricked us, promising us subsistence plots which we have never received." In this statement, the peasant is referring to the fact that he served for the patron under the traditional tenancy system and during that time he was told that he would receive his own subsistence plot. He retired from his job with the hacienda however, and his son replaced him in his former position, shortly before the advent of the local agrarian reform. Thus when agrarian reform was implemented in 1962, it was his son's name that was shown on the payroll of the hacienda, so that the son received the official title to the land instead of his father. In this particular case, the father argued that his son, upon receiving the land title, had dismissed his advice, allowing him no say with respect to the allocation of the plot.

In another, more extreme case, when a male head of household who was a titular owner died, his brother attempted to dispossess the widow and her children from the plot, arguing that he held sole rights of possession because he had undertaken cultivation of the plot for the past three years and had also upgraded the value of the land by building his own house on this site. A law passed in association with the national agrarian reform bill stated that all subsistence plots are family patrimony, belonging jointly to the titular, his or her spouse and their descendents, and that this land, if under five hectares in size, cannot be subdivided. The legislation further specified that, in the event of the death of the titular, 50% of the plot should remain in the hands of the widow/widower and the other 50% should be cultivated by the children of the deceased tenant. Since the agrarian reform, many intra-family disputes have arisen concerning the allocation of the subsistence plot, largely due to the peasantry's lack of familiarity with these laws and as a result of multiple claims to a single, small piece of common land.

Factions: Divisions Within the Community of Quimsa

During the third community meeting in Quimsa, convened on April 18, 1983, there was a call for the election of a body of individuals who would be responsible for handling many of the administrative decisions associated with the proposed Pre-Cooperative. Several names were immediately suggested for the directiva (administrative council). At this time, A. Sandoval, the man who had convened the first meeting, spoke up and attempted to place restrictions on the eligibility of certain nominees. He argued that membership in the proposed cooperative should be limited solely to the sueltos; thus jornaleros would be excluded from membership in the Pre-Cooperative. This attempt to restrict membership provoked a flurry of debate and controversy, ultimately creating two separate factions in Quimsa.

Several individuals whose names had already been suggested for leadership positions in the directiva would have been disqualified if the Pre-Cooperative had included only former hacienda workers. A. Sandoval, a suelto himself, argued that the owners of Hacienda La Miranda were most obligated to sell or award land to former workers who had not received title to land in 1962. He backed his position for restricting cooperative membership to sueltos only, by pointing out that many of them were now too old (most were 35 years of age or older) to receive any additional training that would prepare them for obtaining employment outside Quimsa. In addition, he stated that sueltos received no wage income from the hacienda today and therefore their need for land to ensure minimal subsistence needs was critical. He also noted that the jornaleros, by contrast, could rely on their wages from the hacienda to meet some of their living expenses. Furthermore, unlike the sueltos, many of the jornaleros had received some "on-the-job" training, paid for by the Hacienda La Miranda, and if they were to lose their jobs, they had expertise that would enable them to find work outside the parish. Behind his remarks was Sr. Sandoval's assumption that the hacienda owner would react more favorably to a land sale to sueltos than to a larger Cooperative venture that would include sueltos, jornaleros, and perhaps even individuals who had never worked for the hacienda.[6]

Opposition to A. Sandoval's proposed limitation of membership in the Pre-Cooperative brought age-old conflicts to the fore. Peasants who favored equal participation by all groups hurled insults at Sandoval, calling him a huarmi-siki (a man who acts like a woman; a more literal translation of the term would be a woman's behind or rear end). These community conflicts also had geographical, ethnic and political dimensions. A. Sandoval, along with his small coterie of allies, which will be referred to as Faction A, lived in the callejon de Quimsa (lower Quimsa), in which inhabitants' homes were crowded in between the hacienda pastures on the one side and a one-lane cobblestone public thoroughfare on the other. The majority of the members of Faction B, those who favored a more inclusive Pre-Cooperative membership, lived in El Alto de Quimsa (upper Quimsa), perched on the slopes of the Andes. While A. Sandoval's supporters professed a self-identification as mestizos (non-Indians, persons of stipulated European and indigenous American descent) supporters of Faction B largely identified themselves as campesinos indigenas (indigenous peasants). Furthermore, both at this meeting as well as in other social contexts, A. Sandoval and

223

his followers were labelled caciques (bosses) and
gente con palancas (people with pull or important connections) by
the residents of El Alto.[7] Upper Quimsa peasants resented the
control that Faction A had maintained over Quimsa's town council
and over provincial and national politics. Since the first
agrarian reform in 1962, it had been primarily individuals from
Faction A who had been elevated to the town council. As
"brokers" between community concerns and the various government
ministries and national political parties (cf. Adams 1970 and
Wolf 1956), these individuals had acquired political experience
outside the community that members of Faction B lacked. One
peasant from El Alto commented on this domination:

> The zone of El Alto here has always been controlled by the
> people from the callejon,... the mestizos... Before, it was
> worse; before, the people of El Alto were more passive and
> accepted all kinds of discrimination.. In those days the
> caciques ordered us around. Only now are things changing.
> Now people are becoming aware and are finding their own voice.

The term "cacique," used in the preceding to allude to A.
Sandoval and several other mestizos of Quimsa's callejon, was the
name given by the early Spanish colonists to rulers of the Andean
chiefdoms in the Quimsa area as elsewhere. This term has
acquired a second meaning since then, and has emerged as an
important idiom that Quimsenos use for individuals who exercise
political control over the peasantry. In its popular circulation
in Quimseno conversations, "cacique" refers not only to mestizos
but also to hacendados. This term has been associated with the
hacienda system in various discourses that describe "the national
past." Hurtado describes the cacique:

> The phenomenon of caciquismo also had its roots in the
> hacienda structure. The local chief or cacique emerged when
> certain hacendados, because of the great extent of their
> territorial possessions, acquired sufficient economic and
> social status to permit them to rise above other owners and to
> exercise such overwhelming political power as could not be
> countered even by the central government, the cacique used
> Congress and municipal governments to channel patronage among
> his followers and to shower favors among his electoral
> clientele; he used his power to ruin his adversaries... and he
> opposed any public works project that might have enhanced
> national integration [Hurtado 1980:54].

In a variety of political contexts, indigenous peasants of
Quimsa frequently juxtaposed the term "cacique," with its
connotations of power and authority vested in one-man-rule, to a
form of communal solidarity in which the community at large
decides issues of local concern. Much of the antagonism that

developed between Factions A and B revolved around this underlying conflict between privileging individual authority and a consensual, communal authority.

During the course of this third community meeting, several residents of El Alto accused A. Sandoval of acting solely out of individual self-interest, arguing that what motivated his desire to restrict Cooperative membership was his ambition to head the Cooperative and acquire some additional land "under the table" for himself. A few El Alto residents chose this occasion to accuse Sandoval of graft. They reminded him that during his recent term as a member of Quimsa's town council, which had also included several other members of Faction A, the council had "robbed El Alto peasants blind" by embezzling a hefty sum of 23,000 sucres (approximately $290.00 U.S.) that had been collected from the residents in one sector of El Alto for the installation of electricity in that locale. These peasants reminded Sandoval that although their money had mysteriously vanished, they were still without the promised electric lines.

Following this heated debate, the majority of those present backed the proposal that the Pre-Cooperative should be open to jornaleros, sueltos, and non-hacienda peasants. Nominees for the directiva were then proposed for a second time. A. Sandoval's name was suggested along with the names of several individuals from Faction B. An election was held and three men from Faction B were chosen to head the directiva of the Pre-Cooperative Farm of Quimsa. A. Sandoval was not elected to any position.

The Emergence of Concientizacion

Quimsa's fourth community meeting was held on April 27, 1983. Members of Quimsa's new directiva contacted the Ecuadorean Agricultural Aid Program (EAAP) asking that individuals from that organization be on hand to offer advice regarding the formation of the Pre-Cooperative and to share knowledge of the experiences of nearby peasant communities that had been successful in obtaining hacienda land.[8] The meeting also proved to be an excellent window into peasant ideological practices, in which conflicting and sometimes contradictory ideological positions were aired.

The meeting was opened by one middle-aged suelto, S. Amado, who offered several suggestions regarding various political alternatives that community members might pursue. Many of these encouraged the development of strong horizontal ties based on class interests. He pointed out that most Quimsenos were aware

225

of the experience of the neighboring communities of La Yema and Chaupi, in which peasants had been able to buy land from Quimsa's patron. He remarked that, in comparison to Quimsa, La Yema and Chaupi were mas unidos (were more unified, had more solidarity) and he felt that Quimsenos should learn from their experiences. These communities had formed a Pre-Cooperative, bargained collectively with the patron and, with help from EAAP in the case of Chaupi, had succeded in purchasing approximately 135 hectares of land from him. Peasants from Chaupi and La Yema began to grow potatoes and other tubers on this land. Revenues from the sale of these agricultural products enabled them to gain a new independence from the owners of the chicherias and cantinas (bars where chicha and aguardiente were sold) in nearby San Marcos, to whom they had formerly been indebted.

One hacienda jornalero, Manuel Ricali, also contributed to the discussion at this point. He told Quimsenos gathered in the Casa Comunal that he had a grievance against the owner of the Hacienda La Miranda. He stated that, as S. Amado had just reminded them, the patron had sold a tract of hacienda land located near La Yema and Chaupi to some of the peasants residing there. Furthermore, the owners of the neighboring haciendas, La Margarita and El Cisne, had also eventually agreed to a sale of a portion of their respective estates to a group of ex-workers. Ricali argued that, in summary, there was no good reason why Sr. Rodriguez should not follow suit, by selling or donating land to Quimsa's campesinos. Ricali also mentioned that Sr. Rodriguez had stated many times his intention to sell a piece of land to the Quimsenos but he had never done so.[9]

At this time, several Quimsenos mentioned that they had held earlier conversations with the patron, in which they expressed their interest in purchasing a sector of the Hacienda La Miranda known as Loma Linda. Quimsenos were quite conscious of their efforts to obtain this particular tract of land. The Quimsenos insistence on Loma Linda is indicative of a wider struggle between the peasant community and the hacienda owners with respect to control over local production zones (cf. Mayer 1979). Of the three ecological zones in Quimsa (the Bajio, El Alto and the Paramo), the majority of peasants lacked access to the bajio or valley floor of the Andes. Most of this bajio is owned by the five large haciendas in the parish, and it is the only production zone with irrigable land. During the last twenty-five years, production on the bajio lands has become increasingly specialized and dedicated to commercial dairying. The pastures of the valley floor are sown in fodder crops of alfalfa, rye, and bluegrass, and Holstein cattle have been imported to upgrade the local dairy stock. Capital investments have also been high; most hacienda owners argue that dairying involves fewer risks than agriculture in this region and is more profitable. Many peasants in Quimsa resent the estate owner's monopolization of the bajio lands and the latter's ability to engage in a lucrative dairy operation with which peasants are not able to compete. Only the jornaleros of Hacienda La Miranda have been able to gain access to this land through rental of pastures from the hacienda on a monthly basis; but even this access is limited by ceilings on pasture rentals enforced by the hacienda.

The area known as Loma Linda is approximately 90 hectares in size and stands in close proximity to the dirt road leading to the Comuna del Cerro, Quimsa's communal lands, awarded to the peasantry at the time of agrarian reform. The communal lands are located in the paramo, a windswept mountainous region located above the tree line. Much of the land in this production zone is on an incline and only a small portion of the total area can be used for agriculture. During 1982-1983, indigenous peasants from El Alto worked two hectares of paramo land, planting potatoes and onions. Quimsenos stressed the potential benefits of acquiring Loma Linda. First, they noted that most of this land is flat enough that a tractor could enter and plow the area. One Quimsena remarked that Loma Linda is not critical for the operation of the hacienda, as it is only used occasionally to pasture their herds of sheep. She also stated that although not presently irrigated, the land is not far from the Nomo River and water from this source could be diverted to Loma Linda.

The Casa Comunal discussion returned the floor to S. Amado, who argued that along with the formation of a Pre-Cooperative, a sindicato or union should also be organized in Quimsa by all the peasants who still worked for the Hacienda La Miranda. At this point, an individual in the audience, C. Bernal, brought up the issue of negative sanctions, pointing out that the patron might resort to dismissing those Quimsenos who were responsible for organizing the sindicato and he might also bring in outside labor to replace them. Amado responded to this remark, stating that "... we should not fear the patron so much ..." and he argued, "... where else is the patron going to get workers from if we do not agree to work for him?" S. Amado was of the opinion that the patron would probably have to pay outside laborers twice as much as the going daily wage in Quimsa.[10] Amado also mentioned that a successful sindicato should negotiate a written contract, endorsed by workers and the patron, containing clauses that would protect local workers from being dismissed from their jobs without adequate review and would not allow the patron to bring in outside laborers to replace Quimsenos.

This fourth meeting provided an open atmosphere for discussion as well as self-reflection. Initially a few peasants seemed uneasy; they stammered as they began to speak up and describe their problems in the presence of "city folks." Ashamed by their lack of educational preparation, many peasants, demonstrated their own feelings of inadequacy by prefacing their remarks to the EAAP officials with "Mr. Engineer and Mr. Promotor, our distinguished guests, you are more prepared than us peasants, the poor ones. Please excuse our manner of speaking and expressing ourselves." As the meeting progressed, many peasants gradually became more outspoken. The EAAP personnel who were present at this meeting provided the Quimsenos with an outside perspective on local problems. EAAP had begun working with the community in 1982, offering technical assistance with agricultural production and providing advice on matters such as the control of soil erosion, reforestation, and the eradication of certain pests. This organization had also made agricultural equipment, such as tractors and threshers, available to peasants at a low rental cost. The agency's own policy convictions were to encourage independent problem-solving among peasants in rural communities and to establish collective self-help projects. EAAP hoped to foster a "team spirit" in Quimsa that might counter certain features of daily life in the community that directly or indirectly divided the peasantry. These divisive features included a mistrust of fellow peasants and a sense of isolation stemming from the fact that most peasants tended to work on their parcels of land alone, separated from others. EAAP was also interested in "concientizacion," the process of raising the political awareness of the peasantry in rural Ecuador (cf. Freire 1970). Of the two members of the local EAAP team, one was an agronomist and the other was trained as a Promotor Social (people's advocate). It was the specific responsibility of the Promotor Social to work with the peasantry on issues relating to concientizacion. He was assigned the tasks of promoting cooperative work among campesinos and providing them with some understanding of the larger political picture. This picture included a sketchy outline of the national class structure and it made peasants increasingly aware of their position within that structure.

At this fourth community meeting, the EAAP advisors explained that they were there to listen to the Quimsenos first. They urged peasants to describe and share their work experiences with one another, to air their grievances and to try to formulate potential political goals, such as the formation of the Pre-Cooperative Farm. In response, several other peasants then rose to the floor, and began to speak about their early work experiences. An intergenerational dialogue unfolded in which many of the older peasants, who had formerly worked for Hacienda La Miranda, described their living and working conditions under the traditional tenancy system that prevailed before agrarian reform. These labor testimonies emphasized the issue of landlessness and pointed to the fact that many community members had worked long years for the hacienda but they had nothing to show for this servitude. In delivering these testimonies, many individual peasants made a logical connection between their former service and their understanding that, in return, they were entitled to receive a small family subsistence plot of their own from the patron of the hacienda. One woman spoke of her life under traditional tenancy:

We were on call both day and night. At 3:00 a.m. we were frequently aroused by the mayordomo of the hacienda and sent off to fetch water from La Yema. I often had to leave my crops and my children and go off for domestic service for 2 months at the owners' home in Quito. I remember the patrona Anna telling me "... when the agrarian reform comes, Rosa, make sure you get your own subsistence plot." But I never received any land.

Another woman spoke to community members about her rightful claim to land: "For many long years in the hacienda, my husband and I worked. Because of that I have my rights. Because of that I am not afraid to enter the patron's house. He cannot deny me the land."

After listening to these labor testimonies as well as the earlier comments that various peasants made, the EAAP representatives had a clearer understanding of the local political problems. They responded by raising certain issues for discussion and suggesting ways the community might organize. The EAAP team made Quimsenos aware of the many forces that might divide or fragment their attempts at political mobilization. For example Alfaro Mina, EAAP's Promotor Social, pointed out that many of the peasants attending this meeting still worked for the Hacienda La Miranda and he enumerated several ways in which this might weaken their organization. He presented the following scenario for his peasant audience, suggesting that:

Tomorrow, Senor Robles, the administrator of the Hacienda La Miranda may approach a worker and ask him about exactly what had occurred last night in the Casa Comunal. Then this worker, in order merely to assure favorable relations with Sr. Robles, or perhaps in hopes of receiving a small cash bonus, might disclose information about the political movement which we have been discussing here tonight.

The spokesman's discussion was interjected by one Quimsena who appealed to hierarchical norms as she rose to defend the patron, stating "... we can't betray the patron because he has given us work and has helped with the education of our children." In response to this woman's appeal for loyalty to the patron, A. Mina told the Quimsenos that peasants in the nearby community of Chaupi were also once afraid to struggle. He noted that peasants

229

there had feared the patron, viewing him as a cuco (a demon or devil) and they felt incapable of organizing against such a powerful figure. Through their own political efforts in conjunction with outside support from both EAAP and CEDOC (a national labor confederation), the peasants of Chaupi formed an Association of Agricultural Workers, which was ultimately successful in acquiring hacienda land from the patron. Mina argued that in Chaupi, the peasant's image of the patron as an omnipotent figure changed, once they saw that their cumulative efforts had achieved positive results.

Mina also informed the campesinos that one of EAAP's many objectives was to promote a dialogue among peasants about political issues. He stressed that, however, EAAP was not primarily a political organization. He suggested that to gain "outside support" for the local political movement Quimsenos should contact such national organizations as the Ecuadorean Indian Federation (EIF) or Ecuarrunari (Ecuadorean Indigenous Peoples) (cf. NUEVA 1983).

Following this discussion, the EAAP spokesman asked me to address the community members assembled in the Casa Comunal that night. My reception by EAAP personnel had been somewhat cool initially, when I visited their regional offices in Chalapa, because the team working there had immediately taken me for a U.S. Peace Corps volunteer (of which there were many in rural Ecuador), and also as a "friend of the hacendados." Only after several visits, in which I described the nature of my field research to them and listed my affiliation with several institutions in Quito, was I able to gain their trust, and they agreed that I might attend any of the community meetings of Quimsa in which EAAP was also present. Somewhat suprised by EAAP's request that I participate in the meeting, I decided to share knowledge gathered from my field research that was pertinent to the discussion of political mobilization that night. I reminded those present that my study concerned changes in the landlord-peasant relationship and that consequently I had conducted several interviews with both the local patron as well as with the other hacienda owners in the parish. I reported that most of these estate owners had informed me of their future plans to increase the mechanization of their farm operations. I also explained that in my house-to-house surveys of each peasant home in Quimsa, one of the most frequent responses to my question of "What do you think is the biggest problem in the community of Quimsa?" was that "there is a lack of union (unity or solidarity) among the peasants here." Envisioning a future in which fewer wage positions on the local haciendas would be available to peasants, I spoke of the importance of establishing union. I argued that peasants would increasingly have to create their own alternatives that would ensure their subsistence needs and would attend to caring for the elderly when they were no longer able to work. I stated that, in my opinion, one of the most viable local options for the peasantry would be an expansion of their existing land base. I suggested that this additional land could be used to grow both subsistence crops and cash crops for sale in the regional markets. I told them that I therefore endorsed their efforts to form a Pre-Cooperative and I would try to support them in fulfilling these efforts.

Following my statement, D. Moreno, a jornalero, addressed the community and spoke of the difficulties both in organizing local peasants and in creating union. He remarked: "People here say they want to organize and have union. But then they make it only halfway up the hacienda road. Quimsenos retreat, the closer they come to an encounter with the patron."

Commentary

An analysis of the dialogue that arose during these meetings demonstrates the ambivalence Quimsenos have about initiating and supporting a movement for social change. That this meeting, and the others preceding it, occurred at all, in the absence of landlords and other social superiors, set a precedent in Quimsa, indicating a subtle shift in peasant consciousness. Peasant informants reported that this was the first time in which: a) community meetings had been held for such a lengthy period of time; b) the objectives discussed during the meetings were for the most part, political in nature; and c) peasants had encouraged an outside group such as EAAP to become involved in their mobilization efforts. The presence of EAAP also lent a new authority and legitimacy to the demands of the peasantry. Seeing outsiders who were willing to challenge the local power structure created new ways of thinking about their problems among the peasantry.

Two contradictory ideological orientations emerged in the various statements aired by individual peasants during the series of community meetings. The proposals and discussion concerning the formation of both a Pre-Cooperative to acquire land and a peasant union that would increase the laborer's bargaining power, suggest at least a nascent ideological orientation based on shared class interests that are perceived as distinct from the interests of the owners of large estates in the parish. Other statements voiced during the meetings indicated that some peasants were still inclined to appeal to a hierarchical ideology that acceded to the inequalities of the existing social structure. This ideology was characteristic of the deference and loyalty that Quimsenos had shown toward the landlords under traditional tenancy arrangements.

231

Visions of Justice

After participating in many hours of public and private discussion related to this period of politicization, I arrived at several conclusions regarding what social justice might mean to the majority of peasants who were involved in this mobilization. First, peasants feel they have a right to some portion of hacienda land. At minimum, peasants argue that each family without land today should have a subsistence plot, or as an alternative, they believe the hacienda should sell them a portion of land, such as Loma Linda, that they can work collectively. The sueltos view their claim to land as a repayment for work performed for the hacienda in the past. The jornaleros justify their need for land by pointing to the fact that their present positions do not provide them with any type of unemployment compensation or old age pension. From the peasants' standpoint, the legitimacy of the existing agrarian social structure and the patron's position of authority within it depend on the latter's willingness to take some form of action that will enable peasant households to meet their basic subsistence needs. What is perceived as "immoral" from the vantage point of the peasantry is a person who controls a vast extension of land within the community while at the same time others are deprived of this resource and consequently may go hungry (cf. Scott 1976). At present, the peasant conception of justice does not call for a society of equals in Quimsa. Interestingly enough, although peasants have not been able to obtain the hacienda land they need, other hacienda resources, available on a regular basis, do contribute to the daily sustenance of the peasant community. These resources, all found inside the grounds of the hacienda, are particularly critical for the poorer peasants. They include wild fruits, nuts and vegetables as well as special pasture grass gathered for animals, and fallen branches that are used for firewood. Furthermore, on a few select tracts of hacienda land, communal grazing after the crop is harvested is also allowed. Although indigenous peasants defend their access to these resources as "their rights," I was informed by two members of the hacienda management that these are not really "Indian rights" at all but merely "concessions," temporary favors bestowed by the hacienda that may be taken away at any time. The decision on the part of the hacienda owner to continue to allow campesinos their customary access to these resources, has bolstered his image in the eyes of the peasantry. I would suggest that these practices are one of many mechanisms by which peasants resist the pressures of privatization and commercialization associated with hacienda production. In this scenario, hacienda resources are appropriated by the peasantry as community resources that enter the realm of the public domain.

The Dissipation of Political Mobilization

During the six months following the March and April meetings the collective efforts to form a Pre-Cooperative and a sindicato dissipated. Community meetings came to a grinding halt and after several unsuccessful attempts by EAAP to contact the directiva of the Pre-Cooperative, the EAAP personnel finally reduced their visits to the community. Although coordinated political activity was suspended at this time (and until my departure in October 1983), this does not mean that a resurgence of this mobilization might not occur in the future. Furthermore, I would argue that although this series of political meetings did not lead to the formation of a Pre-Cooperative or a sindicato, they did encourage the growth of a new critical consciousness. This new consciousness allowed peasants to gain a different perspective on their problems by beginning to view what were formally individual and private problems as collective problems shared by fellow peasants. The discussion during these meetings of the victories and successes of other peasant communities that had been able to acquire hacienda land opened new horizons for Quimsenos, enabling them to concede that the existing rural social structure in Quimsa was not the the only possible social structure. It is quite plausible that insights gained from these attempts at mobilization can be drawn upon by local peasants and used to inform future struggles. Turton speaks of the development of self-confidence and a sense of autonomy arising among Thai peasants:

> When poor peasants are able to organize their own meetings, shielded from the presence of richer farmers and village officials (who may try to monitor and deliberately inhibit such meetings) then their self-confidence increases and the poor dare to show their feelings ... [and]... there is a constant effort to overcome fear by subordinant parties to relations of domination.... In this light, every assertion which reduces fear and increases boldness, takes on new significance [Turton 1984:48,61].

Acknowledging that one outcome of these meetings may be a recognition on the part of Quimsenos of their capacity for independent organizing, a central question remains to be asked: What were some of the forces at work that limited political mobilization at the time and that also deterred a more complete class conflict from developing in Quimsa, or as D. Moreno put it earlier, "Why did Quimsenos make it only halfway up the hacienda road?" Many Quimsenos evaluated their initial efforts at collective organization in light of an almost predictable retaliation by the local patron. Feder has described the

233

landlords' response to the political organizing of their rural laborers, noting:

The severest sanctions are reserved for efforts to unionize the farm workers. The opposition of the hacienda owners to collective action is systematic and accompanied by drastic counter-measures which seem warranted only as an expression of the principle that to admit to rightful claims in an individual case is tantamount to the landlord's surrender of authority to determine unilaterally the working and living conditions of his farm people [Feder 1971:91].

Quimsenos, although acutely aware of their shrinking land base and thus interested in acquiring any new land, had to weigh this need in light of the material benefits of paternalism that many still received. Peasants felt that a continuation of their political organizing might result in the loss of jobs at the Hacienda La Miranda, a cutback or curtailment of the patron's gifts and donations to the local primary school, and a severing of the patron's personal ties with the peasantry, that included his participation in certain community rituals. Households in which several family members worked for the hacienda or which had many children in the local primary school would be the first to feel the impact of any withdrawal of the patron's aid.

There were other obstacles that mitigated against further political action and the growth of class solidarity based on that action. Conflicts within the community, often apparent in the resurgence of Factions A and B, also divided the peasantry on many issues. Although Faction B seemed to have the backing of the majority of peasants in Quimsa, this did not mean that it was free from political wrangling with Faction A. Faction B feared that the latter group, hoping to ingratiate themselves in the patron's favor, would spread rumors about their activities to the patron. Instead of promoting a popular front in which peasants might unite together to obtain a common end, such as securing land, the resurgence of these factions almost always resulted in the vertical fragmentation of the community. Differentiation of the peasantry also discouraged a unified course of political action. Not all peasants in Quimsa shared the same class situation or a similar relation to the means of production. Instead, individual peasants held different relations to the means of production and a complex landholding system with its own internal hierarchy prevailed within the peasant sector. This hierarchy was noted previously, in the case of the sueltos and the jornaleros, many of whom were dependent on the titular (who owned the means of production, which in this case was "land") in order to gain access to the means of production.[11] This hierarchy, prevalent to varying degrees within the peasantry, replicated many of the patterns of domination and subordination typical of earlier relations between hacienda owners and peasants. It generated cultural values of submission and deference that did not facilitate social change.

Conclusion

During the process of political mobilization and consciousness-raising that swept the community of Quimsa, peasants began to question both the legitimacy of some of the patron's actions as well as the validity of their "hierarchical belief system," one that arose under traditional relations of tenancy on the hacienda. In the aftermath of the mobilization however, peasants have not replaced the ideology of hierarchy with an alternative, class-oriented scheme of apprehending the world (cf. Brow 1981). Instead, these undercurrents of change represent a partial breakdown of the peasantry's traditional hierarchical outlook and social imagery. As intimated earlier, there is the possibility that in the future the hierarchical ideology will lose further credibility among the peasantry, and be replaced by an alternative ideology (cf. Alavi 1973 and Sharpe 1976). At present however, cross-cutting ties such as patron-client relations, hinder class formation and counter the existing class imagery of the peasantry (cf. Brow 1981, Newby 1978, and Alavi 1973). Peasants today evaluate their continued appeal to hierarchical norms as the strategy that offers the best guarantee for their long-term security. The attachment of the Quimseno peasantry to hierarchical norms can be explained in light of Scott's thesis regarding "the moral economy of the peasantry," in which the principles of securing "subsistence first" and "risk aversion" motivate much of peasant action (Scott 1976).

Acknowledgments

My fieldwork in Quimsa, extending from January 1982-October 1983 was supported by the Doherty Foundation at Princeton University, with supplementary funds from the Institute of Latin American Studies at the University of Texas at Austin. I would like to thank the Ecuadorean Instituto Nacional de Patrimonio Cultural in Quito for sponsoring my research. This paper, written while I was a visiting scholar at Bolivar House, Stanford University, received helpful comments from James Brow and George Esenwein.

Notes

[1] For obvious reasons, all of the names of places and persons in this paper are fictitious.

[2] The response to high demographic pressure on available land resources marked a precedent in one parish case in 1975. IERAC ruled that some 70 hectares of private hacienda land were to be sold to a nearby peasant community. Ever since the successful resolution of this case, other communities have also appealed to IERAC, asking that a government investigation of local man/land ratios be undertaken, in hopes of obtaining hacienda land (see JUNAPLA 1975).

[3] For example, IERAC turned Hacienda X over to peasants who became owners and workers at that point. The state agency specified that approximately 90% of the production unit should be worked collectively, with the remaining 10% of the land divided into small household plots allocated to each individual family.

[4] In 1962, during Quimsa's agrarian reform, only 110 individual heads of household, the labor service tenants, received title to Hacienda La Miranda's plots. These were individuals employed at that time by the hacienda, who held customary rights to the use of subsistence plots on hacienda land. Former employees who had already retired or who had left their positions for a period of time, were not included in this land reform. In 1983, Quimsa had approximately 315 households.

[5] Although agrarian reform in Quimsa was the result of a private initiative, its content coincided with the policy outlined in the national agrarian reform bill of 1964. The majority of private haciendas in Ecuador were subject to State intervention during 1964, in order to implement the reform process.

[6] In my interviews with hacienda owners in the parish, several estate owners disclosed to me that when possible, they continue to acknowledge an obligation to provide jobs or sell land both to former workers, such as the ex-tenants and the sueltos, and to the sons and daughters of the ex-tenants. These hacendados clearly regarded other peasants not included in these two groupings as gente ajena (outsiders) or gente del pueblo (townspeople) toward whom they felt little or no responsibility.

[7] The term gente con palancas translated literally signifies a person with a stick or lever. In its figurative connotation implied in this context, it refers to someone who has leverage or

236

important connections with individuals who hold important positions in the social structure.

[8] The Ecuadorean Agricultural Aid Progran (EAAP) is an agricultural institution based in Quito that receives support from the Catholic Church. EAAP teams work with peasant communities throughout Ecuador providing assistance in some of the following areas: helping with the legalization of individual and communal land titles, informing peasant communities of various lines of government credit they may be eligible for, and offering technical assistance regarding agricultural matters such as soil erosion and pest control.

[9] As early as 1976, peasants of Quimsa wrote to the National Peasant Federation of Ecuador (NPF), asking for advice regarding efforts to negotiate a land sale from the patron of Hacienda La Miranda to the community of Quimsa. During that same year, NPF responded to the peasants plea and wrote a letter directly to Sr. Rodriguez about the situation. Sr. Rodriguez responded, thanking NPF for demonstrating an interest in the situation of local peasantry. He informed them that their help would not be needed, however, and that he would take charge of these matters himself.

[10] Many peasants had told me that the wages paid in the Quimsa area were significantly lower than those paid by the large landowners in closer proximity to Quito.

[11] Within the peasant society of Quimsa, norms of reciprocity govern relations among kin. In general, the titular, or peasant smallholder, cannot deny a kinsman access to his plot of land, as he has a moral obligation to help more unfortunate kin. As owner of the land however, the titular has the power to determine the exact terms of the exchange between the two parties. The titular usually decides whether his kinsman will return his generosity by sharecropping his entire plot or by working only a small portion of his land in exchange for a monthly contribution of money or other services to his household.

References

Adams, Richard N. 1970. Brokers and Career Mobility Systems in the Structure of Complex Societies. Southwestern Journal of Anthropology 26(4):315-327.
Alavi, Hamsa. 1973. Peasant Classes and Primordial Loyalties. Journal of Peasant Studies 1(1):23-62.
Brow, James. 1981. Class Formation and Ideological Practice.

Journal of Asian Studies 40(4):703-718.
----- 1985. A Sketch of Some Conceptual Issues in the
Ethnographic Study of Agrarian Change. In: MS from the SSRC
Conference of Symbolic and Material Dimensions of Agrarian
Change held in Sri Lanka, summer 1984.
Feder, Ernst. 1971. Latifundia and Agricultural Labor in Latin
America. In: Peasants and Peasant Societies. Theodor Shanin,
ed. Great Britain: Penguin Books.
Freire, Paulo. 1970. Pedagogy of the Opressed. New York: Herder
and Herder.
Herring, Ronald. 1982. Fear, Loyalty and Attachment: Local
Understandings of Class Relations in South India. Paper
presented at the annual meetings of the Association for Asian
Studies in Chicago, panel of Ideology and Consciousness in
Legitimations of the Social Order in Peasant Societies.
Hurtado, Osvaldo. 1980. Political Power in Ecuador. Trans. Nick
Mills. Albuquerque: University of New Mexico Press.
Junta Nacional de Planificacion y Coordinacion Economica
(JUNAPLA). 1975. Determinacion de la Presion Demografica en
las Haciendas NN. Quito, Ecuador.
Mayer, Enrique. 1979. Land Use in the Andes: Ecology and
Agriculture in the Mantaro Valley of Peru with Special
Reference to Potatoes. Lima, Peru: Centro Internacional de la
Papa.
Newby, Howard, et al. 1978. Property, Paternalism and Power:
Class and Control in Rural England. London: Hutchinson &
Company.
NUEVA. 1983. La Cuestion Indigena en el Ecuador. In Cuadernos de
NUEVA. June 1983, Quito, Ecuador.
Rude, George. 1980. Ideology and Popular Protest. New York:
Pantheon Books.
Scott, James C. 1976. The Moral Economy of the Peasant: Rebellion
and Subsistence in Southeast Asia. New Haven: Yale University
Press.
----- 1977. Protest and Profanation: Agrarian Revolt and the
Little Tradition. Theory and Society 4(1):1-39 and 4(2):210-42.
Sharpe, Kenneth E. 1977. Peasant Politics: Struggle in a
Dominican Village. Baltimore: Johns Hopkins Press.
Stark, Louisa. 1981. Folk Models of Stratification and Ethnicity
in the Highlands of Northern Ecuador. In: Cultural
Transformations and Ethnicity in Modern Ecuador. Norman
Whitten, ed. Urbana, Illinois: University of Illinois Press.
Turton, Andrew. 1984. Limits of Ideological Domination and the
Formation of Social Consciousness. In: History and Peasant
Consciousness in South East Asia. Andrew Turton and Shigeharu
Tanabe, eds. Senri Ethnological Studies 13.
Wolf, Eric R. 1956. Aspects of Group Relations in Complex
Society: Mexico. American Anthropologist 58:1065-1078.

14. THE ECONOMICS OF DEVELOPMENT THROUGH SERVICES: FINDINGS OF THE MCGILL PROGRAMME AMONG THE CREE

Richard F. Salisbury

In high-income countries over half of the labor force works in the service sector, and much smaller proportions work in farming, resource extraction, or manufacturing; development in the Third World always involves a disproportionate increase in service employment. Materialists since the eighteenth century have decried this as "parasitic" on the "real" sources of wealth -- farming or industry. This paper suggests, by contrast, that increasing service employment may, under certain circumstances, be a highly effective way of inducing greater productivity in both primary and secondary industries, and thus of achieving the higher living standards and diversified economy that constitute development. In remote or colonial areas where services are planned and staffed by non-local metropolitans an increase in local service employment is best accomplished by establishing local control of service delivery within the region.

This proposition was suggested by earlier studies in Papua New Guinea (Salisbury 1969, 1971). The present paper reports on a longitudinal study of emerging regional autonomy in service delivery in Northern Canada between 1971 and 1981. During that period the staff and graduate students of the McGill Programme in the Anthropology of Development (PAD) were able to assist and advise the 6,000 Cree of Quebec as they organized and then took over the regional administration of their area. Before 1971 the PAD (Chance 1968, 1969) had studied several of the isolated, colonially administered villages of the region as mining and forestry expanded into the forest in which the Cree continued their hunting existence. Between 1971 and 1975 regional unity emerged in opposition to a major hydro-electric project, and in 1975 the Federal and Provincial Governments signed the James Bay Agreement (JBNQA) with the Cree leaders granting them regional control and finance, in return for accepting governmental sovereignty in general, and the hydro project specifically. A book is in press (Salisbury 1986) analyzing the changes of the decade 1971-1981 (and the involvement of anthropologists in the changes). The present paper focusses on the economic aspects of emerging regional self-government: its benefits of increasing employment and incomes, improved services, and a build-up of infrastructure and demand for primary and secondary industry; also on its costs, to the wider society and to the local area. It argues that creating regional political unity and improving service delivery have had major impacts as a multiplier of local demand and as a builder of the infrastructure needed for

239

diversified economic development.

Cree History 1964-1983

The growth of modern-style services of education, health,
justice, etc. to Cree living in villages long antedates 1971,
even if films like Cree Hunters of Mistassini (1973) vividly
portray the continuity between 1971 lifestyles and pre-1945
hunting patterns. Between 1945 and 1964 there was a steady
sedentarization of hunters around the foci of Hudson's Bay
Company (HBC) posts, as Canadian government services were
officially extended to native people equally with other
citizens. Before 1964, however, more than half the Cree had no
permanent residence in a village, but hunted in the bush all
winter, and lived in tents or teepees during their summer visit
to the village/post. By 1964 the building of village housing and
the expansion of forestry and mining industries in the south of
the Cree region meant that half had a permanent residence (in a
village or near a non-Cree settlement) even if 80 percent still
hunted in the bush in the winter. By 1971 about 70 percent of
the Cree had permanent housing, and the portion living in
hunting camps in winter had declined to about 70 percent.
Between 1971 and 1983 permanent housing had been built for 100
percent of the Cree population. The proportion spending winters
in the bush had dropped to 50 percent by 1975. It rose to almost
60 percent in 1976, and since then the number of winter hunters
has stabilized, though the overall increase in Cree population
means that winter hunters now form less than 50 percent of the
total.

The build-up of services in the villages implicit in
sedentarization was, before 1971, both slow and paternalistic.
It was provided for the Cree, by outsiders. Schools started
earlier by the Anglican or Oblate missions were taken over,
either by the federal Department of Indian Affairs (DINA) or by
the provincial Department of Northern Quebec (DGNQ). Small
primary schools and nursing stations were built in the smaller
villages. DGNQ built a hospital in Fort George in 1971; in 1972
the former Anglican primary school in Fort George was converted
by DINA into a residential high school for the region. Each year
DINA built a few more permanent houses in each village. The HBC
had converted its trading posts into retail stores before 1964,
and had closed the posts of Nemiscau and Waswanipi, but only
three Co-operatives had emerged by 1971 to supplement the HBC.
Only in the two largest villages of Fort George and Mistassini
were there small convenience stores, a restaurant, and a few
other local businesses.

240

Though the eight administrative bands had elective chiefs and councils, until 1971 these were mainly agencies for requesting DINA to provide more services, and for distributing housing and welfare money to individuals within bands. All planning of schools and houses was done at the District Office in the town of Val d'Or. All administrative staff other than band chiefs -- the teachers, nurses, and store managers -- were non-Cree.

Money had been used increasingly in the villages after 1945, as family and old-age allowances were paid to native people directly. The HBC had increasingly paid for furs in cash, rather than in "credit," though credit accounts were a regular part of its retail business. Salaries from employment had also grown. Casual summer work, unloading supplies for the HBC or in government construction projects, had provided cash to equip winter hunters even before 1945, and the HBC and missions had employed a few Cree as "homeguard" for over a century. Both types of employment were increasing.

Table 1 shows the economic situation of 1971. The subsistence sector produced most of the production, and most people worked in it. Even a conservative valuation of food and housing produced gave a value of twice the value of salaries, even if the sale of furs provided very little cash. Two thirds of the total cash obtained came from salaries, while transfer payments including welfare provided the other third. But overall it is a picture of poverty -- of a GNP per capita of only $1150 -- even if the Cree did not see themselves as poor.

The wage employment sector gave every indication that the Cree were destined to become a proletariat (LaRusic 1969). In southern villages the proximity of mines and forestry operations meant that temporary unskilled jobs were available, but few permanent skilled jobs. Village employment was mainly janitorial in schools and band offices, with a few positions as store clerks and secretaries. In the bigger villages to which children came as boarding-school pupils, many people worked in dormitories or as foster parents. The very few more skilled jobs were as radio-telephone operators, airline agents, teacher's aides, band managers, and a few entrepreneurs.

Into this slow paternalistic growth of sedentarization and services came the shock of the Premier of Quebec announcing in April 1971 that a hydro-electric project costing $5.6 billion would be built on Cree lands. Cree felt threatened, but did not know what to do. There were no pan-Cree structures, and band chiefs met only sporadically at meetings of the Indians of Quebec Association (IQA). The IQA agreed to protest on behalf of the Cree, as did various ecology groups and the McGill PAD.

241

Table 1.

Table 1

CREE INCOMES 1971 AND 1981

		1971[1] ($000)	%	1981[2] ($000)	%
Hunting	in cash (furs)	300	4	642[3]	2
	in kind (meat etc)[7]	3,864	57	5,700[5]	20
	Income Security	-	-	6,046	21
	Total	4,164	61	12,388	43
Salaries	Government, industry, and local businesses	1,580[4]	23	14,891	52
Transfers	Welfare	683	11	800[5]	3
	Old Age, Family Allowances	305[6]	5	600[5]	2
	Total	6,732	100	28,679	100

Sources 1. Salisbury (1972a) Table 8, except as noted.
2. Various sources; basically Cree Village Profiles, with omissions corrected from other sources, such as LaRusic (1982) ISP Annual Reports, and Salisbury et al(1982)
3. Figure for 1980
4. In Salisbury (1972a) Table 8 the figure for this item was based on an underestimate for Fort George, as data were then lacking on Fort George salaries. A sum of $600,000 has been added on the basis of Salisbury (1972b)
5. 1981 figures for smaller populations have been extrapolated for the total Cree population, using census data on ages and NHRC (1982) for overall game harvests.
6. No figure was given in Salisbury (1972a). Estimate is based on number of children and aged.
7. The estimates of total Cree harvests of fish and game in Salisbury (1972a) and NHRC (1982) -- the latter modified to account for the change in number of hunters between 1978 and 1981 -- are multiplied by the average price for meat in Cree village stores, 1971 and 1982.

Environmental and social impact studies were no "normal procedure" before 1975, but the protests did elicit a governmental ecology review, and a social impact study by the PAD for the James Bay Development Corporation, reporting in October 1972.

A group of Cree -- mainly young people who had attended high school together in southern Canada -- received a grant from the Arctic Institute of North America to meet formally in Mistassini. But not until May 1972 did the IQA obtain Federal funding to set up a Task Force on Ecological and Social Impacts, under John Spence (biology) and the author (anthropology). Its field study in August 1972 involved outside experts, but also most of the emerging Cree-educated activists.

In both its reports the PAD recommended as follows: 1) that the Cree hunting economy be explicitly supported, as its viability was currently threatened by poor infrastructure, although it could continue to support most of the population, even after reservoir construction, if its infrastructure were improved, 2) that damages to the hunting economy be compensated for, 3) that damage to village life be minimized by isolating construction camps from villages, and by making then removable after use, and 4) that the Cree would be best served in the long run, not by temporary employment as unskilled construction labor, but by using the project as a time to train local people to take over administration of the region, after construction was completed. We spelled out demographic projections of the labor force, and the employment and training policies that could lead to the Cree administering the region. In 1985 those projections proved very close to reality, and over three quarters of the recommendations had come to pass.

However the recommendations were not smoothly accepted. After a month of negotiations over the reports, the Cree and the developers became deadlocked. Injunctions, a court case, appeals of the verdict, and two years of hard bargaining, in which the Quebec negotiator was an ex-deputy minister of Indian Affairs, finally resulted in an Agreement -- the James Bay and Northern Quebec Agreement (JBNQA). In it the Cree accepted the project and Government sovereignty; the Government agreed on compensation and on providing support for Cree regional autonomy. But not before opposition to the project had unified and politicized the Cree villages. The Cree had developed a structure, first under the IQA and the Task Force, but finally independently of the IQA as the Grand Council of the Crees of Quebec. It signed an agreement in principle in November 1974, and, after legal haggling and a referendum of all villagers, the JBNQA Agreement in November 1975.

This agreement recognises a Cree Regional Authority (CRA) as administering regional services to Cree villages, and Cree boards for health, social services, schools, environment, housing, economic development and other services. They are staffed by Cree, and have the status of municipalities, and school or other boards under Quebec ministries. Importantly their employees are paid by the Province at standard rates of pay. The GCCQ remains a non-statutory body and the political forum of Creeland; the CRA constitutes its elected administrators. The core of both are the activists of the 1972 research who also negotiated the Agreement.

The territory administered by the CRA is an area surrounding the eight separate villages, comparable to Indian Reserves, but now termed Category 1 lands. The remaining land was transferred to the Province, which recognized Cree rights to hunt over all of it, except towns and hydro-installations. Over almost a quarter (termed Category 2 lands) Cree hunting rights were exclusive, but over the large remainder (Category 3 lands) the Cree accepted that non-Cree could hunt some species (not those of main Cree concern), but only if Cree food needs were satisfied. To make these rights effective the Cree jointly control decisions over sport-hunting quotas, and are taking over outfitting operations in the region. They have monitored hunting catches for five years to establish what Cree food needs are before any flooding by the Project. The Agreement establishes their right to this yield of meat, and includes a special program, the Income Security Programme for Cree Hunters and Trappers (ISP). This provides the funds to outfit winter hunting for food and furs; it has largely eliminated the need for welfare payments (except to people unable to hunt): it is administered by the Cree themselves, within an indexed maximum total payout, who see it as a "salary for hunting work," even if it is technically a transfer payment.

For the diminution of Cree rights through codification, and for permitting development to proceed, the 7,000 Cree were awarded $150 million, half being paid over five years, and half as a royalty payment as hydro generating is installed. Most funds are in non-transferable government securities. Neither principal nor interest can be distributed to individuals. The interest (and some lump sums) may be used for program, administrative services, and investment. The Finance Board has acted conservatively, but has already set up Cree Constructions, invested in an airline Air Creebec, and speeded up rehousing by "topping up" funding obtained through regular channels. The GCCQ is exploring other investments in businesses to create northern employment, such as tourism, mining, and forestry. It is able to buy the best technical advice, but is not obligated to follow it. Where previously government officials made decisions, the Cree at first used non-Cree consultants (including anthropologists) but a technical staff now exists among the Cree themselves. Even where consultants are still used, Cree decision-makers include Cree who can evaluate the advice that is given.

In short, the twenty years 1964-1984 have seen the steady build-up of modern administrative structures for the region, planning and delivering services to 7,000 people scattered over 150,000 square miles of land. The period 1971-1984 is distinctive as the time when these structures came to be run by the Cree. Constructing (for $15 billion as it turned out) the hydro project had relatively little effect on the villages, for these were off-limits, and few Cree worked in construction. Its main legacy is the super highway cutting through Cree-land from south to north, with branches to each of the four dams. Flooding of 50 hunting territories has hurt three northerly bands. Transmission lines have cut swathes through more southerly forests, but logging for pulp has had more profound effects. Some hunting territories, recently logged, are desolate; some, cut twenty years ago and now reforesting, are producing abundant game, mainly moose. The 1982 depression severely hit lumbering and mining, and cut Cree employment also. Nor has electricity given the Cree a base for industry, as no villages are linked to the high-voltage transmission lines. The development that has indeed come to Cree villages is attributable to the service industries, and to the delivery of services by the Cree themselves.

Economic Assessment

The Internal Economy

Table 1, Cree Incomes 1971 and 1981 provides a first approximation of the changes in the Cree economy. The figures are, it is true, approximations based on data collected in individual villages at varied dates, projected to give overall figures for the particular years mentioned. The estimates could undoubtedly have been improved had monitoring of the project been funded, but neither Cree nor government liked the idea of research studies in 1973. The figures are thus the best available, but they are consistent with more impressionistic data. They include amounts in dollars for the value of meat and housing produced by hunters, and for transfer payments made to Cree individuals. They omit transfer payments to Cree organizations that are not individuals, Cree income from investments, and the salaries of non-Cree working in villages.

The figures do not consider, either, the flows out of the region to southern Canada and the USA -- billions of dollars worth of hydroelectricity. These elements will be considered in the next section, the political economy.

Overall the increase in total incomes over the ten-year period is 426 percent. This increase, when adjusted for population increase (25 percent) and cost-of-living increase (186 percent) becomes a change in constant dollar per capita terms of 83 percent over ten years. The Cree have got wealthier at a faster rate than most Canadians or Americans. But in 1971 per capita Cree incomes were just over $1,000; by 1981 per capita incomes were still generally at the poverty level, but per-family incomes (given the larger Cree families) were within the Canadian range, at $14,366. In doing better the Cree have caught up from a point below the poverty level, to a level comparable with that found in many rural communities across Canada.

The source of income by sector -- subsistence, salaries, and transfer payments -- has changed markedly. Welfare and family allowances have dropped from 16 percent to 5 percent of total income; salaries have increased from 23 percent to 52 percent. The total of the former has increased absolutely but by less than inflation: the latter has increased tenfold. The hunting sector has tripled in product, but declined -- from 61 percent to 43 percent -- as a proportion of the total product. Wage work is now the major activity of the Cree, surpassing the formerly dominant hunting.

1) Hunting

The decline of the hunting sector is only relative, however, and in part reflects our calculating a dollar value for meat. Thus the volume of meat produced (in pounds) has risen almost as much as population, by 20 percent. But the price of store-bought meat in Creeland has not increased as fast as inflation, largely because transport costs (and store mark-ups) have reduced with the construction of roads. In constant dollars the price of meat has declined, and even the increased production forms a greatly decreased proportion of total income. But including the ISP payments as salaries to hunters (and this is how the Cree define them) brings the total return to hunters to more than double the meat value. Without ISP payments subsistence hunting would not be viable. Almost half the ISP goes to pay for air transport to hunting territories, and for equipment to set up camp and to hunt and trap. One could interpret the figures in Table 1 as meaning that the half spent on equipment is a business expense, and so deduct it from income. But I do not attempt such detailed interpretation of

246

what are approximate figures. I use them merely to indicate that hunting remains a major focus of Cree life; that ISP plays a crucial role in maintaining local food-production, and that the Cree, by deliberately opting for ISP, see it as vital for cultural survival and -- not as a handout to those unable to get a wage job -- but as a fair return for the most skilled and respected Cree job, that of the productive hunter.

The rate of return per hour of hunting labor may indeed have increased between 1971 and 1981. In 1971 a good hunter could have earned much more per hour hunting (even using the cited dollar values for meat) than as unskilled labor in mining or forestry. Certainly this was true for moose-hunting under favorable snow and weather conditions, which can yield $200 per hour; regular trapping of beaver, walking a trapline, and chopping through the ice at beaver lodges, provided a steady return of meat and fur at about twice the unskilled wage rate (and also provided information about other game); periods of unsuccessful hunting, or of fishing and snaring small game lowered the average return but enabled the hunter to subsist in the bush and to be on the spot when favorable hunting periods occurred. For an unskilled hunter in 1971 it may well have paid to switch to wage labor, and some observers (e.g. LaRusic 1969) felt that such a switch was occurring, and was likely to continue.

By 1981 the technology and the economics of hunting have changed. Snowmobiles, chain saws, and radios have reduced the drudgery of walking traplines, hauling home meat and fuel, and maintaining a home in the bush. The hours of work needed to produce a comparable amount of meat have been reduced, perhaps by as much as a third. The months that hunters now spend in winter camps thus involve more time with their families -- leisure in our terms, "investment in family life" in Cree terms. Though hunters cannot earn very high incomes, ISP ensures that all hunters earn a minimum. The minimum without any meat would be well below the earnings of an unskilled wage earner, but a successful hunter is well rewarded, has an incentive to produce meat, and to maintain the highest Cree status of hunter and provider. The less skilled hunter now has a clearer choice of whether to enter a hunting way of life, or the wage economy, without pressures of poverty pushing him ineluctably to the latter. Above all the standard of living (and comfort) of hunters and their families has increased markedly.

The production of meat has not been commercialized. It is still illegal in Quebec to sell wild game, even in cooked form in restaurants. There is however an exchange between hunters and wage-workers; they reciprocate by caring for hunters' children at school, or by purchasing major items like trucks (Scott

247

1984). Hunting now also leads to cash income through the guiding of white sports fishermen, through summer outfitting camps operated by Cree bands or entrepreneurs. Minor amounts are earned by selling furs and artifacts made while hunting.

In short, hunting remains a vital part of the economy, but not as the engine of change, or the prime mover of Cree development. By maintaining the productivity of the subsistence sector, however, the Cree economy has been able to maintain a high degree of autonomy. As the productivity of labor in subsistence has remained high, local people have been able to refuse low-paying wage labor, and to choose to enter only skilled occupations paying higher rates (cf. Salisbury 1971). If Cree hunting had become unproductive, Cree would have been forced into unskilled wage labor -- the proletarianization foreseen by LaRusic (1969).

2) Salaries

There are fewer problems in interpreting the figures for salary incomes and their tenfold increase. The number of workers has roughly doubled, and the average wage is five times as high, largely because most of the new workers are in skilled or professional jobs. In 1971 the typical worker was a seasonal manual laborer. The number of such workers has changed little since then, but the number in all the more skilled categories has increased many times. Almost a third of the professionals and white-collar workers are now women.

Simply put, the skilled jobs delivering services to villages in 1971 were held by whites. They staffed the schools and the nursing stations; they planned budgets and housing programs; they flew north for a week to repair telephones, install plumbing, or audit stores. Now most of these tasks are performed by local Cree, and Cree staff the offices of regional government, the school board, the health board etc. Localization is not complete, and differs for each service, with between 5 percent and 50 percent of jobs still held by whites. Total numbers of staff have also risen to bring services up to provincial standards, and Cree policy has been to "deconcentrate" regional offices from the town of Val d'Or to individual villages. The result has been that most salaries paid by governmental agencies (at standard salary rates), to provide the services normal in any rural Canadian community, now go mainly to Cree people in villages.

As will be discussed later this has not caused commensurate increases in the ongoing cost to the government (apart from inflation). It was expensive to hire non-local teachers, mechanics, and administrators, to provide them with travel and housing subsidies, and "hardship allowances" for going north. An unpublished Hydroquebec study of 1973 showed that the current costs of paternalistically administering the Cree region, and excluding any payments made to Cree, were equal to 85 percent of the total cash incomes of all Cree, while capital costs were equal to 40 percent of total Cree income. A great deal is saved by higher-level governments hiring local people, though we have no data on whether the savings were realized, and the number of white staff reduced.

Employing local people also has "multiplier" effects on the local economy. Most transient whites spent little of their salaries in the villages. Housing was supplied, and there was little to buy locally except food. At the end of their northern duty employees took south the "nest eggs" they had saved, and fed them into the urban economies of the south. Our figures show about 90 percent of salaries paid to non-Cree "leaking" out of the community, either as "nest eggs," or buying goods imported into the villages; only 10 percent went to pay the salaries of Cree workers in stores. By contrast Cree salaried workers, receiving the same rate for the job, do not receive "hardship" and housing allowances. They live at home and their salaries are spent on goods and services used in the villages. Though many goods are imported (from heating oil to radios and flour), buying them employs local salespeople, while all services and housing bought locally go to provide employment. Consumer budgets suggest that 60 percent of local salaries "leak" directly from villages to pay for imports, but 40 percent is recirculated. Iterating the process of leakage and recirculation yields an implied multiplier of 1.11 for non-Cree salaries, and 1.67 for Cree salaries. Every $1 million paid as non-Cree salaries in 1971 produced another $111,111 locally; payment of $1 million in Cree salaries in 1981 adds to village income not only the $1,000,000 by also another $666,667 in "multiplier effect."

There are also more manual jobs in villages, matching a big decline in the number of Cree leaving villages to work in mining or forestry. This increase in village employment is through businesses owned either by individuals, or, like Cree Construction, by the GCCQ. Cree Construction contracted for some work for the hydro-project (e.g., clearing trees from land to be flooded) and now builds most of the houses for the housing program. Such companies make it possible for Cree with formal training in skills such as machine operation or plumbing to gain the practical experience needed to obtain skilled employment elsewhere. Without experience there are no outside jobs. Villages with available skilled and semi-skilled workers, and local companies prepared to carry out the work, can now plan for summer projects, and obtain funding for them as can all municipalities in Canada. Summer projects have replaced prospecting and forestry as the source of seasonal wage-work for winter hunters. The infusion of money by the housing program (some of it from compensation funds) has built up the local construction industry, and that in turn has contributed to producing the multiplier effect.

Another contribution to this effect is the greater ease of buying things in villages. All HBC stores have expanded and employ more staff. But in addition every village has one or more "corner stores" (depanneurs), one or more restaurants, and (if it has roads) taxi and truck services. Three villages have co-operative stores, and two have banking facilities. Though villagers still use mail-order catalogues, and travel to larger towns for major purchases (including alcohol) most salaries are spent in villages. The interior of many houses approaches those of suburban housing anywhere in North America. As in other suburbias young people complain there is "nothing to do but hang around," but Cree adults focus interests on improving their homes.

By contrast Creeland has so far produced little "industrial" employment. Two village sawmills of the late 1960s proved uncompetitive with imported lumber, even given the protection from high transport costs. One Cree has staked his own mineral find, but development is likely to be jointly with a large firm, and only when the industry recovers from the depression. A few Waswanipi men subcontract for forestry work from large companies; but without the allocation of a quota to supply the Qevillon pulp mill the Cree have no other market for forestry production. Subcontracting is the simplest expansion of Cree interest, but the GCCQ is studying other options, especially if Cree Construction and local repair needs make sawmills viable.

Tourism is the other possibility for an "industry," and it too is helped by a village base. Most villages now have a "motel," either band-owned, or individually-owned, thanks to a band loan. Outsiders coming on official business -- consultants, bank auditors, skilled mechanics -- stay at the motel, when in 1971 they would have stayed at the house of a non-Cree. Rates are exorbitant -- but charged usually to expenses. Sport fishing camps are being taken over by the Cree, and provide a means of capitalizing on hunting skills. Summer courses in guiding, run by the school board, teach how to cope with tourists, and promise to make the industry viable.

In short the past ten years have seen great increases in Cree prosperity -- though no one except other Indians could call them wealthy (NIB 1982). It has involved a great increase in the social services and housing in villages that now conform to a suburban standard. The services have not followed <u>after</u> development of an industrial "base," they have preceded it and facilitated its establishment. The critical change has been that local people now supply their own services. Their salaries, fed into the local economy, have led to diversification in employment. The subsistence sector is strong, and exchanges exist between it and the growing service sector. The economy as a whole has become dynamic, providing the basis for sustained, and locally controlled industrial expansion.

The Political Economy

Who benefits from this increase in Cree wealth? And who pays for it? Many Indian people in Canada believe, as the National Indian Brotherhood (1982) study of the JBNQA, entitled <u>Practically Millionaires</u>, suggests, that the Cree sold their land heritage for money, that the money has been appropriated by a wealthy few, and that it will soon disappear leaving poverty and dependency. Critics of the Alaska Native Claims Settlement Act of 1971 say that this is happening in Alaska. Is it happening in Northern Quebec?

Some unequal sharing of the cash benefits indeed appears in our data, but the inequalities are small and do not split Cree society into antagonistic classes. Increases in white collar and professional jobs provide salaries to educated younger Cree; but the skilled hunters benefit most from Income Security. Everyone now has better housing. Many women have salaried jobs. It has been deliberate policy not to pay Cree administrators at rates comparable to administrators elsewhere in Canada, but at little more than white-collar salaries, though the non-taxable status of salaries paid on Indian reserves makes the lack of marked differentials less significant.

Household budget figures indicate the differences, but also the comparability between salaried and hunting Cree. Hunting families earn, on average, about $1,000 less cash, and must use about $3,000 to generate their hunting income, but they produce food and housing worth some $6,000. The average salary earner has a very small disposable income -- the biggest fixed cost being winter house heating with oil -- and uses some of it to produce about $1,500 of subsistence in spare-time hunting. The villager with insufficient cash to hunt on weekends, like the hunter who must also heat a village house in winter, is in a very difficult position. By contrast the above-average salary earner and the full-time hunter can live well, as the other living costs in a village are low.

Whether the spectrum of village income levels is creating

class divisions between hunters and administrators has been examined by LaRusic et al. (1979), Brelsford (1983), and Scott (1984). All argue that classes have not emerged, partly because Cree ideology stresses equality and reciprocity, partly because Cree policy reflects that ideology, and partly because all extended Cree families include hunters and salaried workers. Meat and goods, money and services, are exchanged among kin, reducing inequality, and blurring lines of division. In principle Cree assert that class divisions reflect "white-man's materialism" and are not the Cree way.

The second focus of scepticism -- that the Cree are spending the money received for their birthright, the land -- is also negated by the data. The Cree have not "sold their land." Over almost all their traditional land they maintain hunting rights, which the Agreement enshrines in legal terminology, and provides mechanisms to ensure remain undiminished -- largely through environmental and conservation regimes run by the Cree. Foregone rights to subsurface minerals and to land involved in hydro-installations have been matched by payment of $150 million, but this is a minor part of the Agreement. Nor is the sum being spent. Most is in non-transferable government bonds, yielding income. Even the income is not distributed but is used, partly for public purposes and programs, but mainly for investment. Overall the assets of the Board of Compensation are increasing, not decreasing.

Cree investment (other than the bonds) aims at strengthening the local economy, in two ways. First is constructing local infrastructure, for example rehousing the villages. With normal Indian Affairs budgets and Central Mortgage and Housing Corporation loans rehousing villages would have taken twenty years. By advancing compensation money (and later reimbursing the Fund from annual budgets) the job is being completed in five years and is creating a local construction industry. Secondly there is investment in industries already in the region. Thus the Cree are now majority share holders in the airline that serves Creeland, Air Creebec, formerly owned by Austin Airways who now is a minority owner. The success of investment in Cree construction has been described, though one venture, organized to retail tools and building materials, has already closed, with major losses. The Cree are studying ways to invest in forestry and mining, but as indicated, subcontracting and partnership with major companies seem the most feasible. The possibility of partnership has emerged only because of the improved Cree infrastructure, and the larger pool of Cree skills, managment, and finance.

But if Cree have few industries and most employment comes via government funding of social services, is this not a situation of "dependency?" Or of false security, should a changing government cut funding? I argue against this at two levels -- the funding is guaranteed, and the funding is not a gift but an exchange.

The guarantee of funding is the 1975 Agreement signed by Canada, Quebec, and the Cree, and enacted into law. The 1983 Canadian Charter entrenches the provisions of such treaties, containing the precedent dating back to 1763 in Canada. Indian people who recognize the sovereignty of Canada receive in return "protection" by Canada. As interpreted, "protection" means the provision of services similar to those given other Canadians, without having to pay taxes on income earned on reserves, for which the Indians permit whites limited access to their land. In the past services have not been comparable with those provided to other Canadians, but as we have seen services are being improved. Though it costs government more to provide services for an individual in the sparsely populated north than it does for an individual in the crowded south, the extra costs of those services are borne by a large population that benefits environmentally, politically, and strategically from Canadian sovereignty over the North. Provision of comparable though expensive service to northerners is part of an entrenched Canadian compact from which all Canadians benefit.

The benefits are not just political, however; there is an exchange of economic benefits between the Cree and the south. If the electrical capacity of the existing hydro-project (8 million kilowatts) operated full-time and the power sold at a price of 40 mil per kilowatt hour, it would earn $2.8 billion each year for Hydroquebec. Operating costs are small, though interest and amortization of the $15 billion investment may take $2 billion. Against these figures the compensation of $150 million, and the annual payment of $28 million to support services to the Cree seem very small amounts to "rent" the land for the project. Whether the exchange is precisely in balance is debatable, but clearly both sides benefit from the contract. Abrogation of such a contract is unthinkable.

But if the Cree have indeed received material and service benefits, have they lost what is more precious, their Cree "cultural heritage"? Elsewhere (Salisbury 1984) I argue that the Cree, like many small but newly affluent groups, are experiencing a cultural "enhancement," as they amplify some features of their previous culture while losing others. The culture is evolving, in ways that many Cree see as a cultural revival, as they become an ethnic regional government within the nation-state. I shall not repeat that argument here beyond considering how far they have moved in the opposite direction -- toward cultural "dependency."

Any increased "dependency" is clearly not the economic dependency of being "a reserve army of labor"; there has been a major decline in the employment of Cree by non-Cree firms, and a period of relatively full employment within villages. The most obvious visible change, as described, is that Cree village lifestyles now approximate "suburban" ones, of involvement in homes and families, of purchase of consumer durables and transportation equipment (snowmobiles, rather than cars however), of television and recorded music, and of central heating by oil for houses. As described, the purchase of goods imported from the rest of Canada absorbs 60 percent of every dollar of local income, even though this percentage has declined markedly from the time when village service providers were transients from the south. The inflow of goods is even more dramatic if one considers the capital investments that have been made over the past ten years, and that have not been considered in our treatment of the ongoing local economy. These have included roads, communications, and electricity supply provided by government, and housing provided jointly by government and villages. There has been a positive encouragement to the Cree to become consumers, as a banking system has begun to develop, and credit has become available to people who now have a steady income. Elberg et al. (1977) documents the millions of dollars of credit used to buy trucks and television sets in Fort George, when the highway was opened up, and satellite antennae installed. Several years disposable income was spent in advance of its receipt. So too the use of compensation funds to speed house building has committed the Cree to import immediately the goods involved in that housing, and to pay for what they have bought from their future income.

But if this is "cultural dependency" the Cree are no different from other Canadians who use money to buy goods that they do not manufacture. What has happened is better described as the emergence of the Cree from what Paine (1982) has described as "paternalism," to a situation where they are participating as partners in the national Canadian economy. They indeed consume manufactures made elsewhere, which they pay for with money earned predominantly through the service sector, though they contribute to the national economy also as the landowners of northern Quebec. In 1985 they now make their own consumer choices, in ways they could not do when they were only the recipients of services provided by white administrators, and not the providers of the services themselves. Though the Crees may have abdicated some sense of "independence" in becoming part of the wider Canadian service economy, what they have gained in becoming a regional government within Quebec and Canada is the ability to use the service economy to produce local development.

This is the message that the Cree case provides. The

provision of more services, and not more material goods, is the inevitable trend of post-industrial society. In all "developed" societies over 50 percent of economic activity is in the service sector. If local, and particularly rural, communities are to "develop" and to participate in post-industrial society they need not merely be provided with local services, they need to have local control over those services. It is when they do not have control that "dependency" becomes likely. The Cree indicate how the service economy can indeed be locally controlled, to produce development.

Notes

[1] For a review of the work of the Programme in the Anthropology of Development, and of its experiences in training for applied (or action) anthropological work, see Salisbury 1978. Clearly the present paper builds on the work of all previous members of the PAD, starting with that of Norman Chance, its first Director. References in this paper are principally to work done by Programme students and to their theses, but no attempt has been made to be comprehensive. Any attempt to spell out the colleagues and Cree who have contributed to this review of fifteen years work would be necessarily incomplete; it is not, perhaps, invidious to pick out a very few whose discussions have been most productive, namely Harvey Feit, Ignatius LaRusic, Colin Scott, Alan Penn, Philip Awashish, Billy Diamond, Abel Kitchen, Peter Gull and Matthew Coon-Come. I am nonetheless grateful to the hundreds of friends and helpers whose names are omitted.

References

Brelsford, T. 1983. Hunters and Workers among the Nemaska Cree. MA thesis, McGill University.
Chance N.A. ed. 1968. Conflict and Culture Change. Ottawa: Canadian Research Centre for Anthropology.
----- 1969. Developmental Change among the Cree Indians of Quebec. Ottawa: Department of Regional Economic Expansion.
Elberg N. Visitor R., and Salisbury R.F. 1977. Off-Centre: Fort George and the Regional Communications Network of James Bay. Montreal: McGill University PAD Monographs, No 9.
Feit, H.A. 1968. Mistassini Hunters of the Boreal Forest. M.A.

255

thesis, McGill University.
----- 1979. Waswanipi Realities and Adaptations. Ph.D. thesis, McGill University.
LaRusic, I.E. 1968. The New Auchimau: Patron-client relations among the Waswanipi Cree. M.A. thesis, McGill University.
----- 1969. From Hunter to Proletarian. In: Developmental Change Among the Cree Indians of Quebec, N. Chance, ed., Annex 2, pp. 1-59.
----- 1979. Negotiating a Way of Life. Ottawa: Department of Indian and Northern Affairs.
National Indian Brotherhood. 1982. Practically Millionaires: A Report on the James Bay Agreement. Ottawa: National Indian Brotherhood.
Native Harvesting Research Committee. 1983. The Wealth of the Land: Wildlife Harvests by the James Bay Cree. 1972-1979. Quebec City: James Bay Native Harvesting Research Committee.
Paine, R.P.B. 1982. The White Arctic. Memorial University Press, St. John's Newfoundland.
Salisbury, R.F. 1969. Vunamami: Economic Transformation in a Traditional Society. Berkeley: University of California Press.
----- 1971. Development through the Service Industries. Manpower and Unemployment Research in Africa 4:57-66.
----- 1972a. Development and James Bay: Social Implications of the Proposals for the Hydroelectric Scheme. Montreal: McGill University PAD Monograph 4.
----- 1972b. Not By Bread Alone; The Use of Subsistence Resources by the James Bay Cree. Montreal: Indians of Quebec Association.
----- 1978. Training Applied Anthropologists: The McGill Programme in the Anthropology of Development 1964-1976. In: Applied Anthropology in Canada. S. Weaver, ed. Proceedings of the CES, 4:58-78.
----- 1984. Affluence and Cultural Survival. American Ethnological Society Proceedings, Spring 1981. Washington, D.C.
----- 1986. A Homeland for the Cree: Regional Development in James Bay, 1971-1981. Montreal: McGill-Queens Press (in press).
Scott, C. 1984. Between "Original Affluence" and Consumer Affluence: Domestic Production and Guaranteed Income for James Bay Hunters, In: Affluence and Cultural Survival, R. Salisbury, ed., pp. 74-86.

15. COOPERATIVE MANAGEMENT OF LOCAL FISHERIES: A ROUTE TO DEVELOPMENT

Evelyn W. Pinkerton

Development is usually defined on a national level as an increase in per-capita gross national product. Judging development in the fishery sector in the Pacific Northwest (Alaska, British Columbia, Washington State) requires finer judgement: although salmon fishermen in the 1970s often increased their gross incomes, both their net incomes and the resource, in many areas, were diminished to dangerously low levels. Increased capital investments in boats, increased indebtedness, and increased overfishing threatened to eliminate both fishermen and many stocks of fish.[1] Meaningful and desirable development in the salmon fishery--if this were considered separately for the sake of discussion--would have to involve an increase in per capita net income without a resulting decline in the resource, so that development could be sustained.[2]

Anthropologists have a history of concern for local fisheries development and have documented ways that communities or local groups have circumvented these problems of stock depletion and overinvestment. Most of the cases described have involved local groups asserting informal "rights" over territory, access, effort, and information (Acheson 1975, 1981, Andersen 1979, McCay 1980, McCay and Acheson 1987). Successful local fishery "management" resulted: an appropriate number of fishermen and fish were able to prosper.

The present discussion documents a different approach to the same problems--one that does not necessarily involve altering the common property or the high seas nature of the fishery, but that can work within the structure of common property. This approach involves the creation of new institutions through which fishermen participate in government management. This might be seen as an extension of the analysis of Wilson and Acheson (1981) concerning fishermen's institutions of cooperation among themselves, which serve to share information, reduce uncertainty, and sometimes to limit conflict, reduce costs, or reduce overexploitation, but do not involve government.

Demands for cooperative management of the fishery that have arisen from fishermen in the Pacific Northwest were often a response to crises in resource depletion or overinvestment. The desire to participate in government management of the resource stemmed not simply from a perception that government management was heretofore ill-advised, but also from the sense that adversarial relationships between fishermen and government as well as competitive individualism among fishermen condemned the fishery to underdevelopment. The study of cooperative arrangements is particularly appropriate for anthropologists, because it concerns the setting up of new institutions that create incentives for cooperative behavior and reduce incentives for certain types of competitive and adversarial behaviors and attitudes. Co-management arrangements are thus a laboratory for relations among institutions, ideology, and behavior, and show how people respond to differing rules of the game with differing attitudes and behaviors. For example, in the fishery the institution of cooperative management demonstrates that fishermen are not by nature and for all time the relentless predators who will eliminate the last fish in a "tragedy of the commons," as Hardin and Gordon (1954) conceived them. Instead, the failure to constrain individual fishing effort--where this sometimes occurs and sometimes produces a tragedy of the commons--is a response to specific institutional arrangements. Similarly, the failure of government and of individuals to constrain overinvestment in fishing equipment results from the way property rights have been defined in the fishery, as I discuss below.

Cooperative management is a concept familiar to sociologists and labor historians through the issue of workplace democracy, practiced when workers in factories gain significant control over or participation in decision-making about the labor process or the allocation of profits and investments. Such arrangements have arisen often at the initiative of management, in an attempt to unlock the potentially greater productivity of workers (Edwards 1979).

The management of a natural resource such as the fishery is not usually organized in North America by capitalist owners hiring workers to harvest the fish, because fish, like many forests and waterways in North America, are government property in the sense that the state is held responsible for executing management in the common interest of all citizens. Under British common law since the Magna Carta, however, the state does not have the right to exclude citizens arbitrarily from the fishery, and has always justified such exclusions on grounds of conservation for the good of the resource and the common good (Wildsmith 1985). In this sense all citizens who purchase fishing licenses from government have a "common property" right not to be excluded.[3]

Economists and biologists term fish "common property" in a different sense when they discuss the particular structure of competition in the fishery. A fisherman may own a license, but he does not own the fish until it is captured. Therefore, even if the government successfully holds the harvest in many areas at an acceptable level for conservation and perpetual sustained yield, and limits the number of fishermen, some fishermen will overinvest in gear in an attempt to assure themselves first capture (Guppy 1984). Furthermore, experience in many fisheries suggests that fishermen under severe competition and dissipation of profits tend to overfish, underreport their catch, or fish illegally in areas closed to fishing (e.g. Langdon 1977, Kearney 1983). Illegal fishing is by nature very expensive and difficult, often impossible, to control, when control is exercised by government agents. In summary, institutional arrangements in the fishery have permitted both excessive competition (to the detriment of many fishermen) and excessive pressure on the resource.[4]

The owners of large capital in this industry, usually the four or five largest fish processors (who are also the marketers), have no control over harvesting management decisions, although they may attempt to influence government authorities, and may exert some control over license-holding fishermen who are indebted to them. In the salmon industry in British Columbia, in which both fishermen and processors have incentives to reduce risks by entering into contracts, processors have been in a position to influence prices offered to fishermen and to reward fishermen differentially through private bonusing arrangements (Pinkerton 1985). Because many fishermen had not the solvency or the ideological inclination to form processing and marketing cooperatives, they are not in a position to bargain for the highest prices.[5] Relations between processors and fishermen can thus be seen as another form of underdevelopment, at least from the fishermen's perspective.

Cooperative management of the fishery, hereafter called co-management, involving principally the cooperation of government agencies and fishermen, has not developed merely or usually from an intent to unleash greater productivity (as it has with experiments in workplace democracy). Sometimes "productivity" (harvest) was in fact greater than the resource could sustain. Rather, initiatives have more commonly stemmed from the perceived need to effect a management regime superior to the existing one. Specifically, fishermen and/or the government wished to do some or all of the following: (1) improve the quality of information about the resource so that more fine-grained decisions could be made, (2) make the information public so that harvesting rationales would be based on known data, (3) reduce overinvestment for first capture by rationalizing access of individual fishermen, of fishermen's groups, and of gear types,[6] or through equitable sharing of total harvest, (4) involve fishermen in allocation decisions and in enforcement, as well as in collecting data about the harvest

259

and the condition of the resource.

Co-management arrangements have involved, then, specifying certain rights on the part of fishermen or fishermen's groups. Such arrangements tend to alter the structure of five sets of relationships in the fishery: those between the province and fishermen, those between fishermen and processors, those among individual fishermen and among fishermen's groups, those between fishermen and the fish, and those between fishermen and other water resource users. In this preliminary examination of co-management innovations in the salmon fisheries of the States of Alaska and Washington I argue that these co-management arrangements have the potential to (1) increase the responsible sharing of information and management effort with consequent reduction in conflicts between government and fishermen; (2) reduce the oligopsonistic power of the traditional salmon processors, and increase the bargaining power of fishermen; (3) increase cooperation among fishermen, fishermen's groups, and gear types for their mutual advantage; (4) conserve or increase the resource base; (5) increase long-range planning and the accommodation of other water resource users to fish habitat needs.

These findings are preliminary because official co-management arrangements are still relatively new and little documented. However, they parallel in part the findings of Kearney (1984) in the Bay of Fundy herring fishery co-management experiment by the Canadian Department of Fisheries and Oceans, which was discovered when this stage of research was nearly complete. They also parallel findings in the British Columbia salmon fishery, where in some places informal and ad hoc co-management situations have arisen spontaneously (Pinkerton 1984). What follows is an examination not only of changed behaviors and attitudes among fishermen, fishermen's groups, and government agents resulting from co-management arrangements, but also an analysis of how these arrangements influence all the other actors involved in the fishing industry or fishery resource.

The Regional Aquaculture Associations in Alaska

The regional aquaculture associations in Alaska were the product of a fishermen's lobby that brought legislation in response to an historic low point in salmon abundance in the early 1970s.

It is the intent of this act to authorize the private ownership of salmon hatcheries by qualified nonprofit corporations for the purpose of contributing, by artificial means, to the rehabilitation of the state's depleted and depressed salmon fishery. The program shall be operated without adversely affecting natural stocks of fish in the state and under a policy of management which allows reasonable segregation of returning hatchery-reared salmon from naturally occuring stocks [Section 1, ch.111,SLA 1974].

To be "qualified" to become incorporated, an association must include all users or user groups in the region, including commercial fishermen (licensed for a specific area in Alaska), subsistence fishermen, sport fishermen, processors, and representatives of local communities. All these groups must be represented on the corporation's board.

This discussion focuses only on the Southern Southeast Regional Aquaculture Association, which incorporated in 1976 and by 1978 had built a hatchery on Neets Bay to release coho and chum salmon. By a majority vote of all the salmon fishermen licensed in this area,[1] who automatically became association members, the association mandated the state to tax its fishermen 3% of gross catch at the delivery point; the tax is then returned to the Association. The additional funds required to build and operate the hatchery came from low-interest State loans. In 1981-1983, adult salmon returning to Neets Bay were coho harvested mainly to provide eggs to continue hatchery production. 1984 was the first year that many fish in excess of broodstock needs returned to the hatchery site: these excess chum and coho were harvested by vessels on contract for the hatchery, and sold for cost recovery. In addition, an estimated 75% of the returning salmon were intercepted by locally licensed fishermen before approaching the hatchery, and contributed to the welfare of all association fishermen in this way. The chief purpose of the hatchery has been to increase overall production by 10-15 percent, and to even out the yearly fluctuations in wild salmon runs. Because it was run by fishermen, the hatchery also created opportunities for their greater involvement in specific and overall management.

The innovation in harvesting and management that was felt for the first time in 1985 was the common property fishery managed by the Association inside its Special Harvest Area. The Special Harvest Area is Neets Bay, where returning hatchery stocks are clearly separate from other wild salmon stocks. The Association's 1985 management plan for this area was accepted by the Alaska Board of Fish, a citizens' body appointed by the governor to make general fishery policy. The Alaska Department of Fish and Game then made regulations appropriate to the harvesting plan, and enforced them. The Association had thus earned the right to co-manage the common property fishery inside its Special Harvest Area for that season. Holding a common

261

property fishery inside the Special Harvest Area means that after enough broodstock has been taken for the hatchery, the area is thrown open to all licensed fishermen, who are of course automatically members of the Association and thus benefit from increased fishing opportunities. However, there is an orderly allocation of returning fish to all three gear types by openings for each, interspersed with closures for hatchery harvests. Since all three gear types are represented on the Association Board, whose objective is to manage the fishery for the common benefit of all fishermen, and ensure sufficient hatchery production for future growth, conflict over allocation to gear types is reduced.[8] Instead of lobbying government for special privileges, each gear type must work directly with the others to develop mutually acceptable arrangements. For example, under the latest management plan, trollers have opted to fish chinooks in June but traded away their fishing time for coho in September. Gear groups know that if they do not reach agreement among themselves on allocation and other policy matters, their ability to influence government in all areas will be greatly diminished. Operating as a united front, however, they are likely to get their way with government. In addition, since all fishermen have equitable access to hatchery fish in the common property fishery, the incentive for investment in competitive gear may be weakened. (Area licensing may also play an important role in reducing competition, and some comparable way of linking community or regional interests to specific stocks might be considered a precondition to workable co-management).

In addition to earning the right to co-manage the Special Harvest Area through submission of a plan to the Board of Fish, the Association also has important input into broader management decisions through its Regional Planning Team. Legislation permitting formation of such teams was passed at the same time as the legislation affecting the formation of aquaculture associations. This team is composed equally of Association Board members (fishermen and local citizens) and Alaska Department of Fish and Game members, and functions as if it were a subdivision of the latter. The team plans the enhancement activities of the region, develops goals and priorities, and gives or refuses permits for the building of hatcheries and for the release of particular species. In this way Alaska fishermen have a strong voice in the choice of what species to enhance in the area they fish, as well as who is allowed to build hatcheries, an area of conflict between fishermen and government in other areas (e.g. British Columbia).

The Southern Southeast Regional Aquaculture Association plays two more roles in co-management. It collects data on all returns and all harvesting in the Special Harvest Area, as well as tagging and keeping records of fish it produces that are caught before they enter the Special Harvest Area. The Association also serves as marketer for the fish it harvests in the Special Harvest Area to cover costs, and repay its loan. In this capacity it acts as joint marketer for all the Association fishermen. As such it bargains for the highest price with processors and can act beyond the capacity of individual fishermen in establishing long-term marketing arrangements with buyers. In so doing, it allows individuals to sell part of "their" catch corporately, unencumbered by relations of indebtedness to processors. Although this does not immediately enhance the overall bargaining position of fishermen in their private sales, it has an impact on price expectations and could open the door to the development of collective negotiation where such an ideology did not previously exist. In Prince William Sound, which has a history of strong union activity (but where strike and picket have been illegal since the 1950s), the Cordova Aquatic Marketing Association has continued to act as the bargaining arm of fishermen who are also now in the local regional aquaculture association (Payne, personal communication).

The Southern Southeast Regional Aquaculture Association appears to be in the process of altering five relationships in the following manner. (1) Through their association fishermen contribute financing, expertise, time, and energy toward the increase of the resource base. Instead of being simply predators on the resource, they have committed themselves to a long-range planned interest in the enhancement of the resource. (2) In so doing they abandon some of their individualistic competitive stance, a stance that would press mainly for more fishing time for a particular gear type at the expense of others. They accept some restrictions on their fishing time through the promise of equity from their own fishermen board in return for the rational planning of the common good. They have an incentive to work together for their common interest, because united in an association they can operate a hatchery. As an organized group, they can work with government and contribute to planning in a far more powerful way than they could as individuals. (3) Local fishermen as a unit have certain bargaining power with fish processors for the percentage of their catch that is sold through the hatchery as cost recovery. Because this is a large, predictable, and assured amount of fish, the association receives competitive bids from several processors and enjoys a strong bargaining position. It may establish long-term marketing relations with Korea for its chum harvest. The incentive structure also exists for them to form new bargaining units, or achieve greater economic independence from processors because of their stronger economic position as an association. (4) Experience in the association enables fishermen to go beyond their formerly adversarial relationship with the government to a position of partnership and sympathy with administrative

263

problems. This is possible only because the government has ceded them certain authority in areas in which they have superior knowledge. The fact that they are responsible for their own management plan creates incentives for good data generation and support for enforcement. (5) The aquaculture association staff represents the fishermen's concerns over habitat protection in public hearings and committees. If activities such as logging or mining threaten to affect fish habitat, the association can have input into decisions about these developments through the Regional Planning Team. The Alaska situation will now be compared to the one in Washington.

The Treaty Tribes of Washington State

Although co-management is practiced by some twenty fishing tribes in Washington State whose right of access to 50 percent of the fish that passed their usual and accustomed aboriginal fishing locations was affirmed in 1974 in US vs. Washington, this discussion will focus mainly on only one of the treaty tribes, the Lummi. This level of co-management might be considered three steps more particularized than the Alaska situation, in that it is confined to one user group (commercial fishermen), to one class of commercial fishermen (Indians), and to a sub-region of Puget Sound. The regional operation of co-management in Puget Sound is important, of course, because both non-treaty fishermen and other treaty fishermen are potential interceptors of each others' salmon. Area licensing in Puget Sound is not practicable as such, given treaty rights, the geography of the region, and the consequent mixing of stocks. Therefore, pan-tribal and higher-level organizations are partially involved in articulating local co-management efforts with regional management. Because regional co-ordination is complex and only partially resolved, this discussion is limited to one case of local co-management.

Despite the court decision in their favor, the Lummi tribe (with some 1,700 on-reserve residents) has not achieved a co-management position easily or completely because of a decade of resistance on the part of the State of Washington and the Washington Department of Fisheries to policies and procedures that would permit both the treaty allocation of fish and sound management at the stock level (U.S. Commission on Civil Rights, 1981). Still, the most recent developments give a glimpse of what co-management in Washington might eventually look like. Despite the fact that co-management in this particular situation is forced by the belated recognition of treaty rights, and thus encounters unique forms of resistance and controversy from other fishing and non-fishing interests, the examination of co-management among the Lummi illustrates important general principles.

The Lummi situation differs from that of Neets Bay, Alaska in that Lummi co-management affects stocks that are at times available to the entire Puget Sound salmon fishery. (For simplicity this discussion excludes the treaty fishing by other tribes outside Puget Sound). This is because the areas where the Lummi fished aboriginally involved reef-net interception of British Columbia's Fraser River sockeye and other salmon, as well as more local bay and river fishing. The US vs. Washington decision specified that treaty tribes were entitled to opportunities to harvest 50 percent of the salmon runs that passed their aboriginal fishing locations, requiring the generation of information on specific runs, information that did not exist in 1974. Formerly the State had managed the Puget Sound fishery based on area-wide data on the five salmon species, usually divided into north and south Puget Sound, with one biologist assigned to each salmon species in the entire Sound. There was very incomplete knowledge of the eight drainage areas of Puget Sound that in 1985 were finally made into management areas isomorphic with the treaty areas, and of the intra-watershed fish population dynamics, as well as the effects of mixed stock fishing far from rivers on specific river systems. There was not sufficient staff in the Washington Department of Fisheries (WDF) for research and development of management plans that account for the differential contributions of each river system and run to the overall fishery. Nor was the knowledge of fishermen, frequently mentioned in the literature as complementary to and in some aspects superior to the knowledge of government agents (Langdon 1977, Morrell 1985, Pinkerton 1984), integrated into management. Instead, adversarial relations characterized the industry at large and the relations between the tribes and the WDF in particular (U.S. Commission on Civil Rights 1981).

The major accomplishment of the co-management system that evolved in Washington was the infusion of federal funds to the tribes to generate a data base for run-by-run management (following the court order), the tribes' eventual ability to institute data sharing among all the tribes and the WDF, and the joint production of a management plan taking into account far more considerations. This required the willingness of the WDF to extend some trust rather than endure continual lawsuits. Although the WDF systematically lost lawsuits with the tribes over openings that frustrated treaty allocations and sound management, Lummi informants observed that the WDF was not willing to share meaningful management planning with the tribes until a few key new appointees in the WDF brought in new attitudes. For example, they became willing to take the chance that the tribes would be able to discipline their fishermen and not eliminate a particular run if allowed an opening they desired in a shallow bay where the fish were more vulnerable.

The tribes were confident they could discipline their fishermen, because they had their own enforcement officers, tribal licensing, tribal fish tax, and had all begun to participate in management of the fishery soon after the 1974 court decision. They did not seek a license to eliminate fish runs, but the flexibility to practice more appropriate and fine-grained management as data permitted. Although relations among the tribes and between the tribes and the WDF are still contentious, some general procedures have been established through which differences can be diminished without sacrificing the fish in the process. There remains a major conflict between treaty fishermen and non-treaty fishermen who are reluctant to relinquish some of the fishing privileges they held before the delayed recognition of treaty rights, but this question is not central to the concerns at hand.

The question of Lummi fishermen's relationships to processors also differs from the Alaska situation, because by 1974 the Lummi had lost nearly their entire fleet, composed of some 19 purse-seines in the early 1950s (Taylor 1969: 50-52; Deloria 1978), and these were lost in much the same way Indians lost purse-seiners in British Columbia. As the industry became more highly capitalized, Indians were unable to maintain payments for the new investments and the vessels were repossessed by the companies (Pinkerton 1985).

After treaty rights to fish were recognized in 1974, loans were available from the Federal government to acquire a fleet. By 1985 the Lummi fleet consisted of some 30 purse seiners, 90 to 100 motorized gillnetters, and some 200 skiffs, many of which used hand-pulled gear (and some had no motors), primarily fishing the rivers and bays. This last category of boat had survived as a fishing method when the larger boats had been lost. In building up their fleet to take 50 percent of the catch, the Lummi did not limit license applicants, but competed with other tribes in Fraser sockeye and pink interceptions, because as late as 1981 (Lummi Fisheries Annual Report) the sockeye treaty tribes did not have enough capacity to take their treaty share of the Fraser River sockeye and pinks in a "high" year. (The purse-seine vessels primarily fish sockeye and pinks in the Fraser River interception fishery, while the smaller gear takes most of the coho, chum, and about a third of the chinook in rivers and bays.) The Lummi had to choose between having the right capacity for an average sockeye year or not having enough for the exceptional years, and have consequently developed overcapacity. They no longer assist in loans for new boat purchase and discourage further entry into fishing by young people.[9] By 1982 they passed a regulation that prohibited any Lummi fisherman from fishing with a boat that was leased from or partially owned by or mortgaged to a non-Lummi. Although this regulation was intended primarily to prevent Lummis from selling or leasing any part of their fishing right to non-Lummis, it also effectively ended any linkages with processors that would affect the competitive position of the fishermen.

The Lummi have also asked for the cooperation of processors in collecting their 4 percent (of gross sales) tribal tax, to be paid at the time of fish sale. Because some processors have not collected the tax, or have collected it and not passed it on to the Lummi, the Lummi are working toward a system whereby all the treaty tribes will boycott those processors who do not cooperate. They have already instituted a system whereby processors post a bond that the Lummi can collect if tax payment is not made. All of these arrangements underline the bargaining power of the group that has taken over some management responsibility for its own fishery and can exert certain controls over its own fishermen.

One of the uses of the tribal tax has been the operation and expansion of the two Lummi hatchery operations, in which coho, chinook, and chum are reared in that order of importance. Since 1969 when this program began, over 52 million juvenile coho, chinook, and chum have been reared and released by the Lummi into the waters of the Nooksack River and Lummi Bay. The Lummi estimate that 15 to 20 percent of returning hatchery coho are caught by commercial and sport fishermen in Puget Sound, whereas one-third to one-half of those that escape capture are taken by the tribe in a terminal fishery (Lummi Fisheries Annual Report 1983). A microtag program enables the tribe to fit releases into its harvest management regime. As in Alaska, the co-management situation has provided further incentives and funds to enhance the natural runs and to reintroduce runs (spring chinook) that had been eliminated previously by overfishing.

The Lummi situation is particularly important in illustrating how co-management contributes to planning the accommodation of other water resource users to the needs of the fishery. In the Lummi's Nooksack River watershed, there are many competitors for use of the water or the watershed in ways that conflict with fish-rearing use: farmers needing irrigation water, small hydro-electric generators, logging companies, shoreline developers, etc. In Phase II of the Boldt decision (1980) the initial decision ruled that the Lummi have a strong voice in decisions about the quality of the environment, since their treaty rights to fish are meaningless without an environment that can continue to support fish. Thus the Lummi and other tribes have been in court many times to intervene in developments they viewed as detrimental to the fish. Environmental groups that were previously without power in such developments were able to get standing in the courts through their alliances with the Lummi (Harper 1982). (Recent appeals of

267

this case have not supported the decision, and relitigation may result.)

As an alternative to continuous litigation with the tribes, the "developers" formed the Northwest Water Resources Committee in 1981, to explore more constructive methods of dispute resolution. According to the 1984 Annual Report of the Committee, joint corporate-tribal meetings over the last three years have produced a degree of respect for existing data on the fishery and the impact of other resource use, and a feeling that more can be gained by pooling research efforts than by continued litigation. While it is still unclear what the accomplishments of the committee might be, Lummi leaders stated in interviews that at least attitudes are changing with greater communication and the establishing of a common knowledge base on the issues.

Overall, the Lummi co-management situation appears to have ccntributed to changes in the five areas where change was noted in Alaska: (1) The resource base has clearly been improved, both because the Lummi are rehabilitating specific streams, but also because the tribes have been insistent about the necessity to generate adequate information about the watersheds to enable fine-grained management. Through a system of cross-checking of delivery slips and through sharing information on specific stocks, far more funding and human energy has been devoted to management than existed previously. (2) Fishermen members of individual tribes relate to each other more through their own tribal management now, in contrast to former days when they related chiefly to government authority. Through their tribal government they can influence tribal management decisions. Explicit catch allocation among different gear types has been avoided by the tribal leadership, although it may be argued that the larger, more capitalized gear have more successfully influenced tribal policy and gained access to boat-building loans, thereby taking the large majority of the catch.[9] This inequality may be partially balanced by the fact that the most successful enhancement effort has been on coho, which are caught exclusively by the small gear fishermen, and cannot be intercepted by the large Lummi purse-seines and gillnets. ("We wonder if they swim in tunnels under the ocean floor, because we can't catch them even with our nets dragging the bottom," notes one gillnetter.) (3) Co-management has enabled Lummi fishermen to gain individually competitive positions with processors and even to demand processors' cooperation in the collection of their tribal tax. (4) Lummi relations with the Washington Department of Fisheries have been altered in that they have at least partialy been accepted as co-managers. Instead of struggling over the reconciliation of two conflicting plans after each has been made, the Department and the Lummi now share more data and they work more as a team to develop a joint management plan. The

268

Lummi feel that they will never relinquish their role in
co-management because "we're on those rivers all the time, and we
know what's going on." They believe that their role in
co-management will certainly not decrease, and may increase. (5)
The Lummi treaty rights have clearly contributed to their ability
to co-manage not just the fishery, but the fish habitat, in
co-operation with other users of that habitat. This is
co-management in its largest sense.

Conclusion

In the two co-management arrangements described above, five
relationships appear to have been altered: fishermen--fish,
fishermen--fishermen, fishermen--processors,
fishermen--government, and fishermen--other water-resource users.
The changes in relationships have been accompanied by certain
changes in behavior or attitudes on the part of fishermen and
government that have led to redefinitions of the meanings of
roles and of relationships. Fishermen can no longer be viewed by
government in these situations only as individualistic and
competitive predators, whose behavior follows simple bio-economic
models. Changes in institutional arrangements have altered both
behavior and perceptions of roles. In addition to territorial
rights and other property rights that fishermen have exercised
informally and formally, co-management emerges as a very
important path by which fishermen's rights can be specified
without altering the common property nature of the resource.
Rather, by altering the five relationships noted above,
co-management alters the institutional arrangements that have led
to underdevelopment in the fishery because they allowed fishermen
to become enmeshed in the tragedy of the commons and adversarial
relationships with government and others.

Changes wrought by co-management arrangements in the Pacific
Northwest salmon fisheries have important implications for the
way anthropologists, economists, and biologists might think of
the relations among institutions, ideology, and behavior in
fishery management. If we choose to think of fishermen as
economizing individuals, it is crucial to include in our analysis
the question: in terms of what do they economize? With
co-management arrangements the rules of the game have changed.
The same fishermen may still "economize," but no longer simply as
individuals nor with the same strategy. In the short term they
can now economize by fishing at appropriate times for efficiency
with less fear of not getting their share of the catch, while in
the long term they economize by ensuring the long-term
productivity of the resource. Institutional changes alter the
nature and expression of their self-interest, which is now more
clearly linked to the interests of other local fishermen, and to

269

the long-term planning of mutual interests. Their behavior changes, and certain attitudes as well.

In addition, co-management implies some transfer of power from state authorities and from large capitalist enterprises to fishermen and fishermen's groups. This becomes possible mainly because the co-operation of fishermen in data collection, enforcement, and in management decisions is necessary to prevent the degradation of the resource that conventional management and resource development threatened to produce. Sharing power with the fishermen has prevented a loss of the resource to government, and promises to reward government with an eventual increase in resource productivity. The processors, and other large capitalists, stand to benefit as overall catches grow and stabilize in the future, increasing the total national income. But most importantly, per capita income of fishermen, the index of development in the fishery, appears likely to grow. Development becomes a reality if individual fishermen are given a stake in decisions affecting the resource; their knowledge and participation under co-management can indeed make the harvesting appropriate, while under conventional resource management fishermen feel exploited, are forced to exploit the resource, and so recreate the "tragedy of the commons."

Notes

[1] Stock decline was not necessarily region-wide, nor concentrated in the 1970s. In B.C. it has been notable in Rivers Inlet, the West Coast of Vancouver Island, the Queen Charlotte Islands, and in chinook salmon throughout most of the coast (see Shirvell & Carbonneau 1984). Indebtedness and its relation to overfishing are documented in McMullan (1984) and Langdon (1982). For purposes of discussion at this point, other factors contributing to stock decline, such as damage to spawning habitat by industrial development are not considered.

[2] This paper originally was presented at the meetings of the Society for Economic Anthropology, Warrenton, Virginia, April 1985. I would like to thank E. N. Anderson of the Department of Anthropology, University of California-Riverside, and Richard Salisbury of the Department of Anthropology, McGill University, for very helpful comments on an earlier draft. I am also indebted to Dan Boxberger, Department of Anthropology, Western Washington University and Fay Cohen, Institute of Resource and Environmental Studies, Dalhousie University, for useful editorial comments on the Washington treaty tribes situation.

Conversations with Don Amend, Fikret Berkes, Mike Blanchard, Norman Dale, John Dunker, Gary Freitag, Ward Griffieon, G.I. James, Jewell James, Steve Langdon, Dominipus LeVieil, Jim Payne, and John Sutcliffe contributed a great deal. Finally, I am indebted to members of the University of British Columbia Fish and Ships Research Project, Department of Anthropology and Sociology, for debates that contributed to the basic theoretical formulations underlying this paper, and to the Anthropology departments at the University of California-Riverside and University of California-Los Angeles for logistical support during the research and writing.

[3] In the 1980s Canadian fishermen and fishing groups have taken the Federal Department of Fisheries to court to protest arbitrary exclusion or allocation of fishing opportunities to other groups of fishermen. One such group has already won its case in a lower court, on the grounds that the Department of Fisheries does not have the constitutional right to allocate for reasons other than conservation. See: Gulf Trollers Assoc. vs. Minister of Fisheries and Oceans, F.C.T.D. 1984 (unreported). Although this decision may be overturned in an appeal, Wildsmith (1985) argues that the right of the state to allocate is ambiguous.

[4] Elsewhere I have argued that provincial policies in British Columbia (more than the nature of competition) have created and exacerbated overinvestment and overfishing of certain stocks through interception (Pinkerton 1984). Nonetheless I concur with fisheries economists to the extent that I believe the nature of competition in the fishery tends, under some circumstances (especially expanding markets), to produce overinvestment and dissipation of profits.

[5] Unionized small boat skippers and deckhands on seiners influence minimum prices set for the entire season, but are not able to bargain directly during the season.

[6] In the salmon fishery, the main concern here, the three major gear types are trollers, who catch fish on hooks dragged behind the vessel; gillnetters, who catch fish in stationary nets suspended from corklines; and purse-seiners, who catch fish by surrounding a school with a mobile trap-net. The government often regulates the harvest by permitting only one gear-type access at any particular time; questions of equitable access are thus raised, and fishermen's associations to lobby for greater access are often formed along gear lines.

[7] There are about 50 seine, 500 gillnet, 1,000 power troll and 4,000 hand troll permits in southeast Alaska, although the number of fishermen is less, because many fishermen are multiple permit

holders.

[8] See Johnson 1985 for a discussion of conflict between gear types. The way allocation has been handled in the 1985 management plan makes it clear the Association board learned from this and is making every effort to avoid future conflicts.

[9] For a discussion of the consequences of differential access to fish by gear types, see Boxberger 1984. However, the existence of inequalities within a tribe and the ability of the larger gear to dominate policy may be more the result of the structure of representation (whether there are enough positions on fisheries management bodies to represent poorer river fishermen as well as wealthier ocean fishermen) than anything related to co-management.

References

Acheson, J. 1975. The Lobster Fiefs: Economic and Ecological Effects of Territoriality in the Maine Lobster Fishery. Human Ecology 3:183-207.
------- 1981. The Anthropology of Fishing. Annual Review of Anthropology 10:275-316.
Andersen, R., ed. 1979. North Atlantic Maritime Cultures. Mouton: The Hague.
Boxberger, D. 1984. Traditional Fishers in a Modern Industry: Allocation of the Salmon Resource among the Treaty Indians of Washington State. Paper read to the American Fisheries Society meetings.
Deloria, V., Jr. 1978. The Lummi Indian Community: The Fishermen of the Pacific Northwest. In: American Indian Economic Development. Sam Stanley, ed. Mouton: The Hague
Edwards, R. 1979. Contested Terrain. New York: Basic Books.
Gordon, S. 1954. The Economic Theory of a Common Property Resource: The Fishery. Journal of Political Economy 62(2):124-142.
Guppy, N. 1984. Property Rights and Changing Class Formation in the Social Organization of the B.C. Commercial Fishing Industry. Paper presented to the Western Regional Association of Sociology and Anthropology, Regina, Saskatchewan.
Harper, J. 1982. Indian Fisheries Management in the State of Washington. Socio-Economic Development, Indian and Northern Affairs Canada, MSS.
Johnson, T. 1985. Heavy Hatchery Return for SSRAA Pose Problems. National Fisherman 65(10).
Kearney, J. 1983. Common Tragedies: A Study of Resource Access in

the Bay of Fundy Herring Fisheries. Master of Environmental Sciences thesis, Dalhousie University.
------- 1984. The Transformation of the Bay of Fundy Herring Fisheries 1976-1978: An Experiment in Fishermen-Government Co-Management. In: Atlantic Fisheries and Coastal Comunities: Fisheries Decision-Making Case Studies. C. Lamson and A. Hanson, eds. Dalhousie Ocean Studies Programme, 1321 Edward Street, Halifax, Nova Scotia, Canada B3H 3H5.
Langdon, S. 1977. Technology, Ecology, and Economy: Fishing Systems in Southeast Alaska. Ph.D. dissertation, Stanford University.
Lummi Fisheries Annual Report. 1981, 1983.
McCay, B. 1980. A Fishermen's Co-operative, Limited: Indigenous Resource Management in a Complex Society. Anthropological Quarterly 53(1):29-38.
McCay, B. and J. Acheson, eds. 1987. Capturing the Commons: Anthroplogical Contributions to Natural Resource Management. Arizona:University of Arizona Press.
Morrell, M. 1985. The Gitksan and Wet'suwet'en Fishery in the Skeena River System. Final Report. Gitksan-Wet'suwet'en Fish Management Study, Box 229, Hazelton, B.C. V0J 1Y0.
McMullan, J. 1984. State, Capital, and Debt in the British Columbia Fishing Fleet from 1970 to 1982. Journal of Canadian Studies (Spring 1984) 19(1):65-88.
Payne, J. 1985. The Effects of the 1964 Alaska Earthquake on The Cordova Alaska Commercial Salmon Fishery: An Anthropological Perspective. Ph.D. dissertation, University of Alaska, Anchorage.
Pinkerton, E. 1984. Intercepting the State: Dramatic Processes in the Assertion of Local Co-Management Rights. Paper read to the Applied Anthropology Meetings, Toronto, to be published in: Capturing the Commons: Anthropological Contributions to Natural Resource Management. University of Arizona Press, forthcoming.
--------- 1985. Competition Among B.C. Fish Processors. In: Uncommon Property. P. Marchak et al. eds. Methuen, forthcoming.
Shirvell, C.S. and C. Charbonneau. 1984. Can Stream Indexing Improve Salmon Escapement Estimates? Fisheries Research Branch, Rm 117, 417--2nd Ave. West, Prince Rupert, B.C. V8J 1G8
Taylor, D. N. 1969. Changes in the Economy of the Lummi Indians of Northwest Washington. M.A. thesis, Western Washington State College, Bellingham, Washington.
U.S. Commission on Civil Rights. 1981. Indian Tribes: A Continuing Quest for Survival. Washingtion, D.C.
Wildsmith, B. et al. 1985. Individual Entitlements in the Tidal Fisheries: Some Legal Problems. Report prepared for the Department of Fisheries and Oceans, February 1985. Faculty of Law, Dalhousie University.
Wilson, J. and J. Acheson. 1981. A Model of Adaptive Behavior in the New England Fishing Industry. Report to the National Science Foundation, Vol. III.

16. CHEAP FOOD: POLITICIZATION AND PROVISIONING PATTERNS AMONG THE URBAN POOR IN MANILA

Susan D. Russell

Introduction

Food policy is a subject of interdisciplinary interest owing to the many theoretical and social dilemmas posed by efforts to solve entrenched hunger in Third World countries. Whatever the economic form of a society, a need usually exists for some form of state intervention in the domestic food situation. Policies designed to increase growth in the agricultural sector are generally long-term, whereas even efficient market allocation of resources does not necessarily result in affordable prices for the poor in the short-term. State interventions to protect consumers from high or fluctuating food prices usually occur through the establishment of fair price food shops, marketing programs, food stamps or rationing, price controls, and other forms of food subsidy. Although it is essential to target the intended beneficiaries of such programs carefully to prevent needless waste of scarce development resources, designers of subsidized food distribution projects often fail to recognize the heterogeneity of consumption and purchasing constraints among urban residents. Yet in any large metropolis, diversity in food preferences, market outlets, and buying strategies characterize people of different ethnic and regional backgrounds, class levels, and intra-urban geographic residence.

A general assumption exists among technical experts that the types of food consumed are more homogeneous in urban areas than in rural (e.g., Lele and Candler 1985). Policymakers also assume that purchasing constraints among the urban poor are primarily a function of fluctuations in income or food prices (e.g., Timmer, Falcon and Pearson 1983). Such universalistic economic models of social behavior overlook how the poor in any country establish their own culturally and economically appropriate solutions to problems of obtaining food in reaction to a variety of local and national institutions that continually impinge on their livelihood opportunities. Cultural perceptions of appropriate shopping outlets and strategies vary among social classes and subtly reflect the historical diversity of political and economic encounters that the poor experience in their relationships with the wider urban milieu. Targeting food subsidy programs efficiently, then, requires prior information about the attitudes, consumption strategies, and purchasing constraints

275

that influence how, when, and where the poor obtain their food.
In addition to these "micro" concerns, the larger political and
cultural context also represents a diachronic, "macro" dimension
of considerable significance.

In this article, I discuss the various local and external
constraints that influence the food purchase and consumption
patterns among residents of a squatter community in Manila.
Although my fieldwork coincides with a unique and politically
disruptive period of Philippine history, e.g., prior to the
civilian-backed military revolt that exiled Ferdinand Marcos,
this case study has relevance for other Third World urban areas
experiencing political unrest and widespread dissatisfaction with
current regimes. In the first section, I review anthropological
studies of market outlets in the Philippines. In the second
part, I discuss the strategies used by low-income residents to
obtain food and their reactions to various food outlets,
including those operated by the government. In the final
section, I raise several political implications of this case
study that illustrate the important role that cultural processes
can play in what otherwise appear to policymakers as
straightforward forms of development aid.

Market Utilization Patterns Among the Urban Poor

Anthropological studies can strengthen the awareness of
policymakers about the need to design food subsidies in ways
appropriate for low-income consumers. Studies of petty trade and
marketing stress the socioeconomic heterogeneity within the
informal sector and its complex linkages with formal sector
enterprises (e.g., Roberts 1978; Scott 1979; Bromley and Gerry
1979). In the Philippines, market studies in secondary cities
have clarified how personalized trading ties (suki) among
wholesalers, retailers and consumers are rational responses to a
lack of capital, limited access to formal credit sources, and the
legal difficulties of enforcing credit repayment (e.g., Szanton
1972; Davis 1973). Dannhaeuser's (1977, 1983) analyses of the
differential structure and growth of trading channels between
Manila and Dagupan City have examined formal linkages between
higher order wholesaling firms and lower order retail outlets.
His approach illustrates the utility of examining specific
product subsectors as opposed to the more general commercial
sector in order to clarify the socioeconomic dynamics of
distribution channels.

Many empirical studies of Philippine food distribution have
focused on the employment characteristics and coping strategies

276

of street vendors and small neighborhood store operators (e.g., Guerrero 1975; McGee and Yeung 1977; Dannhaeuser 1980; Silverio 1982). These studies underscore the important contribution of small-scale trading enterprises in providing food conveniently and in small quantities to the urban poor. The large number of food-related trading enterprises relative to the population is due to the high percentage of household income spent on food and to a marked degree of specialization (Dannhaeuser 1977). Small-scale enterprises also represent a resilient and expandable source of underemployed labor absorption, thus serving as a barometer of wider economic conditions (Dannhaeuser 1980; Barth 1984). Barth's studies (1982, 1983, 1984) of Davao City and Iloilo City also point out the role of an efficient food marketing system in stimulating regional food self-sufficiency geared to local demand. Although greater government investment in market infrastructure can help induce food production for regional consumption, thereby promoting cheaper food prices and market-related employment (Barth 1982), whether such investments translate into cheaper food for the poor is dependent on a variety of cultural and economic preferences.

Food purchase patterns among the urban poor reflect not only their limited income, but also a variety of food preferences and time constraints. Retail outlets in the Philippines vary in the quantity, quality, price, and variety of food and services offered to consumers. Supermarkets in Manila cater to higher income urban residents owing to their greater range of imported, canned, and processed food. They also attract higher income residents by providing parking space and cleaner facilities compared to most public marketplaces. Still, the primary food outlets even for higher income residents are public markets. The heavy reliance on marketplaces for food purchases reflects both a local preference for fresh food and the greater variety of local produce available in markets.

Grocery products tend to be purchased by low-income consumers at small neighborhood stores (sari-sari) rather than at supermarkets or groceries. Neighborhood stores typically have higher prices than larger establishments, but sell goods in infinitely divisible quantities and in convenient locations (e.g., Dannhaeuser 1980; Silverio 1982). Street vendors that sell prepared food also are important retail agents. In Iloilo City, 30 percent of household food expenditures are for prepared food, two-thirds of which is purchased from street vendors (Barth 1983).

Although anthropological studies in the Philippines provide many insights into the employment characteristics, trading relations, and the variety of food outlets, the urban poor's strategies for obtaining cheap food have not been a specific

277

focus of study. In the next section, I discuss some of the purchasing and consumption patterns that characterize the residents of a squatter community in Manila.

Purchase Constraints in a Manila Slum

Santa Elena is a densely populated squatter settlement along the banks of one of the Pasig River Canals in Binondo, Manila. This area is indistinguishable in physical appearance from the nearby Tondo district, which is one of the largest slums in Southeast Asia. The residential settlement comprises an area of less than one hectare, but has more than 600 households with an estimated population of 3,345. Over the last 15 years, Sta. Elena residents have forcibly driven off government demolition teams who tried to evict them, as the land is legally owned by a Chinese businessman. Although part of the slum has been destroyed by the government, a tentative compromise was reached in 1980 and the area was targeted for urban improvement. This program remains a fairy tale so far, and residents lack a distinct sense of security in their living arrangements. Insecurity also is evident in the income-earning opportunities in this neighborhood. About one-third of the productive household members are "variable" income earners, such as street vendors and the irregularly employed, which inhibits families from maintaining regular consumption patterns or planning for long-term financial obligations.

The average monthly household income for a family of five in 1983 was 1,073 pesos, where as the median income was 906 pesos (11 pesos to $1.00). Of the total household expenditures, 62 percent was allotted to food. For Metro Manila, the share of food in total household expenditure increased from 40.4 percent in 1965 to 52.23 percent in 1983 (National Economic Development Authority 1983). Sta. Elena residents, then, represent some of the poorest of the urban poor in Manila.

The daily per capita food expenditure in Sta. Elena is 4.23 pesos, well below the Food and Nutrition Research Institute of the Philippines' recommended minimal daily per capita food threshold of 6.93 pesos. Given their limited food budget, many of the poorer residents in this neighborhood survive on only two meals a day. The meals most frequently eaten are lunch and dinner. Although most households purchase food once a day, the poorest families purchase food twice a day. For street vendor households, the food consumed at lunch often depends on the magnitude of sales during the morning, and the rate of sales similarly may determine the composition of the evening meal. In addition, daily food expenditures have to be conservative enough to allow for stock purchases early the next morning.[1]

Filipinos, like most Asians, have a strong preference for fresh foods over processed or packaged foods (Table 1). Fresh fish is preferred over dried fish, despite the widespread belief that dried fish is "the poor man's food" in the Philippines. This assumption may be true in inland rural areas where sources of fresh fish are more limited and expensive. In Metro Manila, however, fresh fish is relatively cheap and perceived by the poor as more nutritious, even though during certain seasons dried fish is a cheaper source of protein. Pork is the primary meat item consumed, partly because it is cheaper than beef or chicken, and also because it contains more fat.

Although both meat and fresh fish constitute the largest expenditure share among fresh foods, these figures mask the heterogeneity of consumption even in a very poor neighborhood. Among street vendors, for example, the average amount of fish purchased per week is only 3.5 kilos for a family of six, while the poorest households buy less than one kilo a week. Meat is not consumed on a weekly basis among the lowest income households, who prefer to substitute less expensive fish for meat. Even in the larger sample, the average amount purchased is less than one kilo a week. Cultural preferences are also partly responsible for the degree to which fish is substituted for meat. Many residents in Sta. Elena are migrants from coastal areas in the Visayas, and are accustomed to diets oriented around sea protein.

This consumption basket is biased toward starch and protein rather than vegetables and fruits, and reflective of food preferences and budget balancing among the poor. Although in terms of general food groups the main difference between what the poor and the wealthy consume is in quantity, the type of foods eaten are different. The fish usually consumed by the poor are cheaper (e.g., third class fish), as are the various cuts of meat (e.g., pork backbones, chicken feet) and vegetables (e.g., swamp grass, sweet potato tops). Similarly, the kinds of grocery items consumed by the poor are limited, even though they compose the largest food expenditure share. Coffee, canned milk, sugar, cooking oil, snacks and cold drinks are significant in the diet, with canned meat and fish purchased only irregularly.

A variety of other coping mechanisms have been observed that allow the urban poor to subsist on marginal incomes (e.g., Eames and Goode 1973; McGee 1979). One common pattern is to have as many household members as possible engaged in earning an income, often from multiple sources, in order to spread risks. Credit also is heavily relied on, although McGee (1979:55) observes that

Table 1.

Table 1

COMPOSITION OF FOOD CONSUMPTION EXPENDITURE
SANTA ELENA, BINDONDO -- OCTOBER 1983

FOOD GROUPS	AVERAGE WEEKLY EXPENDITURE*	EXPENDITURE SHARE (%)
Fresh Foods	(70.72)	(42.69)
Fresh Fish	24.81	14.98
Meat	20.84	12.58
Vegetables	13.72	8.28
Fruits	7.45	4.50
Eggs	3.90	2.35
Starchy Foods	(42.41)	(25.67)
Rice	33.29	20.16
Bread	9.12	5.51
Processed Foods	(43.68)	(26.38)
Grocery Items[1]	38.27	23.11
Dried Fish	5.41	3.27
Cooked Food	(8.71)	(5.26)
Average Weekly Food Expenditure	165.62	100.00

*In pesos

[1]Grocery items include canned milk, coffee, sardines, refined sugar, cooking oil, condiments, and other packaged food items.

the poorest of the urban poor cannot borrow money often because lenders consider them poor credit risks. Other strategies include minimizing transport costs and sharing food through reciprocal exchanges with neighbors (Eames and Goode 1973; Lomnitz 1977). Logan (1981) also stresses the partial reliance on rural resources and the minimization of waste through the consumption of day-old or wilted food.

Such generalizations are useful, but significant differences exist among the urban poor in the extent to which these, or other strategies, prevail. Food sharing, for example, is more common in Sta. Elena among close relatives than among neighbors. Due to their extremely low income, the poorest families usually exchange food with other households only on holidays or special occasions. Among the households that share food more than once a month, the amounts exchanged tend to be either very small, such as a piece of fruit or fish, or they are equivalent exchanges designed to vary the side dishes consumed with rice. Rice sometimes is loaned or given to relatives in emergencies, but these cases are rare among people with extremely limited food resources for their own families. Because most residents are migrants from depressed rural areas quite far from Manila, they also never or rarely receive food from relatives in the provinces.

The poorest of Sta. Elena's residents occasionally find themselves without any money to purchase food, although for street vendors this is less common than for fixed-income earners. Vendors were able to cope with the price increases that followed the heavy devaluation of the peso in 1983-84 by increasing their own prices or, more often, decreasing the amounts served or using cheaper ingredients in food preparation. Many fixed-income earners reported greater decreases in consumption because their wages remained the same and payments were often delayed. Skipping meals, begging, and theft are strategies most frequently resorted to by variable income earners, while fixed income earners usually borrow from a moneylender when they have no money for food.

Moneylenders in this community perform essential services, despite their high interest rate of 20 percent (which increased to 40 percent after the 1984 peso devaluations). This informal credit source is most commonly used for school, rent, business, or emergency food and medical expenses, and is more extensively relied on than any other source of loans. Although the poorest residents have little difficultly obtaining small amounts of credit from neighborhood store owners as long as they do not have reputations as delinquent payers, well-to-do usurers are able to loan larger amounts of capital to them over a longer period.

While variabiltiy exists in the choice of primary food

outlet, the majority of Sta. Elena residents buy food from public markets. Proximity and low prices are equally dominant in their preference for public markets, largely due to the nearby presence of Divisoria, the largest retail-wholesale market complex in Metro Manila. Unlike in slum areas some distance from the commercial food wholesaling centers in the city, however, Sta. Elena Filipinos have access to a greater variety of sources of food.

Although most Filipinos patronize public markets, the urban poor's shopping strategies are innovative in order to ensure their access to cheap food. Many residents, especially vendors, purchase fresh food directly from truckers (viajero) that are delivering produce to market wholesalers. These transactions occur late at night or early in the morning, because truckers are anxious to dispose of unsold items before dawn. The traders that dispense goods in this manner park in illegal areas near the wholesale market complex to avoid parking and unloading fees. Even for residents who purchase food once or twice a day from regular market vendors, the prices paid are reduced by shopping at strategic times. Right before closing time, for example, market vendors sell fresh produce more cheaply in order to dispose of produce that will spoil or to avoid excessive storage. Also, some market vendors offer discounts early in the morning to their first customers, as an early sale is considered auspicious for a profitable daily turnover.

Supermarkets tend to carry higher quality items that appeal to upper-class customers. None of the Sta. Elena residents use supermarkets or groceries as primary food outlets, partly because such outlets are several minutes farther than the public market. A few households rely heavily, however, on neighborhood stores and street food outlets. Such outlets are very close by, and some neighborhood stores sell fresh vegetables in addition to grocery items. Although prices are slightly higher at these stores than in the public markets, owners are very competitive in terms of prices and extra services. Mark-ups are usually no more than 10 to 20 percent over the wholesale price, and often much lower. The extra services extended to customers by neighborhood store owners are also innovative. Besides selling food in tiny amounts (such as a spoonful of margarine or an ounce of cooking oil), store owners often informally watch over customers' children for short time periods and allow special customers to store food in their refrigerators. They also encourage socializing (and hence eventual sale of snacks and drinks) by playing radios and allotting space in front of their stores for people to congregate. Most stores owners extend some credit to customers, although selectively and in relatively small amounts. The screening process for credit extension in this neighborhood of generally poor residents, however, depends less on the customers' income than on their reputation for paying off small debts quickly.

A few members of the lowest income classes in Santa Elena obtain their food primarily from street food outlets. These individuals are mobile vendors themselves, and their prime hours of selling coincide with meal times. Rather than lose time every day by shopping and returning home to cook food, they simply purchase a side dish at a cooked food outlet that can be consumed with rice they have brought with them, or they purchase entire meals away from home. Street food patrons also claim to prefer having a diverse range of foods from which to choose their meals.

The availability of personalized trading ties (or suki) is another significant reason why Filipinos prefer public markets. Although this factor ranks below proximity or low prices, its lesser significance is partly due to the large number of residents who purchase food from the illegal wholesale unloading district. It is not feasible to develop suki relations with truckers, because their trips are variable and they only retail goods in small quantities if they have not disposed of their produce to wholesalers. Even for those who usually purchase goods in the unloading areas, shopping in the public market periodically is necessary.

Many individuals consider fair pricing to be one of the significant advantages to having a suki in the market. A reliable market vendor is important, especially because of the volatility of food prices at the time of this study. In this sense, suki vendors dispense more than just goods; they also provide reliable information on price changes. This service is significant for the urban poor, many of whom do not have up-to-date knowledge about published sources of price changes. Residents are very cautious about being overcharged or having their produce inaccurately weighed by unscrupulous sellers, and having a regular market vendor is considered a necessary shopping tactic. Suki relationships are not cast in stone, however, and many individuals maintain more than one regular vendor relationship to facilitate price comparison. If other vendors are found to have cheaper prices, then the former suki vendors are simply dropped.

Other services offered by suki market vendors, street vendors, and neighborhood store owners include friendly socializing and occasional "extra amounts." Although the quality of fresh food is just as important to most of the urban poor as it is to higher income consumers, a few of the lowest income residents have suki market vendors who reserve lower quality produce for them. Some vendors sell wilted or nearly spoiled merchandise, especially vegetables, to special customers at considerably reduced rates. Ostensibly, retailers reserve this produce for suki customers, but some items I have seen exchanged would be impossible to sell to higher income shoppers. Similarly, Keyes (1974:5) found that trash scavengers in Manila maintain suki relations with individuals who reserve paper products for them that would otherwise be thrown away.

This case study of food purchase constraints illustrates several microlevel points. First, proximity and low prices are the two most significant determinants of preferred market outlets. Given the high opportunity cost of time for many low-income earners, especially the informally employed, proximity is a more significant determinant than prices. Neighborhood stores and street food sellers are all within a 1-5 minute commuting distance on foot from Santa Elena, while the public market is within 6-10 minutes. In contrast, groceries and supermarkets require 11-15 minutes commuting time, while the nearest Kadiwa outlet is 15-20 minutes away. Secondly, the resourcefulness of the food-purchasing strategies relied on by many of the poor, such as buying food twice a day, shopping during hours when market vendors sell food at reduced prices, purchasing food at night from illegally parked provincial wholesalers, and occasionally consuming wilted produce, suggest that access to cheap food is neither a primary nor a homogeneous problem in all parts of the city. Greater variability in shopping strategies exists in low income commercial districts near major wholesale markets or ports compared to more isolated sections of the urban area. Although limited income is a serious problem among the poor, many of them ensure their access to cheap food by circumventing normal retailing channels.

Residents of Sta. Elena are subjected to a variety of external constraints imposed by the state that influence their provisioning patterns. State interventions into the food market system include price controls, licensing and sanitation requirements, geographical restrictions on retail food selling, and time limits on the hours of market wholesale and retail operations. Many of the strategic characteristics of food purchasing in this community have developed in response to these external institutions and to the structural problems of underemployment. By forming personalized relationships with food sellers in market places and neighborhood stores, the urban poor extract a number of benefits that otherwise would be difficult to obtain. The small amount of credit or leftover produce that they are able to claim through these relationships may seem negligible to an outside observer, but is representative of a larger strategy wherein people with extremely limited resources forge social institutions that minimally support their reproduction or help tide them over during emergencies. Seeking out illegal wholesale food sources at night, when government restrictions are negligibly enforced, effectively bypasses state regulation and taxation efforts.

Similar actions characterize income-earning patterns. The graft paid by food vendors daily to corrupt police officers allows them to operate their businesses in geographically restricted areas that are nonetheless commercially rewarding. Such payments also enable them to avoid restrictions on sanitation and licensing. During periodic city crackdowns on mobile food sellers, the vendors association designates a quota of individuals to be arrested. All members chip in to cover the foregone earnings of temporarily incarcerated vendors, and collectively protect the vending territories of such individuals from absorption by outsiders. These examples, and the repeated physical confrontations in the past wherein residents successfully asserted their rights to remain in an illegally claimed area, illustrate that people do not passively abide by externally imposed constraints, but mold and adjust their behavior intelligently to maintain their carefully constructed niche in the urban milieux.

Ideology and the Politicization of Food

Government-sponsored food retail outlets, or Kadiwa Centers, represent another market option for the urban poor. The Kadiwa Program is designed to ensure a steady supply of cheap food to the urban poor population by eliminating unnecessary middlemen. More than 60 percent (roughly 300 outlets) of the Kadiwa Centers are located in Metropolitan Manila. All centers are modeled in appearance after various private retail outlets and ostensibly sell food more cheaply. The largest Kadiwa Centers resemble modern supermarkets with their gleaming interiors, advertisements, spacious shelves, and orderly check-out lanes.[2] This food subsidy program primarily represents a form of geographic targeting, in that the outlets are ostensibly set up in low- and middle-income areas.

In our larger food market study, which also included low income areas in Kalookan City and Marikina in Metro Manila, only 2.3 percent (n=324) of residents rely on Kadiwa Centers as major food outlets (see Diokno 1985).[3] This pattern of underutilization occurs even in the areas where Kadiwa Centers are of nearer proximity than a public market. In Sta. Elena, only one resident purchases food primarily from a Kadiwa Center, and she is from the highest income category. This person buys her rice and grocery items from the Kadiwa Center, but shops at the public market for fresh foods. She also commutes to the

285

Kadiwa Center on public transportation rather than on foot -- an extra expense few of the poorer residents can afford.

A variety of technical reasons partly explain why the urban poor in Manila fail to patronize Kadiwa Centers. First, Kadiwa Centers are situated on government property that is often not in sections of the city where the poorest Filipinos are residentially concentrated. To save on rent, the state locates outlets on government property next to municipal buildings or in the business districts, which are some distance from the congested slums.[4] The location of Kadiwa Centers on state property tends to reinforce the social distance the poor already perceive in western-style shopping environments staffed by well-dressed cashiers. Second, the quality of fresh products retailed through the cumbersome government marketing channels is often low. Beef and pork often are a brownish, unappealing color due to erratic freezing conditions and poor packaging methods at the government's refrigerated warehouse. Numerous Filipinos express a reluctance to buy frozen meat or fish based on its visual appearance, which they surmise might cause illness if consumed. While low-quality vegetables might appeal to some of the poorest consumers, their inability to bargain for lower price discounts makes purchasing these commodities at Kadiwa outlets uneconomical. This disparity between the quality and price of retail products basically belies the government's argument that Kadiwa food is cheaper than the fresher food in private markets.

Technical reasons alone never entirely explain the success or failure of any government program among the poor. The attitudes of people toward the project are equally important and even more complex. In the Philippine context, these attitudes directly relate to questions concerning the legitimacy of projects sponsored by what was increasingly perceived by people as a corrupt regime. During the years that Imelda Marcos was governor of Metropolitan Manila, a variety of projects were sponsored that, although ostensibly for the poor, actually benefited mostly middle- or upper-class individuals. Such projects were designated by political slogans intended to advertise the government's compassionate concern for the poor. Examples include subsidized housing loans, or Pag-Ibig ("to love"); small enterprise loans, or Kilusang Kabuhayan at Kaunlaran ("Movement for Livelihood Improvement"); and subsidized food outlets, or Kadiwa ("oneness" or "unity"). In the reemergence of political demonstrations among Filipinos following the assassination of opposition leader Benigno Aquino in 1983, such slogans typified more than ever the empty rhetorical concern offered to the poor during the latter years of Marcos's rule. Political commercials advertising these projects were booed and jeered in public movie theaters and urban signs were defaced. The Kilusang Kabuhayan at Kaunlaran program was cynically referred to as the "Kanya Kanyang Kurakot," or "raking it in," in reference to the perception that Marcos's wealthy friends were primary beneficiaries.

The increased political awareness of corruption and neglect was not confined to the lower classes, but was also apparent among the middle class. The glamorous Rustan's department store, which Filipinos suspected was owned in part by Imelda Marcos, had long been referred to locally as "Imelda's sari-sari," or neighborhood store. Many middle-class patrons voluntarily boycotted this store in protest over her alleged involvement in the Aquino assassination.

Food in the Philippines has a long history of being used as a political tool for manipulating the poor during crises of government stability and credibility. Right before elections, large quantities of free rice often are doled out in the poorer areas in return for votes. Similarly, food price controls are raised or lowered during periods of political unrest in a pattern of selective support-seeking that is by no means unique to this country. The Kadiwa program itself was co-opted by the Metro Manila Commission after its initial launching and the number of such outlets increased substantially in the early 1980s. The heavier subsidies required to operate these outlets were deemed worthwhile given the state's need to placate politically the capital city's population.

The Kadiwa project in Manila, partly because it was a project supported by Imelda Marcos and also because it involved the sensitive issue of subsidized food, came to symbolize urban Filipinos' feelings of powerlessness against economic inflation triggered by Benigno Aquino's assassination. Politicization of the urban poor varies considerably in different countries and at different times, but even within Sta. Elena alone there was substantial diversity. Some of the poorest residents tended to be politically apathetic altogether; for them, using state-subsidized food outlets would have meant jeopardizing the security offered by their existing and conscientiously cultivated patterns of obtaining cheap food. Another group was quite vocal, however, in articulating their views that the Marcos government was systematically denying them rights to better housing, income and living conditions. They felt the Kadiwa Centers represented just another useless project designed to benefit those Filipinos who least needed help, and many suspected that the Marcos family was benefiting financially from the program. These attitudes stem from the larger historical context of neglect and exploitation that the urban poor encountered as a part of everyday life during the Marcos era. Squatters and slum dwellers repeatedly experienced repressive relations with government officials, and were especially incensed over the Marcos policy of demolishing squatter areas. Almost half of the vendors in Sta. Elena, for example, moved there due to previous demolition of their homes by the state. Many of them also paid a substantial portion of their earnings daily to corrupt police officers and city officials due to their inability to obtain licenses. Repeated experiences of eviction, relocation, restrictive ordinances, and graft caused many poorer Filipinos to perceive the Marcos government more as an enemy than as a potential source of aid (e.g., Keyes 1974; Jocano 1975; Doherty 1985).

Given the perceptions of this latter group of highly politicized urban poor, their denunciation of this state project is a necessary part of the explanation for its failure to distribute food to the poor effectively. Noncompliance with state programs is itself a form of resistance that is a well-known phenomenon in studies of peasants (e.g., Scott 1986). Resistance to government projects and feelings of disentitlement to a fair share of society's resources are often equally apparent among the urban poor. Although illegally occupying land is a common form of passive resistance shown by urban squatters, it also reflects their own demands and expectations to be accorded a minimum respect and decent livelihood.

Passive resistance also lays the groundwork for more violent acts of opposition. In the political demonstrations and riots that occurred prior to the revolt that tumbled the Marcos regime from power, the Kadiwa Centers became a primary target of bombs and looting. Because they visually represented the state's manipulatory attitude of false compassion for the poor during a time of volatile food prices, they became the symbol of what people perceived as the ruling family's inequitable and immoral pattern of resource distribution and monopolization. As such, they crystallized sentiments prevailing among people of many different income classes and backgrounds in Manila, thereby serving as one example among many that helped set the stage for later political, extra-class fusion of interests.

Conclusion

Most governments have implicit or explicit food policies that subsidize different groups in their societies. The motivations behind selective subsidization may be political, economic, social, or a combination of all three, because food policy can encompass a variety of development goals. In this sense, the analysis of why certain policies and projects are maintained requires more than simply technical explanations. It is equally essential to identify and incorporate the political and social constraints that influence their design, perpetuation, and the reactions of people to them.

A common problem of many development programs is that they fail to discover and incorporate the heterogeneity of purchasing and consumption constraints among the lowest income classes. The urban poor engage in a variety of strategies to obtain food cheaply, and their specific needs vary according to just how poor they are and where they reside in the city hierarchy of market places. Urban market behavior is influenced by many variables, such as transport infrastructure, seasonality, level of commercial intensity, and the physical distribution of marketplaces. Groups with generally similar rules of appropriate buying strategies may vary in their actual patterns of obtaining food in the city because they are differentially affected by such conditions and because they develop alternative solutions to cope with external constraints. Low-income Filipinos are remarkably resourceful not only in their income-earning strategies but also in their patterns of searching out cheap if unconventional food sources. This does not imply that the urban poor are not in need of subsidized food aid, but the strategy for channeling such food to them must take into account existing patterns of obtaining food and the cultural preferences and attitudes that generate such patterns. Government attempts to sell low-quality fresh food at low prices, for example, rest on the naive assumption that the poor will eat anything as long as it is cheap. Yet only the poorest residents may be willing to buy low-quality merchandise, and only if the price is even further reduced.

The urban poor's access to cheap food cannot be guaranteed simply by offering low prices, because their shopping strategies reflect minimal but frequent purchasing patterns, time constraints, and social perceptions of appropriate environments and customer services. Shopping environments with modern check-out lanes and cashiers may seem appropriate to Western-oriented consumers, but the urban poor often prefer the crowded, informal, and more socially heterogeneous milieux of public marketplaces. Although neighborhood store owners and market vendors exhibit flexibility in the quantities retailed, the extension of credit, and the provision of extra services in order to increase sales, personnel in state projects are usually paid a wage and have little incentive and autonomy to introduce more competitive and appropiate innovations.

Policy analysts' unawareness or disregard for the urban poor's socially and politically conditioned perceptions of appropriate shopping environments also reflects a general misconception of the nature of behavior patterns. Understanding market behavior involves much more than simply collecting statistics on observable actions or assuming that price and

289

income are always the best predictors of behavioral change. The conceptual system that structures people's subjective experiences within a larger political and economic system presents an equally important analytic dimension. For some Sta. Elena Filipinos, for example, Kadiwa Centers represented more than simply a cheap food outlet. Over time, these stores came to signify political manipulation by the state, profit-making for the ruling family and their close associates, and yet another extension of the state bureaucracy into their lives. These perceptions are quite different from the government's viewpoint, wherein the project was technically intended to channel subsidized food effectively to the urban poor and politically designed to illustrate the state's responsiveness to the basic needs of the urban lower classes.

The technical solutions to allocation problems that are inherently political are unlikely to resolve problems of hunger and malnutrition, nor are they likely to deceive people locked into structural conditions of inequality and poverty. In these contexts, the larger cultural dimension of how people perceive the legitimacy of their government and their changing interpretations of manipulative state rhetoric provide important lessons for our understanding of political and economic processes.

Acknowledgments

The data in this paper were collected during an interdisciplinary project on the urban food market system in Metropolitan Manila. The International Development Research Centre funded that project under the direction of Benjamin Diokno, School of Economics, University of the Philippines at Diliman. My participation was sponsored by the Rockefeller Foundation while I was a postdoctoral research fellow and Visiting Assistant Professor at the School of Economics in 1983-84. I owe special thanks to Joseph Soriano for his research assistance in Sta. Elena.

Notes

[1] I conducted this research during the rainy season, which for some vendors is a period of lower income compared to other times of year. Hence, the findings should be viewed in that context.

[2] Other outlets range from more moderate grocery stores to small neighborhood stores and mobile units. Due to the huge subsidies this program requires, the Aquino administration is now planning to sell most outlets to the private sector or simply reserve a few for the retail distribution of rice.

[3] Kadiwa outlets in suburban residential areas of the city may provide more services than we found to be the case in our study of urban commercial districts. Suburban areas are generally not populated by the poorest urban residents, however, which was the determinant of the research areas we chose.

[4] This pattern is reminiscent of the problems of rural health dispensaries in the Philippines, whose location in towns makes them largely inaccessible to many of the rural poor (e.g., Florentino, Adorna, and Solon 1982).

References

Barth, Gerald A. 1982. Food Supply, Distribution, and Marketing in Davao City, Philippines. Ph.D. dissertation. Ann Arbor: University Microfilms.
------ 1983. Street Foods: Informal Sector Food Preparation and Marketing. Iloilo City, Philippines: Equity Policy Center.
------ 1984. Employment and Earnings in Food Marketing in a Philippine Regional Center. Human Organization 43(1):38-43.
Bromley, R., and C. Gerry. 1979. Who Are the Casual Poor? In: Casual Work and Poverty in Third World Cities. R. Bromley and C. Gerry, eds. pp. 105-129. New York: John Wiley & Sons.
Dannhaeuser, Norbert. 1977. Distribution and the Structure of Retail Trade in a Philippine Commercial Town. Economic Development and Cultural Change 25: 471-507.
------ 1980. The Role of the Neighborhood Store in Developing Economies: the Case of Dagupan City, Philippines. Journal of Developing Areas 14: 157-174.
------ 1983. Contemporary Trade Strategies in the Philippines: A Study in Marketing Anthropology. New Brunswick, New Jersey: Rutgers University Press.
Davis, William G. 1973. Social Relations in a Philippine Market: Self-Interest and Subjectivity. Berkeley: University of California Press.
Diokno, Benjamin. 1985. Urban Food Markets in Metropolitan Manila: Analysis and Recommendations. Final Report. Canada: International Development Research Center. (ms)
Doherty, John F. 1985. The Philippine Urban Poor. Philippine Studies Ocasional Paper No. 8. Honolulu: Center for Asian and

291

Pacific Studies, University of Hawaii.

Eames, Edwin and Judith Goode. 1973. Urban Poverty in a Cross-Cultural Context. New York: Free Press.

Florentino, R., C. Adorna, and F. Solon. 1982. Interface Problems Between Nutrition Policy and Its Implementation: the Philippine Case Study. In: Nutritional Policy Implementation: Issues and Experience. N.S. Scrimshaw and M. B. Wallerstein, ed., pp. 247-268. New York: Plenum Press.

Jocano, F. Landa. 1975. Slum as a Way of Life: A Study of Coping Behavior in an Urban Environment. Quezon City: University of the Philippines Press.

Keyes, William. 1974. Manila Scavengers: the Struggle for Urban Survival. Quezon City: Institute for Philippine Culture, Ateneo de Manila University.

Lele, U. and W. Candler. 1984. Food Security in Developing Countries: National Issues. In: Agricultural Development in the Third World. C. Eicher and J. Staatz, eds., pp. 207-221. Baltimore, Maryland: Johns Hopkins University Press.

Logan, Kathleen. 1981. Getting By With Less: Economic Strategies of Lower-Income Households in Guadalajara. Urban Anthropology 10(3): 231-246.

Lomnitz, Larissa. 1977. Networks and Marginality: Life in a Mexican Shantytown. New York: Academic Press.

McGee, Terence G. 1979. The Poverty Syndrome: Making Out in the Southeast Asian City. In: Casual Work and Poverty in Third World Cities. Bromley, R. and C. Gerry, eds., pp. 45-68. New York: John Wiley & Sons.

McGee, T. and Y. Yeung. 1977. Hawkers in Southeast Asian Cities: Planning for the Bazaar Economy. Canada: International Development Research Centre.

National Economic Development Authority. 1983. Philippine Statistical Yearbook. Manila: Republic of the Philippines.

Roberts, Bryan. 1978. Cities of Peasants: the Political Economy of Urbanization in the Third World. London: Edward Arnold.

Scott, Alison MacEwan. 1979. Who Are the Self-Employed? In: Casual Work and Poverty in Third World Cities. R. Bromley and C. Gerry, eds., pp. 105-129. New York: John Wiley & Sons.

Silverio, Simeon G., Jr. 1982. The Neighborhood Sari-Sari Store. In The Philippine Poor I: Two Monographs. M. S. Fernandez, ed. pp. 59-135. Quezon City: Institute of Philippine Culture, Ateneo de Manila University.

Scott, James C. 1986. Everyday Forms of Peasant Resistance. Journal of Peasant Studies 13(2): 5-35.

Szanton, Maria C. 1972. A Right to Survive: Subsistence Marketing in a Lowland Philippine Town. University Park: Pennsylvania State University Press.

Timmer, C. P., W. Falcon, and S. Pearson. 1983. Food Policy Analysis. Baltimore, Maryland: Johns Hopkins University Press.

17. DEPENDENT DEVELOPMENT AND THE MARGINALITY THESIS: A CASE STUDY FROM MANAUS[1]

Leo A. Despres

This is a first report on a continuing study of social aspects of economic development initiatives in the city of Manaus, Brazil. The basic methodology includes the collection of economic data, with the social implications and explanations of their parameters researched by intensive field work with the concerned population groups, including interviews and observation. I emphasize the current implications of the study for certain key issues concerned with dependency theory.

Roberts (1978:60-87) has emphasized that urban-based, dependent industrial development has become the dominant economic force in Latin America. So far as the industrially employed and other working-class elements are concerned, it is not entirely clear what social, cultural, and political forces this process of change has set in motion. Two issues have engaged theoretical discussion. One concerns the meaning and significance of dependent development for understanding the dynamics of change in societies that are in the process of acquiring a capital intensive mode of production (see e.g., Cardoso 1973; Chilcote 1982: 3-16). The second concerns the impact of dependent development on the labor process and its consequences for the organization and cultural formation of working-class populations: i.e., the marginalization thesis (see Quiano 1974; Roberts 1978: 159-177; and Evans 1979:28-29). Paralleling these discussions are those relating urbanization and industrialization to the so-called "informal sector" of the economy.[2]

Urban-based dependent development underscores a process of industrialization associated with the widespread penetration by external capital and the implantation of multinational or (depending upon the particular context) national firms. Cardoso (1973) relates this process to a regressive profile of income distribution, an emphasis on the capital-intensive production of luxury consumer durables as opposed to basic necessities, and the social marginality of large sectors of the working class. By "social marginality" it is meant that, as producers, large sectors of the working class are excluded from employment in the newly established capital-intensive industries. Frequently composed of migrants and relegated to earning their livelihood by self-employment in the informal sector, this aggregate of workers is also excluded from the consumption benefits presumably attached to employment in the formal sector. Thus, these workers form a relatively permanent underclass that is excluded from the economic and political life of the larger society.

In the literature, there is not complete agreement regarding this thesis. Roberts (1978:159-177), for example, underscores the disagreements that exist between Quijano and Nun and the group of researchers associated with the Brazilian Institute (Central Brasileiro de Analise e Planejamento). Quijano and Nun tend to argue that the surplus population that is attracted to urban centers as a consequence of dependent development becomes permanently marginalized and does not function as an industrial reserve army: in effect, it forms a parallel or separate economy. By way of contrast, the Brazilian researchers maintain that workers in the informal sector are not, in the final analysis, marginalized: rather, they are a necessary and functional part of dependent capitalist development. The position of Quijano and Nun has received some empirical support (e.g., Lopes 1964; Berlinck 1975). However, the position of the Brazilian researchers has also received considerable empirical support (see e.g., Leeds 1974; Leeds 1970; Oliveira 1980; Faria 1976; Perlman 1976). Roberts (1978:136-157) suggests that the structural relation between the formal and informal sectors, and thus the relation between dependent development and marginality, may vary regionally within particular societies as well as among societies with different historical and development experiences.

How do these propositions apply to Manaus? In light of the data to be presented, suggest that self-employment in the informal sector in Manaus is, and perhaps always has been, an integral component of the urban economy. The workers involved are not so much marginalized by developments in the formal economy as they are attracted by the opportunities they perceive in the informal economy. However, under the conditions of dependent development there exist structural constraints with respect to these opportunities and these constraints affect not only the selection of workers employed in the formal sector but also the self-selection of workers who seek to establish themselves in the informal sector. Finally, in the context of these constraints, the choice of self-employment in the informal sector expresses not only the mobility aspirations of the workers involved, but also their desire to participate more fully in the consumer economy that has been created.

Dependent Development, Economic Sectors, and the Labor
Process

With respect to the Amazon, the prevailing policy of the Brazilian government has been one that generally views the increasing concentration of population in urban centers and in non-agricultural employment as a necessary condition of economic development (Cardoso and Mueller 1977; Davis 1977; Mougeot and Aragon 1983; Bunker 1985). Manaus, an old port city and the capital of the State of Amazonas, provides a showcase example of this policy. With Decree-Law 228 in 1967, the government created SUFRAMA (Superintendency for the Development of the Free Port of Manaus) and provided a powerful program of fiscal incentives to make the city the center and major entrepot for capital-intensive industrialization within the region (Mahar 1979:154). By 1983, SUFRAMA had established 208 industrial projects in the Free Trade Zone of which 193 were located in Manaus (SUFRAMA 1983:16).

The public sector aside, the urban economy created in Manaus enjoins a large number of enterprises, many of which are assemblage-type industries engaged in the production of a considerable variety of goods and services. In the industrial sector, most of these enterprises may be classified in two general types. One includes those that are operated by nationally based or multinational firms. The electronics firms are the best example. These firms engage few linkages with the resources of the region. Combined, they contribute approximately 67 percent to the 47,194 jobs that SUFRAMA (1983:16) claims to have directly created by virtue of its development efforts.[3]

The second category of enterprises comprises firms engaged in the production or processing of products that have been traditionally produced or processed in the region (e.g., lumber, furniture, textiles, clothing, food products, beverages, and rubber). These enterprises create both backward and forward linkages with local resources and markets. Many of these firms already existed in Manaus and have been expanded with funds provided by SUFRAMA. Some of these enterprises are new in the sense that they have relocated from other regions of the country in response to SUFRAMA's fiscal incentives.[4] Whatever the case, most of these firms are locally owned and family-operated enterprises.[5]

The administrative and production divisions of the electronics firms are hierarchially arranged and bureaucratically organized. Approximately one percent of their personnel consists of engineers and top-level management, all of whom have been recruited outside the region. Less than 10 percent are accountants, bookkeepers, and office workers. Among production workers, three percent or less are low-level technicians, line inspectors, and the like: 97 percent are assembly workers and, depending upon the firm, between 40 and 60 percent of these are women. The recruitment of these production workers usually involves the administration of examinations that give emphasis to the digital dexterity of applicants and to their ability to read and follow instructions. Workers generally believe that to be successful at the interview that follows they should be deferential and avoid asking questions about pay, benefits, rank, and especially the prospects for promotion. In fact, these firms do not encourage workers to believe that they might make a career in their employ.

The personnel directors of the electronic firms studied underscored a strong preference for hiring women, for workers under thirty years of age, and for workers who were born or raised in the city rather than migrants from the interior. Regarding the latter, one director said, "People from the interior are a source of too many problems. They are not accustomed to urban life and they have no technological affinity. The work they do is dull and stupid work: it requires little intelligence. Still, they do not do it well. They are too independent. They do not like to take orders.... They are particularly troublesome if you have to dismiss them."

It is the policy of these firms to dismiss or hire workers in response to periodic national and international market assessments delivered from Sao Paulo. As a consequence of this policy, there now exists in Manaus a pool of assembly workers that these firms can draw upon when needed. Accordingly, employment in these industries is insecure and workers feel they must carefully guard their behavior in order to avoid dismissal.

The wage and benefit structures of these industries are uniform. They conform to what is minimally required by federal legislation. With the exception of low-level technicians (who may receive several minimal wages), practically all production workers are paid two minimal wages or less and most are paid one.[6] On-line production performance is mechanically regulated and measured. Industrial discipline is strict. Absenteeism requires medical certification and tardiness can result in dismissal. Promotions are few in number, non-existant beyond the rank of technician or office worker, and they do not come often. Work tasks preclude extensive socializing among workers outside of scheduled breaks and this socializing almost never includes higher-level managers or supervisors. In fact, many of the workers interviewed had never seen and could not name the local director of the firm or his immediate subordinates. In general, workers were poorly informed regarding the ownership, organization, and direction of these firms. In fact, most did not know precisely the recruitment criteria of these firms, the full range of benefits they provided, how their work was evaluated, or what was expected of them in order to earn a promotion.

By comparison, the more traditional industries (e.g., wood-processing) are more heterogeneous in their organization, the character of the work they provide, and in their recruitment preferences. Sawmills and, to a lesser degree, compensados are among the most numerous of these enterprises.[7] Except for some compensados, virtually all of these enterprises are family-managed firms. Employment in these traditional industries is relatively stable. Sixty-five percent of the workers interviewed at two sawmills had been in the employ of these firms six years or longer (67 percent of the electronics workers interviewed had worked less than two years for their respective firms). As a result of their size (most sawmills employ less than 200 workers) and the stability of their labor force, a majority of the workers employed by these firms had had personal encounters with their patroes (as the owners were called).

These personal connections with owners and supervisors extend to the recruitment process. For the most part, recruitment by these firms proceeds by word-of-mouth and frequently involves the hiring of relatives or close friends who are recommended by trusted employees. Apart from sales persons, office personnel, and a few supervisors, the only qualifications for employment are physical maturity and fitness. Except for some compensados, the recruitment process is highly selective for males. It also tends to be selective for individuals who have migrated to Manaus from areas that are predominantly rural.

Although employment in these industries is relatively stable, the work they provide is dirty, arduous, and sometimes dangerous. The workday is long (usually 10 hours) and the workweek is five and one-half days. Promotions in these industries are almost non-existant. At the same time, the wage and benefit structures of these industries do not differ significantly from those of the capital-intensive industries. Virtually all of the production workers in the wood-processing industry (and also in the jute, food-processing, and beverage industries) are paid two minimal salaries or less. Forty percent of the workers inteviewed were paid two minimal wages or more but most of these were employed by one firm.[8]

These types of industries aside, the formal sector in Manaus engages more than 35,000 white collar workers, mainly in the commercial and public sectors. Informants considered the public sector to provide the most stable, secure, and financially rewarding wage employment available in Manaus. Workers interviewed in this sector averaged seven minimal salaries per month and reported benefit structures that were in some respects better than those available to industrial workers. However, the commercial sectors of the economy present a somewhat different picture. Except for management-level employees, the wage and benefit structures of family-owned firms in these sectors are no better than those provided by industrial firms. In fact, most white collar workers in the commercial sectors earn on average less than industrial workers and some of the firms operating in

297

these sectors avoid compliance with federally mandated benefit payments by retaining unregistered workers.

The labor process among self-employed workers assumes an entirely different character than that described for the above categories of wage workers. For one thing, self-employment in the informal sector appears to be as much a matter of choice as it is a consequence of structures resulting from dependent development. For example, among the 47 self-employed workers included in the study, more than half had once worked for wages (mainly in the traditional industries of the formal sector) and only two of these became self-employed as a result of unemployment.[9] The remaining 45 either quit jobs in favor of self-employment or they had never sought any type of wage-employment.

This exercise of choice is, in part, related to the family origins of these workers. Slightly more than 80 percent of these workers reported that one or both of their parents also had been (or were) self-employed--mainly as regateiros (hucksters who sell goods along the river), street peddlars, artisans, or comerciantes (i.e., owners of small shops or commercial enterprises). Also, 64 percent of these 47 workers were either heads of households or they lived in households whose declared heads were self-employed. In addition, 57 percent of all the economically active workers included in these households were self-employed. By comparison, only 14 percent of the self-employed workers interviewed lived in households whose declared heads were employed for wages. In other words, self-employment appears to be not only a matter of choice by also something of a family or household tradition.

Family tradition aside, based on observation and interview data, three sets of factors related to the work process seem to influence the preference for self-employment. One concerns the economics of self-employment. In terms of economic consideration, self-employment tends to be not only more secure, but it is economically more rewarding than wage employment in the new or traditional industrial sectors. Data supportive of this contention may be summarized: 82 percent of the 17 government-employed functionaries interviewed report incomes in excess of four minimal salaries. This level of income is achieved by less than 13 percent of the 117 industrial workers included in the study and only 10 percent of other white collar workers. However, more than one-third of the comerciantes interviewed, and 23.4 percent of other self-employed workers, report four minimal salaries or more. Conversely, only 13 percent of the former and 46.8 percent of the latter report one minimal salary compared to 73.3 percent of other white collar workers, 58.7 percent of new industrial wage workers, and 53.7 percent of the wage workers in the traditional industries. In other words, unless one works for government in Manaus, it is mainly by way of self-employment that workers are somewhat able to free their labor from the expropriative wage structures that obtain in the formal economy.

What workers in the informal sector seem to like most about their economic situation is that they generally have money in pocket. As informants noted, they are not "caught short" while waiting for pay envelopes that are mostly consumed by credit payments. At the same time, these workers are not without access to the most critical benefits that industrial workers are provided. Virtually all of the self-employed workers interviewed had access to public health care by self-registration with INPS or by listing as a "dependent" of a registered worker.

A second set of factors concerns the work itself. Self-employed workers, compared to most wage workers interviewed, held extremely positive attitudes concerning the character and organization of their work. Inter alia, they considered that their work provided them with freedom of movement and a sense of self-reliance. They perceived that it afforded them the opportunity for advancement, to "reward their own initiative." They were their own bosses. They did not have to take orders, submit to authority, or worry about relationships with patroes. They did not have to worry about layoffs or dismissals for reasons they considered arbitrary. Most of them, particularly those who worked the street, also emphasized that their work was interesting and challenging. It provided them the opportunity "to meet people who come to Manaus from all parts of the country." They had to "study" and "understand" these people in order to sell. Above all, these workers emphasized, they "enjoyed" working the streets. As several informants noted: "I have many friends in the streets and everyday, except when the weather is bad, I look forward to being with them."

Except for functionaries and other white collar types, a majority of the wage workers interviewed expressed varying degrees of dissatisfaction with, among other things, the wages they earned, the conditions of their work, or with the firms that employed them. Among the self-employed, the opposite was the case. Many of the hucksters and vendors interviewed indicated that their work provided them with the experience or the capital they needed to become "comerciantes"--to someday "own a shop" or "become more important in business." "Comerciantes," they noted, are more respected and "they are not always being bothered by the authorities." As comerciantes, they could "give work to the family." Moreover, as comerciantes, they could make more money and "live better." Indeed, based on a special study that was made of 22 small-scale enterprises operated by comerciantes, if they could "own a shop," the self-employed could do almost as well

299

economically as most low-level government functionaries.

What emerges from these data is the fact that self-employed workers in the informal sector do not generally consider themselves to be marginalized as producers: i.e., excluded from employment in the formal sector. Many have worked for wages in the formal sector and very few have been forced to vacate these positions because of unemployment. Others have never sought employment in the formal sector. By an exercise of choice, most have preferred to be self-employed. By comparison to all but the middle and upper echelons of white collar employees, most self-employed workers report higher incomes, more job satisfaction, and more opportunities for advancement than wage workers in the new or traditional industries of the formal sector.

Dependent Development, the Labor Process, and Marginality

In light of these data, the question of marginality appears to be considerably more complicated than is suggested in the current literature. Various discussions (see e.g., McGee 1973; Singer 1975; Merrick 1976; Faria 1976; Roberts 1976: 116; 1978: 61-87; Oliveira 1980; Alves de Souza 1980; Vianna, et al. 1980; Mingione 1983) have directly or indirectly linked the problem of marginality to such factors as migratory flows stimulated by urban-industrial growth, to chronic unemployment, or to the survival strategies of low-income households involving the employment of women, the young, and the unskilled. What significance do these factors have in Manaus?

The most visible consequence of dependent development in Manaus is its impact on population growth. Census data reveal that between 1960 and 1980, the population of Manaus increased from 173,703 to 634,756, a relative increase of 265 percent. Most of this growth is attributed to migratory flows originating within the state (Bentes 1983). During the same period, the number of Manaus' economically active population increased by 602 percent, from a total of 28,280 to 198,732. Clearly, the percentage increase in Manaus' economically active labor force was significantly greater than the percentage increase in its urban population. Accordingly, dependent development in Manaus does not seem to have stimulated a migratory flow of labor that could not be absorbed by the employment opportunities that were created.

Concomitant with this growth, however, there has been a profound shift in the distribution of the labor force by sector of employment. Our data contain several key points. First, prior to the process of dependent development there already

300

existed in Manaus a substantial number of self-employed workers in the informal sector. This aggregate of 9,446 workers contributed 33.4 percent to the economically active labor force. Second, while SUFRAMA's development project served to increase employment in virtually all sectors of economic activity, the relative increase in wage employment (from 18,834 to 156,646) was 732 percent as compared to the relative increase in self-employment, 346 percent (from 9,446 to 42,086). In other words, while the number of self-employed workers increased substantially during the course of this development process, the percentage contribution of such workers to the economically active labor force actually declined from 33.4 percent to 21.2 percent of the total.

Two possible interpretations may be offered in explanation. One, workers who might have been unemployed in the less dependent economy of 1960 may have been drawn out of the informal sector and into various forms of wage employment as a consequence of the expanded economy of 1980, in which case the unemployed already living in Manaus as well as more recent migrants found opportunities for work.[10] Or, alternatively, the expanded and more dependent economy of 1980 created structural constraints that may have significantly affected the choice of workers seeking wage employment. The data suggest that both sets of factors have been operative and that they are not unrelated.

As noted in the previous section, self-employment in the informal sector is largely a matter of choice. The exercise of this choice, however, does not exist independently of structural constraints. Structural constraints prevail mainly at three levels. One has to do with the recruitment preferences of firms previously described. The second concerns the relation that has materialized between the formal and informal sectors as a consequence of the government's industrialization policy. The third relates to the organization and economy of households. With regard to the first, what types of workers appear to be excluded from what types of employment and, thus, are more or less compelled to seek a livelihood by self-employment?

Consider, first, the problem of migrants.[11] Of the 88 households included in the author's study, 60 percent are headed by migrants (defined as individuals born outside of Manaus). Combined, these households include 211 economically active workers. Virtually no difference was found to exist in the distribution of migrants (84) and non-migrants (80) among wage workers. Moreover, although the proportion of migrants who are self-employed (68 percent) is slightly greater than their overall proportion in this particular sample (60 percent), this difference seems not to have been affected by whether migrants arrived in Manaus before or after the creation of the Free Trade

301

Zone. If migrants, on the whole, have not been significantly
excluded from the wage employment opportunities that have been
created by SUFRAMA, are there any particular categories of
workers that have been excluded? In this regard, two previously
mentioned factors are particularly significant: sex and
education.

First, the sex factor. The dependent industrial development
of Manaus has been accompanied by a significant growth of female
wage employment in virtually all sectors of the economy.
Computations from census data indicate that between 1960 and 1980
the number of women included among wage workers in the formal
sector increased from 24 to 36 percent while the number of
self-employed women in the informal sector declined from 23 to 18
percent. By way of contrast, among males, the number of wage
workers declined from 76 to 65 percent while the number of
self-employed workers increased from 77 to 82 percent. The
increase of women employed in the industrial sector, reflecting
the recruitment preference of assemblage-type industries for
female labor, has been particularly significant, increasing from
less than 10 percent in 1960 to almost 29 percent in 1980. Thus,
dependent development in Manaus has drawn female labor from the
informal sector while diminishing the proportion of males
occupied in the formal sector.

Similarly, education cannot be discounted as a structural
constraint. Of the 174 wage workers interviewed by the author,
38.5 percent had completed no more than four years of formal
education. Among self-employed workers, this number reaches 66
percent (31 of 47). At the other extreme, only 4.2 percent of
the self-employed workers interviewed had completed high school
as compared to 29.3 percent of the wage workers interviewed.
Moreover, among those wage workers who had completed primary
school (eight years), the vast majority were employed in the
newly established electronics industry, whereas those who had
completed less than four years of education were employed in the
more traditional industries (e.g., 65 percent of the sawmill
workers interviewed reported having one year or less of formal
schooling). Thus, self-employment in the informal sector is the
principal avenue of mobility for males who have little formal
education and who wish to avoid a lifetime of work at low wages
in the more traditional sectors of the economy.

Perhaps one of the most significant changes resulting from
SUFRAMA's efforts to create an industrial pole in Manaus has been
the extent to which it has also encouraged a consumption economy.
The new industrial sector, particularly with its emphasis on the
production of expensive consumer durables (e.g., television sets,
stereophonic units, digital watches, air conditioners, etc.) has
stimulated consumer wants among all categories of workers. At

302

the same time, firms in virtually all sectors of the economy have used the government's minimal wage policy to maintain uniformly wages at levels that are barely sufficient to provide basic necessities. Workers in large numbers purchase television sets and stereophonic units even when they cannot provide their families with adequate housing, clothing, potable water and, in some cases, sufficient food.

If the workers have not been marginalized as producers (i.e., excluded from employment), they are certainly marginalized as consumers (i.e., given very limited access to the consumer economy that has been created). Two structural consequences have followed from this type of marginalization. First, in order to sustain their purchase of a few consumer durables, most wage workers must orient their consumption behavior to the low-price markets (for food, clothing, and services) that self-employed workers maintain in the informal sector. Thus, the economic well being of workers in the informal economy is significantly dependent upon the economic well being of firms (not workers) in the formal economy. This structural interdependency most certainly affects the decision of particular workers to establish small-scale enterprises in the informal sector.

A second consequence of the marginalization of workers as consumers is evident with respect to working-class households. In order to enhance their limited purchasing power, most working class households have adopted a multiple income strategy. Only 31 percent of the 88 households investigated were found to be completely dependent upon the income produced by only one of its members. Thirty-three percent contained at least two economically active persons and 36 percent contained more (22 percent actually contained four or more). This too provides a structural linkage between the formal and informal sectors. For example, no less than 40 percent of the households investigated contained wage workers as well as self-employed workers. These 34 households reported a total of 152 minimal salaries of which self-employed workers contributed 66 percent. Moreover, among the households that were totally dependent upon wage workers for their incomes, 44 percent are headed by individuals employed in traditional industries. It is these households that were found to be most dependent upon a single breadwinner (60 percent) and it is also these households that were found to be most marginalized as consumers (as measured by their consumption of expensive durables).

Marginalization and Political Culture

Numerous observers have suggested that because of their exclusion from employment in the formal sector of the dependent

303

economy, workers in the informal sector form a relatively permanent underclass that is also excluded from the political life of the larger society. At issue here is the extent to which the processes of dependent development in Manaus have served to transform what was traditionally a predominantly rural, semi-proletarianized population, organized in terms of relatively unstratified social communities, into an urban-based, politically conscious, and politically active social class. It is not possible to provide a detailed discussion of the data collected in this regard. However, a few pertinent observations:

First, virtually no differences were found to exist in the political consciousness of wage and self-employed workers. The communal attachments that once characterized a substantial proportion of the working-class population that has migrated to Manaus no longer exist.[12] These attachments have not been reformed within bairros or even neighborhoods. In general, social networks do not extend beyond kin and small friendship circles formed at work or close to home. Even networks among kinsmen who live widely dispersed throughout the city are extremely fragile. In the bairros investigated, there existed no church-related basic communities, no social movements, and very little civic involvement.

Second, the work process that obtains in different sectors of the economy has itself contributed to the fragmentary composition of working-class elements by deflecting the formation of social networks from neighborhood communities to the workplace where individuals spend most of their waking hours.

Third, although most registered workers belong to unions, less than 15 percent of those interviewed considered unions to be of any benefit to themselves or their families. Only two of the workers interviewed had ever participated in any of the social or political programs that their unions sponsored on a weekly or monthly basis.

Fourth, the overwhelming majority of the workers interviewed considered political parties to be of no benefit. Similarly, except for the creation of the Free Trade Zone, approximately half considered the state and federal governments to have contributed little of value to the working class in Manaus. When asked what changes they would have the federal government institute to the benefit of the working class, two-thirds would have it increase the minimum wage, control inflation, and lower the cost of food.

In summary, without exception, there is little evidence to suggest that the working-class elements in Manaus have become in any significant way politically active or incorporated. However, this may be as much a function of the regional social and cultural origins of this population as it is a result of dependent development. Alternatively, the political marginalization of this population may be related to the oligarchical system of politics that is so deeply rooted in Brazilian history, or to the authoritarian political milieu that came into being with the military coup of 1964.

Conclusions

In light of this particular case, it may be concluded that self-employment in the informal sector in Manaus is and always has been an integral component of the urban economy. However, dependent capitalist development engages a more complicated structure of marginality than perhaps previously existed.

Specifically, the migratory pulses attending this development process have not resulted in the creation of a reserve of surplus labor that has been excluded from wage employment and, thereby, relegated to the informal sector in order to maintain wages at the lowest possible level for the purpose of attracting new industry. Firms have not needed a surplus of labor to maintain a low level of wages. Given the government's wage policy, for most workers, the minimum wage has become the maximum wage. As a consequence, there exists more wage employment now than previously existed.

Currently, if not also in the past, self-employment in the informal sector is a strategy elected by certain categories of workers in order to circumvent low wages and minimize their marginalization not as producers, but as consumers. However, the self-employment of these workers is itself dependent upon the growth and stability of wage employment in the new and more traditional sectors of the formal economy. It is also dependent upon maintaining the wage level in these sectors at or slightly above the minimum, thereby sustaining the dependence of wage workers for their consumption purchases on the low-priced goods and services produced in the informal sector.

Thus, although the urban economy now combines hegemonic with more traditional and small-scale modes of capitalist production, it is structurally integrated. Regarding its integration, the Brazilian state emerges as a key element. The state not only has provided the fiscal incentives with which large-scale industrial firms have been attracted to the Free Trade Zone, but it also has instituted wage and benefit policies that largely free these firms from the economic and political costs of a competitive labor market. As an effect of these policies, very few workers in Manaus have been marginalized as producers: most have been marginalized as consumers. This type of marginalization has not

305

yet become problematic for the state or for the firms that have come to Manaus. Three factors may be offered in explanation of this:

1. The expropriation of labor in the formal sectors of the economy is being subsidized in large part by the self-expropriation of labor in the informal sector.

2. The absorptive capacity of the expanded urban labor market, both with respect to wage and self-employment, has allowed a substantial number of households to minimize their marginalization as consumers by electing a multiple-income strategy to which the informal sector makes a significant contribution.

3. And, as a class, workers in Manaus are not yet politically formed. They disclose little corporate or political organization. They maintain few associational ties. They reveal little sense of civic interest in their neighborhoods, their bairros, or the city. They articulate problems but only vaguely in political or class terms. In these respects, the depth of their political marginalization is matched only by their marginalization as consumers. If a political movement is to take shape in this context, it is more likely to be energized by issues relating to income redistribution than by ideologies of class or state formation.

Finally, it needs to be emphasized that, given the peculiarities that obtain in Manaus and other parts of the Amazon region, it is difficult to know the extent to which these conclusions can be generalized. However, the data presented here lend support to those theorists who have argued that self-employment in the informal sector "... is an integral component of peripheral capitalist economies and its development is mandated by the conditions in which these economies are incorporated into the contemporary world system" (Portes and Walton 1981:67-106).

Notes

[1] The data presented here were collected during the course of fieldwork conducted between June and December, 1984, in respect to industrialization and the formation of working-class culture in Manaus, Brazil. This research was made possible by a grant from the National Science Foundation (BNS 83, 17543). The author wishes to express his gratitude to the Instituto Universitario de Pesquisas do Rio de Janeiro for its assistance in facilitating the research. He is also grateful to Rosalvo Machado Bentes and his colleagues at the Nucleo de Altos Estudos Amazonicos,

Universidade Federal do Para, and at the Universidade Federal do Amazonicas, for their assistance. he also wants to thank Drs. Regis S. de Castro Andrade, Paulo J. Krischke, and others of the Central de Estudos de Cultural Contemporanea in Sao Paulo, Dr. Lorissa Lomnitz (Universidad Nacional Autonoma de Mexico), and members of the Kellogg Institute, University of Notre Dame, for their helpful comments on earlier drafts of this paper.

[2] The conceptualization of the informal sector seems to have originated in the dual economy notion developed by Geertz (1963) and extended by McGee (1973). As Bromley (1978) and Moser (1978) have noted, the "two-sector terminology" has become the theoretical basis of an extensive literature. For discussions relating this terminology to Brazil, see Tolsa (1978) and Vianna (1980). In the final analysis, at issue in these particular discussions is the structural relationship between various sectors of the economy (see Portes and Walton 1981:67-106).

[3] Among these enterprises, the author's research gave focus to two electronics firms that, combined, employed approximately 2,500 workers. Although the electronics industry accounts for only 18 percent of the firms established by SUFRAMA, it contributes almost 45 percent to the 47,194 jobs it claims to have created.

[4] In this category, the author's research concentrated on a comparative study of two sawmills, one of which was originally established in Manaus.

[5] Without relating details, this classification of enterprises may be extended to the commercial sectors of the economy.

[6] At the time of research, one minimal wage represented approximately US$59. Over a period of six months, the value of the minimal wage declined to approximately US$37.00.

[7] Manaus contains approximately 20 sawmills and seven compensados. The latter employ more than 60 percent of the workers engaged in the industry and in some of these almost half of the workers employed are women. Compensados are factories where logs are processed mainly for the fabrication of laminated wood, most of which is of low quality and sold for concrete forms.

[8] This firm also provides all of its workers with housing, electricity, and potable water. As it turned out, this particular firm is an exception. It recruits almost all of its production workers from among the friends and relatives of employees who relocated in Manaus when the firm was moved there by its owner.

307

[9] This particular sample of workers was recruited for interviews off the streets of the central city or the neighborhoods in which they worked or, in some cases, they were members of households in which industrial workers were interviewed.

[10] Current unemployment data were impossible to obtain in Manaus. However, in a survey of 5,336 household heads living in seven public housing schemes, constructed by SHAM (Sociedade de Habitacao do Estado do Amazonas 1978:108), only 5.4 percent were counted as unemployed.

[11] The best available study of the migratory process in relation to establishment of the Free Trade Zone in Manaus is one recently made by Machado Bentes (1983).

[12] For descriptions of rural-based communities in the Amazon Basin, see Meggers 1950: Wagley 1953; Watson 1953; Galvao 1959; Moran 1974; Ross 1978; Ianni 1978; Sawyer 1979; Bunker 1985.

References

Alves de Souza, Guaraci Adeodato. 1980. Urbanizcao e Fluxos Migratorios para Salvador. In: Bahia de Todos os Probres. Angela Ramalho Vianna, et al., pp. 103-28. Caderno CEBRAP No. 34, Petropolis, Brasil: Editora Vozes, Ltda.
Bentes, Rosalvo Machado. 1983. A Zona Franca o e Processo Migratorio para Manaus. Dissertacao de mestrado, Universidade Federal do Para, Brasil.
Berlinck, Manoel T. 1975. Marginalidade Social e Relacoes de Classes en Sao Paulo. Petropolis, Brasil: Editora Vozes.
Bromley, Ray. 1978. Introduction - The Urban Informal Sector: Why Is It Worth Discussing? World Development 6(9/10):1033-39.
Bunker, Stephen G. 1981. The Impact of Deforestation on Peasant Communities in the Medio Anazonas of Brazil. Studies in Third World Societies, No. 13, pp. 45-60.
----- 1985. Underdeveloping the Amazon. Chicago: Univ. of Illinois Press
Cardoso, Fernando Henrique. 1973. Associated-dependent Development: Theoretical and Practical Implications. In: Authoritarian Brazil. Alfred Stephan, ed., pp. 142-78. New Haven: Yale University Press.
Cardoso, Fernando Henrique and Geraldo Mueller. 1977. Expansao do Capitalismo. Sao Paulo: Editora Brasiliense.
Chilcote, Ronald H. 1982. Issues of Theory in Dependency and Marxism. Latin American Perspectives (3 & 4), Series No. 1,

Boulder, Co.: Westview Press, pp. 3-16.

Davis, Shelton H. 1977. Victims of the Miracle. Development and the Indians of Brazil. New York: Cambridge University Press.

Evans, Peter B. 1979. Dependent Development: The Alliance of Multinational, State, and Local Capital in Brazil. Princeton: Princeton University Press.

Faria, Vilmar E. 1976. Occupational Marginality, Employment and Poverty in Urban Brazil. Ph.D. dissertation, Harvard University.

Galvao, Eduardo. 1959. Acultracao Indigena no Rio Negro. Boletim Museu Paraense Emilio Goeldi, No. 8, Belem, Brasil.

Geertz, Clifford. 1963. Peddlars and Princes: Social Development and Economic Change in Two Indonesian Towns. Chicago: U. of Chicago Press.

Ianni, Octavio. 1978. A Luta Pela Terra. Petropolis, Brasil: Editora Vozes.

Leeds, Anthony. 1974. Housing-settlement Types, Arrangements for Living, Proletarianization, and the Social Structure of the City. In: Latin American Urban Research. Wayne Cornelius and Felecity Trueblood, eds. pp. 67-99. Vol. 4. Beverley Hills: Sage Publications

Leeds, Anthony and Elizabeth Leeds. 1970. Brazil and the Myth of Urban Rurality: Urban Experience, Work, and Values in 'squatments' of Rio de Janeiro and Lima. In: City and Country in the Third World: Issues in the Modernization of Latin America. A.J. Field, ed., pp. 229-85. Cambridge, Mass.: Schenkman,

Lopes, Juarez Rubens Brandao. 1964. Sociedade Industrial no Brasil. Sao Paulo: Difusao Europeia do Livro.

Mahar, Dennis J. 1979. Frontier Development Policy in Brazil: A Study of Amazonia. New York: Prager.

McGee, T.G. 1973. Peasants in cities: a Paradox, a Paradox, a Most Ingenious Paradox. Human Organization 32:135-42.

Meggers, Betty J. 1950. Caboclo Life in the Mouth of the Amazon. The Anthropological Quarterly 23: 14-28.

Merrick, T.W. 1976. Employment and Earnings in the Informal Sector in Brazil: The Case of Belo Horizonte. Journal of Developing Areas 10: 337-54.

Mingione, Enzo. 1983. Informalization, Restructuring and the Survival Strategies of the Working Class. International Journal of Urban and Regional Research 7(3): 311-39.

Moran, Emilio F. 1974. The Adaptive System of the Amazonian Caboclo. In: Man in the Amazon. Charles Wagley, ed., pp. 136-59. Gainesville: University of Florida Press.

Moser, Caroline O.N. 1978. Informal Sector or Petty Commodity Production: Dualism or Dependence in Urban Development? World Development 6(9/10): 1041-64.

Mougeot, Luc J.A. and Luis E. Aragon, eds. 1983. O Despovoamento do Territorio Amazonico. Belem: Cardenos NAEA, Universidade Federal do Para

Oliveira, Francisco de. 1980. Prefacio: Salvador: Os Exilados da Opulencia (expansao capitalista numa metropole pobre). In: Bahia de Todos os Probres. Angela Ramalho Vianna, et al., pp. 9-22. Caderno CEBRAP No. 34, Petropolis, Brasil: Editora Vozes, Ltda.

Portes, Alejandro and John Walton. 1981. Labor, Class, and the International System. New York: Academic Press.

Perlman, Janice E. 1976. The Myth of Marginality: Urban Politics and Poverty in Rio de Janeiro. Berkeley, University of California Press.

Quijano, Anibal. 1974. The Marginal Pole of the Economy and the Marginalized Labor Force. Economy and Society 3, pp. 393-428.

Roberts, Bryan R. 1976. The Provincial Urban System and the Process of Dependency. In: Current Perspectives in Latin American Urban Research. Alejandro Portes and Harley L. Browning, eds., pp. 99-131. Austin: The University of Texas Institute of Latin American Studies.

----- 1978. Cities of Peasants. The Political Economy of Urbanization in the Third World. Beverley Hills: Sage Publications.

Ross, Eric. 1978. The Evolution of the Amazonian Peasantry. Journal of Latin American Studies 10: 193-218.

Sawyer, Donald R. 1979. Peasants and Capitalism on the Amazon Frontier. Ph.D. dissertation, Harvard University.

Singer, Paul 1975. Urbanization and Development: The Case of Sao Paulo. In: Urbanization in Latin America: Approaches and Issues. Jorge Hardoy, ed., pp. 435-56. Garden City, N.Y.: Anchor.

SHAM. 1978. Realizada nos Conjuntos Habitacionais da SHAM (Sociedade de Habitacao do Estado do Amazonas. Manaus, Brazil. Unpublished report, pp. 1-161.

SUFRAMA. 1983. Perfil dos Projetos Aprovados na Amazonica Ocidental. Manaus: Ministerio do Interior, Superintendencia da Zona Fraca de Manaus

Tolasa, H.C. 1978. Causes of Urban Poverty in Brazil. World Development 6(9/10): 1087-1101.

Vianna, Angela Ramalho, et al. (eds.) Bahia de Todos os Pobres. Caderno CEBRAP No. 34, Petropolis, Brazil: Editora Vozes, Ltda., pp. 185-214.

Wagley, Charles. 1953. Amazon Town - A Study of Man in the Tropics. New York: Macmillan.

Watson, James. 1953. Way Station of Westernization: The Brazilian Caboclo. In: Brazil: Papers Presented in the Institute for Brazilian Studies. James Watson, et al., eds., pp. 9-59. Nashville: Vanderbilt University Press.

18. WATER WATER EVERYWHERE IN IRRIGATED AGRICULTURE, AND NOT A DROP WITH CONSTANT MEANING

David M. Freeman

In Asia, Latin America, and Africa irrigated agriculture accounts for more than two thirds of all food production (Svendsen, et al., 1983). This proportion will increase because most of the improved agricultural technology coming out of the international research centers will be tailored to irrigated conditions and will require predictable controlled water supplies to approach its potential. Only 37 million hectares out of a total of 127 million hectares are irrigated in India, but the irrigated area produces one half of the total grain production (Keller, et al., 1981). Third world nations typically have predominantly agricultural economies and are increasingly dependent on controlled irrigation water supplies. Hopes for economic growth in agricultural sectors depend heavily on further development of irrigation, and aspirations for social justice are fundamentally dependent upon how irrigation systems are designed and organized.

Despite costly investment in major irrigation capital works over the past century, water delivery and application efficiencies, cropping intensities, and yields have generally not fulfilled planners' expectations due to poor water management within local command areas. Everywhere the picture of poor water management unfolds around details of low levels of water use efficiency, marked inequities in distribution, disappointed cropping intensities, poor yields, and irrigation bureaucracies that perform functions with little regard to needs of farmers to control water for production of food and fiber (Keller, et al., 1981; Lowdermilk, et al., 1978; Bottrall, 1981; Reidinger, 1974).

Some envisage a "water revolution" brought about by rehabilitated irrigation systems and reformed administrative structures that would be analagous to the "green revolution" in its capacity to bring about large increases in crop production at very favorable cost-benefit ratios (Bottrall, 1981). In addition, there is the thought that a water revolution might well increase social justice as benefits can be delivered to least-advantaged small farmers who obtain redistributions of critical resources in their favor, because existing systems tend to work heavily against their interests. There can be little doubt that there are immense opportunities for improvements in performance of irrigation water management. The key to this revolution lies in securing greater control over water for the

311

ultimate user of the resource--the farmer. Water control is the
most important factor to farmers in determining what crops to
grow and their willingness to adopt new technologies such as
fertilizers, pesticides, and high-yielding seed varieties.
Because the least-advantaged farmers must pay the highest prices
for insecure water in high demand periods, and because the poor
and powerless are, by definition, least able to influence water
distribution, the increase of irrigation water control for such
farmers is potentially a powerful tool in the policy makers' kit
for promoting agricultural development with social justice.

It is the central thesis of this analysis that:

    a)   the meaning of water control importantly
        shifts as water flows across units downward
        in irrigation systems from central
        bureaucracies to farmers; and
    b)   the shift in the meaning of water control
        across units of analysis has significant
        implications for the design and operation of
        irrigation systems.

It is our purpose to show how the social meaning of
irrigation water significantly shifts across units of analysis
common to large-scale gravity flow systems, and to erect a
framework for the comparative social analysis of irrigation
systems.

The Problem

Water Control and Units of Analysis

Water control by farmers, the capacity to apply the proper
quantity and quality of water at the optimum time to the crop
root zone to meet crop needs and soil-leaching requirements, is a
fundamental yardstick used to measure effectiveness of irrigation
systems. Irrigation water management in large-scale gravity flow
systems is the process by which bureaucracies capture and control
water in central irrigation works and pass it on to the farmer
who must control it "on farm" and in particular fields, to place
it in crop root zones. Doorenbos and Kassam have plainly stated
the problem in its technical aspects:

The upper limit of crop production is set by the climatic conditions and the genetic potential of the crop. The extent to which this limit can be reached will always depend on how finely the engineering aspects of water supply are in tune with the biological needs for water in crop production. Therefore, efficient use of water in crop production can only be attained when the planning, design and operation of the water supply and distribution system is geared toward meeting in quantity and time... the crop water needs required for optimum growth and high yields. (Doorenbos, 1979).

The extent to which the water supply is in tune with crop biological requirements is a function of the organizational operations at the three levels of Figure 1. The effectiveness with which irrigation water gets to root zones in a productive manner is a function of the organizations that have been created to rehabilitate, operate, and maintain works, and to resolve conflict at all three levels.

Farmers in irrigation systems around the world are faced with the common task of hitting a moving target--a crop root zone moisture deficit--in technically dynamic and socially tumultuous environments, within irrigation systems that may have been designed by engineers and politicians whose professional responsibilities were to do little more than aim a quantity of water in the general direction of a command area. In most large-scale systems, especially in Asia where the preponderance of global irrigation occurs, the upstream control systems are designed without regard for the problems faced by farmers in securing local control (Kathpalia, 1981). Engineers, historically, have provided a transport system for water using rivers, canals, reservoirs, and diversion structures. They have assumed that if water were moved in the general direction of command areas, water control at the local level would automatically evolve, simply because it was needed. In the light of history, this optimism is now known to have been naive. In the light of pressing needs for increased production and social justice, this optimism has been badly misplaced.

Types of Knowledges and Units of Analysis

The knowledge of irrigation officials educated in the professions, who inhabit central irrigation bureaucracies, depends heavily upon generalized principles abstracted from the rich flow of natural and social processes (i.e., nomothetic knowledge). Highly processed, abstract organizing principles have pride of place in science and in the training of irrigation

313

engineers--they are the essential prerequisite of parsimonious explanation. This general, cross-culturally viable, scientific knowledge, available to educated professionals, proceeds on the basis of rendering propositional knowledge out of particular facets of the whole system, but does not comprehend the richness of the whole; it is limited to shedding light on particular, abstracted slices of reality as in supply and demand curves, bars of tension, pounds of pressure per square inch, yield responses to fertilizer, thermodynamic behavior, channel hydraulics, velocities and scouring, principles of capillary action, soil intake dynamics, and evapotranspiration processes. Theoretical science in general, and irrigation engineering in particular, abstract general rules to construct logically connected sets of propositions about relations among phenomena. These are employed in central planning units in the design and operation of those parts of the irrigation system under the management of the central bureaucracy.

On the other hand, there is the extensive idiographic knowledge, built up over long experience, and encoded in tradition and custom in the possession of local people who in all probability have little access to the world of scientifically processed knowledge. Theirs is the knowledge of unique, local circumstances, and of their particular situation relative to those circumstances. Whereas the central bureaucratic analyst may be content to hypothesize about general tendencies, the local individual is intensely interested in specific outcomes in his or her particular situation. Whereas the central manager obtains knowledge for decision-making by employing methodological devices to control extraneous variables that might confuse the analysis of central tendencies in the system, the local individual responds to the very factors excluded by central management that operate in an important way in specific local contexts. Irrigation is practiced under a great variety of conditions (e.g., social, political, economic, topographic, soils, climatic and crop). These vary within a farm, they vary widely among farms and among command areas within a given irrigation system. Given the distinctiveness of each setting, and given that each represents a unique arrangement of the generalizable properties known by central management, what seems to be a condition across the whole system is not necessarily a condition in any specific sub-set of that system. Farmers, employers of rich idiographic knowledge, have much reason to distrust the nomothetic understandings of main system managers.

The problem, then, is that the generalizations of irrigation managers in large, remote bureaucracies are often inappropriate where farmers' individual and unique settings are concerned. The lack of mutual understanding is rooted in differences in types of knowledge and experience. There need be no hypothesis of

irrationality on the part of any party to account for
differences.

The Problem Defined--Units of Analysis and Shifting Means of Water Control

It is now possible to generate the outlines of a
cross-cultural, comparative analysis of behavior in irrigation
systems--focusing on the implications of three units of analysis
distinguished by level--by employing the concepts of water
control and the distinction between knowledge types.

Figure 1 presents a set of simplified concepts and
distinctions that define units of analysis at three levels in
large-scale gravity flow irrigation systems.[1] The message of
Figure 1 is that water is captured and controlled by formal
irrigation bureaucracies constructing, rehabilitating, and
maintaining large-scale "lumpy" collective goods in the form of
large dams, reservoirs, barrages, canals, and diversion
structures. At some point in every system, the large volumes of
water managed by the state bureaucracy must be broken down into
the small volumes manageable by individual farmers. Irrigation
bureaucracies vary widely in their approaches to this problem of
managing the transition from state bureaucracy to farm, but in
every instance some form of routine, organized interaction
emerges to manage the breaking down of large volumes into small
volumes between the state bureaucracy and the farm. At the farm
level, water must be moved to the plant root zone at the proper
time, in the required amount, so the micro-environment of the
plant j⁻ ⟋⟍ ⟍ production. Controlling water to
provid⟋ ⟍rops requires a great deal
of dif

common activities must be
perfo⟋⟍ ruction and rehabilitation
of works, rout⟍ location and drainage of
water. Each of these tn⟍⟍ ⟍s is the source of social
conflict as conduct of such activi⟍⟍es generates profiles of
advantage and disadvantage. Interests of people, meanings of
water control, and types of knowledge brought to bear on
irrigation problems, vary as one moves across units of the system
at the several levels of Figure 1.

At the main system level, good water management means
controlling the flow of large water volumes in large-scale
capital works within key parameters so that water moves
predictably toward aggregated demands of many farmers. The
emphasis is upon dealing with farmers in large categories by
focusing upon average needs and conditions. Main system managers

Figure 1

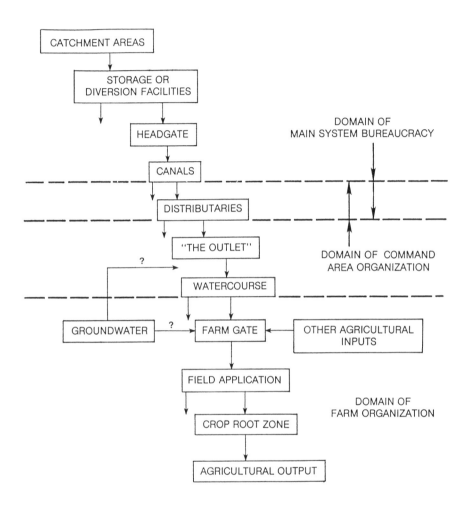

FLOW OF WATER IN TYPICAL IRRIGATION SYSTEM

almost everywhere are civil service employees and are almost nowhere rewarded or punished in a manner directly connected with farm productivity of the water. This is understandable given that the variables determining irrigation water productivity cannot be controlled by main system operators (e.g., variability in soil moisture holding capacity, soil moisture availability, root zone depths, crop depletion allowances, and evapotranspiration rates). Main system operators, although adapting their system to local topography and to a history of demand, depend heavily upon the processed disciplinary knowledge of engineering, public administration, economics, and the like without have the time or the particular need to know specific local details of individual farms. Water control, at the main system level, means managing water for daily operational smoothness so as to avoid sharp fluctuations that would threaten to exceed physical limits of systems operating within narrow tolerances.

Moving to the bottom of Figure 1, good water management at the farm level must focus on controlling water such that relatively small volumes are productively placed in particular crop root zones in specific and unique individual settings. Above all, farmers must rapidly adapt their irrigation water management on farms as they work to move water to various crops planted in different soils, at different stages of growth, under variable weather conditions, all the while bonded to the diverse and variable expectations of kinship networks and neighbors. The compelling fact at the farm level is that water delivered too early, too late, too little, or too much, seriously compromises production and, thereby, farm life. Delay of a water issue for three or four days, under quite typical conditions of crop, soil and climate, at a critical period in plant growth can cause severe decrements (e.g., thirty percent or more) in plant yields. As farmers witness their plants moving toward the permanent wilting point, they actively seek ways to obtain water, authorized or not, from the main system. On the other hand, a water issue from the main system that cannot be stopped, coming after a rain, can cause severe flooding to the micro-environment at critical stages of plant growth and also impose severe losses. Given the importance of water control, a study of irrigation in Pakistan revealed that farmers seek all possible ways to gain water control. Such control comes at high cost through illegal purchasing, theft, bribing of officials, and by investing heavily in relatively expensive private tubewell technology. Evidence is overwhelming that tubewell water is of much higher value than canal water because of its openness to control (Carruthers and Stoner, 1981; Lowdermilk, et al., 1978).

At the farm level, much idiographic knowledge of specific conditions beyond the awareness of main system managers must be

317

brought to focus on the precise control of small volumes so that water is placed in crop root zones in a way that sustains micro-climates required for crop production. Lack of sufficient water control at the farm level imposes severe costs:

1) Because high yielding plant varieties are much more demanding of adequate, timely water applications, farmers with inadequate water control will refrain from investment in such varieties, and the associated costly inputs of fertilizers and pesticides that high yielding varieties require.

2) As control over water diminishes, it becomes necessary to apply increasing quantities of water whenever available to attempt to assure survival of at least a portion of the plant population. Over-irrigation, and associated waterlogging and salinity problems are exacerbated by poor water control.

Farmers are less persuaded to act on central tendencies in the irrigation system, and are more attentive to unique conditions of particular fields and crops. Farmers cannot depend heavily upon processed disciplinary knowledge except as it is adjusted to their particular situation. Unlike main system managers, farmers are directly rewarded and punished according to the productivity of water.

Yet, farmers cannot control the variables central to main system management (e.g., watershed yields and distributions, river and canal hydraulic, storage capacities, interactions of control, measurement, and drainage). Farmer requirements for water control, served by idiographic knowledge about crop micro-environments, must be melded with main system management requirements for water control with altogether different meanings attributed to components of nomothetic disciplinary knowledge.

Social organization at the middle level must emerge to provide a link between farm and state bureaucracy. Organizations are systems of jointly negotiated agreements for bringing people together to do things collectively, which they cannot accomplish individually. Given problems of tight interdependence between farm and main system in large-scale surface gravity systems, what people cannot do individually at the middle level is to break main system water into volumes suitable for particular fields. This requires jointly negotiated agreements with main system operators and among neighbors sharing channels--agreements about obtaining main system water and "retailing" it to particular farmers. These negotiated agreements, written or unwritten, formal or informal, are essential to the integration of farm

318

water control requirements with main system requirements. The
question is not whether such negotiated joint agreements appear
at the middle level, but whether extant joint agreements serve
any defensible conception of agricultural development and social
equity.

At the middle level, water control refers to ways of
converting large volumes of main system water into small volumes
for farm use under conditions allowing farmers to control it for
productive purposes. Local, middle-level organizations must
disaggregate central supply tendencies of the main system into
specific flows meeting particular requirements of individual
farms. Good water control, at this level, must weave the
particulars of local circumstance organized idiographically with
the requirements imposed by the general tendencies and nomothetic
standards of the main system.

A Framework For Comparative Analysis

The analysis that follows is based upon observations in the
South and Southeast Asia and in the Western United States. The
author is also deeply indebted to the work of many other
scholars, the efforts of whom have been most stimulating (Hunt;
Wade, 1979; 1981; 1982; Wade and Chambers, 1980; Bottrall, 1978;
Coward, 1980; Bromley, 1982).

If one accepts that different requirements for control and
knowledge of main and farm systems must be fused in the
functioning of mid-level organizations, then it becomes necessary
to advance specific propositions regarding the attributes of such
organizations. Figure 2 summarizes the nature of the
propositions to be advanced.

Staff Responsibility

A critical variable in mid-level organizations is that of
establishing authority relationships. Shall the staff of the
local organization be fundamentally responsible to the
authorities of the main system or shall they fundamentally defer
to farmers? Responsibility to main system authority is indicated
by dependence upon the main system for remuneration, by
affiliation with the civil service, and by job specifications
defined by main system managers. Responsibility to farmers, a
posture of looking downward in the system, is typically indicated
by the fact that farmers can hire and fire staff without regard

319

Figure 2.

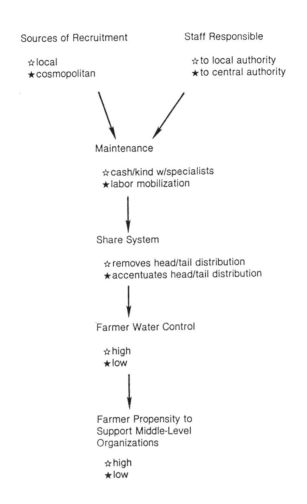

Sources of Recruitment Staff Responsible

☆local   ☆to local authority
★cosmopolitan   ★to central authority

Maintenance

 ☆cash/kind w/specialists
 ★labor mobilization

Share System

 ☆removes head/tail distribution
 ★accentuates head/tail distribution

Farmer Water Control

 ☆high
 ★low

Farmer Propensity to
Support Middle-Level
Organizations

 ☆high
 ★low

STRATEGIC VARIABLES IN ANALYSIS OF MIDDLE-LEVEL
IRRIGATION ORGANIZATIONS

to civil service regulations, and by the fact that rewards for services are established by farmers. It is hypothesized that as staff members of the local, mid-level organization "look down" for direction and definition of success, they become tuned to the local idiographic requirements and acquire incentive to seek creative methods to fulfill local water control needs within main system constraints. As staff members "look up" to main system authority for definition of adequacy, they become local agents of main system nomothetic principles without substantial incentive to be concerned in sustained ways with seeking the most workable fusions of nomothetic and idiographic understandings in the service of water control.

Staff Recruitment

A mid-level irrigation organization may be staffed by "cosmopolitians" who are recruited from outside the local command area, who are typically selected on the basis of educational qualifications with a high emphasis on comprehension of nomothetic generalizations of a given discipline, who are characterized by considerable social distance from local farmers, and whose aspirations are for upward mobility and departure from the local irrigation command. On the other hand, the staffing choices may emphasize the hiring of "locals" who are recruited on the local labor market by employing criteria having to do with local experience, local social connections, virtually no social distance from the farmers being served, and aspirations to spend a lifetime of work in the local area. The greater the proportion of staff recruited on the "local" pattern, the greater the propensity for staff to integrate idiographic understandings of the particular setting into implementation of main system operational requirements to serve local water control needs.

Maintenance

An important sub-set of the general staffing problem to be addressed by mid-level organizations is how routine maintenance is organized. There are two strategic options.

The first option is that routine maintenance be performed by staff hired full or part time, paid in cash or kind, and thereby develop specialized competencies in aspects of irrigation work. Secondly, such tasks may be performed periodically by mobilizing farmers, or their surrogates, who perform work within specified time periods or are subject to penalty.

It is hypothesized that as routine maintenance is performed by specialized and paid staff as employees of the organization, the farm water control will be enhanced because:

321

1) Individuals who spend full or part time in such work acquire specialized skills, job related contact, and knowledge not available to the general farm membership and not developed by annual or semi-annual general labor organizations.

2) Paid staff can promptly respond to problems in the local command area as they develop, whereas the mobilization system tends to defer to slack seasons much routine maintenance too large in scope for the voluntary efforts of any few farmers.

3) The system of general labor mobilization provides much opportunity, even incentive, for organizational "free riding." Farmers who are "free riders" often schedule other activities during the time that labor is mobilized so as to secure benefits of maintenance without contributing a "fair" share, however defined. The organization is then on the defensive; it must proceed against "free riders" in ways that threaten to erode support for the organization or at the very least impose substantial costs on the organization. Costs will be high because those with sufficient influence and power to attempt "free riding" strategies are those who are most difficult to keep harnessed to organizational norms. It is much less disruptive to the organization to collect maintenance revenue according to some legitimate conception of water shares and to use the payments in cash or kind to support a paid maintenance staff.

Water Share Systems

Water shares are central to the life of viable irrigation organizations. A share is always a two-sided concept: it confers a resource within certain prearranged rules; and it imposes an obligation or assessment upon the user. The concept of share, therefore, unites two essential aspects of organizational life--the delivery of the water resource and the gathering in of payments in cash, kind, or labor with which to support organizational operations. Productive and equitable resource distribution in general, and water distribution in particular, is not just a matter of good intentions; it is primarily a function of the way organizational rules resolve the problem of defining and allocating shares. The problem is complex and only brief mention of the possibilities can be made here. This listing of water share types is influenced by, but not identical to, that proposed by Raymond Anderson and Arthur Mass (1978). Essentially, mid-level organizations can specify water shares in some combination of the following ways:

1) Shares may be organized by fixed percentage allotments:
   a) by volume (e.g., a percent of the total acre feet estimated to be available)
   b) by time period rotation (e.g., a percentage of a day or week)

2) Shares may be organized by a priority system:
   a) priority by location (e.g., head to tail of a channel)
   b) priority by farm characteristic (e.g., time of settlement)
   c) priority of crop (e.g., market or subsistence value)

3) Shares may be organized by user demand:
   a) demand placed upon storage in a surface reservoir
   b) demand placed upon storage of groundwater

Many combinations are possible depending on local circumstance. Share systems may be combined by constraining one type of share by another. For example, shares by volume may be subjected to crop priorities. Share systems may employ two share types simultaneously as when shares by time rotation are supplemented by higher priced demand water. Share systems may shift within seasons in response to change in environment as in cases where shares by volume are shifted to shares by time of settlement or crop priority during severe drought. It is suggested here that the great diversity of irrigation allocation arrangements are various combinations of these basic share types.

Water Share Systems and Control

Problems of water control at all levels--main system, mid-level and on farm--will assume different forms depending upon which combination of share types is employed to distribute the resource from the middle level to the farm. Different kinds of uncertainties face farmers and system managers depending upon choices made in the establishment of share types. The most important single facet of the problem, however, can be abstracted out of the complexity and briefly examined here. The problem can be stated as a question: does the share system reinforce or defeat the problem of "head" and "tail" given by geography? Water must flow in channels from point A to B. Farmers toward point B are, by definition, nearer to the tail and--all else equal--will be disadvantaged in the matter of receiving water allocations relative to those near point A. The more one proceeds to locations toward the tail of an irrigation channel, the more one is vulnerable to:

1) losses due to leaks, seepage, and
   evaporation;
2) self-interest manipulations of others toward
   the head as the number of irrigators
   intervening between farmer X and the
   head increases; and
3) non-routine breakdowns in the system--there
   is simply more to go wrong when one
   is dependent upon longer channels.

Engineers must construct canals with potentials for head and
tail positions, but it is up to designers of social organizations
to decide whether the potentials for head-tail distinctions are
to be realized by share systems. The Pakistan and Punjab
warrabandi share systems accept, reiforce, and solidify the
head-tail distinction (Reidinger, 1974). When one combines water
allocations by time and location, one immediately reiforces what
engineers and geography have already done, and one creates a
fundamental difference in interest between irrigators with which
any local, mid-level organization must cope. Namely, irrigators
toward the head do not experience the same control problems faced
by their neighbors toward the tail and find their relatively
advantageous situation to be typically threatened by the desires
for reform on the part of tail-enders. Tails are, however, a
problem only to extent that organizational design of the share
system fails to overcome them. If the mid-level organization
should employ a combination of share types that impose the costs
of "water shrink" on all members without respect to location,
then all members have equal incentive to pay costs of maintenance
and operation of the system as a whole. If losses toward the
tails of channels are distributed by the share system to all,
irrigators at all locations have equal concern to reduce losses
at any point. If, for example, the organization should employ a
definition of shares by volume, or by volume combined with some
form of demand, and if volumes are measured so that losses
anywhere reduce volume to all irrigators, and if assessments
against shares are proportionate to volume received, then all
farmers absorb the "shrink" and all have an incentive to reduce
losses. Views of "head" and "tail" as inevitable natural
phenomena must be set aside. Uncritical willingness to accept
"heads" and "tails" in irrigation commands is a function of poor
organizational analysis of share types, and is not a reflection
on universal physical necessity.

I cannot, within the confines of this paper, perform an
analysis of the complexities of analyzing, selecting, and
defining the physical tools and organizational rules for
implementing share types. However, a critical question can be

raised: does the particular share type actualize all the
negative potentials for problematic water control inherent in a
reiforcement of the head-tail distinction among farmers, or does
the share type distribute the water shrink to all members without
respect to location? As share types are of the former variety,
one expects to witness severe problems of local water control in
the system. As one finds share types of the latter variety, one
expects to find superior water control.

Farmer Propensity to Support Mid-Level Organizations

The final variable on Figure 2 is that of farmer propensity
to support local, mid-level organizational arrangements between
farm and main system. Support here is taken to mean an
investment of personal resources to sustain arrangements by the
middle level for controlling water. It is posited that farmers
are willing to make such investments insofar as their
idiographically apprehended water control requirements are at
least minimally fulfilled. For this to occur, the mid-level
organization must provide a security zone for the sustenance of
those particular needs.

The argument of Figure 2 can now be summarized as follows:
the more the mid-level organization is staffed by locals who look
downward in the system to the authority of farmers, and the more
that it provides continuous maintenance performed by employees
using a share system that distributes the water shrink to all
members without regard to location, the greater the water control
that can be afforded, and the better the opportunity for farmer
involvement and investment. Farmers will display a higher
propensity to deliver sustained support to the mid-level
organization because it hypothesized to have a higher probablity
of fusing nomothetic requirements and central tendencies of the
main system with locally comprehendedd realities.

Conclusion

The meaning of irrigation water shifts dramatically as it
flows from main systems, through mid-level organizations, to
farms. In the social division of labor within large-scale
gravity flow irrigation systems, those who work with idiographic
knowledge on farm are faced with fundamentally different water
control problems than those, in central bureaucracies, who work
to control great volumes of water by relying heavily on
nomothetic principles and respond to demands known primarily in

the form of central tendencies. One cannot assume a commonality
of interest between main and farm system operators. One must
assume just the opposite. To note that interests differ is not
to suggest that mutual cooperation is not possible or desirable,
but that programs designed to promote effective farmer
participation in irrigation system operations must be rooted in
careful analysis of the organizational link between main system
and farm operations. Comparative analysis of irrigation systems
may be usefully informed by examination of the variables advanced
in the analysis of mid-level organizations.

There is a tendency, when middle-level arrangements are
defective, for central irrigation authorities to blame farmers
for problems. Irrigation bureaucracies gravitate toward strong
paternalistic behavior, justified by finding farmers to be
uncooperative and in need of stronger regulation to mold them in
directions required of technical solutions devoid of
organizational thought. The consequence has been enormous
centralization of bureaucratic power to manage irrigation
development and to by-pass local farmer experience. As authority
centralizes, communication gaps widen, local action is stifled,
dependency of farmers increases, opportunities for coercion and
corruption expand (Wade, 1979;1981;1982), and more authority is
swept by the bureaucracy. Frustrated attempts at corrective
bureaucratic action, aided and abetted by international donor
agencies--speaking in terms of computerized and intensified
management, coordination, monitoring, and evaluation--simply
intensify the destructive spiral.

Rehabilitation of poorly performing irrigation systems is
not simply a matter of reconstructing physical facilities such
that they meet orginal design standards. It is a matter of
examining defects in the extant mid-level organizations to
determine why they could not deliver the water in sufficiently
controllable ways so as to earn the support, and investment of
resources, on the part of irrigators.

If there is any prospect for authentic water revolution, it
will come as a result of increased water control for farmers by
building improved mid-level organizations whose arrangements
satisfactorily link farms to state bureaucracies. What is
required is a policy-relevant social science that can work with
other disciplines and local people in order to diagnose and
overcome constraints on farmer water control by examining
properties of irrigation systems. It is hoped that analysis of
the kinds of variables and propositions advanced here will be
viewed as a step in that direction.

Notes

[1] Figure 1 was created with the assistance of Dr. Alan C. Early, Professor, Department of Agriculture and Chemical Engineering, Colorado State University, Fort Collins, Colorado.

References

Anderson, Raymond and Arthur Maass. 1978. A Stimulation of Irrigation Systems. Revised edition. Washington, D.C.: U.S. Department of Agriculture, Economics, Statistics, and Cooperatives Service, Technical Bulletin No. 1431.
Bottrall, Anthony. 1978. The Management and Operation of Irrigation Schemes in Less Developed Countries. Water Supply and Management 2.
------- 1981. Comparative Study of the Management and Organization of Irrigation Projects. Washington, D.C.: World Bank Staff Working Paper No. 458.
Bromley, Daniel W. 1982. Improving Irrigated Agriculture: Institutional Reform and the Smaller Farmer. Washington, D.C.: World Bank Staff Working Paper No. 531.
Carruthers, Ian and Ray Stoner. 1981. Economic Aspects and Policy Issues in Groundwater Development. Washington, D.C.: World Bank Staff Working Paper No. 496.
Coward, E. Walter, ed., 1980. Irrigation and Agricultural Development in Asia. Ithaca: Cornell University Press.
Doorenbos, J. and A. H. Kassam. 1979. Yield Response to Water. Rome: Food and Agricultural Organization of the United Nations.
Hunt, Robert C., n.d., Water Work: Community and Centralization in Canal Irrigation. Unpublished manuscript. Waltham, Mass.: Brandeis University, Department of Anthropology.
Kathpalia, G. N. 1981. Rotational System of Canal Supplies and Warrabundi in India. In: India/USAID: Irrigation Development Options and Investment Strategies for the 1980's. Jack Keller et al. Appendix B. Logan: Utah State University, Water Management Synthesis Project, Report No. 6.
Keller, Jack, Wayne Clyma, Mathew Drosdoff, Max K. Lowdermilk, and David Seckler. 1981. India/USAID: Irrigation Development Options and Investment Strategies for the 1980's. Logan: Utah State University, Water Management Synthesis Project, Report No. 6.
Lowdermilk, Max K., Alan C. Early, and David M. Freeman. 1978. Farm Irrigation Constraints and Farmers' Responses: Comprehensive Field Survey in Pakistan. Ft. Collins, Colo.:

Colorado State University, Water Management Technical Report No. 48.

Reidinger, Richard B. 1974. Institutional Rationing of Canal Water on Northern India: Conflict Between Traditional Patterns and Modern Needs. Economic Development and Cultural Change 23.

Svendsen, Mark, Douglas Merrey, and Worth Fitzgerald. 1983. Meeting the Challenge for Better Irrigation Management. Horizons: United States Agency for International Development Publication, (March)18.

Wade, Robert. 1979. The Social Response to Irrigation: An Indian Case Study. Journal of Development Studies 16.

----- 1981. The Information Problem of South Indian Irrigation Canals. Water Supply and Management 5(1):40.

----- 1982. The System of Administrative and Political: Canal Irrigation in South India. The Journal of Development Studies 18(3).

Wade, Robert, and Robert Chambers. 1979. Managing the Main System: Canal Irrigation's Blind Spot. Economic and Political Weekly 15 (September): A-111.

19. PROPERTY, PERSISTENCE, AND PARTICIPATION: THE STATE AND TRADITIONAL IRRIGATION SYSTEMS

E. Walter Coward, Jr.

Throughout Asia, the State is increasingly involving itself in the affairs of traditional irrigation systems -- usually in small works that are the product of some previous local effort and that follow principles of property and operation that have been derived and reproduced locally rather than principles imposed by the current State apparatus. Typically, this government intervention is legitimized in modernization terms -- replacing primitive with sophisticated technology, improving efficiency in water use, or increasing agricultural production. However, many of these government efforts produce negative effects. Not only do such assisted systems often fail to perform better, the facilities frequently become wards of the State -- their upkeep and repair discontinued by local people with the assumption that the State will be the responsible party.

The process can be seen as one in which actions of the State alienate local groups from the hydraulic property that they have created or acquired -- most important, the rights to the hydraulic works and the water that they supply.[1] This occurs because the State's irrigation development activities rearrange the structure of hydraulic property rights in the "assisted" system.

From a research point of view, it is possible to use these government intrusions as a research strategy. By focusing on specific intrusion events and analyzing the reactions of the local group to the government activities, it may be possible to uncover the basic structures of action, which often will be property relations, that form the group and that are being infringed upon by the development program. This paper draws on several contemporary studies of traditional irrigation systems in Southeast Asia, both assisted and non-assisted, to explore the hypothesis that such groups are bound together and derive their persistent ability to mobilize collective action from the connections that occur among them as co-property holders.

Zanjeras in Ilocos Norte

There are several studies of traditional irrigation systems in the Ilocos region of the Philippines -- locally called

329

zanjeras (Christie, 1914; Lewis, 1971; Coward, 1979; Siy, 1982). The most recent work by Siy (1982) has further illuminated the social organization of these groups and the centrality of property rights to this organization. Two ethno-property concepts underlie the social arrangements of the zanjera.

Biang ti daga.

Based on a review of historical documents and discussion with older informants in the Ilocos Norte region, Siy (1982) suggests it is useful to distinguish the origin of three types of zanjeras. First are those that were organized by farmers with the common interest of irrigating those lands that they already cultivated. It is this type that Christie (1914) seems to have in mind in referring to the zanjeras as "irrigation societies" -- small holders with a common need that could not be met by any one of them acting independently. A second situation is that in which the zanjera group is formed to bring irrigation water to territories not previously cultivated. In Siy's (1982) study of a federation of several zanjera units, he found that two of the zanjera units were created after "new" lands became available as the result of shifts in the course of the Laoag River.

The third circumstance is that in which a zanjera group is formed to provide irrigation water to unirrigated lands owned by persons other than the zanjera members. The zanjera group agrees to provide irrigation services in exchange for usufruct rights to a portion of these newly irrigated lands. The arrangement between the landowners and the zanjera group is formalized in the biang ti daga (literally, sharing of the rice land) agreements. The actual division of land between the landowners and the zanjera would vary from case to case, but it seems that the arrangements permitted the zanjeras to use from one-third to five-sixths of the total area to be irrigated. The terms of the agreement were that ownership of the land would be retained by the landowners and use rights would be granted to the zanjera as long as the land of the owners continued to receive adequate irrigation from the zanjera.[2] For those zanjeras formed on the basis of biang ti daga agreements, the basic purpose of group formation appears to have been providing irrigation services in order to acquire access to land.

Atar.

The second property concept, atar, has characteristics that fit with the biang ti daga processes discussed above. An atar is essentially a membership share that is composed of several different dimensions -- land, claimants, water, and member responsibilities. As a unit of land an atar is typically composed on several separate parcels that are noncontiguous. All the atars in a single zangera have equivalent land sizes per atar -- but may be different across zanjeras. For each atar share there is a claimant, or sometimes claimants. Alternatively, some persons have claim to more than one atar.

The atar also represents a right to a portion of the zanjeras' water supply. Because the supply of water in the system will vary, the actual volume of water delivered to each atar will fluctuate, but ideally the proportion to each atar will be similar. Finally, the atar also signifies membership responsibilities in the zanjera. In most instances, when resources such as labor or cash are required for system operation and maintenance, these resources are mobilized on a per atar basis -- the exception being times of emergency when all able-bodied persons are expected to contribute the labor needed to correct the problem.

The dispersion of the parcels of land associated with an atar may be explained by the biang ti daga processes discussed earlier. Because each of the landowners benefitting from the irrigation service were required to provide a portion of their land for use by the zanjera members, the acquired blocks of land would be scattered across the landscape. In each of these blocks acquired for zanjera use, some practical number of parcels would be created and assigned to the zanjera members as part of their atar share. Thus, an atar holder would be assigned parcels in several, or all, of the blocks provided by the landowners.

In summary, one can note that the social relations among the zanjera members are supported by their connections as co-owners of the hydraulic facilities that they or their ancestors created and that they act to reproduce continually In those zanjeras that have been created through the biang ti daga process, those connections are also based on the common position that they occupy relative to the usufruct rights to some of the lands they farm.[3]

Muang-fai Systems in Northern Thailand

There are a number of thorough ethnographies of the traditional irrigation systems of northern Thailand -- locally called muang-fai systems (literally, canal-weir systems) (Sirivongs, 1983; Tanabe, 1981; Cohen, 1981; Calavan, 1974; Tan-kim-yong, 1983). Tan-kim-yong's work provides considerable detail about a muang-fai system in the district of Chomthong allowing some inferences about property.

331

Construction of the system Tan-kim-yong studied, Fai Muang Mai, was begun late in the nineteenth century under the direction of one of the local elite (phaya).[4] At this time, the traditional sources of power and economic support of the phaya were being eroded by the inclusion of the Chiengmai kingdom into the Bangkok-based Siamese kingdom and many turned to irrigation development as a means to supplement their dwindling state incomes.

The present system has a main canal 22 kilometers in length and serves an area divided into two sections -- head and tail. The arrangements for building these two portions of the system were quite different and require brief discussion. The head portion, or first phase, was built between 1870 and 1880 under the leadership of the phaya. During this ten-year period, every year the total new irrigation command was divided among those who had participated in that year's construction -- with a larger share going to the phaya and his assistants. The annual distribution of land resulted in cultivators having scattered parcels in this first section of the system rather than concentrating some farmers close to the water source while others were distant. Instead, the general pattern was for farmers to have some parcels close and others far from the diversion weir.

Work on the tail section of the system was begun around 1930. This portion of the system was built under a contract between farmers who already had claims to the land in this tail section (some of whom were members of Fai Muang Mai) and a Chinese contractor from Chiengmai City. The arrangement was that in exchange for extending the canal system the contractor would be given land in this tail area.

Property Rights

There are three important activities in the contemporary system that illustrate the fundamental property base of the muang-fai group. One is the process for selecting and replacing leaders in the system. The rule is that all those currently cultivating land in Fai Muang Mai, owners or tenants, can propose candidates for the various offices, but only the owners of rice land are permitted to vote. Those who are only tenants or only owners of orchard lands have no voting right -- though they may be nominated to hold office.

The arrangements for mobilizing resources to reproduce the physical irrigation works also reflect property relationships. Tan-kim-yong (1983:189) identifies the following categories of "members" in the irrigation group: rice land owners, orchard land owners, tenants on the rice lands.

The rules for mobilizing resources from these three categories of users mirror the different relation that each has to rice land and, thus, also the varied connections they have to the hydraulic apparatus. Recall that the original property relation resulting from construction of the head section of the system in the nineteenth century was that builders of the system became individual owners of the rice lands that were thereby created. Thus there was an intertwining of hydraulic and agrarian rights that continues into the present. Regarding resource mobilization, these categories define the following responsibilities:

1) the cultivators of the rice lands, owners or tenants, are responsible for providing labor and local materials, such as bamboo, in proportion to the system's need and the amount of rice land that they are cultivating;

2) owners of rice land, in addition, must provide cash for certain emergencies and any special projects that result in substantial improvements in the hydraulic works; and

3) owners of orchard lands are occasionally called upon for cash contributions for special project needs.

I suggest that property relations also are embedded in the key group ritual of Fai Muang Mai -- the piti phi fai. This prepared for the start of a cropping season. The activities occur at a small shrine (hoh phi fai) close to the diversion weir. Tan-kim-yong (1983:165) indicates that the ritual has elements of both recognition of the "spirit of the weir" and the "spirit of the former leaders." The latter may be seen as representing the original property creators and the ritual serves to recall the investment efforts of prior generations and to confirm the continuity between those previous property-creating activities and the contemporary ones. It can be suggested that the ritual activity provides the irrigation group legitimation for collective action not based in common biological ancestors but in common property builders. It is from the actions of that prior group and the relationships that they created among themselves that the present group derives its own relationships, rights, and responsibilities.

Overall, it seems plausible to suggest that a number of the organizational arrangements and processes observed in Fai Muang Mai are expositions of an underlying property grid. That property grid, formed during the initial period of constructing the hydraulic works and continually reproduced, provides the logic both for the persistence of certain old practices and the creation of new procedures as circumstances require.

The State and Traditional Irrigation Systems

The brief discussions above illustrate the property connections in two types of traditional irrigation systems. These cases, and others, suggest that this property dimension is fundamental to the persistence of these sociotechnical groups. As suggested above, observation of government intrusions into such systems may be an especially rich context for identifying property structures. Two additional examples illustrate this point.

The Ataran Systems of South Sumatra

In the western section of the province of South Sumatra (Indonesia) close to the Barisan Mountains, one can find numerous small, traditional irrigation systems -- locally called ataran -- largely used for rice production. Recent research has described the sociotechnical organization of these systems and provided information on the impact of government assistance (Pusat Penelitian Universitas Srivijaya, 1984).

One such system is ataran Bagindo, which serves an area of about 60 hectares. Oral tradition suggests that this system was created about 300 years ago. In Bagindo, as in other traditional irrigation networks, there is a careful attempt to deliver water equitably to the water users of the system -- who are, in fact, the co-owners of the facilities and co-shareholders of the water rights. To achieve this end the atarans use a combination of concepts, roles, and physical apparatus. These include the following.

The direction of the ataran is in the hands of a locally selected person, the mantri siring (literally, canal chief). This individual, usually himself a water user in the system, is responsible for mobilizing the labor required for system maintenance and repair, coordinating the timing of planting activities, and managing the water distribution. The mantri siring is paid for these services. Payment is based on the number of water inlets (locally called mata air) serving each farmer. As Tanabe (1981) has suggested for the system he studied in northern Thailand, these inlets represent the point of contact between the "public" portion of the system and the "private" portion -- the spot where water control is transferred from the mantri siring to the individual farmer. The mata air symbolizes the hydraulic and agrarian rights of the individual -- it signifies his right to a proportion of the system's total water supply and to an amount of land irrigated by that inlet. It also serves as the accounting unit for mobilizing labor and other resources required to reproduce the physical works. As in the

334

system described above, the rights originally were obtained through participation in the construction of the works. Farmers who opened additional rice lands after this creation phase were required to make a payment to the ataran group, thus mimicking the investment of the original builders.

To move the correct amount of water from the diversion point on the river through the canal network to the various water inlets scattered across the irrigated area, a device called a penaro is utilized. This device, which we can think of as a proportional weir, is placed at each location in the canal network where a division occurs. It consists of a board, or log, placed perpendicular in the channel and with appropriately sized notches to divide the stream of water into two, or more, portions. This division is designed to supply equitably the number of water inlets that lie along each canal below the division point -- thus if the divided streams are serving a different number of water inlets the notching in the penaro will reflect this different supply requirement. A key point to be understood is that the penaro and mata air, while simple in appearance, are artifacts manifesting fundamental, and enduring, property rights and relationships.

It is into this complex social space, with its simple hydraulic artifacts, that the government intruded -- actually, on more than one occasion. In the 1950s, assistance was limited to making part of the temporary diversion structure permanent. However, in 1979 the government's "assistance" was more comprehensive. In addition to further improvements in the diversion weir, the government now replaced the penaro structures with "modern" division boxes and imposed new organizational arrangements for managing the system -- both boxes and organization following standard designs being used throughout Indonesia. It seems clear that in neither case did the government understand what it was replacing. Neither the logic of the penaro nor the mantri siring was known; in fact, the concept of the ataran as an indigenous irrigation arrangement was either unrecognized, or known but not valued.

The effort of the ataran members to preserve their fundamental property rights and relation is illustrated by their response to a particular "modern" device installed by the public works agency. In this case, the new division box replaced a penaro that divided water into two channels: one serving 20 mata air and the other serving 26. However, the new box did not allow accurate enough adjustments to permit the farmers to divide the water in a 20:26 ratio. To deal with this problem the farmers took the two streams of water from the new box and rejoined them immediately below the box. At this point they reinstalled the traditional penaro, thus allowing the water supply to be divided

335

in a ratio consistent with the hydraulic rights of those downstream from this location (see Figure 1).

As can be seen in this example, the modification of the physical apparatus of these systems, often done without the discussion and participation of farmers, can have the consequence of de-structuring existing property relation and ultimately the viability of local collective action. Government actions, which directly rearrange property rights and relationships, can disrupt, confuse, and muddle social organization that rests on prior investment activities and previously created objects of property.

The Bagindo case allows one to see the persistence of property arrangements in the face of technical changes. Farmers in Bagindo took action to restore the technical capability to divide water in a manner consistent with the architecture of hydraulic property rights. Thus, adjustment of the division box can be seen as a property rights protection strategy. Without the ability to restore the 20:26 ratio property principles, represented in the notion that each mata air in the system should receive an equal share of water, would be violated. The inability to produce this water supply ratio would endanger the ability to reproduce the social organization of tis section of the ataran because the social arrangements are reciprocal with the individual-held water rights.

Local Hill Systems in Nepal

Pradhan (1982) has recently provided an instructive discussion concerning State intervention in an existing irrigation system in Nepal locally called a kulo. This case is a small-scale hill system diverting water with a simple weir to lands that produce rice in the wet season and wheat and corn in the dry season.

The present system is an amalgamation of two previously independent kulos. The consolidation occurred after one of the systems, Tallo Kulo, experienced system damages that could not be repaired. Through a series of negotiations with the other system, Taplek-Pokhariya Kulo, it was agreed that Tallo Kulo could join its canal network to the works of Taplek-Pokhariya. The Tallo Kulo system had originally been developed by two individuals using their own and some borrowed capital to hire construction specialists to build the irrigation works. After construction was completed they sold shares in the system to landowners whose land could be served by the canals. These shareholders formed into an irrigation society (samaj) which jointly owned and operated Tallo Kulo.

336

Figure 1.

10

Figure I: Farmer Adjustments to Government Structures

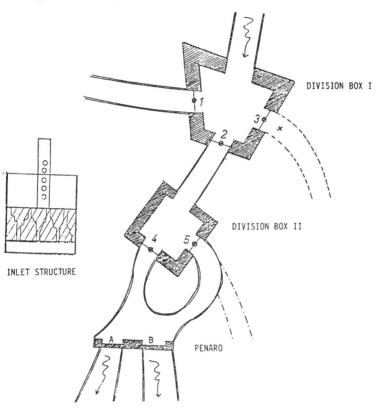

Explanation: 1-5 = Inlets

A:B = 20:26 Ratio

≡≡≡ = Delivery canal

‑‑X‑ = Canal planned but not built

‑·‑·‑·‑ = Canal built but closed by the farmers

Source: Srivijaya University Research Center (1984).

The negotiations that led to the formation of this consolidated system seem to clearly recognize hydraulic rights. As a conditon to Tallo Kulo joining with the other system, it had to agree to the following:

1) to widen the main canal from the diversion point on the river;
2) to assume all responsibility for routine work and maintenance of the entire system -- the Taplek-Pokhariya group could be called for in times of emergency;
3) to give priority in water distribution to the Taplek-Pokhariya group -- originally Tallo Kulo was only to irrigate at night.

These tough terms of agreement reflect the prior investments that the Taplek-Pokhariya group had made in their system. The newcomers, the Tallo Kulo group, were to pay their shares of these costs by assuming the extra duties and accepting inferior water rights. As was said with the Bagindo case above, it was this complex social and historical space into which the government intruded.

The development project that the State implemented was an extension project -- a project to modify the existing main system and extend the canal network beyond the fields of the Tallo Kulo group to serve a completely new set of lands farmed by other people. Although the modifications to the existing canal system were accomplished (perhaps because it did increase the water supply for both the Taplek-Pokhariya Kulo and Tallo Kulo groups), the project has been completely unsuccessful in enforcing any actual distribution of water to the new area. Pradhan (1982:20) gets at the central problem with the following comments:

> The feeling of ownership of the system entails many consequences in terms of effective resource mobilization and management. [Tallo Kulo] . . . feels that for nearly half a century they have put sweat and toil, life and risks, money and labor into the system. It is a private kulo, not a state-owned or state-constructed one. It is quite irreconcilable for (one group of) people to just give water to (another group) simply because of some development program of a lakh rupees. . . . Whatever it is (Tallo Kulo) feels it is their duty to be responsible for their system and thus will take all measures to safe-guard it and, moreover, own it.

The resistance to expansion can be understood as resisting the loss of property rights without compensation. When Tallo Kulo joined with Taplek-Pokhariya the latter was compensated in a variety of ways -- including the assignment of inferior water rights to the newcomers. As with Bagindo, in this case also the Nepal authorities seemed to have little understanding of the socio-historical context in which they were operating. Thus, not surprisingly, their acts contradicted the property connections existing in the project area. People in the existing system were asked to enter into property relations with a new group but without material, or symbolic, recognition of the prior investments that had occurred and that formed the basis for their collective actions in reproducing the hydraulic artifacts of the system.

Summary

These cases illustrate the following important points. First, the persistence of many of the traditional systems appears to be conditional on the social cohesion that derives from the property-forming and property-reproducing activities of these groups. Each of these four cases illustrates the fundamental importance of the property formation phase of developing the hydraulic works. It was during this phase that the basic property relations were established -- perhaps building on preexisting social relations of one form or another.

The second point derives from the two cases of government intervention. In both cases government has used processes that are centralized or nonparticipative in style. The outcome frequently is a basic breach of the structure of property rights. The infringement of rights and responsibilities can result in various corrective local actions -- either hostile or passive in form and having the consequence of allowing the facilities to go unused or fall into disrepair.

What is needed are project strategies that are capable of generating location-specific solutions consistent with broad political goals and objectives (and also economical of scarce resources such as finances and staff capacity). Viewing traditional irrigation systems as property groups could have an important impact on the strategies that governments use to "assist" these systems. Present strategies used by government reflect the view that these systems have ineffective technical equipment and obsolete social arrangements -- thus legitimizing government modifications. A property conceptualization could emphasize the resources that exist, both material and organizational, and lead to a property-based strategy of assistance. This strategy would (1) begin with a concern for identifying existing property relations and the fit between these claims and the artifacts and management procedures in the system, (2) attempt to fit technical and management "improvements" into these property patterns, or (3) where existing property rights were judged to be "unfair" explicitly define the rights to be modified.

Notes

[1] The theoretical arguments regarding property-rights are not detailed here but have been discussed in other recent papers (Coward, 1985a,b; 1986). Conceptual ideas for the discussion come from discussions of irrigation by Tamaki, 1977; Leach, 1961; and Bloch, 1975. From the general anthropological literature, I have used Goody, 1962. Useful ideas are also found in present writing in institutional economics (see for example Demetz, 1967) and in Marxian conceptualization of property.

[2] A recent report on irrigation organization in the Lake Toba region of North Sumatra (Lando, 1979) gives additional insight as to how this process might have operated. Here, groups (often a single patriclan) act to construct the basic facilities of an irrigation system -- a weir at the water source and a canal(s) to convey water to the potential sawah area. Those who are not members of this "investment" group can use water from the irrigation canals to form their sawah fields and thereafter to irrigate them. But the cost of doing so is that the user provide one-fourth of the newly created rice-lands to the group that created the irrigation works. This one-fourth is reported to be held in "trust" -- which I presume may mean having usufruct but not ownership rights.

[3] While not discussed in the paper, there is a project underway to "modernize" a number of the zanjeras in Ilocos Norte. This project, called the Palsiguan River Multi-Purpose Project, is discussed by Visaya, 1982.

[4] Phaya were local elites operating as appendages of the kingdom that centered in Chiengmai. They had control of territories -- roughly equivalent to present subdistricts in this region and comprising a number of hamlets. Their livelihood was obtained by collecting revenues on the land and forests in their territory -- a portion of which they retained while submitting the remainder to the Chiengmai center.

References

Bloch, Maurice 1975. Property and the End of Affinity. In:
Marxist Analyses and Social Anthropology 203-228. M. Bloch,
ed. London: Malaby Press.
Calavan, Sharon 1974. Aristocrats and Commoners in Rural Northern
Thailand. Unpublished Ph.D. dissertation. Urbana: University
of Illinois.
Christie, Emerson B. 1914. Notes on Irrigation and Cooperative
Irrigation Societies in Ilocos Norte. The Philippine Journal of
Science 9(2):99-113.
Cohen, Paul T. 1981. The Politics of Economic Development in
Northern Thailand, 1967-1978. Thesis, University of London.
Coward, E. Walter Jr. 1979. Principles of Social Organization in
an Indigenous Irrigation System. Human Organization
38(1):28-36.
----- 1985a. Traditional Irrigation Systems and Government
Assistance: Current Research Findings from Southeast Asia.
DVWK Bulletin 9:1-30. ----- 1985b. State and Locality in Asian
Irrigation Development: The Property Factor. In: Current Issues
in and Approaches to Irrigation Water Management in Developing
Countries. R. K. Sampath and K. C. Nobe, eds. Boulder: Westview
Press. ----- 1986. Direct or Indirect Alternatives for
Irrigation Investment and the Creation of Property. In:
Irrigation Investment, Technology and Management Strategies for
Development. K. William Easter, ed. Boulder: Westview Press.
Demsetz 1967. Toward a Theory of Property Rights. AER Papers and
Proceedings 57:347-352.
Goody, Jack 1962. Death, Property and the Ancestors. Stanford:
Stanford University Press.
Lando, Richard P. 1979. The Gift of Land: Irrigation and Social
Structure in a Toba Batak Village. University of California,
Riverside: Unpublished Ph.D. dissertation.
Leach, Edmund R. 1961. Pul Eliya: A Village in Ceylon.
Cambridge, England: Cambridge University Press.
Lewis, Henry T. 1971. Ilocano Rice Farmers: A Comparative Study
of Two Philippine Barrios. Honolulu: University of Hawaii
Press.
Pradhan, Ujjwal 1982. Irrigation Development: Whose Panacea?
Unpublished paper.
Pusat Penelitian Universitas Srivijaya 1984. Pola dan Dampak
Bantaan Pemerintah Terhadap Oranisasi Irigasi Tradisional:
Pengalaman Desa Tanjung Agung, Sumatera Selatan [Types and
Impacts of Government Assistance for Traditional Irrigation
Systems: Experiences from Tanjung Agung Village, South
Sumatra]. Paper presented at Workshop on Government Assistance
to Traditional Irrigation Systems. Bukittingi, West Sumatra.
Sirivongs, Abha 1982. A Comparative Study of Traditional

341

Irrigation Systems in Two Communities of Northern Thailand. Second edition. Bangkok: Chulalongkorn University, Social Research Institute.

Siy, Robert Y. Jr. 1982. Community Resource Management: Lessons from the Zanjera. Quezon City: University of the Philippines Press.

Tamaki, Akira 1977. The Development Theory of Irrigation Agriculture. Tokyo: Institute of Developing Economies, Special Paper No. 7.

Tanabe, Shigeharu 1981. Peasant Farming Systems in Thailand: A Comparative Study of Rice Cultivation and Agricultural Technology in Chingmai and Ayutthaya. Ph.D. dissertation, The School of Oriental and African Studies, University of London.

Tan-kim-yong, Uraivan 1983. Resource Mobilization in Traditional Irrigation Systems of Northern Thailand: A Comparison Between the Lowland and the Upland Irrigation Communities. Ph.D. dissertation, Cornell University, Ithaca.

Visaya, Benito P. 1982. The Palsiguan River Multi-purpose Project and the Zanjeras. Paper presented at conference on Organization as Strategic Resource in Irrigation Development, Makati, Metro Manila, Philippines, November 15-19.

SECTION IV: OUTSIDE INTERVENTIONS: THE ACTIVITIES OF
               DEVELOPMENT ORGANIZATIONS

The essays in this section focus on the interventions of
development organizations: the U. S. Agency for International
Development, the Institute for Development Anthropology, and the
Land Tenure Center at the University of Wisconsin. (Two other
such organizations are the Harvard Institute for International
Development and the Programme in the Anthropology of Development
at McGill University.)

Dolores Koenig describes the process of implementing a
USAID-funded project, cosidering it as a series of negotiations
among local and international persons and agencies. Koenig's
study is of the type called for by Robert Bates in his essay.
Thayer Scudder gives us a history of the Institute for
Development Anthropology, and makes a case for anthropological
involvement in development work. Don Kanel and his associates at
the Land Tenure Center of the University of Wisconsin describe
recent research and advisory activities on land reform and
emphasize the importance of an inter-disciplinary social science
perspective.

343

20. THE CULTURE AND SOCIAL ORGANIZATION OF USAID DEVELOPMENT
PROJECTS IN WEST AFRICA[1]

Dolores Koenig

Since Laura Nader (1974) wrote about the importance of
"studying up," anthropologists have begun to address the power
structures that affect our lives. This has been true
particularly among applied anthropologists who have learned that
their work can be most useful when they understand the
organizations for which they work.

Much of the work already done concentrates on central levels
of policy making and project design. This paper complements that
work by its focus on the organization of the development project.
In the process of implementation, each development project
becomes a distinctive social system. Although not separate from
the larger social systems of which it is a part, it is
distinguishable. To make this social system, the actors
participating must negotiate among themselves a set of shared
meanings and goals on which the project's actions will be based.
This paper will look at some aspects of that process of
negotiation.

                          The Culture of Policy

As the culture of policy has become an important part of
anthropological study, a series of studies and review articles on
general issues have appeared (e.g., Britan and Cohen 1980;
Hinshaw 1980; Chambers 1985) as well as those that focus more
specifically on international development (Hoben 1980 and 1982;
Almy 1977; Partridge 1984; Practicing Anthropology 1981). These
studies have concentrated on selected parts of the development
process, paying less attention to others.

In the best of these studies, the focus has tended to be on
central policy levels and within government agencies, and on
planning rather than implementation. Among the first was
Tendler's (1975) study, which stressed the importance of
Congressional funding and legislation for development decisions.
This was later followed by Hoben's (1980) analysis of the project
design process. Both emphasized the importance to personnel
within development agencies of obligating money for
organizational survival and for individual career advancement in
the bureaucracy.

That some of these anthropological analyses concentrated on

the central administration seems to reflect the fact that many of
the authors worked there. Hoben (1980:339) for example, worked
in a policy bureau for the Agency for International Development
(USAID) in Washington. As more anthropologists have begun to
participate in field activities, some material on this part of
the development process has begun to appear.[2] Studies range
from Green's (1981) anecdotal account of short-term consulting
work to Epstein and Ahmed's (1984) short, rather programmatic
discussion of monitoring. There have also been a number of
sector or project specific accounts (e.g., Boyle 1984; Horowitz
1979; Merrey 1984; Painter 1985; Stevens 1978). However these
have only begun to scratch the surface of the vast problem of
implementation: translating policy and project design into real
activities of social change to improve beneficiaries' lives.

Although anthropologists are only beginning to analyze field
activities, administrators have been interested for a longer
time, because implementation is a daily issue for development
managers. An important problem of development administration has
been the gap between the plan and the results of that plan
(Honadle 1979:3). Once projects begin to operate they are
subject to forces that pull them away from their original design;
Honadle (1979:9) labels this process "mutation" and sees it as an
essential feature of implementation that the good administrator
must understand and manage.

Although the mutating development project may be normal,
there is also a tendency to see it as something potentially
disruptive. Honadle (1979:9,10) talks of it as a process by
which local organizations attempt to "absorb" project resources,
often diverting benefits from the intended beneficiaries. One
way to deal with problems of implementation is through better
design (Rondinelli 1979). Implementation will never directly
follow design, but it is worthwhile to pursue good design, which
should lead to a smaller gap between implementation and
development. In particular, good design should focus on the
necessary uncertainties of implementation to help managers better
deal with them (Rondinelli 1979:31).

The problem of the gap between design and implementation
would seem to be one where an anthropological contribution would
be useful, because it concerns the difference between ideal
representation and real behavior. An anthropological approach
that sees aspects of culture and social systems as the created
product of transaction and interaction among individuals would
seem to be one of the more useful approaches for understanding
the social process of implementation and why a plan's translation
to reality inevitably differs from the plan.

As Rosen (1984:ix) says of the people in the small Moroccan

346

town he studied, they "create their social reality by constantly bargaining over and through the terms that compose it." Moreover, "concepts ... appeared to acquire meaning not as the result of mechanical application but as the result of a distinct process of negotiation" (Rosen 1984:4). Rosen places his analysis in the specific context of a particular Muslim town, but this process would seem to occur not only there, but within all social systems, including development projects as they are implemented.

The idea that a development project ought to be viewed as an arena for creating a new social system through interaction and negotiation is hardly a new one. For example, Epstein and Ahmed (1984:34) have noted that there are various different sets of project participants, each with its own needs, and each subject to its own set of pressures. They (1984:36) note further that "intraset cleavages and alliances across sets (of development project participants) need to be carefully examined. Their study will unveil much of the 'mystery' of successes or failures of various projects." Or, as Chambers (1985:183) describes it, a policy setting is a situation in which different intentions come into conflict and where some attempt to negotiate or mediate is called for. Yet, while this approach has been used to look at policy formation, it has not yet been used to analyze project implementation systematically.

A view of the development project as a negotiated social system should ultimately provide an analytic tool for understanding a variety of implementation issues. For example, from this point of view, while it is surely important to have good design, that will not necessarily close the gap between plan and implementation. Rather good design will provide a useful framework for the negotiations to follow. In the limited space of this paper it is possible to follow only a few of the implications of the suggested approach.

The Setting

This paper is grounded in my experience with USAID projects in the West African Sahelian countries, especially Mali. Both USAID and the Sahelian countries have particular characteristics that affect the ways in which development projects are done.

The AID Development Project

In his article, "Agricultural Decision Making in Foreign Assistance," Hoben (1980:349-350) discusses the long road from general policy to actualizing that policy in an actual project design document (the Project Paper, or PP). Even once the design is approved however, the project remains to be done, translated from the general document to particular development actions. Of this he has little to say, simply outlining the procedure:

It is only after the PP has been approved that AID can issue a Request for Proposals to solicit bids for project implementation from prospective contractors and negotiate a Program Agreement with the host country. During the period of project implementation the mission must submit a Project Evaluation Statement annually and an indepth Evaluation at a scheduled date.... In all, it takes at least 2 years for a project to pass through the program and budget cycle from the PID (Project Identification Document) stage to the beginning of implementation -- usually considerably longer (Hoben 1980:350).

It is perhaps not surprising that a writer whose subject is the central AID agency does not discuss implementation in detail, because the central agency does not actually do implementation. Rather implementation is usually done by a host country agency assisted by a group of American technical assistants.

While the host country chooses which of its agencies will be responsible for a particular project, AID is responsible for selecting an organization to provide technical assistance. Contractors are usually chosen on the basis of competitive bids, and judged on both technical capability and cost.[3] Once chosen, contractor personnel enter the field, and a kind of informal management/decision making unit is set up that includes three major sets of actors: USAID mission personnel (who remain interested in the project even though they do not implement it directly), host country agency personnel, and contractors.

AID mission personnel are primarily those who work at the local mission. They include Americans who work directly for the agency as well as host country personnel who are AID local employees. Their primary loyalties are to AID and its requirements, although the relationship of Americans and nationals to host country government agencies usually varies somewhat, due to the larger cultural heritage and national identity of each. They are primarily responsible for ensuring that the project conforms to AID guidelines. Their formal role is that of managing the interface between donor and recipient agencies.

Host country agency personnel are primarily civil servant nationals of the local country. Their loyalty is primarily to their own agency and secondarily to their national governments. In addition, they may also want to promote the interests of political party, region, or ethnic group. Their national

348

governments may also put various formal and informal requirements on them that they must follow in project negotiations (cf. Doornboos and Lofchie 1971). This group may also include third country nationals working as technical assistants in the host country agency, not uncommonly funded by some other donor organization.

This group is usually the one formally responsible for project implementation and must see that the project is congruent with their own country's policy priorities. Both AID and host country personnel normally sign all budget authorizations and retain the right to veto contractor personnel. In French-speaking West Africa, host country agencies may and often do refuse to authorize contractor personnel who do not speak adequate French.

Contractors are a more diverse group than these other two. Although the personnel of these other two groups have often worked together in readying the project for approval over a significant period of time, contractors are usually hired by the firm for the particular project after approval of the project and the award of the contract. They have not necessarily worked either with the firm or with any of the other groups prior to the project.[4] Their backgrounds are varied, and they often represent a mix of disciplines. Some have considerable prior experience in the country but others have little and are hired primarily for their technical expertise.

Because AID funds are bilateral foreign assistance that must ordinarily provide some benefit to the United States (Tendler 1975; see also USAID 1978: Appendix O) as well as to the recipient country, Americans are usually hired. Non-Americans are hired when necessary, i.e., when qualified Americans cannot be found. This is particularly likely to occur in highly technical fields in which it is often difficult to find appropriate personnel. The problem is even more acute in non-English speaking countries, as the appropriate person needs not only a technical skill, but also the ability to express it in some language other than English. Their formal role is usually that of the "technical assistant," serving as a counterpart to someone in the host country agency whom they advise on technical matters.[5]

Once in the country, these three groups must work together to implement the project. Although the PP offers a framework for this, it is not always clear how to translate that framework into particular concrete actions. In making decisions about which actions to take and how best to do them, these three groups create a project through interaction and negotiation in a way analogous to the way in which culture is created and recreated by

349

individuals. Although they all come from larger cultures, they form their own arena of action in project implementation where a new social system is formed through an ongoing process of interaction.

The Sahel

Sahelian countries are among the poorest in the world. Affected by continuing drought from the 1970s until very recently, stagnant economies and poor social service systems, the countries are poor both financially and in terms of the trained and educated human resources necessary to implement projects. Accordingly, they are viewed as greatly in need of foreign assistance.

Four of the six major Sahelian[6] countries are considered by the World Bank to be in the category of "low income economies" (World Bank 1985). Of these, three (Mali, Burkina Faso, and Niger) are among the eleven poorest countries as measured by GDP/capita. Of the two countries (Senegal and Mauritania) that are considered to be "middle income economies," both fall in the bottom five of this classification. In addition, foreign reserve balances for most of these countries are negative and declining; exceptions were Niger during its uranium boom and Burkina Faso (Gray and Martens 1983). Although many of these countries are under International Monetary Fund pressures to improve their economies, they are finding this to be very difficult.

The trained and educated human resource base of Sahelian countries is also small. Total population is low, ranging from 1.6 million in Mauritania to 7.2 million in Mali, with the population spread over large areas. Moreover, education has not developed as quickly as in some of the coastal countries, and the proportion of educated individuals remains only a small part of the total population. The number of individuals aged 20 to 24 in higher education ranges from less than one-half percent in Niger, Mali, and Chad to 3 percent in Senegal, and primary school enrollment ranged from 23 percent in Niger to 48 percent in Senegal (World Bank 1985:222). There is a link between educated human resources and economic development (World Bank 1981) and a greater trained human resource base is needed to encourage economic development in Sahelian countries.

The combined lack of financial and trained human resources makes it very difficult for Sahelian economies to absorb large amounts of project foreign assistance in a sustained fashion. As Gray and Martens (1983) point out, Sahelian countries simply do not have the funds to provide for the recurrent costs (operation and maintenance) of projects begun with outside funding. This leads to a greater dependence of these countries on outside foreign aid for continued funding of projects than is found in many of the more developed countries who also receive foreign assistance.

Furthermore, given the problems of the Sahel there has been a tendency to attempt very large projects that will attack these problems in a significant way, despite the fact that there is still little basic information on the costs and benefits of strategies. This had often led to projects being done on an inappropriate scale (Gray and Martens 1983:105). In this situation, the period necessary to establish a workable project is much longer than in some other parts of the world where knowledge, trained management, and local investment capacity are greater. Basically, the unavoidable uncertainties of project implementation are much higher in the Sahel. In the terms of this paper, more aspects of projects need to be negotiated, and this negotiation is likely to occur over a longer period of time.

Goals and Strategies

The basic project documents, such as the Project Paper, form a framework in which negotiation takes place. Despite attempts to formulate a clear and concise plan of action for a particular project, many issues are left vague or unclear. Thus a number of issues must be negotiated as the project begins. Basic among these are the meaning and goals of the project and the strategy to be used to achieve those goals.

Project Papers specify goals in only very general terms. For example, the stated goal of the Mali Renewable Energy Project was two-fold: 1) to improve the quality of life by energizing tasks accomplished by human muscle power; and 2) to alleviate Malian dependence on fossil fuels and firewood (USAID 1978:1). That of the Manantali Resettlement Project was to resettle the people of the Manantali region in a way that would re-establish their pre-project quality of life. In fact, the goals tend to be much more complicated and often multiple. Negotiation focuses on how these general goals ought to be interpreted and which are more important.

For example, in the Mali Renewable Energy Project, the day-to-day goals were somewhat different from those in the PP although there were still two: to solve the energy problems of the rural poor and to increase the institutional capacity of the Solar Energy Lab (Laboratoire d'Energie Solaire) in Bamako. The first of these more or less combined the two PP goals. The second goal of laboratory support however, was initially seen as a strategy to achieve these goals, but during implementation, it became a goal in and of itself.

It soon became apparent that it would be very difficult to pursue these two goals simultaneously, and one needed to be given priority. Among project participants, different actors valued each of these goals differently. In fact, there never was total agreement among all participants on the primary goal of the project.

In the Manantali Resettlement Project, the goal problem was somewhat different, as extended negotiations took place over the question of whether the purpose of the resettlement was to re-establish or improve the quality of life of the resettled population. Although officially the goal was to re-establish the quality of life, certain participants continued to manipulate the project to improve the quality of life of the individuals insofar as possible.

According to some administrators (Landau and Stout 1979), negotiated goals tend to be vaguer than decisions handed down by fiat from a single authority, and do not and cannot exhibit great clarity and precision. However, they are more likely to lie within the "zone of acceptance" (Landau and Stout 1979:151) of the participants, allowing enough agreement for action to be taken.

Once working agreement has been reached about pursuing a particular goal in a particular situation, the negotiation then turns to the subject of how best to reach that goal with the financial and human resources available. Here things are even less constrained by the larger plan, and decisions are constantly made and remade as conditions change. A part of the Mali Renewable Energy Project was village-level studies of energy use. During the project design, various agencies had carefully negotiated a plan of village and regional choice by which all major areas of the country would have been touched by the study. Once implementation started, participants summarily threw out this plan as a poor use of human resources because it required unrealistically high levels of travel by supervisory personnel. Those involved in designing the elaborate earlier plan were not consulted, although some were informed of the decision.

Changing circumstances tend to make the negotiation process more or less continuous. During the process of implementation, emphasis on the various goals changes, particularly when there was never a single goal negotiated in the first place. Secondly, strategies on how to reach a particular goal change as flows of resources change. Finally, the outside environment of the project changes, sometimes substantially over the period of implementation. For example, in the Renewable Energy Project, the solar lab was initially seen as a government research and development agency. During the time the project took place, the Malian government changed its overall policy about the balance between public and private sector development, and the issue of user fees for government agency goods and services became important. For the lab, this meant a reorientation from a research and development agency to one that also sold its technology to the general public. Needless to say, this had an impact on how project implementation was pursued. Goals, meanings, and strategies are not simply negotiated once and accepted by all, but rather they are continually re-negotiated through the life of the project, as long as there are decisions to be made.

The Conditions of Negotiation

How particular meanings and strategies will be bargained and negotiated depends to some extent upon the conditions under which they are negotiated. Some of the major conditions that affect the way in which negotiation takes place in AID projects in Sahelian West Africa are the fact that the project is not an independent social system, the small size of the project group and its reliance on oral communication.

Dependence on Larger Social Systems

The cultural arena formed by a development project is not an independent social system. All the individuals involved are also members of many other overlapping social systems. Although the bureaucratic culture in which each is involved is likely the most salient in development work, individuals also belong to various other social systems associated with ethnic group, political alignment, academic training, and of course, national identity.

These form what Honadle (1979:9) refers to as "hidden agendas," but often they are not so hidden. For example, Doornboos and Lofchie (1971) note the disagreement among different Ugandan ministries over participation in a ranching project funded by AID as each ministry judged the project according to its own criteria. In Mali, there is one particular research agency that is well known for evaluating potential participation in foreign assistance projects by the amount of capital goods the agency will be able to procure through the project.

Although examples of hidden agendas whereby local agencies attempt to use projects for their own ends abound, the issue is not confined to the question of subversion of projects. It is simply normal that each participant's involvement in a project is conditioned not only by his or her role in the project and by personal career considerations, but also by roles in all the other social systems of which the participant is a member. Boyle (1984:4) for example notes one project in which problems arose because American technical assistants tended to see themselves as independent professionals but Sahelian professionals tended to see themselves as government civil servants. In the Mali Renewable Energy Project, I tended to have a very different point of view from the engineers because my discipline led me to concentrate on the people involved while theirs led them to look at the technical efficacy of certain decisions. Although I kept telling them that the villagers would not be very interested in their innovations, they told me that they could not do anything about what the villagers did need. What the villagers needed was more appropriately done by another organization (e.g., procuring better agricultural equipment) or was not both economically and technically feasible (e.g., better water distribution systems).

Differing agendas may affect project goals and strategies in different ways. First, despite differing agendas, a truly negotiated goal may be pursued by all, when a workable "zone of acceptance" is found. Secondly, participants with different agendas may agree on a single goal or strategy, yet manipulate it in different ways to achieve ends corresponding to their differing agendas.[7] For example, in the West Africa Projects, where farm-level studies were done, a single research strategy was agreed upon and pursued. Yet although the goal of project management was to get usable data to produce an overall model of Sahelian farming, my goal was to get data to better understand farm constraints in a particular region and ecological zone. Fortunately these different goals were both consistent with the basic research strategy. Finally, mutual coexistence may result, with participants pursuing different strategies to reach different goals. This was the result in the Renewable Energy Project, where the social scientists went about studying village-level energy needs and the engineers worked on their technology, and we both stopped worrying too much about the fit between the these two facets of the project.

Small Size

The project negotiating group is usually quite small. It includes a few people in management positions in the host country agency, several technical assistants and several AID mission personnel. Because the group is so small, individuals tend to develop "diffuse" rather than "specific" relationships with one another. This is especially true when the project is carried out in a rural area, but even in the capital, project personnel are likely to associate with one another socially and to depend on one another for help in arenas outside the project, as well as to work together in project activities.

The diffuseness is most clear in the case of vehicle use in rural areas, where it is often assumed that vehicles are an important regional resource. Negotiations about vehicle use concern not only project but also private use, and uses not only by project personnel but also by assorted friends and colleagues outside the project. Even in urban areas, project personnel are often called upon to feed, clothe, or otherwise aid project personnel in ways not directly associated with the project.

In addition, the larger groups from which each of the three groups (AID mission personnel, host country personnel, contractors) are recruited are relatively small. This is particularly true in the Sahelian countries where the number of educated nationals is relatively small as is the number of French speaking American technical assistants. Therefore, the people who form a group for a particular project are likely to have some prior experience with one another, often having worked together on a previous project, in that or some other country. This tends to mean that the social systems created by separate projects tend in fact to have some continuity from project to project as individuals find themselves renegotiating similar issues with similar individuals as they move from project to project.

Because of the intense interaction of the three groups of people directly involved in project decision making, and because decision making is so diffuse, overlapping public and project arenas, it is sometimes difficult for people not directly involved in this interaction to participate to any great degree in project decision making. Specifically, it makes it difficult to have much participation by local people who do not interact with AID personnel, host government personnel, and contractors to the same degree that these groups interact with one another.

It often seems that the local population remains peripheral to decision making in projects even where participation is formally highly valued. This is not surprising when they also remain peripheral to the tight social group formed by project personnel. On a field trip, it is common for the different members of the team to eat dinner together and socialize afterwards, but it is much less common to do this with the villagers.

An Oral Culture

Despite the fact that the three major groups of people involved in the development project are well educated and literate, the primary means of carrying and communicating the

355

development project culture is oral. Although these groups
produce great quantities of paper, the function of written
communication is protection, i.e., to protect oneself as a member
of the larger bureaucracies of which one is a part. The purpose
of writing is not primarily to communicate new ideas; rather new
ideas are proposed, discussed, and decided upon without writing
them down. Once decisions are made, the results can be written
in whatever bureaucratic or legal form is necessary.

The emphasis on oral communication is related to the
relatively small size of the social system, and the relative
importance of face-to-face interaction and negotiation among its
members. In any situation of this type, cultures are made and
passed down in oral fashion. The particular situation in which
this culture finds itself has several particular characteristics
that strengthen the need for oral communication.

First, and most important, most development workers are
overworked and tend to place a greater premium on doing rather
than reading. To read everything takes a great deal of time away
from either getting projects done or necessary administrative
demands, and often development workers simply do not want to
spend time wading through great quantities of written documents.
They feel they can learn more and in a clearer fashion through
oral dialogue with others involved than they can through reading
the relevant material. Face-to-face dialogue allows the actual
working out of a "zone of acceptance" and agreement, in a way
that written communication cannot.

Secondly, the fact that the major actors in this social
system come from a variety of cultural traditions also
accentuates the importance of face-to-face verbal interaction.
In this case, host country nationals have an interesting
combination of traditional African and French, bureaucratic and
international training to form their cultural background.
Americans come with their own culture, and usually some kind of
international experience. Thus, all communication is
inter-cultural at one level while being intra-cultural at
another. It is often difficult to communicate when native
languages are not shared, even when people are quite proficient
in additional languages.

Finally, in international relations, the exact phrasing of
written documents is crucial, and precise use of language is
necessary to avoid ambiguity. Alternatively, oral communication,
particularly in more informal situations, is much more flexible.
Questions may be asked and clarifications offered, and much of
the discussion can be off the record. Finally, a formally worded
document can be agreed upon which says all that the participants
want to say but no more.[8]

One of the results of this emphasis on face-to-face verbal interaction is the development of a project language, based largely but not completely on AID and host government jargon. It serves as a kind of shorthand to facilitate communication among the project participants, while at the same time it serves to separate the project group from outsiders. Again as locals do not participate in the same day-to-day fashion, they often do not share this language. Where much of the local population does not speak the national language, as in the Sahel, this can further separate them from project conversations and decision making carried out in this language. Insiders and outsiders can be distinguished by whether they can understand and speak the project jargon.[9]

It is in this context that the whole problem of local participation must be seen. Even in projects where local participation is required, it often becomes peripheral to the process of interaction and negotiation that leads to specific project decisions. Local participants are less likely to attend central meetings, more likely to have language difficulties and more likely to be only intermittently involved in project decisions. Real participation would require more involvement of representatives of the local population in a greater number of project activities and arenas. This is unlikely to happen as long as a development project is only one part of their lives while it is the major professional commitment of the other three groups involved.

If project decisions are negotiated, there needs to be an arena for negotiation. While much negotiation is done informally, the major formal arena is the meeting. Here decisions can be negotiated in a series of face-to-face meetings where a consensus is reached. Sometimes these meetings include large groups; other times they consist of a series of one-to-one meetings and the overall decision is an amalgam of these. This results in the feeling common to development workers that they are always going to meetings. Not only are these meetings interminable, but they often repeat the same ground over and over again. Everyone involved must have an opportunity to contribute, however, for otherwise, a negotiated consensus could not be reached.

Forms of communication, size and context all set conditions for the negotiation of the goals and strategies of development projects. However, it is the people participating who do the negotiation and bargaining through their words and actions. That the development project becomes a social system through the extended negotiation of these people has implications for the choice of development personnel, particularly contractors.

357

Contractor Choice: Looking for Good Negotiators

If everyday or instrumental culture is negotiated and bargained, then all human beings participate in this process to some extent. But effective participation depends in part on the ability to discover hidden agendas and distinguish between overt and covert arguments, and individuals do seem to have different predispositions and capabilities for this. As Bailey (1983:20) notes, the different capacity of individuals to make use of what "officially" does not exist is one of the factors regulating relative power.

Most important among the skills of development workers is the ability to work in small face-to-face decision making groups in forging a consensus. Persons who cannot or will not do this cannot successfully work on development projects, and will not make an impact. The person who at least implicitly recognizes the negotiated quality of development implementation and accepts it is likely to be more successful in participating in those projects. On the other hand, individuals who maintain that there is some "truth" about a particular project or approach, or who resist being manipulative are likely to have a difficult time once they are in the field.

To the extent that some anthropologists at some times have refused to compromise on their suggestions, then they too have been isolated or ignored. On the other hand, very subtle uses of language and very complicated maneuvering may be necessary to find a path that all can agree upon. Insofar as anthropologists are more prepared for this because of their own work, they should be more likely to be successful at this sort of thing than other participants.

In addition to individual abilities in negotiation and compromise, certain behavioral aspects of contractor selection make more sense if they are linked to the negotiation perspective. This includes the emphasis on extra-disciplinary skills; reliance on networks to choose contractors; and the importance of continued involvement at different stages of the project.

As a member of the last group to join the implementation team, the contractor is in a special position. AID and host country agency individuals have normally worked with one another throughout the project design and already know each other. They are then joined by a contractor team, composed of individuals with varying levels of country experience, technical competence, and previous relationships with AID and host country personnel. The success of a project depends heavily on the ability of this group to join the other two in the common endeavor of creating a development project.

If development projects are seen as a series of negotiated decisions among persons of differing agendas, then it comes as no surprise that the skills required of someone involved in a project are more than simple disciplinary competence. The ability to negotiate successfully, to discover covert agendas, to understand the relation between overt and covert agendas, and the ability to manipulate are all essential skills.

Furthermore, negotiating ability is not enough. Although consensus may be forged orally in the small-scale, face-to-face social system, it must be communicated to the larger national systems through a great variety of written documents. The ability to write quickly and clearly is important, as is the ability to know what should and should not be written down. The ability to do one's technical task is only a part of what is needed to participate successfully in development projects.

These additional skills cannot be listed on resumes or evaluated in a simple and direct way. Thus, the major way to know a (potential) contractor is through direct personal knowledge. In fact, the only way to know whether an individual has the negotiating and bargaining skills necessary is by knowing that person, or through the personal testimony of someone who knows that person, in other words, through the networks established by prior development work.

Virtually everyone who has worked on development projects has either met or heard stories about someone whose resume looked good but who turned out to be a total disaster once he or she arrived in the field. The problem is usually based on inability to work with other members of the team/mission/government in constructive ways rather than disciplinary incompetence, although the latter is not unknown. Alternatively, I was once told that a year-long position for an anthropologist would be written into a project extension if I would take the job; otherwise the position would be for six months or less and somehow combined with a technical position. Interestingly, this was on a project where the anthropological contribution was judged to be less than a success. Evidently, a known slightly flawed participant, or a known participant flawed in a predictable way is preferable to a person whose qualifications may look perfect but is unknown.

If the project is not simply negotiated once, but renegotiated again and again over the life of the project as conditions change, any particular agenda can be put forward more successfully by those with long-term involvement in a particular project. This too is a direct corollary of the focus on face-to-face negotiated decision making. The more decisions involve a person directly, the more that person is involved in forming the final product. Conversely, the less one is involved, the smaller the impact.

Many anthropologists have stressed the importance of being involved at the design stage, which forms the basic framework and direction of the development project. From the perspective of this paper, being involved only in design is not sufficient. Rather more participation through all phases of design, implementation, and evaluation is needed if anthropologists wish to have a real impact on how development is done. Anthropological input need not come from only one person in one kind of position, but may come from different individuals involved in different ways over the life of the project.

Conclusions

This process of extended negotiated decision making implies another aspect of development projects; they rarely seem to be consistent or coherent. This is directly attributable to the process of continuing negotiation discussed above. Because each decision must be renegotiated, and because outside constraints change over time, it is not surprising that decisions made at different points are often made in light of different agendas; hence they produce different results. This leads to inconsistencies and even contradictions among the different components of the project.

Several tendencies within project funding tend to make this result even more likely. First, the tendency to do ever larger projects, with ever more components, implies ever more meetings and negotiations among interested parties, and thus ever more inconsistencies and incoherence. Secondly, there is a tendency to view existing development projects as "overplanned," and thus, unable to respond to changing circumstances. In light of this concern, there is a tendency to try for less planning and more adaptability, allowing project implementors to respond to on-the-ground conditions. Although this will likely lead to more flexibility in regard to project implementation, it is also likely that it will lead to more time used for ad hoc decision making, to more inconsistent decisions, and in the worst cases, lead to projects that begin to lack all coherence. However, understanding the social process that produces the inconsistencies may help us deal with them in a more productive fashion.

To this end, this paper has looked at some of the conditions underlying the process of negotiation of goal and strategy within AID development projects in Sahelian West Africa. Although based on one particular set of data, the general process of negotiating and bargaining is likely to be universal. However the extent to which both goals and strategy must be negotiated, as well as the conditions forming the framework of that negotiation, are likely to vary with the level of development of the country and with donor policy. For example, in more developed countries with a track record of projects in a given sector, strategies may not need to be negotiated to the degree that they are in the Sahel, where the technical answers to many questions are simply not available. The "open-endedness" of many Sahelian projects that give large sums of money for vague goals to governments with poor absorptive capacity may well lead to a much higher level of continued negotiation than is the case in other parts of the world where host governments have clearer priorities and are able to fulfill most of those without reliance on foreign assistance.

Notes

[1] This paper is based on my work since 1977 on a variety of development projects funded by the US Agency for International Development (USAID) in the French-speaking countries of West Africa. The major projects on which I have worked include the Purdue University West Africa Projects (AFR-C-1257 and AFR-C-1258), the Mali Renewable Energy Project (688-0217), and the Manantali Resettlement Project (625-0955), all in Mali. I owe much to all those project personnel with whom I have worked over the years, and who helped me understand in many ways how the system really did work. I wish to extend thanks to Allan Hoben and Thomas Painter for their useful comments. The views expressed in this paper are mine alone and should not be attributed to the Agency for International Development, the Government of Mali, or any contracting agency with which I worked.

[2] There are in fact two separate issues here: the perspective of the person in the central agency vs. the perspective of the person in the field; and the problems of implementation vs. those of planning, design, or evaluation. In fact, the existing work tends to focus on the central agency perspective as well as on the problems of planning, design, and evaluation. Although the problem discussed in this paper is that of implementation, the perspective is definitely that of the person in the field.

[3] There are a number of alternatives to a formal competitive bidding process through which smaller projects may be funded. These include such things as Indefinite Quantity Contracts and

Cooperative Agreements where competition occurred on general capability prior to awarding a specific contract. Certain projects are set aside for bidding by only certain kinds of entities, e.g., Minority and Small Businesses, or Land Grant Universities. A formal competitive bidding process has strict legal requirements that makes it very expensive as well as time consuming and thus it is often avoided.

[4] But see below, on the effects of the small pool from which development workers are drawn. While contractors do not necessarily know anything about the project or participants until they are hired, they often are familiar with both beforehand.

[5] There are also variations on these basic groups. For example, in some countries, the host country uses AID funds to contract directly with technical assistants, in contrast to the more common Sahelian procedure where AID contracts directly with the technical assistance firm. This will lead to somewhat different perceptions of reward structures by the technical assistants.

[6] West African Sahelian countries can be defined by their membership in CILSS (Comite Permanent Inter-Etats de Lutte contre La Secheresse dans le Sahel). These countries are Cape Verde, Chad, Gambia, Mali, Mauritania, Niger, Senegal, and Burkina Faso. The World Bank's economic indicators do not cover the countries of Cape Verde or Gambia. In addition, the 1985 version has minimal information on Chad, so its precise ranking on many of their indicators cannot be determined; presumably it is quite low.

[7] In other words, while groups may agree upon a certain symbol, they may agree to disagree on the interpretation of that symbol. Ardener (1975) shows how the symbol of "the wild" is important to both Bakweri men and women, but has significantly different meanings for each.

[8] Doornboos and Lofchie (1971) illustrate the power of written communication in international affairs. Their discussion of Ugandan interpretations of an AID director's letter shows the damage that may be caused by formally writing certain things. Their discussion of information written by the AID mission to Washington shows, on the other hand, how writing can be used to cover one's actual position.

[9] Host country participants may in turn use local languages to reinforce their identity and solidarity with the project population while at the same time separating themselves from foreign participants.

References

Almy, Susan. 1977. Anthropologists and Development Agencies. American Anthropologist 79(2):280-292.

Ardener, Edwin. 1975. Belief and the Problem of Women. In: Perceiving Women. S. Ardener, ed. London: Malaby.

Bailey, F.G. 1983. The Tactical Uses of Passion: An Essay on Power, Reason and Reality. Ithaca, NY: Cornell University Press.

Boyle, W. Philip. 1984. On the Analysis of Organizational Culture in Development Project Planning. Binghamton, NY: Institute for Development Anthropology.

Britan, Gerald and Ronald Cohen, eds. 1980. Hierarchy and Society. Philadelphia: ISHI.

Chambers, Erve. 1985. Applied Anthropology: A Practical Guide. Englewood Cliffs, NJ: Prentice-Hall.

Doornboos, Martin and Michael Lofchie. 1971. Ranching and Scheming: A Case Study of the Ankole Ranching Scheme In: The State of the Nations: Constraints on Development in Independent Africa. M. Lofchie, ed. Berkeley and Los Angeles: University of California.

Epstein, T. Scarlett and Akbar Ahmed. 1984. Development Anthropology in Project Implementation. In: Training Manual in Development Anthropology. W.L. Partridge, ed. Washington: American Anthropological Association and the Society for Applied Anthropology.

Gray, Clive and Andre Martens. 1983. The Political Economy of the 'Recurrent Cost Problem' in the West African Sahel. World Development 11:101-117.

Green, Edward. 1981. Have Degree Will Travel: A Consulting Job for AID in Africa. Human Organization 40:92-94.

Hinshaw, Robert. 1980. Anthropology, Administration and Public Policy. Annual Reviews of Anthropology 9:497-522.

Hoben, Allan. 1980. Agricultural Decision Making in Foreign Assistance: An Anthropological Analysis. In: Agricultural Decision Making. P. Barlett, ed. NY: Academic.

----- 1982. Anthropologists and Development. Annual Reviews of Anthropology 11:349-75.

Honadle, George. 1979. Implementation Analysis: The Case for an Early Dose of Realism in Development Administration. In: International Development Administration. G. Honadle and R. Klauss, eds. NY: Praeger.

Horowitz, Michael. 1979. The Sociology of Pastoralism and African Livestock Projects. Program Evaluation Discussion Paper No. 6. Washington: US Agency of Internationl Development.

Landau, Martin and Russell Stout, Jr. 1979. To Manage Is Not to Control: Or the Folly of Type II Errors. Public Administration Review 39:148-156.

363

Merrey, Douglas. 1984. Myth and Reality: Approaches to Developing LDC Capacity for Improved Irrigation System Management. Paper presented at the Meetings of the American Anthropological Association, Denver.

Nader, Laura. 1974. Up the Anthropologist - Prespectives Gained from Studying Up. In: Reinventing Anthropology. D. Hymes, ed. NY: Random House.

Painter, Thomas. 1985. Development Management in Africa: An Evaluation of the Management Impact of the Niamey Department Development Project (NDD), Niger. Binghamton, NY: Institute for Development Anthropology.

Partridge, William, ed. 1984. Training Manual in Development Anthropology. Washington: American Anthropological Association and the Society for Applied Anthropology.

Practicing Anthropology. 1981. Special issue on Anthropologists in the Agency for International Development 3(2).

Rondinelli, Dennis. 1979. Designing International Development Projects for Implementation. In: International Development Adminstration. G. Honadle and R. Klauss, eds. NY: Praeger.

Rosen, Lawrence. 1984. Bargaining for Reality: The Construction of Social Relations in a Muslim Community. Chicago: Unversity of Chicago Press.

Stevens, Phillips. 1978. The Social Sciences and African Development Planning. Special issue of The African Studies Review 40:1-110.

Tendler, Judith. 1975. Inside Foreign Aid. Baltimore: Johns Hopkins University Press.

US Agency for International Development (USAID). 1978. Mali Renewable Energy Project Paper. Washington, DC: Agency for International Development.

World Bank. 1981. Accelarated Development in Sub-Saharan Africa. Washington, DC: The World Bank.

----- 1985. World Development Report 1985. NY: Oxford University Press for the World Bank.

21. THE INSTITUTE FOR DEVELOPMENT ANTHROPOLOGY: THE CASE FOR ANTHROPOLOGICAL PARTICIPATION IN THE DEVELOPMENT PROCESS[*]

Thayer Scudder

Starting in 1956, the first 20 years of my career were devoted largely to documenting the adverse impacts of development projects on local populations (Scudder, 1972 and Scudder and Colson, 1982). Those projects were dominated by the construction of large-scale dams, which to date have caused the compulsory relocation of millions of low-income people in the tropics and subtropics. Though in some cases local people were supposed to benefit (and indeed over the long run some have), generally speaking the main beneficiary of dam construction was the urban-industrial sector as opposed to the rural areas in which the dams were built.

Large-scale engineering projects are only one example used by ecologists and social scientists to show how development can adversely effect millions of people. Bodley (1982), Eder (in press), Goodland (1982) and many others have documented the negative impacts of development, and incorporation into a wider sociocultural system, on small-scale societies in which gathering, fishing and hunting continue to be important activities. Horowitz (1986) and Salem-Murdock (1984) have done the same for transhumant pastoralists, while the Fleurets (1980) and have noted how the introduction of case cropping and other forms of agricultural change have adversely affected nutrition and consumption among farming populations. Schneider, in this volume, critiques still further the impacts of development on the very people who are supposed to be the main beneficiaries.

---

[*] Editors' Note: In the Preface and elsewhere, we note that this book lacks a separate paper on the ecological aspects of development, and that the field has not been well represented in anthropological research on development. We should note that as the book MS was nearing final editorial treatment, the IDA published Lands at Risk in the Third World (edited by Peter D. Little, and Michael M. Horowitz, Westview, 1987). Thirteen of the eighteen contributors are anthropologists, most of them consultants or research associates of the IDA or similar organizations. This is the first symposium produced by anthropologists on an eco-development theme. Most papers are country case studies of issues such as soil depletion and forest destruction.

Although anthropologists are well aware of the fact that development as planned and implemented has not worked out as it was supposed to and have documented adverse effects in case studies and general articles, there is little agreement in the profession as to what should be done about the situation. Some anthropologists largely ignore it, concentrating on less painful topics. Others are effective critics on paper who choose, however, not to get further involved. Still other anthropologists attempt to work within "the system" to increase the advantages that they believe development could bring to local populations and to mitigate against the disadvantages, while a fourth category, as advocates for disadvantaged people, become adversaries of the developers.

In this paper I describe how the Institute for Development Anthropology is attempting to increase the beneficial impacts of development for low-income populations, and decrease the adverse effects, by working with the very development agencies that are accused (see, for example, Numbers One and Two, 1985, of the Ecologist) of worsening their lot. The major justification for this stance, I believe, is the fact that the large majority of the world's population want development for themselves and their families. Because anthropologists have documented so carefully adverse effects on people who may wish to continue former lifestyles, we run the risk of forgetting that such people constitute a very small minority of the world's population.

During my career I have had the good fortune of visiting and researching some of the more isolated people in the old world tropics (eg., Scudder, 1981a, 1985; Scudder et al., 1982), including the Tonga in Zambia, the Dinka and Nuer in the Sudan, the Bhils in the Indian states of Gujarat and Madhya Pradesh, and low income-spontaneous and government-sponsored emigrants to the frontier zones of Indonesia, Malaysia, the Philippines, and Sri Lanka. Although in many cases development did not allow those involved to meet their expectations for the present and the future, without exception the large majority wanted development.

People's desire for development was especially emphasized for me during several consultancies for the United Nations Development Programme that took me to the Central Sudan. There I worked closely with Sudanese colleagues who were designing and executing socioeconomic surveys among the various Nilotic peoples who would be affected by the construction of the Jonglei Canal. Though some of the scenes that I photographed in Nuer and Dinka cattle camps were almost identical to those pictured in Evan-Pritchard's trilogy on the Nuer, much had happened to the people during the intervening fifty years. Both Nuer and Dinka had been caught up in a 17 year civil war in which they were active participants. After the war, they headed north as labor migrants, Nuer becoming well-known construction workers in the cities. Members of both Nilotic groups invested their profits in cattle, some of which they drove to Malakal and Juba markets for sale, and in shops and other businesses. As Lako (1985) has noted, their problem was not development as such -- for the majority wanted improved schools, and improved medical facilities for themselves and their cattle -- but rather the failure of policy makers at the national level to deliver the type of projects and programs they wanted.

It is important that anthropologists pay close attention to what the people they study want, as opposed to what the anthropologist thinks is "best" for them, but it is also important that we do not gloss over sociocultural constraints to development. More knowledgeable than other professionals about the nature of sociocultural systems, anthropologists have been in the forefront of those showing, on the one hand, that the main development constraints do indeed lie at the center as opposed to the periphery.

In correcting the record, however, we must not forget that sociocultural constraints at the community level also interfere with the realization of local goals for raising living standards. Although we must continue to emphasize the need for local people to participate in all stages of the development process, we need pay more attention to how such participation can be achieved on a continuing basis. In Africa, for example, a major participatory problem is the difficulty that communities of producers have in operating and maintaining viable production and marketing systems. It is one thing for community members to cooperate in building a school or clinic. It is far more difficult, however, to get them to cooperate over the years in efficiently running an irrigation scheme on which their livelihood depends. Factionalism, jealousies, and the persistence (indeed, spread) of sorcery can, and do (Scudder, 1984), pose serious constraints to the achievement of a people's own development goals. Anthropologists need not only research such problems in a rapidly changing world, but also facilitate the emergence of socially sound institutions to cope with them.

THE INSTITUTE FOR DEVELOPMENT ANTHROPOLOGY: INCORPORATION, GOALS, AND MILESTONES

1. Incorporation and Goals

I think four factors explain the speed with which the founding directors (Brokensha, Horowitz, and Scudder) established

367

IDA. First, soon after we met we learned that we all shared the same assumptions and the same goal. The assumptions were that development and equity were not incompatible and that an organization run by anthropologists could focus its attention more on people as opposed, for example, to water management and land productivity. Assuming that improved social analysis could prove beneficial, our goal was to use our anthropological understanding to help low-income populations better realize their aspirations through greater involvement in planning, implementing, managing, and evaluating development projects and programs in which they were the principal risk-takers.

Second, we knew from our own experience as individual consultants that we would have more influence if we had the backing of an organization like IDA behind us. Also, we were convinced that through such an organzation we would be able to play a brokering role by involving more anthropologists in development work. That has proved to be the case. The anthropologists and other scientists who have participated in IDA contracts number well over 100.

Third, I think each of us realized that, personally speaking, it was now or never. In my own case, I had collaborated with four colleagues during 1962-64 to set up an even more ambitious Institute for Development Planning (IDP). In preparing this chapter I went through our 1962-64 correspondence and was rather amazed by similarities in conceptualizing IDA and IDP. In the 1960s we drew up position papers, solicited CVs, approached foundations for establishment grants, and considered affiliating with a number of European institutions to get us off the ground. Three of us (George Appell, Francisco Benet, and me) were prepared, we thought, to work full time for the Institute if it got off the ground. But it never did. Much of the time we were isolated from each other: Appell in the Pacific, Benet in the Middle East and Europe, and me in Africa and the United States. This made it difficult to reach a consensus on our goals and how to realize them. As time passed we drifted apart. Then Benet, who had been the driving force, died in a tragic accident in Iran. This experience taught me that one can overplan an idea. So when a second chance came to establish an institute in the mid-1970s, I was prepared, as were Brokensha and Horowitz, to incorporate immediately.

The fourth factor explaining our early success was Michael Horowitz's willingness to take over the administrative responsibility for incorporating IDA in the state of New York.

2. Milestones

During our first few years of existence, IDA was little more than the sum of its three directors, with annual revenue not rising above $50,000 until 1979. Looking back on our history today, I can see a number of major milestones that I would like to mention briefly. They are ordered chronologically rather than in order of importance. Our first grant was to organize a workshop for the United States Agency for International Development (USAID) in Washington, D.C., on Rural Development in Yemen (Brokensha et al., 1977). I mention it as a milestone not so much because it was our first contract but because it was our first workshop and produced one of our first publications. Since then we have organized seven workshops, shared responsibility for another three with Clark University, and, for an eleventh workshop, developed a reader, provided resource personnel, and written the final report. The first nine workshops were funded by USAID and were largely for AID personnel. The tenth was a workshop on Planning Fuelwood Projects, which was convened by the Food and Agriculture Organization of the United Nations (FAO) in Lilongwe at the invitation of the government of the Republic of Malawi (Brokensha et al., 1983, 1984).

We are proud of our record with workshops, which we believe have played an important role in raising the consciousness of government officials not just about the importance of relating development interventions to local ecological and sociocultural conditions, but also about the need for local participation at all stages of the project cycle. Although I suspect my colleagues have different rankings, I would list our two workshops on Pastoralism and African Livestock Development (Horowitz, 1979), the Malawi workshop on Planning Fuelwood Projects, and our most recent workshop, on lands at risk in the Third World, as our most important. The pastoralism workshops were important because they raised AID consciousness about the efficiency and effectiveness of existing livestock management systems for arid and semiarid habitats.

The fuelwood workshop was important because for the first time the participants were officials from Third World countries. Lasting three weeks, that workshop drew 29 participants from 11 eastern and southern African nations. Its purpose was to familiarize them with how to integrate fuelwood into farming systems planning at household and community levels and with the sorts of information that are necessary to plan effective fuelwood projects. Looking to the future, we hope that this workshop will be a prototype for more of the same kind to familiarize host-country personnel -- not just officials but also producers -- with procedures for planning and implementing better production systems for farmers, herders, and fishermen, as well as for the landless. The conference on lands at risk dealt, in an interdisciplinary fashion, with complex interrelations between ecology and development. Topics discussed included the ecological implications of unequal access to resources, the future of indigenous resource management systems, and the penetration of farming households into the Sahelian drylands of Africa.

We are also proud of IDA's publications. In addition to shorter reports, we expanded into books in 1982 with a volume on the effects of compulsory relocation on Navajos (Scudder, 1982). Currently we are in the process of bringing out a series of Monographs in Development Anthropology with Westview Press. The inaugural monograph deals with development anthropology in West Africa (Horowitz and Painter, 1985), while the second volume will present the results of the lands at risk workshop. The third volume will address development anthropology in East Africa. Other publications include IDA's newsletter Development Anthropology Network (first published in late 1981), which carries short articles on development topics as well as news about the Institute, and a Working Paper series.

The next milestone was a joint field trip that the three directors took to the Sahel over the 1976-77 Christmas holidays. Funded by AID, and intended to identify "grassroots" projects in a number of Sahelian countries, this trip enabled us to evolve our common perspective in the field and to write up together the results of our efforts. Though there have been no further opportunities for all three directors to work together overseas, currently Horowitz and Scudder are co-directing a major activity in the Senegal River Basin of West Africa.

A third milestone was reached in 1979. This was our global state-of-the-art evaluation of the development potential of land settlement in the tropics and subtropics with special emphasis on policy implications. It was important to IDA not so much because it was our first large funding but because it was a self-directed policy study that enabled IDA to sponsor fieldwork outside of Africa. IDA's settlement proposal was unsolicited: we designed it because we thought it was important. Although the funding process took two years, the eventual grant served as recognition that IDA personnel had topical expertise with worldwide comparative implications in addition to our demonstrated, but geographically constrained, areal and linguistic expertise. The global settlement evaluation also enabled us to fund intensive field research in Egypt, Sudan, Nepal, and Sri Lanka by Third World students working for higher degrees. Moreover, it gave us the chance to evolve a procedure for working with senior host-country colleagues that we have tried to build into our subsequent contracts.

370

The year 1981 proved to be a milestone for us -- a real watershed in IDA's short history. During that year we were awarded by AID our first Indefinite Quantity Contract (IQC) for rural development design and evaluation. In collaboration with Clark University we were also awarded by AID a Cooperative Agreement on Area Development. Renamed the Settlement and Resource Systems Analysis Cooperative Agreement (SARSA), this was renewed in 1984 for a four-year period (during 1984 we also were awarded our second rural development IQC).

ETHICAL ISSUES

Because our main sources of funds are USAID, the World Bank, FAO, and the United Nations Development Programme (UNDP), we are occasionally asked whether there is an inconsistency between our stated goals and our reliance on agencies that "are part of an imperialistic establishment seeking to promote western dominance around the world." Relating specifically to AID, that phrase was put to IDA's directors when they were interviewed by an editor of The Anthropology Newsletter (see "Profile of an Anthropologist," 21, no. 9:4-5).

Although problems are associated with such sponsorship, I consider them to be more institutional and developmental than ideological. Generally speaking, we are not uncomfortable with our sponsors. As we noted in the newsletter interview "foreign economic assistance of no Northern industrial country is disinterested. . . . But it is a gross mistake to look on AID . . . as homogeneous; there are many AID officers who are genuinely committed to human rights, to income redistribution . . . and to development from below." We actively seek, or are sought by, such individuals, in AID, the World Bank, and other funding agencies. In working closely with them we try to strengthen their hand by offering them useful perspectives and information. Furthermore, we can and do reject invitations to participate in projects or to work in countries that make us uncomfortable. That said, it is important to state that to date we have had little difficulty in finding worthwhile projects that are largely compatible with our goals. As national and multilateral funding agencies go, AID compares very favorably in regard to our major areas of concern. AID, for example, was one of the first development agencies to include social and environmental impact studies as part of its project planning process. AID was also a pioneer in institutionalizing the monitoring and evaluation of its projects and in directing them toward low-income populations. Our problems are not so much with the goals of such agencies as AID and the World Bank as they relate to social and environmental soundness, to focusing assistance on the household and community level, and to local participation, but with the difficulties these agencies face in implementing those goals.

Up to this point I have tried to present an IDA answer to the question of working with agencies like AID. Let me now follow with a more personalized answer. To me, the main question is whether development anthropology funded by agencies like AID and the World Bank actually has the potential of helping low-income populations to raise their living standards and quality of life in a nonenvironmentally degrading way, and to increase, through local institution building, their ability to compete for scarce resources.

Development anthropology, like any field of knowledge, can be beneficial or destructive to local populations and their habitat. I have satisfied myself that most of the work done by the Institute for Development Anthropology is in the short- and medium-term interests of local populations. I am less certain, but somewhat optimistic, that it is also in their long-term interests.

Throughout my career most of my research has dealt with the local impacts of such large-scale engineering projects as dams and irrigation schemes. Often, impacts have been negative, and in my writings I have emphasized that fact and criticized the projects' implementing agencies. So how is it that I now justify working for the very agencies that I have criticized previously?

The answer is relatively simple. Large-scale engineering projects the world over are very difficult to stop. Furthermore, they have very little, if anything, to do with structural reforms in political economies at national and international levels. Let me be more specific. When the World Bank decided not to fund the Kossou Dam in the Ivory Coast, the United States stepped in for political reasons, with then Vice President Humphrey being sent over as the President's personal emissary to show the U.S. flag in a formerly French-dominated area. Construction then proceeded. When the World Bank, under pressure from the United States, withdrew as a funder of the Aswan High Dam, the Soviet Government stepped in as a bilateral donor. Since that date the USSR has designed and planned implementation of some of the largest water-resource development projects in the world. China currently is formulating a complicated mathematical model to "optimize" development of the lower basin of the Yellow River, a model involving major water transfers that will have a tremendous impact, for better or worse, on local peoples and their habitats. Throughout the War for Zimbabwean Independence, the Central African Power Corporation, with joint membership from Rhodesia and Zambia, continued to meet regularly not just to run the

372

Kariba Dam installations but also to plan future downstream dams. And throughout the Vietnam War, the Mekong Secretariat, with representatives from all the member states, including at that time North Vietnem, continued to plan the development of the Mekong River.

At present a number of bilateral and multilateral donors (including the World Bank, UNDP, UNICEF, the United Kingdom, Sweden, the Federal Republic of Germany, Japan, the United States, and Saudi Arabia) are involved in funding Sri Lanka's Mahaweli Ganga Project. Saudi Arabia and other gulf states are relatively recent funders of Third World development, but since the increase in petroleum prices over a decade ago their cultural and developmental impact has been considerable. They are major backers of the International Fund for Agricultural Development, which carries out feasibility studies of, and provides funding for, projects designed for the rural poor. Gulf funds are especially evident in the Islamic nations of West Africa, where Saudi assistance has funded new mosques in various capital cities and Gulf States have contributed to dam construction along the Senegal and Niger Rivers.

The point is this: regardless of its ideological stance and the nature of a nation's political economy, large-scale river basin development projects are going to continue. The options, therefore, are to stand on the sidelines complaining about the negative impacts of such projects but having relatively little effect on their number, location, design and purpose, or to try to influence -- both from within and, where necessary, from without -- their planning, implementation, and management in ways that incorporate local populations in project benefits in an environmentally sound way. That is what the Institute for Development Anthropology is trying to do.

We select development projects and countries that we believe have potential for low-income populations. Though such populations do not hire us, do not pay us, and more often than not do not know of our existence, we nonetheless see them as our clients. That means we try to expand project benefits to reach the local population in culturally relevant ways while trying to minimize negative impacts. Within development agencies we work closely with individuals whom we believe are sympathetic to our views and are in a position to push them, knowing full well such agencies and individuals have their own agendas that may not be compatible with "people-first" projects. In writing our reports, we have never changed our conclusions under sponsor pressure, responding rather to substantive and editorial critique in the same way in which one responds in redrafting academic papers.

IDA is tax-exempt and takes no partisan political positions.

But IDA staff members do get involved as private citizens in causes of concern to them. Let me give two examples. When opposition leader Amos Sawyer, who had worked on an USAID-funded IDA agricultural sector assessment, was imprisoned by the Doe Government in Liberia, Horowitz and Salem-Murdock lobbied for his release, receiving an appreciative letter from Sawyer after he left prison. In my own case, I have lobbied against projects or plans that involve forced community relocation. In 1978 the Navajo Tribe hired IDA to assess expected impacts of forced relocation on thousands of Navajo should Public Law 93-531 be passed. In our 1979 report we emphasized that Congress had grossly underestimated the numbers of Navajo involved, the financial costs of their relocation, the multidimensional stress that would be inflicted on the relocatees, and the adverse relationships that would embroil the relocatees, the receiving host population, and the Navajo tribal authorities for years to come. Although IDA involvement stopped with the issuing of the report, I personally have continued up to the present, and without fee, to help the Navajo Tribal Council's Navajo and Hopi Land Dispute Commission build constituencies to influence Congress to opt for other ways for resolving this dispute over land in the arid and semi-arid west. It is not that I am pro Navajo, but rather that I am opposed to forced relocation as a solution to a dispute for which there are clearly more acceptable options that are in the interests of both the Hopi and the Navajo.

In summary, I believe it is possible to work within the system, although the risk of providing merely "window dressing" to meet unpopular requirements for what USAID calls "social soundness analysis" is ever present. Yet if my assessment is correct that many projects are going to go ahead regardless, then it is worth trying to make them more relevant to local populations and to improve their long-term environmental soundness. Should it become clear subsequently that the agencies involved are operating in bad faith, informed development anthropologists have the option of using their knowledge to bring pressure to bear on the offending organizations.

IMPACTS

At IDA our intention is to do work that will have both academic and developmental impacts. On the academic side, we believe that our efforts to date have improved our knowledge of how local production systems operate, of how societies respond to development interventions, and of how development agencies impose constraints on the very development that they are supposed to foster. We believe that we have contributed methodologically to the formulation of procedures for rapid rural appraisal. Developmental impacts are harder to assess because it is difficult to disaggregate the factors that lead to project failure and success. Another problem is that ten years is too short a time period after which to assess impacts, with any degree of reliability, because the development process takes time. Early successes, for example, can turn into failures and vice versa.

Although analyzing IDA's impact on development outcomes would be premature, two points have become increasingly clear since IDA's incorporation. First, done by competent social scientists, social analysis "for economic development is not simply socially desirable; it is demonstrably cost effective" (Kottak, 1985:326). Second, IDA activities to date have had a favorable impact on the development process. Three of those activities are described below.

1. Workshops on Pastoralism

IDA's two workshops on African pastoralism and livestock development -- the second of which "formed the basis for the USAID Africa Bureau's 1982 Livestock Development Assistance Strategy" (Atherton 1984) -- constitute along with various IDA publications perhaps the first major effort to demonstrate to policy makers from USAID, the World Bank and other development agencies the importance of building on existing production systems of pastoral communities and the necessity of predicating interventions on clear understandings of socioeconomic and ecological realities. In Horowitz's words (personal communication 1986), IDA's impact "has been first to demystify pastoral practice," by striving, for example, "to provide evidence contrary to the tragedy of the common notion which (in concert with the mythical understanding of pastoral practice) led to coercive attempts at sedentarization, privatization of range, and stock reduction."

Another key issue IDA has raised is the need to take account of the multiple uses and multiple users of an area, which produces a complex set of ethnic, ecological, and socioeconomic exchange relations. Behind this issue, and often implicitly ignored by development planners, are the different sets of values different groups employ to manage their lives, which give rise to goals that may conflict with those of development.

In an influential document, The Sociology of Pastoralism and African Livestock Projects (Horowitz 1979), IDA provided a critique of many assumptions commonly made by USAID projects

375

about the sociology and ecology of pastoral production and analyzed the consequences of the discrepancy between these assumptions and reality. Stating that "we ignore the local scene at our peril" (p. ix) -- by top-down development and the effort to replicate Western commercial livestock production systems -- the paper raises various points including questioning the assumption of pastoral responsibility for range degradation, identifying an anti-nomad ideology as behind efforts at sedentarization, and signaling the role of sedentarization and agriculturalist usurpation of rangelands in causing overgrazing. Thus, one of the most consistent themes of IDA's involvement with pastoral development has been the critique of the poor understanding that prevails of pastoral production systems, particularly the myths of pastoral mismanagement of resources along with various unexamined ideas about "typical" herders that ignore real variation. For example, Horowitz (1986) critiques a pastoral development project in Niger, in which plans for the establishment of pastoral associations and pastoral land units were based on the assumption that a pattern of large-scale social groupings found in neighboring Chad also applied to southeastern Niger. Horowitz states, "As social analyst on the appraisal team, drawing on several years of intimacy with the area, I concluded that the sociological conditions claimed for Chad did not obtain in the proposed project region, and that neither pastoral associations nor pastoral units were likely to be successfully introduced" (p. 260).

By contrast with donors, IDA finds numerous highly rational and adaptive aspects of traditional management and advocates their incorporation in development. These include pastoral mobility, indigenous systems of control over water and pasture, decentralization of decision making on issues of animal husbandry, the herding of multiple animal species and age groups, animal exchange and circulation within the society, and complex interrelationships with other users of the territory. Given that few interventions, other than veterinary actions, support traditional management, Horowitz (p. 272), in a depressing but accurate assessment of development projects, finds that "none of the range management, hydrologic, genetic, and marketing . . . interventions had measurably increased production, enhanced producer income, or retarded environmental degradation."

Finally, in addition to the critique of pastoral development, IDA has recently been concerned to alert planners to the significantly changing role of women in the pastoral household economy and production system in general. As a result of the male out-migration for wage labor, a process of "feminization" of pastoralism is occurring. The increased burden of labor on the women affects many aspects of the pastoral economy. For example, the capacity to make long-distance migration is reduced, and this situation significantly affects herd structure and composition. The implications of this for development must be carefully followed and worked out. In particular, projects must avoid falling into the trap of communicating with only the men, as the women may in fact be carrying on the actual work now.

2. Resettlement and Settlement

IDA's resettlement and settlement expertise has had a measurable impact on donor policies. In 1977, Michael Cernea, Sociological Adviser to the World Bank, contracted with IDA to prepare a paper on "Policy Implications of Compulsory Relocation in River Basin Development Projects" for a Bank seminar series dealing with sociological contributions to development planning. Critical of the Bank's record, some of the ideas in that paper, along with ideas generated by the research of others -- including David Butcher, Elizabeth Colson, Jasper Ingersoll, and Hussein Fahim, were subsequently incorporated within the Bank's 1980 Operational Manual Statement (OMS) on "Social Issues Associated with Involuntary Resettlement in Bank-Financed Projects" (OMS 2.33).

While I do not believe that the Bank's Statment goes far enough, nonetheless, as a significant step forward, it has had an impact on resettlement plans formulated by member countries. In a recent review, for example, Cernea (oral communication) concluded that the 1980 OMS has been associated with improved treatment of resettlement issues by both national and local governments. He noted that, furthermore, projects using anthropologists and sociologists produced better resettlement plans.

In regard to land settlement projects, AID published the 1981 Executive Summary of IDA's global evaluation (Scudder, 1981b), distributing several thousand copies around the world. IDA's more recent evaluation of the World Bank's experience with land settlement projects was published by the Bank in 1985. In these reports we argue that much more attention should be paid to both host and settler beneficiaries with respect to such issues as infrastructure, production, and management. Hosts, we argue should be given priority treatment, and development must be better integrated with environmental planning and natural resource management.

In Latin America, IDA reports on land settlement have argued the importance of developing market linkages between settlement areas and the encompassing region and have critiqued large-scale cattle ranches in the humid tropics, arguing instead for more

377

diversified small-holder production systems that include tree crops. Elsewhere, IDA's annual reviews of the settlement component on the Accelerated Mahaweli Project (Scudder, 1980, 1981a; Scudder and Wimaladharma, 1983, 1985) have influenced the relevant government agencies to pay more attention to settler net incomes, diversification of production systems at the household level, employment generation, water-user associations run by settlers rather than by government officials, and regional planning. Furthermore the current governmental emphasis on enterprise development for creating non-farm employment is a direct result of recommendations in IDA reports. In the Sudan, IDA played an important role in establishing within the Rahad Corporation, a social and economic research unit. One of the first, if not the first, of such units to be established within a Sudanese parastatal organization, it served as the prototype for institutionalizing, with World Bank funding, a similar unit in the Sudan Gezira Scheme.

3. River Basin Development

For a variety of reasons (Scudder, 1981b), river basin development in the tropics has yet to realize its potential for environmental rehabilitation, raising living standards among local populations, and catalyzing a process of regional development in river basin and inter-basin areas. While IDA has attempted in a number of publications and reports to broaden the perspective of planners, and to focus that perspective more specifically on the resident population of river basins, currently the Institute has the opportunity to advise the United States Agency for International Development, the Organization for the Development of the Senegal Valley (OMVS), and relevant host country institutions in Mali, Mauritania, and Senegal on development strategies for the Senegal Basin.

When dams are constructed, the technical issues are such that a firm of consulting engineers is selected to oversee the construction process. The task of that firm is not only to make sure that the various contractors build the dam according to specifications, but also to provide advice on unforeseen problems that may arise. Since IDA's inception we have been interested in applying the concept of consulting engineers to river basins as a whole -- with IDA fielding over an extended time period a team of consulting river basin development experts. The USAID mission in Senegal has recently given us that opportunity.

At the invitation of Vito Stagliano, head of the AID Senegal Mission's River Basin Development Office, I was invited to visit the Senegal and Gambia River Basins in March and April, 1985. As a result of that visit, and with the support of Stagliano and

Mission Director Sarah Jane Littlefield, IDA submitted a
proposal, under the direction of Horowitz and me, which was
funded on a one-year basis in the fall of 1985. In March to
April, 1986 IDA fielded its first five-person team, which was
composed of an agriculturalist, an economist, a geographer, and
two anthropologists. In the report of our mission we made a
number of recommendations as to how controlled releases from the
upriver Manantali Dam and development aid could improve local
production systems, and as to how U.S. assistance could be made
more cost effective. Although it is too soon to know the effects
of our recommendations on policy and, if acted upon, on the
resident population, we were encouraged to submit an expanded
five-year program that would focus on how best to use an
artificial flood for developmental and environmental purposes.
In the meanwhile our second team wll be examining a wider range
of policy options in the Upper, Middle, and Lower Basin regions
in June and July, 1986. Once again our focus will be on how the
strengths of local production and marketing systems can be
enhanced, and the weaknesses offset, by environmentally sound
development aid.

PROBLEMS

As I see it, IDA's main problem is that all too frequently
project goals and plans that we support are not implemented.
Reasons for this vary. Such unexpected events as natural
disasters or wars may preclude implementation, or host country
priorities may change following changes in government.
Unfortunate as such circumstances may be, a more common
occurrence is for the implementing agency to deemphasize plans
and goals relating to the beneficiaries and their habitat --
plans and goals of particular concern to IDA. These include, for
example, plans to facilitate local participation, or to
incorporate the host population within a settlement project, or
to provide promised benefits to "development refugees" who must
give up their land and homes to reservoir basins or other
encroaching development projects. Although governments may agree
to such goals and plans because donor agencies insist on them,
once the loan agreement is signed and funds become available, the
implementing agencies proceed with their own agendas in spite of
loan agreements that contain mechanisms for protecting local
populations and their resource base.

Failure of implementing agencies to observe loan covenants
is a very serious and common problem. Though individuals within
the donor agencies may be concerned, and supervisory missions may
complain, very rarely do donors stop loan disbursements once a

project is under way -- especially if major components of the project, like dam and irrigation construction, are proceeding at a "reasonable" pace. IDA does not yet have a policy for dealing with such situations even though they can undermine our efforts -- converting social soundness analysis, environmental analysis, and planning for beneficiaries into fruitless exercises.

IDA's experience has made us well aware of the problem, and IDA staff are trying to develop a successful counter-strategy. Meanwhile we cope on an individual basis. In my case, I have a strategy that emphasizes four approaches. The first is to build partial safeguards into the project plan in the form of required supervision, monitoring, and evaluation of what I consider to be key components. In connection with World Bank contracts, I have concluded that the Bank supervises most carefully those project components it funds; hence, where a project involves forced relocation, it is important that sufficient Bank funds are involved for relocation purposes to ensure frequent supervision. The second approach is to build a training component into the project in hopes of sensitizing the relevant officials to the importance of involving local communities in project benefits.

The third approach is to work closely with concerned individuals, within both the donor agency and the host country, whom one can "bombard with ammunition" if implementation is faulty. In the case of host country colleagues, I have found during my recent work in Asia that these should be of two sorts -- government officials with influence and academics and private citizens (including agents for private voluntary organizations working with local communities) who have ready access to the project area. As for the fourth approach, that is by far the most difficult. It involves formation of a strong constituency to bring pressure to bear on both implementing and donor agencies. For that to be effective, one has to have access to up-to-date information -- hence the importance of monitoring -- and one has to have access to people within (and where necessary, outside) the funding and implementing agencies who can and will make use of that information. Such access is very difficult for someone who is outside of the system. On the other hand, if constituency building and pressure are too apparent and embarrassing to donors and implementing agencies, consultancies may be terminated and the constituency builder may find herself or himself outside the system after all. Our consultants must proceed with caution, bearing in mind their responsibilities to IDA, to the local population, and to the contracting agency or agencies, but I remain somewhat optimistic that the strategy outlined above will prove helpful for implementing development plans in an appropriate fashion.

Acknowledgments

Although this chapter represents my personal assessment of
the history of the Institute for Development Anthropology, I wish
to thank my colleagues at the Institute for their detailed
commentary on an earlier version.

APPENDIX

THE INSTITUTE FOR DEVELOPMENT ANTHROPOLOGY:

NATURE AND HISTORY

The Institute for Development Anthropology (IDA) is a
tax-exempt, independent, and nonprofit scientific research and
educational organization incorporated in the state of New York.
We are headquartered at Binghamton where we have a resident staff
of 13, including a Director, an Administrative, Grants and
Contracts Officer, a Comptroller, four Research Associates (all
with Ph.D. degrees), two Editorial Associates, and two full-time
and two part-time Research Assistants. In addition we have two
full-time Research Associates on assignment in Niger, two in
Tunisia, and one in Mali.

IDA came into existence during 1976. Although the three
founding directors (Brokensha, Horowitz, and Scudder) all played
an equal role as conceptualizers and policymakers during the
Institute's early years, Horowitz undertook the formidable work
of arranging for incorporation and of running IDA out of his
State University of New York, Binghamton office until he found
our present office in 1979. He also hired IDA's first staff.

Vera Beers joined IDA in 1980 as an Administrative
Assistant/Secretary and subsequently became our full-time
Administrative, Grants and Contracts Officer. Our initial
recruits as Binghamton-based Research Associates were Peter
Little and Muneera Salem-Murdock. Though their Ph.D.
dissertations dealt, respectively, with Kenya and the Sudan, once
at IDA they were able to broaden significantly both their areal
and topical skills.

Little worked in Pakistan and enlarged his expertise in

natural resource management, while Salem-Murdock worked in
Tunisia, Niger, and Jordan, and expanded her expertise to river
basin development. They were joined subsequently by Michael
Painter and by Thomas Painter on his return from research in
Niger. M. Painter pioneered IDA's work in Latin America, while
T. Painter consolidated and added to our work in Niger and the
Sahel. Though IDA never has been Africa-bound, sub-Saharan
Africa -- and especially the Sahelian countries from Cape Verde
to Somalia -- remains a major focal point. Two of our overseas
Research Associates (Walter West and Thomas Price) are currently
working on separate projects in Niger, a third (Curt Grimm) is
working with population resettlement in connection with Mali's
Manantali Dam, and the other two (Phil Boyle and Barbara Larson)
are involved with the Central Tunisian Development Project.

Our research associates are fully responsible for managing
specific contracts dealing with both programs and projects, but
policymaking and overall direction is primarily the
responsibility of the three founding directors. Though none of
the directors is salaried (each having a full-time professorial
appointment), Michael Horowitz, as resident director, is
responsible for the day-to-day running of the Institute. As for
David Brokensha and me, we have the much less arduous job of
running our one-person "regional offices" from our University of
California, Santa Barbara and California Institute of Technology
bases.

In addition to the above staff resources, we have access to
Professors Conrad Arensberg and Elizabeth Colson, who constitute
IDA's Advisory Council; more than 30 development specialists who
are members of our College of Fellows; and a computerized roster
of over 580 associates classified according to area, language,
and topical expertise. The roster lists agronomists, economists,
engineers, and other specialists as well as anthropologists.

Our Binghamton office consists of 13 rooms on two floors of
an office building in the city center. The largest room contains
our library of over 8,000 titles, cross-referenced topically and
geographically. Office equipment includes three IBM PC-XTs, an
IBM Displaywriter, an Osborne, six Leading Edge PCs, an online
telex, and a facsimile copier. To improve communications further
we have recently linked up my Caltech office with Binghamton via
modem and increasingly supply field workers with microcomputers.

The Institute's largest single source of funds has been the
United States Agency for International Development (AID). AID
funding comes to us in four ways. Of major importance is a
Cooperative Agreement on Settlements and Natural Resource Systems
Analysis and Management (SARSA), which we share with Clark
University. The purpose of this cooperative Agreement, which has

been renewed through fiscal year 1988, is to provide AID missions abroad with long-term, in-country research and assistance in program planning, monitoring, and evaluation. Core funding from the agreement provides a substantial portion of the salaries of several IDA staff members.

A second significant revenue source for the Institute for Development Anthropology is an AID Rural Development Indefinite Quantity Contract (IQC) for the design and evaluation of rural development projects, awarded to IDA on the basis of competitive bidding. Our present IQC, the Institute's second, runs from August 1984 through July 1986. The IQC mechanism gives AID access to contractors who carry out a variety of short-term assignments, including workshops, project appraisals and evaluations, country profiles, and the like. The IQC adds breadth and depth to our expertise. The other two routes for AID funding are AID-initiated financing of specific activities and self-directed policy studies proposed by IDA to the Agency. Although neither currently contributes greatly to IDA's ongoing operations, both played very important roles in the past. The Institute responds directly to Requests for Proposals circulated by AID; it also contracts with host-country governments that receive program or project support from AID.

After AID, our most important sources of funds are the FAO, the World Bank, and UNDP. We have also received funds from such organizations as the UN Sudano-Sahelian Office, the Ford Foundation, and the Navajo Tribal Council. Such smaller contractors continue to be financially important to us and they enable us to broaden our base of support.

To date our activities have taken us to more than 30 countries in Africa, Asia (including China and India), Latin America, the Middle East, and North America. Overseas activities include involvement in all stages of the project/program cycle including identification, appraisal, monitoring, midterm review, and evaluation. They also include self-directed research, completion of social institutional profiles of specific countries, and training of host country officials. IDA also makes a special effort to include in all overseas activities host country colleagues.

As an IDA director, I have been especially fortunate in getting colleagues to work with me on a number of assignments where their expertise offset my areas of ignorance. Thus, during the land settlement evaluation Dr. Hussein Fahim and Dr. Mohamed el Sammani traveled with me in the Sudan while Professor Tjondronegoro organized a joint tour of settlement projects in Sumatra and Sulawezi. More recently Sammani and I have worked together with Professor Abdel Ghaffar in designing, with Ford

383

Foundation support, a socioeconomic research unit for the Sudan's Rahad Corporation, while Kapila P. Wimaladharma, a senior official in Sri Lanka's Ministry of Lands and Land Development, and I have collaborated in making five annual evaluations of the settlement component of the Accelerated Mahaweli Project. In the Senegal Basin, Michael Horowitz and I began collaborating earlier this year with Papa Dalla Fall, a regional economist based in Dakar.

References

American Anthropological Association. 1980. Profile of an Anthropologist -- Institute for Development Anthropology: Social Equity Must Be Part of Development. Anthropology Newsletter 21, no. 9:4-5.

Atherton, Joan S. 1984. The Evolution of a Donor Assistance Strategy for Livestock Programs in Subsaharan Africa. In: Livestock Development in Subsaharan Africa: Constraints, Prospects, Policy, edited by James R. Simpson and Phylo Evangelou. Boulder: Westview Press.

Bodley, John H. 1982. Victims of Progress. Palo Alto: Mayfield Publishing Company.

Brokensha, David W., Michael M. Horowitz, and Thayer Scudder. 1977. The Anthropology of Rural Development in the Sahel. IDA Publication, out of print.

Brokensha, David W., Bernard Riley, and Alfonso Peter Castro. 1983. Fuelwood Use in Rural Kenya: Impacts of Deforestation. IDA Publication.

-----. 1984. Fuelwood, Agroforestry, and Natural Resource Management: The Development Significance of Land Tenure and Other Resource Management/Utilization Systems. IDA Publication.

Ecologist. 1985. The World Bank: Global Financing of Impoverishment and Famine. Vol 15, No 1/2.

Eder, James F. In press. On the Road to Tribal Extinction: Depopulation, Deculturation, and Maladaption among the Batak of the Philippines. Berkeley: University of California Press.

Fleuret, Anne and P. Fleuret. 1980. Nutritional Implications of Staple Food Crop Successions in Usambara, Tanzania. Human Ecology, 8:311-327.

Goodland, Robert. 1982. Tribal Peoples and Economic Development: Human Ecologic Considerations. Washington, D.C.: The World Bank.

Horowitz, Michael M. 1979. The Sociology of Pastoralism and African Livestock Projects. Washington, D.C.: USAID Program Evaluation Discussion Paper No. 5, No. 6.

-----. 1986. Ideology, Policy, and Praxis in Pastoral Livestock

Development. In: Anthropology and Rural Development in West
Africa, edited by Michael M. Horowitz and Thomas P. Painter.
Boulder: Westview Press.
Horowitz, Michael M. and Thomas M. Painter, editors. 1985. The
Anthropology of Rural Development in West Africa. Boulder,
Col.: Westview Press.
Kottak, C. P. 1985. When People Don't Come First: Some
Sociological Lessons from Completed Projects. In: Putting
People First: Sociological Variables in Rural Development,
edited by Michael M. Cernea. New York: Oxford University Press
for the World Bank.
Lako, George Tombe. 1985. The Impact of the Jonglei Scheme on the
Economy of the Dinka. African Affairs 84(no. 334):15-38.
Salem-Murdock, Muneera. 1984. Nubian Farmers and Arab Herders in
Irrigated Agriculture in the Sudan: From Domestic to Commodity
Production. Unpublished Ph.D. dissertation. Binghamton: State
University of New York.
Scudder, Thayer. 1972. The Human Ecology of Big Projects: River
Basin Development and Resettlement. In: Annual Review of
Anthropology, Vol. 2:45-55.
-----. 1980. The Accelerated Mahaweli Programme (AMP) and Dry
Zone Development: Some Aspects of Settlement. Report No. 2.
IDA Publication.
-----. 1981a. The Accelerated Mahaweli (Sri Lanka) Programme and
Dry Zone Development: Some Aspects of Settlement. Report No. 3.
IDA Publication.
-----. 1981b. The Development Potential of New Lands Settlement
in the Tropics and Subtropics: A Global State-of-the-Art
Evaluation with Specific Emphasis on Policy Implications.
Binghamton, N.Y.: Institute for Development Anthropology.
-----. 1984. Economic Downturn and Community Unraveling,
Revisited. Culture and Agriculture 23:6-10.
-----. 1985. The Experience of the World Bank with
Government-sponsored Land Settlement. Washington, DC: World
Bank Report No. 5625.
Scudder, Thayer and Elizabeth F. Colson. 1982. From Welfare to
Development: A Conceptual Framework for the Analysis of
Dislocated People. In: Involuntary Migration and Resettlement:
The Problems and Responses of Dislocated People, edited by Art
Hansen and Anthony Oliver-Smith. Boulder: Westview Press.
Scudder, Thayer and Kapila P. Wimaladharma. 1983. The Accelerated
Mahaweli Programme (AMP) and Dry Zone Development - Report
Number Four.
-----. 1985. The Accelerated Mahaweli Programme (AMP) and Dry
Zone Development - Report Number Five.

22. THEORY, RESEARCH, AND POLICY: PERSPECTIVES FROM THE LAND TENURE CENTER*

Don Kanel, James Riddell, David Stanfield, Steve Lawry, and John Bruce**

The impact of land tenure on development raises complex socioeconomic issues and poses heavily value-laden choices. Land tenure plays a major role in the distribution of benefits and losses among various groups in rural society. There is a two-way interaction between agrarian structure and development. On one hand the existing tenure system determines which groups in rural society are positioned to capture the benefits of development: on the other hand the tenure system is transformed insofar as some groups can capture benefits at the expense of modifying or terminating leasing and employment opportunities of other rural groups. Losers have included tenant farmers and women. The Land Tenure Center (LTC) has dealt with land tenure from many different perspectives over the years, but there has been a consistent concern with access to resources and equity as well as with productivity.

The Land Tenure Center at the University of Wisconsin was established in May 1962 in a period of increasing United States interest in land reform in Latin America as part of the Alliance for Progress program. Ever since, the Center has been concerned with land tenure and land reform issues and the study of related rural institutions influencing land use and rural development. Although its initial efforts were focused on Latin America, the LTC has more recently expanded into Africa and, to a lesser extent, Asia. The Center is an interdisciplinary unit based in the College of Agricultural and Life Sciences of the University of Wisconsin-Madison. It has a small full-time staff but in its activities associates faculty from the various schools and departments of the University, both from within and outside the College of Agriculture, and from both the Madison and other campuses. The LTC is active in research and consulting, maintains a unique specialized library on land tenure and rural development issues and has a modest publications program. It also administers an interdisciplinary Ph.D. in Development Studies for the University. The LTC is largely funded by sources external to the University, with greatest support from the United States Agency for International Development (USAID).

The LTC has welcomed a great diversity of approaches, and there is no single "LTC method." Certain threads and concerns, however, run through its work. In reading the Scudder paper about IDA in this collection we are impressed by the way it confronts ethical issues and defends the IDA against anthropologists who are more inclined to oppose projects and project impacts on people of the Third World, and by implication research that serves the needs of such projects. The nonanthropologist has the impression, though it may be oversimplified, that the study of precolonial structures in the Third World and the impacts of externally induced change, which change was on the whole disruptive, has generated preservationist sympathies among many anthropologists. The LTC by contrast started in the context of U.S. college of agriculture activities, which include a commitment to serve farm communities reacting to changing conditions and organizing to influence access to opportunities and to policy-making. The U.S. farm population has been undergoing significant change, particularly since the 1860s. U.S. farmers have certainly not been in full control of their destinies, but their experience shows that organizations and political activity help a substantial proportion of farm families in making gradual transitions, rather than confining development benefits to small minorities and generating wide disparities between the development winners and development losers. The academic focus of the rural social sciences in the land grant colleges has been not on resisting change but on understanding new alternatives, assisting transitions, and widening the access to benefits of development.

The University of Wisconsin's strength in land economics was a major factor in the siting of the LTC at this University. The land economics approach that LTC inherited dealt with such institutions and issues as zoning of the cutover timber areas of the northern Great Lakes states, water rights legislation, rules of access for grazing on public land, zoning and land use planning in areas of urban expansion into farmland, programs to promote acquisition of ownership of farms by tenants and to control foreclosures. There was also a sustained interest in policies on the disposal of the public domain and the relation between these policies and other factors that influenced the long-term trends in the rate of tenancy in U.S. agriculture. Out of these preoccupations came a sensitivity to the difficulties that less powerful groups have in getting access to policy-making and program implementation; a realization of the importance of information and of being organized; and an appreciation of research attuned to questions being asked in public policy debates and administration of programs rather than research formulated to answer purely theoretical puzzles. The emphasis on applied research as an aid to policy-makers is central to the "Wisconsin idea."

Another intellectual current influencing the LTC approach was institutional economics. The University of Wisconsin was one of the principal centers of institutionalism. It was developed at Wisconsin by John R. Commons, who studied collective bargaining and various public policy interventions in the economy. Commons and his students were instrumental in developing many programs of the welfare state: workmen's compensation for industrial accidents, unemployment insurance and the social security system. His students in agricultural economics applied his ideas particularly to land economics and to farm price support and production control programs.

The land economics-institutional economics orientation that developed at the University of Wisconsin was in contrast to mainstream economic theory. That orientation has had a strong historical element, and focused on the analysis of the evolution and impacts of basic economic and societal forms. The agricultural economists who started the Land Tenure Center, based on the success of family farming in North America (as well as Western Europe, Japan, and Taiwan), tended to believe that owner-operated farms were the key to successful agricultural development (as in the old maxim that the "magic of property turns sand into gold"). Mainstream economic theories about alternative tenure arrangements tend instead to reach the conclusion that any of the alternatives can be efficient. The interesting theoretical question then becomes, what are the conditions under which a particular arrangement will be used.

Both of these contradictory conclusions respond to the questions raised by development agencies as to whether land tenure influences production and whether there is an "economic case" for land reform. At present the mainstream economic analysis has the more grounded theoretical answers and the LTC contribution to answering these questions has been limited. The questions are, however, too narrowly framed, and the answers to them, although technically accurate, can be misleading in policy terms.

Even with desirable macropolicies, there are many "market failures" as various rural groups reach to capture development opportunities for themselves. Agricultural development is primarily a matter of making improved agricultural technologies available to farmers, and this, by itself, is not a land tenure matter. What is a land tenure matter is who can capture the benefits of new technologies, and whether such capture displaces others. Widespread ownership of rights in land gives the majority of farm families the opportunity to participate in income increases, whereas concentration of ownership may result in benefits to some occurring at a cost to others.

Given this relation between land tenure and developmental transformation and stresses, the issue of land reform becomes highly political and likely to be acted upon in revolutionary situations. Land reform is commonly a tool in the battle for control of a society and is not decided upon on the basis of theories and research results. The LTC's contribution has been in increasing the understanding of tenure issues, in answering specific questions related to policy and project design and implementation, and in understanding the socioeconomic dynamics that lead to tenure change.

Anthropology at the Land Tenure Center

In spite of the major role of land economics and institutional economics in forming the orientation of the Center, LTC's multidisciplinary character has been its great strength. Anthropologists have been part of the program from its earliest days. During the early period the Center relied heavily on help from Richard Patch, Charles Erasmus, Jorge Dandler, and Dwight Heath during research on land reform in Bolivia. Many other anthropologists, both faculty and graduate students, have worked with the Center in Latin America. The Center's Africa Program has had anthropologists John Bennett and Jim Riddell either as visiting faculty or as part of core staff from its beginning in the late 1970s (Bennett, Lawry, and Riddell 1986; Fortmann and Riddell 1985; and Riddell and Dickerman et al. 1986).

The Scudder paper in the present volume raises the issue that there is "little agreement" among anthropologists as to their appropriate role vis-a-vis planned economic development. Why, in light of this disagreement, has it been possible for anthropologists to work productively in a center that focuses its research in policy areas? Ignoring the idiosyncratic motivations, anthropologists were needed to help explain the new cultural contexts in which institutionalists found themselves. Those in the institutional economics tradition were anxious to grapple with the problems of social action and prepared to deal with units of society other than the atomistic individual producer/consumer. They thus found considerable areas of overlapping interest with their anthropologist colleagues. In addition, the anthropologists and economists who associated themselves with the Center had a common concern over how best to ensure the access to land and resources of relatively powerless members of society, and thus empower them to influence their futures.

The major area of disagreement has always been the issue of policy. Anthropologists are rarely policy scientists in the same way as political scientists, sociologists, or economists. If one could simplify the policy scientist's basic paradigm as "the best policy is that under which the greatest number of people benefit over the longest period of time to the greatest degree," the

390

majority of anthropologists who have worked with the Center would find it unacceptable. Land policies that may purport to benefit the largest proportion of a national population have often proved to be detrimental to cultural minorities. Center writings by anthropologists reflect a cautious attitude toward most policy initiatives. They have expressed many of the concerns described in Scudder's chapter and enriched policy debates in the Center. The debate over nation-building, development as a macro process, and cultural diversity is part of the intellectual fabric of the Center, and it is rare today for the Center to plan or initiate research activity without the participation of an anthropologist or rural sociologist.

In the context of policy discussions, the multidisciplinary make-up of the LTC provides something of a buffer between the anthropologist and policy-makers. Many of the concerns of Center anthropologists can be debated in-house and, if other staff members can be convinced as to the validity of the argument, it is possible to mount a united front. Supporting arguments from other disciplines can be developed, and objections to policy cannot be so easily dismissed as mere "anthropological preservationism." In addition, because LTC is a part of the University and almost all of the anthropologists who work in the Center have academic appointments in their home departments, they are secure enough to make strong and vigorous anthropological arguments. Their academic appointments protect them from the pressures from donors, governments, and colleagues in the heat of policy discussions.

The LTC has always felt that the participation by anthropologists in its programs, research, and publication activities is vital to its mission. This recognition of the value of anthropology to land tenure research has survived the many debates at the Center concerning the complex working relationship between the LTC and development agencies.

The LTC in Operation: Some Cases

There follow five examples of LTC research and policy initiatives in the Third World. The first three illustrate ways in which LTC research has influenced policy on the institutional forms adopted in agricultural development and has helped governments plan more viable institutional strategies and mechanisms. The first, an early example from Bolivia, examines how LTC research in the 1960s on land titling in the Bolivian agrarian reform led to recommendations that increased substantially the rate at which titles were distributed to reform beneficiaries. The second case concerns the impact of LTC's research in the early 1980s on the policy debate concerning the partial de-collectivization of <u>asentamientos</u> in the Dominican Republic. The third example looks at recent LTC research on grazing associations in Lesotho and the challenge of creating a workable institutional and regulatory framework for range management.

The fourth example is from Swaziland, and makes a related but quite different point: how the LTC has sought to deal sensitively with the institutional complexities of government itself as the consumer for research. The fifth and final example, from Mauritania, illustrates the LTC's efforts to strengthen Third World researchers and institutions as an integral part of its research efforts.

Titling of Land Reform Beneficiaries in Bolivia

This particular example of LTC activities indicates the usefulness of research into problems of implementation of land reform and, in this case, a direct contribution toward the improvement of procedures for awarding titles to land reform beneficiaries.

The prereform land tenure system in the highlands of Bolivia was dominated by large holdings using a labor force of Indian peasant families who were granted usufruct rights to small parcels of land in return for providing the landowner with three to twelve days of farm labor per week with no compensation. Work animals and tools were also provided by the peasant. Peasant obligations included transporting the landlord's produce to market and domestic services to the landlord's family, both on the farm and in his home in town. On most of the larger holdings, the peasant was virtually a slave: "He was so tied to the land that even when properties were sold, they were listed as including '300 colonos'"[1] (Clark 1971:130).

The Bolivian land reform of 1953 was a major outcome of the 1952 revolution against a military regime. While sixteen months elapsed between the revolution and the land reform law, the process of land redistribution to the peasants was rapid and on a large scale. It included rapidly spreading organization of peasant unions after the revolution and seizure of land by peasant invasions before the land reform. Even after the land reform law, land redistribution was accomplished primarily by the peasant unions and revolutionary party organizers, with peasants becoming owners of their usufruct parcels (Clark 1971:132-36).

However, the awarding of titles to the new owners was a slower process, so that, some thirteen years after the land reform law, only one-half of the peasant families who benefited

from the land reform had received titles to their land. Some of
the problems that resulted from lack of titles were described in
a Land Tenure Center account in 1966:

On many of these properties, a condition of land
tenure insecurity has been created which results in
social instability in the rural areas and prevents
a more efficient and productive use of the land.
Because of the uncertain status of these properties,
conflicts have arisen between the campesinos and the
former landowners and among the campesinos themselves,
particularly concerning their respective boundaries.
A process of social disintegration has also been noted
in many rural communities, which creates barriers to
the introduction of social and economic innovations.

In addition, investments and improvements on the
land are not being carried out to the extent they
could, given the resources and potential of the people
involved. There exist, for example, some 2,000 to
4,000 former landowners who have a legal right to
retain a certain portion of their old properties.
Many of these had been fairly productive and efficient
farmers. But they have abandoned their farms, which
are partially occupied by campesinos, and are
unwilling to return until their legal rights are
definitely established and they receive a secure
and legal possession over a specific amount of land.

Legal problems are also multiplied as a result
of the delays and slowness of the agrarian reform.
Anxious to obtain a title, many campesinos who have
settled on affected properties have grown weary of
waiting and have purchased "titles" from their former
landowners who unscrupulously exploit their ignorance.
These "titles" have no legal validity whatsoever and
only serve to further complicate an already indefinite
title situation, particularly as these transactions
may result in the abandonment of their agrarian reform
cases by the campesinos who no longer feel the need
for proceeding through the Agrarian Reform Agency
(Thome 1966:30-31)

In the 1960s, the Land Tenure Center was engaged in research
on the Bolivian land reform in collaboration with the Bolivian
government and the Inter-American Committee for Agricultural
Development (Comit. Interamericano de Desarrollo Agricola,
CIDA). This was a broad, interdisciplinary program concerned
with economic and social changes resulting from the land reform.
The concern with titling developed from the recognition of

393

problems described above.

This LTC research indicated a number of administrative problems responsible for the long delays in the granting of titles. The titling procedures required action at five levels: in the provincial, departmental, and national levels of the National Agrarian Reform service (Servicio Nacional de la Reforma Agraria, SNRA); in the Ministry of Campesino Affairs; and in the Office of the President of the Republic. A number of steps were involved at each level concerned with land surveying, presentation of conflicting claims, legal analysis and adjudication, appeals, decisions, and registration of titles. The procedures generated delays in several ways. There were opportunities for appeal at each of the five levels. Also, while the SNRA had the legal power to initiate cases, it was in fact not able to do so because of lack of vehicles and staff; action depended on peasant initiative, requiring organization, access to lawyers and government officials, and effort and money to keep in contact and to push the case along. The same complex procedure was used for the typically more difficult cases of determining the applicability of the provisions for expropriation of large properties as well as for the simpler provision called "consolidation," which was for the purpose of giving clear title to small and medium properties not subject to expropriation as well as for transferring titles to heirs of beneficiaries (Thome 1967).

The proliferation of peasant organizations involved in the land reform was one result of the desire on the part of Bolivia's populist leadership to give campesino organizations a greater say in local decision-making. The rapid growth of these organizations was contributing to delays in title registration. But other more compelling political considerations, not least the growth of a guerrilla movement led by Che Guevara, favored acceleration of the process of actual title registration.

Two types of recommendations resulted from the titling study. One set of recommendations suggested simplifying or eliminating some of the steps in the administrative hierarchy as well as providing briefer procedures for cases of "consolidation" and other less complex actions. The other recommendations were concerned with improving procedures in the field by relying on mobile teams composed of an agrarian judge, a law clerk, and two topographers. The purpose of such teams was to make it possible for SNRA to initiate titling actions instead of waiting to respond to peasant initiatives, to save the peasants considerable expense and effort, and to shorten the time required for titling (Thome 1967:68-86).

Most of these recommendations were accepted and the first

three mobile teams were established in July 1967. The improvements in procedure resulted in the awarding of 117,000 new titles in 1968 and 1969, compared with 318,000 titles in the preceding thirteen years, from 1955 through 1967 (Thome 1970:48).

Transformation of the Collective Farming Model in the Dominican Republic

In the first thirteen years of its existence, the Land Tenure Center was little concerned with collective farming. The classic land reforms in the nineteenth and twentieth centuries in Europe and Asia (in non-Communist countries) established peasant proprietorship (or family farming, the successful tenure model most familiar to social scientists in the U.S. colleges of agriculture). The major Latin American land reforms in Mexico and Bolivia, although they attempted to foster collective approaches, also ended up establishing individually operated family farms (even if ownership of land was collective, as in the Mexican ejidos).

Major reliance on collective farming in the Third World developed in the land reforms of Chile, Peru, and Tanzania, all in the 1960s. While the LTC had a major project on the Chilean land reform, it was primarily concerned with production and employment rather than with problems specific to the collective form of organization.

The LTC effort to analyze the problems of collectivization in agriculture began with a conference in 1975, which resulted in the 1977 publication of Cooperative and Commune. It included papers on collective farming in the Third World and in Communist countries and on the collective farms in Israel and those organized by the religious communities of the Hutterian Brethren in the United States and Canada. This brought into the LTC circle of researchers some new associates and new perspectives. Subsequent to the conference, members of the LTC staff conducted research on collective farms in Peru and El Salvador, but the most significant LTC effort has been in the Dominican Republic in the mid-1980s.

The research in the Dominican Republic developed out of a debate about the collective farm model of reform enterprise that had been used following the State's acquisition of large rice farms after 1972. The research combined ideas from previous LTC research with local field studies. The research results provided suggestions for enabling legislation that would accommodate demands from farmers for modifications in the collective farm model.

395

In mid-1983 the LTC entered into an agreement with the Superior Agricultural Institute (Instituto Superior de Agricultura, ISA) of the Catholic University and with the Dominican Agrarian Institute (Instituto Agrario Dominicano, IAD), the semi-autonomous agency charged with implementing the various agrarian laws that comprise the reforms legislated since the death of Trujillo in 1961. Trujillo's overthrow left the new government with the question of what to do with the vast expanses of land that he and his family and friends had controlled. Despite the appropriation of some of this land by private landlords, the Trujillo sugar estates were kept largely intact and operated as state farms. Other lands were assigned to the control of IAD and were gradually turned over to beneficiaries of the agrarian reform and operated through 1972 as individual enterprises.

In 1972, under the government of Balaguer and as a result of substantial political turmoil and pressures, new laws were formulated that allowed the government to take over some of the most productive lands in the country, which were being used for the production of rice. These lands were organized into IAD-managed farms referred to as collectives (also known as asentamientos or fincas) ranging in size from ten to one hundred member-workers.

The IAD technicians and administrators in conjunction with the agricultural bank had a powerful role in the management of these farms. By 1982, however, pressures had mounted from the members of the collectives for more independence from IAD and more individualized decision-making structures. The reduction of state influence on these farms has been resisted by the government. The high priority placed on low-priced rice as a basic staple of the Dominican diet has combined with the long-standing distrust of international food markets to result in a strong political interest in assuring that domestic rice production comes as close as possible to meeting national consumption needs. Who controls the production of rice is, therefore, of great political significance in the Dominican context.

The problem at the beginning of the research project was how to respond to the reform beneficiaries' (asentados) demands for a new "associative" model of rice-farm management, where each asentado would earn according to the production of a specific plot of land assigned to his care. The associative model of agrarian reform settlement included the idea that some group of associative activities were to be retained that had previously been performed by the collective, such as the group administration of production credit, collective purchase and maintenance of machinery, group management of the irrigation

396

system internal to the farm, and the collective marketing of the rice.

This proposal for an "associative model" of enterprise management contrasted with the collective system where each worker participated equally in the profits of the collective enterprise. The overall operation of the enterprise was the responsibility of the administrative committee, whose chair was the administrator appointed by IAD. Much of the labor was organized into work crews formed by the worker-members of the collectives. On many of these farms, serious labor discipline and motivation problems had proved to be difficult to resolve.

With the accumulation of these problems over the years, demands from the asentados, the members of the collectives, had reached serious proportions by the time of the election of the new government in 1978. However, no decision had been reached by the time of the initiation of the LTC/ISA/IAD project concerning how to deal with these asentado demands.

The first objective of the research project was to produce case studies of the variety of asentamiento management structures in the rice sector. These case studies explored the alternatives to the original collective model of farm management that were actually being tried out on a number of asentamientos. Those case studies were done through the direct research activities of people from IAD, ISA, and the LTC, with the central responsibility for preparing the final versions of the case studies being assigned to ISA (Stanfield et al. 1985; Stringer 1985; Carter and Kanel 1985).

The cases were presented in a national-level seminar on the theme of rice asentamiento management. At that seminar numerous officials of the government as well as representatives of the collective farm workers discussed with members of the National Congress the legal and economic implications of the proposed associative model of asentamiento management. In March 1985, legislation was approved by the National Congress to recognize and regulate the associative model of reform enterprise management. The new law stated that the profits of agricultural production, generated by the association of reform beneficiaries, would be distributed "according to the production contributed by each association member and his/her family" (Law No. 269 of 1985). This clause implied the existence of an administrative system whereby the production of each family could be determined. The administrative problems, particularly the challenge of accounting for collective and individual costs of production and the value of what was produced, became of central concern to those asentamientos that immediately adopted the associative model. Some members of the LTC/ISA/IAD research team helped carry out accounting and management training courses for the asentados, despite inherent problems deriving from the low levels of functional literacy of most reform beneficiaries.

The associative model required the individualization of costs and value of production, which in practice has meant the physical subdivision of the collectives and the individualization of the value of production and its cost accounting. The 1985 law does not, however, permit the permanent delineation of parcel boundaries: "No farmer beneficiary of the agrarian reform will be able to divide physically the corresponding work area for which he is responsible in the associative asentamiento." Boundary markings that do not interfere with the use of machinery and the organization of irrigation are used to identify the members' parcels. The associative model, then, is really a mix of individual and collective enterprises.

Following the official acceptance of the associative model of farm organization, significant gains in productivity have occurred on at least some asentamientos. Moreover, the organizational and efficiency advantages of collective action within the asentamientos in certain farming operations have not been lost. In January of 1986, however, a National Committee of Reform Beneficiaries occupied the regional offices of IAD demanding definitive title to the land they had received provisionally through the agrarian reform. In February of 1986 the same Committee presented a list of demands to IAD, all pertaining to definitive title to the land. This demand for title to the land, however, did not necessarily mean individual title. The notion was for IAD to assign title of the land to the association in a way analogous to the techniques of condominium property in urban areas. The association would have some rights to specific parcels of land described so that they would have the right to the goods produced from a specific piece of land and would have the right to pass the land on to their heirs. The Committee of Agrarian Reform Beneficiaries included in their document presented to IAD a draft of the legislation that the Committee considered necessary to carry out this form of titling the land to the reform beneficiaries.

In the midst of this controversy the research teams from ISA, IAD, and LTC that had worked on the associative model problem reassembled to prepare recommendations concerning a titling program and the implications of different approaches to the titling question. Fieldwork was carried out in the rice-producing areas, in the irrigated Azua plain, and in the mountainous areas along the Haitian frontier where colonization projects had been carried out prior to 1961. In none of these areas had definitive titling of the land occurred. On the basis of this field research (see Stanfield et al. 1986 for a summary of the reports), recommendations on titling were made to IAD. The recommendations supported the form of titling outlined in the Committee's statement, and urged that IAD develop criteria for the issuance of associative titles that would give greater incentives for the formation of strong and functional associations of reform beneficiaries. The recommendations also addressed the titling issues in the highly productive Azua plain, where fragmentation was a serious issue, and in the colonization projects on the frontier, where land consolidations and lack of farmer investment were salient problems.

As a result of the focus on a serious policy issue, the titling of agrarian reform land, at least a reasonably informed basis now exists for the design of a titling program that fits the needs and circumstances of the major regions affected by the country's agrarian reform. Subsequent to the preparations of these recommendations in March 1986, national elections and the installation of a new government have delayed the resolution of the titling issue, but attention will undoubtedly return to this question in the near future.

Institutionalizing Grazing Associations in Lesotho

Recent LTC research on communal grazing in Lesotho illustrates the importance of having a perspective on specific economic and political circumstances affecting institutions at both the local and the national level when framing policies toward resource management.

Much of the policy-making on communal grazing lands has been informed by the "tragedy of the commons" paradigm, popularized by Hardin (1968) but expressed in many neoclassical statements of individual use strategies under circumstances of communal tenure. At the heart of the neoclassical perspective is the assumption of the "dominance of free rider strategies"; in circumstances of communal use of grazing, individuals acting in their own short-run interests will build up aggregate stock numbers above what can be supported by the range because their marginal benefits exceed their marginal costs. A typical policy prescription is individualizing grazing rights.

The paradigm failed, however, to take account of considerable historic evidence of institutional arrangements for managing the collective use of common pool resources. In an important article, Ciriacy-Wantrup and Bishop (1975) pointed out that distinctions must be drawn between open access situations characterized by an absence of rules and constraints on individual behavior, and common property situations where formal and informal rules act to define conditions of access and use of

399

common resources. Other research suggested that in precolonial times traditional authorities regulated grazing patterns consistent with long-term carrying capacity of rangelands. Research on contemporary range policies pointed out important equity and ecological problems associated with new tenure arrangements. Many of the policy prescriptions that evolved from this research emphasized the importance of allowing local communities to resolve their resource management problems without outside interference.

Recent LTC research in Lesotho has focused on the interplay between local and nonlocal institutions in communal resource management as a means for gaining a more realistic understanding of the policy problems and options. An LTC researcher was based in Sehlabathebe from 1984 to 1986 to study the effectiveness of a local grazing association, established with technical assistance from the Government of Lesotho and USAID, in regulating the grazing patterns of local stockholders under a pasture rotation plan. It was hoped that the association would become a model for the local management of grazing land in Lesotho, and that the need for direct government involvement in range-use control would be minimized.

A comprehensive range and animal improvement program was implemented in the project area, involving importation of improved breeding animals, a marketing program for beef, construction of a new facility for shearing sheep and goats, and intensive extension assistance to the executive committee of the grazing association. The project leadership took considerable care not to target particular groups within the community for privileged access to communal grazing land, a strategy that in earlier efforts had led to project sabotage by those excluded.

Despite the more open approach exercised at Sehlabathebe, adoption of the pasture rotation plan--which involved sending livestock to distant high mountain cattleposts, away from the village areas, during the summer--was resisted by important segments of the community. The purpose of the rotation was to allow the village pastures to rest during the summer so as to encourage maximum production of forage for use by animals in the harsh winter, when they return to the village from the cattleposts. But smallholders especially lacked the herding labor to establish a second base of operations away from the village. Household-level research on livestock management revealed that less than one-third of livestock owners actually owned cattleposts. Although many stockholders made arrangements to share cattleposts belonging to others, these arrangements involved costs that many others sought to avoid.

The grazing plan was in conflict with other aspects of local

400

grazing practice. It required that, in addition to cattle, all sheep and goats were to be brought to the village grazing area in the winter to minimize grazing pressure in the mountain pastures. But keeping smallstock in the village was resisted by almost all stockholders, usually for sound reasons. Smallstock are destructive of cattle grazing and home gardens, and it was generally felt that hired herdsmen were inattentive when they worked in the village. The design of the original rotational scheme had not taken into account problems of integrated livestock management and the extent to which household labor supply and local livestock production goals influenced range use.

It became clear to the government and project staff that the executive committee of the association was not prepared to enforce the grazing plan vigorously. Part of the committee's reticence was due to natural sympathy toward those being forced to adopt unpopular and, for some, onerous aspects of the plan. The committee's credibility was to some extent compromised by the unwillingness of the chairman to send his expensive Brown swiss milk cows to the cattleposts in the summer. He was afraid of stock theft and was producing large amounts of surplus milk for sale in his village, and so was vulnerable to charges of arrogance of power. Other executive committee members openly violated provisions of the plan. The executive committee was unsure of its real authority on matters of resource control. Chiefs and headmen had traditional responsibilities in this area, but there was a widely shared sense in the community that they were ineffectual in enforcing even modest grazing controls. The role of chiefs in regulating grazing was very modest, and was limited to setting aside winter reserve areas in the villages, known as Leboella. The ability of the chiefs even to manage Leboella has been much diminished because of political and social changes affecting the chieftainship, but also because Leboella is subject to the same kinds of pressures that threaten the grazing plan.

The project was unwilling to see its own efforts in promoting scientific management so easily defeated, and increasingly took over direct day-to-day administration of the enforcement program. The project leadership was aware that the enforcement function must be handled sensitively. Arbitrary imposition of rules from outside without local sanction would be resisted as a matter of principle. Thus, the project did not give up on the grazing association. It continued to work with the committee, from which it received useful guidance on the social feasibility of many features of the plan. Unpopular rules, such as the requirement that all smallstock be brought to the village in the winter, were dropped. But, by providing administrative back-stopping to the enforcement function, clearly reasonable aspects of the plan were seen to be enforced in an evenhanded manner. This gave the plan greater standing in the eyes of stockholders. Stockholders came to see the benefits of increased forage production due to a more disciplined rotation. This helped broaden the constituency in support of grazing management.

Research pointed out the interplay of relationships summarized above. Research on household income strategies, the role of livestock in the household economy, livestock management practices, and cattlepost ownership and use patterns helped develop a better understanding of producer practices and objectives, and provided a framework for understanding resource use and management problems as perceived by range users. This research also revealed the absence of a strong systemic basis for the development of local institutions for regulating resource use. Producers were found to be heterogeneous and independent. Households tended to be highly autonomous economically, and interhousehold interdependencies mediated by livestock--through loans, bridewealth, etc.--were of declining importance. Significantly, though over 85 percent of households owned livestock, livestock were the principal source of income for only about 16 percent of households. Remittances from men working in the mines in south Africa was the principal income source for about half of all households.

This leaves range policy in a potential quandary. The bases for cooperation at the local level are lacking, but rules imposed from outside are likely to be perceived as arbitrary and will often be insensitive to local constraints. However, the rough solution to this apparent dilemma may lie in the project's response to the executive committee's reluctance vigorously to enforce grazing rules. By providing administrative back-stopping to the enforcement program, the project provided the executive committee with an element of sanction that it could not derive locally. It also relieved the committee of some local pressures that it would have otherwise found difficult to bear. The committee enhanced its standing in the eyes of the community by explaining to the project staff the constraints upon stockholders in adopting unrealistic aspects of the plan. The credit for improved grazing conditions was shared by the committee and the project, though it is unlikely that the committee would be able to sustain an effective enforcement program without the continuing involvement of outside authorities.

The research drew out some policy lessons. Local management of common property is made difficult by diverse management strategies, themselves the product of variable income strategies and decreased reliance upon local sources of income in rural areas where households are increasingly dependent upon remittance income. Resource policies promulgated by central authorities

402

must be carefully applied in ways that make sense to resource users. Central authorities must be prepared to provide backing to increasingly weak local institutions.

The client for this research was the USAID-funded Land Conservation and Range Development (LCRD) project, which provided technical assistance to the Range Management Division of the Ministry of Agriculture. The USAID Mission in Lesotho has called upon the Land Tenure Center to provide general assistance in the area of agricultural land tenure. In 1984, three LTC staff participated in a high-level policy workshop in Lesotho that considered how the Land Act 1979 could best be implemented in rural areas. Two LTC staff returned to Lesotho in early 1987 to participate in the inaugural workshop for a national commission established to review Lesotho's land policies.

The Institutional Context of Policy-Making in Swaziland

There is another level on which the Center's focus on institutions is important in an applied research context. LTC research findings eventually reach a wide audience, but the immediate audiences are the national policy-makers and donors whose concerns posed the research task. This is a familiar and comfortable audience for those steeped in the "Wisconsin idea" of university research as service to the government and people of the state. The need to find effective ways to communicate research results to policy-makers is a persistent concern. Overseas, the LTC regularly enters unfamiliar policy arenas, dealing with issues of considerable sensitivity, and its sense of the institutional context of policy-making is critical to the success or failure of its projects. Often several government agencies will need to absorb and internalize the research results if they are to have the desired impact on policy. The best way to ensure this is through involvement of host-country technical staff and policy-makers in the research at all stages of the work.

The LTC's current land tenure research project in Swaziland provides an example of how these considerations can play out in a particular situation. In 1985 the Swazi Ministry of Agriculture and Cooperatives (MOAC) approached USAID/Swaziland concerning research to identify both constraints and opportunities for agricultural development inherent in the customary land tenure systems. The objective of the research is to identify options for the development of the traditional land tenure system as it comes under increasing population pressure and at the same time operates in a more and more diversified economy, in which most homesteads derive substantial income from outside of agriculture and in which agriculture is often seen more as a safety net than

403

as an attractive economic opportunity. The research seeks to move beyond the "rules" of the tenure system to discern in actual behavior the way in which the tenure system is evolving. The issues addressed are fundamental to the structures of power and privilege. Should the land continue to be administered by the chieftainship institutions, or should new local and national institutions take over this task, or should societal control over land distribution be withdrawn to allow market mechanisms to determine distribution?

Swaziland is a very traditional polity, with its traditional tenure system structurally intact though evolving in important ways. The delicacy of the policy issues involved was stressed from the outset. How should the research be organized? Because land tenure research is quite specialized, it was considered that LTC should have a resident research coordinator. On the other hand, it was essential to involve Swazi researchers, for a variety of reasons. First, it would be important to have the benefit of their research experience, skills, and sense of the sociocultural milieu. Second, on-the-job exposure to the LTC's methods could help develop a capability for future land tenure research in a local institution. Third, Swazi involvement in the research planning and implementation gives the Swazi researchers a sense of the way in which empirical research on policy-related issues proceeds and confidence in the integrity of the research process.

Almost immediately there arose a question as to where, institutionally, the research effort should be nested. Four options presented themselves. MOAC's Malkerns agricultural research station was a possibility but was rejected, partly because its staff were already deeply involved in an AID-funded cropping systems research project. The Planning and Research Division of MOAC, the second possibility, seemed to offer a base that was well-situated to feed research conclusions into the policy stream. On the other hand, it had functioned primarily as a planning and budgeting unit for the Ministry and had very limited experience with empirical research. Third, there was a Land Use Division in a newly formed Ministry of Natural Resources, which Division had been shifted out of the Ministry of Agriculture to the new Ministry. Its staff was the most concerned about the issues the research was to address, but it was decided that, if the project was to influence agricultural policy, it was best based in MOAC. Finally, there was the Social Science Research Unit in the University of Swaziland, which had a solid record of policy-relevant survey research. It was, however, staffed largely by expatriate researchers, and relations between government and the university community had been tense.

As the substance of the research required emerged more

404

clearly, it seemed that a compromise approach to the siting of the project was possible. There was a need for a sample survey of landholders under the customary tenure system. This would be a major undertaking logistically, and was seen as the centerpiece of the research program. It was decided to base the LTC research coordinator and this large survey exercise in the Planning and Research Division of MOAC, both to be close to policy-makers and to attempt to develop the research capabilities of the Division. AID/Swaziland inclined to a base in MOAC partly because AID already had several projects with that Ministry and was not anxious to begin dealing with another institution, increasing its staff's administrative workload.

On the other hand, there was also a need for several discrete, more limited research initiatives. They dealt with issues that could not be effectively addressed through the large survey, as where the phenomenon of interest was so infrequent that it would not appear in a random sample in sufficient quantity to permit analysis or where the matter was sensitive and would likely be seriously misreported in a survey. The research experience in the Social Science Research Unit (SSRU) at the University seemed a resource that could be effectively tapped. A series of seven research contracts with university researchers were arranged through the SSRU, as well as two small workshops with university staff, one in the planning stage of the research and one when there were preliminary results that could be discussed.

This left out the Ministry of Natural Resources, however, and a number of other ministries and institutions whose areas of policy responsibility overlapped with those of MOAC in important respects (e.g., Justice, Planning and Finance, and the Tinkundla, which handles chieftainship affairs). It was essential to decrease the dangers of a later turf battle among these ministries over land policy by involving them in the research from the outset. An Interministerial Reference Group for the research project was created by invitation of the Minister of Agriculture and Cooperatives, composed of senior staff from the various ministries and organizations. This reference group meets to review research plans and procedures and to discuss preliminary research results, and will review the final research product.

Do such arrangements smack of institutional overkill? On the contrary, LTC's experience suggests that success in applied research requires a great deal of attention to the institutional siting of the research project and linkages with a variety of institutions (Fortmann 1985). The Swaziland project is still under way, but to date it has been successful in engaging the attention of policy-makers on a sensitive topic and providing a

405

basis for policy discussions. LTC's experience shows: (1) that
policy dialogue on land tenure is likely to be far more fruitful
if it can be based on common ground generated by careful
research, and (2) that good research is in itself no guarantee
that policy discussions will get off the ground, especially if
there are no clear strategies for getting the research results
into the policy stream.

Building Local Research Capabilities: Mauritania

Finally, the LTC's priorities in research planning reflect
its origins and location in a training institution, the
University of Wisconsin. The Center administers an
interdisciplinary Ph.D. in Development Program, and through this
and nondegree training programs seeks opportunities to enhance
the capabilities of Third World researchers and research
institutions. Where research projects are conceptualized by
host-country governments and donors as not involving training,
the LTC generally seeks to incorporate a training component in
some form, whether it be degree training; short-term, nondegree
skills training; or on-the-job training. It also seeks
opportunities to collaborate with local research institutions and
to involve local professionals on its research teams. The LTC
has sought to avoid the research model known among LTC's Latin
America staff as "parachutismo," research conducted by expatriate
researchers in isolation from the local research community--and
usually in isolation from local administrators and policy-makers
as well. The teaching of the processes of inquiry that we know
as empirical research and demonstrating its usefulness in
policy-making should be integral parts of any research project.

A research and training project recently funded by
USAID/Mauritania shows the potential of a well-planned mix of
research and training. The Ministry of Rural Development had
become increasingly concerned about the structure of land rights
in the country, and approached USAID/Mauritania for assistance
with research and training needs. The LTC advised on the
development of a project, which brought four trainees nominated
by USAID and the Ministry of Rural Development to the University
of Wisconsin-Madison to do master's degrees. It was decided that
while they should all focus their seminar papers and theses on
land tenure issues in Mauritania, each should enroll in a
different disciplinary program. LTC assisted in the formalities
connected with admissions--conditioned upon progress in
English--by Rural Sociology, Land Resources, Development
Administration, and Law. An LTC part-time project coordinator
worked regularly with the students and their academic advisors
through informal seminars and other means. After two years the
students were ready to take up the unusual opportunity offered by

this project: the opportunity to return to Mauritania as a team, accompanied by the LTC project coordinator and an LTC research assistant, for six months of intensive field research for their theses.

This research had been planned in Madison by the coordinator, the students, and their advisors. The site selection--two irrigation schemes along the Senegal River--was made by the research team but cleared with USAID/Mauritania and the Ministry. Each researcher had his individual research project and disciplinary research domain, but the research was planned so that these complemented one another and could be drawn together by the project coordinator in a comprehensive report.

The students have now graduated and returned to Mauritania. It remains unclear whether the potential of this project will be achieved, due in part to conflicts that developed between the Ministry and USAID over another project. One graduate has, however, been given specific responsibility for land tenure research and policy, based in the Ministry's Planning Unit. LTC has also been able to put together research teams involving some of the graduates for project design work in Mauritania and Senegal.

Mauritanian capabilities in this area have been dramatically increased, and both government and donors are far better informed of tenure issues in the irrigated sector than was previously the case. The per-student costs were only a little greater than usual; the close supervision provided by LTC kept the students on schedule and, even with the period for field research, the degrees were completed in less than average time for students from Francophone countries.

There are many other ways in which research and training can be integrated, and often this involves short-term nondegree training, either in the country concerned or at the LTC. The LTC has long had the capability to offer training programs in Spanish and has recently achieved the capability to train in French. The search for training opportunities will remain a priority for the LTC, especially those that involve effective integration of research and training.

Conclusion

In those few cases in which major reforms have been carried out, the LTC contribution has been twofold. In the design of the reforms, LTC has been able to provide policy-makers with insights from the relevant experience of other countries, which is very useful in clarifying alternatives and consequences of proposed

actions. In the implementation of land reforms, LTC field
research has often provided feedback about problems of applying
provisions of the reform to local situations and the unintended
consequences of land reform programs.

Another contribution to development programs has involved
design of appropriate tenure rights to facilitate a variety of
development projects: irrigation, resettlement, reforestation,
range management, etc. Depending on the nature of the project,
relevant issues may deal with how existing rights should be
modified to facilitate project implementation and appropriate
rights to be awarded to project beneficiaries.

In both of the above types of activities, LTC facilitates
the grand design of others: politicians in one case, and
development project designers in the other. But much of its
ability to analyze the role of tenure in such cases arises out of
continuing LTC research work on long-term trends involving
spontaneous tenure changes and postreform development, work that
includes specific research studies and interpretative analyses of
land tenure and land reform experience. LTC has completed and is
currently undertaking a number of such interpretative studies
(e.g., Bennett et al. 1986; Bloch 1986; Brown and Dorner in
progress; Bruce 1986, in progress; Dorner 1971, 1972; Riddell and
Dickerman 1986; Thiesenhusen 1986).

The Land Tenure Center has sought to address those issues
which are its special concern through a variety of activities:
consulting, research, training, and synthesis. These can, with
care in planning, be complementary and mutually reinforcing.
They continue to be informed by the institutionalist perspective,
multidisciplinary approach, and tradition of engagement and
public service that have been critical to the intellectual
development of the Center.

Notes

* Revision of papers presented to the annual meeting of the
Society for Economic Anthropology, held at Airlie House,
Warrentown, Virginia, April 11-13, 1985.

** Staff members of the Land Tenure Center, University of
Wisconsin-Madison.

[1] The system was known as colonato, and the peasants, as
colonos.

References

Bennett, John W., Steven W. Lawry, James C. Riddell. 1986. Land Tenure and Livestock Development in Sub-Saharan Africa. AID Evaluation Special Study, no. 39. Washington: U.S. Agency for International Development.

Bloch, Peter C. et al. 1986. Land Tenure Issues in River Basin Development in Sub-Saharan Africa. LTC Research Paper, no. 90. Madison: Land Tenure Center, University of Wisconsin.

Brown, Marion and Peter Dorner. Retrospective Synthesis: Land Tenure in Latin America. (In progress, 1988).

Bruce, John W. Security of Tenure and Land Registration in Africa. (In progress, 1988).

------- 1986. Land Tenure Issues in Project Design and Strategies for Agricultural Development in Sub-Saharan Africa. LTC Paper, no. 128. Madison: Land Tenure Center, University of Wisconsin.

Carter, Michael and Don Kanel. 1985. Collective Production of Rice: Institutional Performance and Evolution in the Dominican Agrarian Reform Sector. Madison: Land Tenure Center, University of Wisconsin.

Ciriacy-Wantrup, S.V. and Richard C. Bishop. 1975. Common Property as a Concept in Natural Resource Policy. Natural Resources Journal 15:713-727.

Clark, Ronald J. Agrarian Reform: Bolivia. In: Land Reform in Latin America: Issues and Cases, Peter Dorner, ed. pp. 129-164. Madison: Published by Land Economics for the Land Tenure Center at the University of Wisconsin, 1971.

Dorner, Peter. 1972. Land Reform and Economic Development. Baltimore: Penguin Books.

-------, ed. 1971. Land Reform in Latin America: Issues and Cases. Land Economics Monograph Series, no. 3. Madison: Published by Land Economics for the Land Tenure Center at the University of Wisconsin.

-------, ed. 1977. Cooperative and Commune: Group Farming in the Economic Development of Agriculture. Madison: University of Wisconsin Press. Fortmann, Louise. 1985. Turning Field Research into Government Policy. Rural Sociologist 4:287-290.

Fortmann, Louise and James Riddell. 1985. Trees and Tenure: An Annotated Bibliography for Agroforesters and Others. Madison and Nairobi: Land Tenure Center, University of Wisconsin, and International Council for Research in Agroforestry.

Hardin, Garret. 1968. The Tragedy of the Commons. Science 162:1243-1248.

Riddell, James C., Carol Dickerman et al. 1986. Country Profiles of Land Tenure: Africa 1986. LTC Paper, no. 127. Madison: Land Tenure Center, University of Wisconsin.

Stanfield, J. David et al. 1986. Evolving Property Relations in the Agrarian Reform of the Dominican Republic. Madison: Land Tenure Center, University of Wisconsin. Prepared for Latin American

Studies Association meetings, in Boston.

------- et al. 1985. El asentamiento campesino Vasquez Quintero: un estudio de caso de un asentamiento asociativo. Santo Domingo: Centro de Administracion del Desarrollo Rural, Instituto Superior de Agricultura, Instituto Agrario Dominicano, Centro de Tenencia de la Tierra.

Stringer, Randy. 1985. Innovations in Group Farming: The Case of Sergio A. Cabrera. Madison: Land Tenure Center, University of Wisconsin.

Thiesenhusen, William C., ed. Searching for Agrarian Reform in Latin America. Winchester, Mass.: Allen and Unwin, forthcoming 1988.

Thome, Joseph R. The Bolivian Agrarian Reform: The Need for a Faster Title Distribution Process. Land Tenure Center Newsletter, no. 24, August-October 1966.

------- Problems which Obstruct the Process of Title Distribution under the Bolivian Agrarian Reform. Preliminary draft. Madison, January 1967.

------- Expropriation and Title Distribution under the Bolivian Agrarian Reform: 1953-1967. Madison, January 1970.

23. CONCLUDING ESSAY

POWER AND MEANING IN ECONOMIC CHANGE: WHAT DOES ANTHROPOLOGY
LEARN FROM DEVELOPMENT STUDIES?

John R. Bowen

"Development" Reconsidered

Readers may have noticed that while the four overview papers
(Bennett, Adams, Schneider, Bates) and the "organization studies"
(Koenig, Scudder, Bruce et al.) take "development" as their
central concept and problem, the empirical studies do not do so.
Indeed, with the exception of the papers by Despres and Salisbury
(who offer critiques of dependency theory), the empirical papers
avoid the concept of "development." If we take these studies as
representative of recent work in "development anthropology," then
this discrepancy is as surprising as would be that of a volume on
kinship in which "kinship" were absent.

I suggest here that those anthropologists who have carried
out the best studies in "development anthropology" find the
concept of "development" particularly inappropriate for thinking
through their results. They therefore turn either to other social
theories, or to a rejection of research and theory itself for the
role of the (oddly named) "practicing anthropologist." In short,
"development" as a heuristic tool has led anthropologists to ask
important questions (as is evidenced in the essays here), but, at
the same time, has not provided them with a theoretical framework
appropriate to their object. In this concluding essay I shall
review the implicit meanings associated with the concept of
"development," and the contributions to anthropology made by our
authors.

Metaphors and images of "development" have shaped social
thinking in the West at least since Aristotle's evolutionary
derivation of the state out of the family and the village ("and
the nature of a thing is its end" Politics 1252:32; see also
Nisbet 1969). Development has been thought of as unfolding, the
yielding of full fruit from an initial kernel, and the
teleological tending of an object to its true end. Development
implies an internal propulsion, a pre-constructed path, and an
end-point--the "developed" state. The metaphor works best for
those areas of study that accept all three of these implications.
Developmental psychology, for example, in Piagetian and other
formulations, assumes an object, the child, who develops into an
adult along a tightly-wired set of stages, each with a clear
behavioral index. Because anthropologists do not, by and large,
assume that current social changes have such a path or goal they

have not formulated an anthropological theory of development or a developmental anthropology.

The theories of development that the anthropologist encounters and sometimes appropriates have been formulated by those social scientists whose paradigms tend toward the universal and the replicable: economists, political scientists, sociologists, and social psychologists (Bernstein 1973 and Seligson 1984 are useful readers). Although anthropologists have written about social change since their evolutionist beginnings, the fieldworking anthropologist starts from his or her experienced particulars and is wary of venturing too far from them. We base our theories, and to some extent our convictions, in what Clifford Geertz (1983) has called the "local knowledge" that we encounter. From this perspective, "development" appears as local struggles for control of land and water, changing and challenged interpretations of rights, duties, and authority, and the appearance of outsiders who seek to implement "planned change" (see Bennett's essay). We tend to consider, first and foremost, the implications of national and international plans to "develop" a society for the people who are supposed to be the subject of the verb.

Not that anthropologists have failed to make use of general theories of development. For the most part, they have borrowed elements of development theories that could be translated into hypotheses about social behavior and cultural orientations. In the immediate post-war years, the anthropologically relevant view of development involved a combined socioeconomic and sociopsychological approach to history. The economic foundation was W. W. Rostow's (1960) theory of "stages of economic growth" with its famous "take-off" point. Despite a series of critiques of the model by economists (e.g., Kuznets 1971), Rostow's model provided an economic starting-point for anthropologists working in the early 1960s on the sociological preconditions for economic growth (e.g., Geertz 1963a). The most comprehensive sociological theory of economic transformation was provided by Neil Smelser on the basis of his study of the English cotton industry during the Industrial Revolution (1958). Drawing on Emile Durkheim's (1984 (1893)) theory of the effects of industrialization on the forms of social solidarity, Smelser (1963) pointed to the emergence of separate, functionally distinct socioeconomic units (the firm, the family, the school) out of earlier multifunctional units (the working-educating family) as the social key to industrial change (1963). Smelser has labeled this process "structural differentiation." Few anthropologists sought to test Smelser's theory directly, but it provided an influential framework for subsequent studies of industrial change (Bellah 1957; see Long 1977).

A sociopsychological alternative theory of development was influenced by Max Weber's study of the "spirit" of European capitalism (1958 (1904-05)), and focussed on the motivations and orientations that make "take-off" possible. David McClelland (1961) suggested that a need for achievement (formulated as "n-achievement") regularly appears prior to a "take-off." W. E. Moore (1963) attempted a more general formulation, based on Weber, of the sociopsychological preconditions for industrialization, emphasizing a rationalist cultural orientation. Weber's isolation of this-wordly asceticism as a fundamental motivation historically for industrial development led a number of anthropologists to consider other instances of a similar psychological drive (e.g., Geertz 1963a) or functional equivalents of asceticism in other sociocultural systems (e.g., Bellah 1957). This approach is often referred to as "modernization theory."

In the 1950s and 1960s both theories of development and empirical anthropological research looked for endogenous sources of social and cultural change. However, in the 1970s and 1980s attention has turned to exogenous sources of political and economic pressure (see also Bennett's essay). The new attention to imposed development has come in two, related forms. Several Latin American economists and sociologists have viewed development as the creation of relations of dependency between the developed countries and their suppliers of raw materials. Andre Gunder Frank called this process the "development of underdevelopment" (1969). A number of anthropologists working in Latin America have sought to refine the concept of dependency, and, in particular, to explore the complex relations among sectors within and across national boundaries (e.g., Orlove 1977; Smith 1978).

Anthropologists also have turned to the nation-state context in which development takes place. From the perspective of the nation-state as a major initiator of development (along with international agencies and major donor nations), development appears not as a process, but as things done by some people to other people in particular relations of power. From this point of view, the powerful metaphorical implications of "development" as an endogenously activated process impede the anthropological understanding of current events. Here stand the majority of the contributors to this volume. In their essays, these authors depict people engaged in a variety of multi-level sociocultural processes: villagers contesting with each other over the proper attitude to take toward their landowning patrons, farmers deciding on crop strategies against ever-shifting relationships of price and supply, bureaucrats at various levels implementing plans that "mutate" (the winning phrase reported by Koenig) continuously from their inception. These actors are caught up in--and, to a certain extent, create--complex and often contradictory pressures and demands.

In their emphases on hierarchy, the heterogeneity of social and cultural systems, and processual aspects of culture, anthropological studies of development in the 1980s conjoin a broad, current theoretical turn toward "practice" (Bourdieu 1977; Ortner 1984) and "process" (Moore 1986) with the emphasis on studying large-scale systems in regions (Smith 1976), the nation (Anderson 1983), and the historical development of the "world system" (Wallerstein 1974; Wolf 1982). But the best of these studies have been cultural as well as politico-economic in their approach: they have studied the phenomena at hand from the actor's point of view as well as from that of the system. James Scott (1986), studying recent economic changes in a Malaysian village, presents the "offstage" challenges of the poor to the system that they cannot safely challenge directly. Richard Salisbury's paper (this volume) shows how Quebec Cree understand the payments they receive from the government in terms of reciprocity and the remuneration due the Cree hunter. Stephen Gudeman's work (1978) links the economic concepts of Panamanian farmers to the changes in opportunities occurring around them. All these studies combine analysis of external, impinging political and economic forces with the elucidation of changing local interpretations of these forces.

The best of the anthropological work on "development," then, is in fact simply good anthropology of a particularly inclusive sort, in which external processes and pressures are brought together with local interpretations of these events. That most of the contributors to this volume wrote their essays either as the result of work on a development project or as a contribution to a conference on development (or, in most cases, both) has led some of them to comment on the concept (in most cases, without attempting to define it). As has been the case with anthropologists generally, the contributors to this volume use the term in one of four ways. The first, most common use is in the sense of economic development, interpreted in one of several possible ways (raising GNP, raising incomes, changing production patterns, etc., see Scherr, Adams, Pinkerton). A second, more specific use of the term is to refer to projects carried out by governments or, more often, by development agencies. In this sense, interventions in the name of development are ipso facto considered as development, without necessarily being directed toward raising production or incomes (see Scudder, Koenig). In a third sense anthropologists use the term with explicit or implicit quotation marks. Adams refers to development itself as an "illusion of progress" (see also Schneider, Bates). Finally, some authors use "development" to refer to the increasing interdependence of local communities within larger-scale institutions and forces (see Adams, Schneider, Despres, Salisbury; see also Long 1977).

"Development" has provided some anthropologists with the practical opportunity, perhaps the interest, and a loose rubric for the study of the control and direction of economic change by governments and agencies. The category has provided an avenue for looking outward from the single village, and both backward and forward from the "ethnographic present." The price of adopting the category has been to reject (or, most commonly, to ignore) its metaphorical roots and unidirectional tendencies. Many anthropologists, including some of the contributors to this book, have "studied development" without wishing to accept that what they saw was "development" in any of the meanings that the term has gained in our own intellectual history. Thus, for intellectual as well as professional reasons, the alienation of the "development anthropologist" that Bennett describes in his essay. But also, I think, some fine contributions to our understanding of how people engaged in multi-level processes of economic change and political control interpret their experience. In what follows, I suggest three such contributions made by the papers in this volume.

The Control and Meaning of Distribution Networks

Central to many government efforts to control production has been the establishment of hierarchies of distribution, trade, and purchasing, which both regulate local activities through control of prices or the distribution of scarce goods (water, fertilizer, seeds) and reinforce state control over society. Two such hierarchies are of great importance in efforts to increase incomes or production: agricultural marketing networks and irrigation systems. In both cases a technical fact (the concentration of population in cities, the concentration of water in rivers, springs, and lakes) becomes a political, economic, and cultural fact: the control of resources and the problem of their just repartition in society.

The relative merits of private and public mechanisms for purchasing and sale of food crops has become a major issue in studies of African production. Although the current literature (e.g., Bates 1981) emphasizes the problems caused by government regulation of prices through marketing boards, Mahir Saul turns to the inefficiencies in the private trading networks in one African nation, Burkina Faso. Saul points out that previous discussions of trading networks have taken for granted an ideal model of the private trader, who collects small amounts of grains, gradually "bulks" them as he moves up the ladder of aggregation, moves grain along lines of least transportation cost, and sells to the next highest level up. In fact, traders in Burkina Faso depended on networks of personal ties for their access both to capital and to stocks of grain, particularly sorghum, for purchase. The personal networks and shortages of capital led traders to bulk and debulk as they sold upward to buyers who had varying amounts of capital themselves, to sell in circuitous routes (a practice that raises the price of grains), and to sell rather than store. Because buyers need personal ties in order to find grain, small-scale traders could compete successfully with the big-city buyers in the villages. However, these small traders were chronically short of capital, and tended to sell their grain quickly, leaving rural areas short of grain for the rainy season. If a local trader did have the capital to hold on to grain into the rainy season, he would often hold back his reserves until rural grain prices had risen well above those demanded in the cities. Saul points out that villagers would benefit from any efforts to help them to stock grains locally.

Saul's analysis remains relatively external to the strategies and interpretations of villagers. Constance McCorkle, however, examines the culture of grain sales in Burkina Faso. For the producers in the Bwa area, the primary choice in the allocation of labor and land was between sorghum and cotton. The government has promoted cotton production through guaranteeing swift and sure payment for all cotton grown. McCorkle's informants contrasted the dependable provisioning and purchasing by the state with the "negative reciprocity" practiced by private grain traders. As cotton production has increased, cereal production has declined, creating regional food deficiencies. McCorkle attends particularly to the response of Bwa villagers to the changing cereal/cotton balance. Villagers were acutely aware of the need to maintain a balance between the social importance of sorghum and the hard necessity of its sale. On the one hand, sorghum is needed to make beer (the social lubricant of Bwa life), to feed livestock, to pay tribute payments to chiefs, and to give gifts to relatives and trading partners. Grain reserves magically prevent future failures, and tithes make one's grains religiously clean: in both cases one's own grain must be used. The association of material continuity of a primary foodstuff and spiritual continuity of nourishment is common in many places (in Indonesia, it is linked to the idea that the soul of rice lives from one rice cycle to the next because one year's harvest is the next year's seed). It is an association that is threatened by either agricultural intensification programs (in which new seed must be purchased each year to avoid reversion to type) or programs that encourage the monoculture of export crops.

On the other hand, sorghum is sold to obtain needed cash reserves. The increasingly precarious balance between local production levels and local consumption needs has made it increasingly important that the wrong kind of grain sales be prevented. In the area studied by McCorkle, villagers had formulated what the author calls a "cereal code of honor" to maintain a balance between culturally prescribed uses and economically attractive sales. Large-scale sales were disapproved of, but sales of "surplus" to the village cooperative were valued, and sales during the rainy season to less fortunate villagers were honorable. From McCorkle's description we can formulate six types of sales in decreasing order of "honor":

1) no sales of grain, rather, gifts to the needy.
2) sales to the needy long after the harvest.
3) no sales but also no gifts.
4) sales of grain shortly after the harvest.
5) purchases of grain in the rainy season, a sign of improvidence.
6) advance sales of grain yet to be harvested, carrying a high rate of interest.

McCorkle's analysis is a fine sketch of a moral economy in flux. A case study of the 1983-84 grain harvest is an ironic case in point: farmers turned to growing more cotton so as to avoid having to sell grain and thus to behave more "honorably." However, this strategy had negative system-wide consequences, as it led to a grain shortage. The following year farmers returned in greater numbers to cereal cultivation.

In her study of food strategies among poor residents of Manila, Susan Russell describes the tension between government attempts to control through centralized food shops, and the diversity and flexibility guaranteed by the use of multiple sources of food. Poor urban consumers obtained food by choosing between a number of alternative plans: purchasing during the day for convenience from legal sellers or at night at slightly lower prices from illegally-stationed wholesalers, buying better or poorer quality foods, trading distance (and hence time) for price, or preparation time for the marginally higher cost of buying prepared foods. These responses were partially shaped by government restrictions on the time and place of sales, but the urban poor perceived their strategies as their own, in contrast to the food supermarkets (called Kadiwa centers) established by the government.

The Manila poor saw certain technical deficiencies in the Kadiwa centers (they were located at some distance and the food was of uncertain quality) and advantages in the local diversified marketing strategy (personal networks among traders and consumers offered stability and security). But popular reactions to the supermarkets were not based on cost considerations alone; the

417

government supermarkets were political symbols as well as food sources. The technical inferiorities of the supermarkets became the ideological raw material for their rejection as exemplars of the Marcos government's manipulation of food and patronage. They were frequent targets for bombings during the 1986 revolution.

The Burkina Faso and Manila situations are quite different, of course. In the former, villagers identified the sales behavior of fellow villagers as the source of local food supply problems (although private traders were the objects of criticism; one would like to know more about villagers' attitudes toward different purchasing hierarchies). In the latter, urban poor identified the government as the source of repression and attempts at cooptation. But the tension between central and local control, and the formulation of the problem as more than just a technical one, bring the two cases together.

The problems presented by irrigation systems are similar: central control versus local demands for flexibility and fine-tuning. And, again, this technical problem is also a cultural and political one. Anthropologists have been debating the relation between the control of water and the origins of power at least since Karl Wittfogel (1957) suggested that the control of irrigation systems was the natural basis for the rise of an "Asiatic Despotism." Both Edmund Leach, in his study of a Ceylon water system (1961), and Clifford Geertz, in his work on irrigation in Java and Bali (1963b, 1972), sought to show that irrigation systems were culturally specific, local adaptive systems, in which both power and meaning were not predetermined by supposedly general characteristics of irrigation. In different settings, the village, the temple, or the state might exercise control of social life by way of an irrigation system.

The articles by David Freeman and Walter Coward examine, not external sources of validation (the state or temple), but the issues of control and rights that arise from the workings of irrigation systems themselves. Freeman contrasts the expertise of "main system" operators, who learn general principles for dealing with "lumpy" collective goods, with that of water users (here, farmers), who deal with the local problems of different soil types and fast-changing weather patterns. Main system operators are rewarded with raises or promotions for keeping water flowing smoothly through the system and for their attention to its "main tendencies," while farmers are rewarded with a good crop for achieving precise control of water flow and for their attention to the unique and changing conditions of particular fields. The power to control water locally can become a valuable resource in its own right. In the Pakistan case mentioned by Freeman, tubewell water was more valuable than irrigation system water, not because of a difference in the water itself, but because the

418

supply of tubewell water could be better controlled by the farmer. As Freeman points out, improvement of local control is particularly necessary for the use of high-yielding varieties of grains, which are more sensitive to variations in water supply.

So far, a technical problem. But Coward shows how it is also the basis for the local formulation of concepts of "property" and "control," and for resistance to attempts by government agencies to regulate these systems. Freeman's is a bureaucratic point of view--incorporate knowledgeable local people into the bureaucracy and achieve a better fit between the two ends of the system. Coward writes from the positions of particular (Thai, Ilocos, Sumatran) farmers who have come to consider rights to land and water as originating from and dependent on the collective production and preservation of a fine-tuned community water system. Within the local "underlying property grids" the state has no claims on water or land. Coward's case of passive resistance in Sumatra might be supplemented by cases elsewhere in Indonesia (e.g., in South Sulawesi) where the Indonesian bureaucracy continues to encounter resistance from local irrigation groups over the right to allocate water. The control of water may be the basis for political control, but it may be equally well the grounds for resisting control. Attempts to assert control over resources, defined more broadly, is a second topic covered by the contributors.

The Definition and Control of Property

Although the efforts by local communities to assert control over their means of production within an established political structure are sometimes reclassified as "development from below," they usually stem from resistance to particular forms of political control from above. They also involve the rethinking of central cultural categories by which control is defined: gender, property, and authority. By studying the debates over the control and meaning of property, we are able to observe changes in those general assumptions that James Scott (1976) has termed the "moral economy of the peasant."

Mary Crain documents how assumptions and concepts of justice, property, and labor in a Quimsa community in highland Ecuador were slowly changing within the context of a national struggle over the distribution of land. The workers and former workers on the local hacienda gathered on several occasions during Crain's stay to discuss the allocation of land under a new land-reform measure. Crain describes multiple claims to land, conflicting principles of distribution (on the basis of need, a "subsistence ethic," versus equal shares for all) and a debate between

419

proponents of two interpretations of property rights and obligations. Advocates of one position, based in the multi-stranded ties between patrons and clients, argued that the former hacienda workers "cannot betray the patron." Those favoring the second, based in a nation-wide idea that everyone has the right to own a parcel of land, objected that owners had become obliged to provide a plot of land for those people who worked for them. Both the national government, through its Agricultural Aid office, and the anthropologist played roles in peasant mobilization. Crain makes explicit her own public stand in favor of community solidarity and the expansion of the land base. While Crain focusses on the dilemma of the peasant, caught between conflicting loyalties and fears, Sara Berry, in her analysis of gender and investment decisions in West Africa, provides a fine-grained examination of a changing and contested "property system." Berry's initial question was: if cocoa trees are the clearly attractive investment that they are, why do women not invest their resources in them more often? To answer she first asked how control of "property" was exercised. She found that, in principle, trees belonged to those who planted them, not to the owners of the land on which they were planted. However, labor on the trees builds up a claim over time, such that a sharecropper or a relative could contest an allocation of ownership on the basis of his or her investment of labor. This provision has been used by owners to skew the eventual inheritance of the trees in the direction of a favored son or nephew, and to attract and retain the services of sharecroppers. To further complicate the situation, men or women who have planted trees often found their claims contested if they were migrants to the area. Berry concludes that "whether or not former laborers assert claims to tree crop farms often appears to depend more on changing economic and political conditions than on the original terms of the labor contract," and that, therefore, "contracts are at most only partial determinants of social outcomes." Berry's essay continues the anthropological insistence that contracts are themselves social facts (Durkheim 1984 (1893)), and are continually subject to renegotiation (Moore 1986).

The association of labor with property rights did not benefit wives, however, because labor contributed by wives to their husbands' plots was considered to be part of their obligations as wives, and generated neither a property right nor a category of joint property. Because women were less able to mobilize labor on a non-paying base than were men (who could call on subordinate kin and on their wives to work for free), women found it more difficult than men to obtain the capital with which to cultivate tree crops. Berry shows how key cultural categories shape relations of power and possibilities of production.

The papers by Crain, Berry, and Coward exemplify the contrasting roles property systems play in Latin American, African, and Asian societies. Each paper isolates a key point of tension within the social system. Crain describes the historically deep-seated moral and economic ties between the hacienda owners and their laborers: land reform runs up against the moral authority of the owner (see also Bruce et al. in this volume). Berry shows how the separate and asymmetric rights and obligations of husbands and wives shape expanding commercial agriculture in West Africa. By contrast, in many Indonesian property systems households control property jointly, often as units within larger property-owning groups. Tensions over property frequently involve the conflicting claims of the household and these larger-scale lineage or village groups. Property is based on such collective categories as the labor invested in irrigation (Coward this volume), the lineage system, or the joint household.

Both Evelyn Pinkerton and Richard Salisbury describe efforts by local communities to construct new middle-level organizations for the internal regulation of production and the guarantee of autonomy vis-a-vis the nation. In both cases the concept of property has been a central cultural feature of the reorganization effort. Pinkerton studied the fishing cooperatives created by Neets Bay fishermen in Alaska and by the Lummi tribe in Washington State. The problem was the technical one posed by common property systems: how to prevent the overuse and exhaustion of resources. The solutions have been of two types: the individuation of property rights, or the creation of a management structure for common property. Her paper is a description of several variations on the second theme. Pinkerton stays close to the organizational issues, suggesting (and, one would hope, leading to a full demonstration elsewhere) that cooperative management has led fishermen to develop new social relations and ideas of property.

Salisbury deftly combines an account of how the Quebec Cree have taken control of their own territory with an analysis of how they view their actions in Cree terms. Protests over the planned construction of a hydro-electric project in Cree territory led in 1975, with the participation of Salisbury and others, to the creation of the Cree Regional Authority. The Authority is staffed by Cree and uses government funds to subsidize winter hunting expenses and promote local development. Salisbury provides an economic assessment of the benefits of the intervention and, most unusual, a cultural assessment as well. The Cree view the subsidization of hunting as "a fair return for the most skilled and respected Cree job, that of the productive hunter." The intervention has stalled the previously sharply felt pressures on the Cree to leave hunting and enter the wage economy. It did not "fuel development," but it preserved autonomy by making a culturally valued occupation economically viable within the context of national economic change. The renewed strength of Cree activities has also strengthened Cree practices of reciprocity and helped to prevent the emergence of marked class differences. Worthy of note is the fact that the new system works only because Cree hunters are able to trade meat to wage earners for goods and services, the sale of wild game being illegal. The combination of state regulations, development plans, and local mobilization has thus led, ironically, to the creation of a barter economy.

The Reproduction and Recreation of Society

The assertion of control over distributed resources and local property is made sharply difficult for communities when they migrate, or are migrated, and must recreate a sense of shared destiny anew. Anthropologists recently have turned to the study of the creation and transformation of culture, traditions, and forms of community on local and national levels. Some of the essays in this volume address this issue within the context of internal migrations and state-directed change.

In his comparative study of social reproduction in frontier communities in the United States and the Amazon, Emilio Moran argues that migration to the frontier, far from promoting an egalitarian social order, has led to the recreation of socioeconomic differences in the new setting. Migrants brought with them cultural knowledge that was ill-suited for the new environmental conditions they faced. They also lacked sufficient capital for investment in farm enterprises, and could obtain relatively high wages for off-farm work. Frontier settlers therefore have looked upon farm land as a source of subsistence and as an object of speculation, but not as an object of investment. Stephen Gudeman, in his comment on Moran, notes that "the set of notions concerning rugged individualism and human equality are not, as Turner might have claimed, a result of the impact of nature within culture, but part of the model that humans within a certain economy bring to their activities upon nature." However, the individuals filling positions in that model are those who have taken advantage of the frontier to assert their authority, often on the basis of their relatively early arrival, a process also noted by Berry for Ghana. The models of frontier settlement appear to be of wider importance than once sought: recent work in African history (e.g., Kopytoff 1987) suggests that the perceptions and processes were often those of frontier settlement.

422

Moran and Gudeman's observations might also be applied to such resettlement programs as Indonesia's _transmigrasi_ and Tanzania's _ujamaa_ program (Hyden 1980; Galaty this volume). In the Indonesian case, Javanese farmers accustomed to cultivating rice on small, well-irrigated terraced plots have been moved to newly-cleared primary forest sections of the "outer islands." While many have attempted to adapt to their new settings, their agricultural knowledge has been out of tune with the new environment, where slash-and-burn techniques with long fallow periods would be necessary to creating a new viable farming system (but ends by destroying much of the land). Furthermore, in many of the new environments, it has become impossible for the settlers to reproduce the culturally satisfying densely-packed living arrangements of their home villages. Many, dissatisfied with the new settlements, have moved to nearby cities or to overcrowded Jakarta. Meanwhile, an additional amount of primary forest has been devastated. According to a recent memo from a group of environmental scientists to the World Bank, 300,000 transmigrants currently occupy "economically marginal and deteriorating" settlements, with plans to clear 3.3 million hectares of primary forest by the end of the decade (Transmigration Memo 1986).

John Galaty reports on the differential impact of Tanzania's villagization program on two of its peoples, the Sukuma agro-pastoralists and Maasai pastoralists. Long migrations to new pasture areas have been made possible by drugs that reduce the effect of tsetse-carried diseases. Trains and roads also make rapid travel possible. However, although the Sukuma have moved south in large numbers, the Maasai have not. Galaty analyzes the implications of specializing in pastoralism versus combining pastoralism with agricultural activities. In particular, villagization has meant that once-dispersed populations now live in smaller village settlements. Finding a balance between grazing cattle and not exhausting the pasture forces herders to travel much longer distances than before resettlement. The opportunity cost of the extra time required for grazing is much higher for the Sukuma, who would use that time for farming, than for the primarily pastoralist Maasai. The Maasai have struck a balance more easily than have the Sukuma; the latter, finding their current pasture insufficient, have responded by migrating south in large numbers.

As did the frontier settlers studied by Moran, Masaai and Sukuma have tried to reproduce their socioeconomic systems in the new conditions of settlement, leading in turn to differential degrees of adaptability and differential attitudes toward further migration. Resettlement policy and the technological advances in transportation and medicine have reshaped the socioeconomic differences between the two populations.

Leo Despres's research concerns a true "development frontier," that of the free-trade city of Manaus, Brazil. Despres also is one of the few authors represented here to address explicitly a current theory of development, namely the "marginality thesis" associated with the dependency school. This thesis predicts that high-capital industries in developing countries will exclude a large share of the work force from the production side of their activities, because of their capital-heavy industrial strategy, and also from the consumption side, because the workers are not able to purchase any of the goods they produce.

Whereas this theory assumes that causality stems from the center, Despres looks at things from the vantage point of Manaus workers, many of whom have intentionally avoided the formal sector because of its hard working conditions and low rates of pay. For most workers, self-employment is more stable and better-paid than is work in either the electronics and other assemblage plants (which employ urban female workers) or the firms that process local products or raw materials (which employ rural male workers). Self-employment in small shops or trade also provides a form of cross-generational social reproduction, in that children often succeed to the trade of their parents. Despres documents how workers are able to control their economic activities more than is envisaged in current models of dependent development.

Both Russell and Despres analyze social relations among the urban poor, but reach opposite conclusions. Russell emphasizes the intricate web of personal ties through which Manila poor obtain their food; Despres, however, found few enduring social networks in the urban communities of Manaus, nor did he see a sense of class solidarity growing out of the workplace. However, many of the residents of Manaus were recent migrants, and, during the period of Despres's fieldwork, Manaus society may have been in a period of transition toward more well-established forms of urban sociability.

The Struggle for Meaning and Control

We can now better understand the paradox cited in the beginning: that anthropologists writing ostensibly on development in fact carry out their analyses without using the concept. The reason is that anthropologists have come to understand socioeconomic change in terms of culturally-mediated struggles between actors engaged in particular productive pursuits and possessing differential degrees of power. There is little room in these analyses for the historical privilege given in mainstream theories of development to the nation-state, to "modern" ways of thought, and to a linear conception of change. But, as Bennett notes in his opening essay, it is precisely these "macro" ideas to which post-war societies, "developed" and "developing," have given pride of place. Economists and other macro-oriented social scientists, not anthropologists, have found their disciplines most in tune with these conceptions of reality. Economists deal in nation-state units; they can compare them and prescribe such development medicine as setting fuel prices at appropriate levels and devising appropriate tax policies. Such measures are formulated in acultural terms. Taken together, they define the path of development.

Anthropologists who take the opportunity to work in development projects or consulting programs are supplied with the correct macro-concepts and asked to fill in the squares. Some anthropologists have struggled to effect changes in particular practices within the economistic context, as in the case of the pressure placed on the World Bank to formulate a policy regarding the rights of tribal peoples. But the guiding category of "development" is not easily subject to anthropological reformulation, because its assumptions--that there is a path, that some kind of development is a good thing, that developers and the developed world will recognize such good things--are not generally acceptable to anthropologists.

What the anthropologist does do, and do much better than the high-flying development experts, is to study how, in a particular place and time, people experience the projects and plans that are decided on elsewhere. They can do so in a way that may be heard and understood by the economists and bureaucrats who meet in the capital cities if they attempt to link up local knowledge with the supra-local institutions, forces, and distributions that the development experts understand. This effort has at least three implications for the kind of work that anthropologists do: it must be comparative, it must include the study of the institutions that link local to national levels, and it must expand to include processes of--at least--medium (rather than the favored longue) term.

The validity of the anthropological enterprise has rested, to a great extent, on a particular part-for-whole relationship: the small community standing for the larger culture, society, or nation. We come to understand a great deal about a small place, and find that, indeed, we can thereby say something about a particular people. However, when studying the effects of development projects on a complex nation, ceteris becomes somewhat less than paribus. Differences in ecology, resources, religious orientation, markets, land tenure patterns, and local-level politics mean that what one anthropologist observes

425

in one village may not say a lot about what other anthropologists, working in other villages, might find. Must we then abandon the possibility of commenting on national development schemes?

Sara Scherr, herself an economist, suggests (this volume) one way in which an anthropologist might plan fieldwork so as to be able to confront the economist on his or her own terms. Scherr urges anthropologists to select study sites with comparisons in mind. She provides a case study in local-level fieldwork that was able to answer a macro-question: why household farmers' responses to the Mexican oil-fed boom of the 1970s were not as expected (production rose, rather than fell, despite high non-farm wages). Scherr selected both the site and crops to be studied with this macro-problem in mind. She found four different "production cultures," each with its own evaluations of the relative desirability of different kinds of work, and with its own estimations of the trade-offs among profit, total returns to the household, and income security. Scherr was able to build a complex model of price response out of her data. Differences between the disciplines emerge even in Scherr's case: an anthropologist might have analyzed to a greater extent the four contrasting "production cultures." But her essay suggests one of several possible comparative strategies.

Scherr's study was of a process of change in prices and production levels, not of a program. As Robert Bates suggests (this volume), the involvement of some anthropologists in development projects has given them an opportunity to study both the organizations that endeavor to implement policies and the cultural assumptions behind development policies. Delores Koenig writes about the continual process of negotiation that characterizes the "implementation" of USAID development projects. Koenig's essay is particularly promising in her attention to the various actors in this process of negotiation. John Bruce and his colleagues similarly focus on local, multi-level political processes in their review of the research and consulting activities of the Land Tenure Center. Their essay is particularly useful for the detailed case studies it provides in the politics of land reform.

These kinds of research emphases should lead to increased anthropological study of agencies and bureaucrats, whether local or foreign, as "development brokers." Some advance has already been made in the anthropological study of bureaucracy (e.g., Britan and Cohen 1980), and Koenig mentions several investigations of U.S. development bureaucracy. These studies tend to be single-agency, however, rather than inclusive of the many institutions that affect the outcome of a particular program. If we are to study governmental attempts to incorporate communities into larger-scale economic systems, then we must study the total range of people who carry out those attempts, including judges, heads of cooperatives, and district officials as well as self-identified "development agents." Such studies are not easy. Between 1981 and 1983 I participated in an inter-disciplinary study of the impacts of Indonesian government development programs in four provinces of that country. The study was to be comparative, and to include the implementing structure itself. The methodology had three analytic components: the anthropological study of village socioeconomic changes, the economic study of costs and benefits at the national and local levels, and the sociological study of how programs were implemented from the center (Jakarta), through provincial, regency, and sub-district levels, down to the village. The last of the three projected studies was the most difficult, because, to be done well, it had to be anthropological in method, comparative in scope, and extremely sensitive to the subject matter. We learned quite a lot about how different the "same" program could be in different parts of the country, but we learned little of a systematic nature about the sociocultural organization of the bureaucracy. Such a study will require the long-term cooperation of Indonesian and foreign anthropologists and other social scientists.

The final desideratum for anthropological studies of development is the adoption of a processual perspective, along with, ideally, longitudinal research methodologies. The central question to be asked is, of course, what changes in local control or welfare result from particular interventions carried out in the name of development. The development agent is neither inclined nor practically capable of answering that question. His or her efforts are successful if the project is completed on time, even if, as was noted in a footnote to a final report on a project in Indonesia, "all the ducks died." The time perspective of the development agent is inherently restricted to the length of time necessary to complete the project. As S. J. Tambiah recently remarked, this is why "prospective feasibility reports will take precedence over postmortem evaluation reports, and why the historian-anthropologist might write the best sociology of development" (1985:351). Yet, to do so, anthropologists will need to set up studies with processes in mind, as suggested recently by Sally Falk Moore (1987). In the short term, these studies would focus on disputes and events that are diagnostic of changes in categories, orientations, and practices. In the medium term, they would track changes in welfare and employment, as well as in the less measurable attitudes and emotions expressed. As Salisbury's essay in this volume shows, from the perspective of community, the difference between autonomy and dependency is ultimately to be sought in the degree of control exercised by a people over their own resources and activities.

427

Here, perhaps, the anthropologist needs to exercise his or her own need for semantic empowerment. One may be working as a "development anthropologist" for an agency or government, but at the same time studying processes, differences, and institutions as an anthropologist tout court. As the essays collected here demonstrate, doing what we do well, understanding how people act on the bases of their local, changing understandings and powers, has the best chance of both accurately representing local views to a wider, powerful audience, and contributing to the anthropological study of the changing world.

References Cited

Anderson, Benedict. 1983. Imagined Communities: Reflections on the Origin and Spread of Nationalism. London: Verso.

Bates, Robert H. 1981. Markets and States in Tropical Africa. Berkeley: University of California Press.

Bellah, Robert N. 1957 Tokugawa Religion. Glencoe, Ill.: Free Press.

Bernstein, Henry, ed. 1973. Underdevelopment and Development: The Third World Today. London: Penguin.

Bourdieu, Pierre. 1977. Outline of a Theory of Practice. Cambridge: Cambridge University Press.

Britan, Gerald M. and Ronald Cohen. 1980. Hierarchy & Society. Philadelphia: ISHI.

Dalton, George, ed. 1971. Economic Development and Social Change. Garden City, N.Y.: Natural History Press.

Durkheim, Emile. 1984. The Division of Labor in Society. W. D. Halls, trans. New York: Free Press. Originally published 1893.

Frank, Andre Gunder. 1969. The Development of Underdevelopment. In: Latin America: Underdevelopment or Revolution? Pp. 3-17. New York: Monthly Review Press.

Geertz, Clifford. 1963a. Peddlers and Princes: Social Development and Economic Change in Two Indonesian Towns. Chicago: University of Chicago Press.

------- 1963b. Agricultural Involution: The Process of Ecological Change in Indonesia. Berkeley: University of California Press.

------- 1972. The Wet and the Dry: Traditional Irrigation in Bali and Morocco. Human Ecology 1:23-39.

------- 1983. Local Knowledge: Fact and Law in Comparative Perspective. In: Local Knowledge. Pp. 167-234. New York: Basic Books.

Gudeman, Stephen. 1978. The Demise of a Rural Economy: From Subsistence to Capitalism in a Latin American Village. London: Routledge & Kegan Paul.

Hyden, Goren. 1980. Beyond Ujamaa in Tanzania: Underdevelopment and an Uncaptured Peasantry. Berkeley: University of California Press.

Kuznets, Simon. 1971. Notes on Stage of Economic Growth as a System Determinant. In: A. Eckstein, ed. Comparison of Economic Systems. Berkeley: University of California Press.

Leach, Edmund. 1961. Pul Eliya: A Village in Ceylon. Cambridge: Cambridge University Press.

Long, Norman. 1977. An Introduction to the Sociology of Rural Development. Boulder: Westview.

McClelland, David C. 1961. The Achieving Society. Princeton: Van Nostrand.

Moore, Sally Falk. 1986. Social Facts and Fabrications: "Customary Law" on Kilimanjaro, 1880-1980. Cambridge: Cambridge University Press.

------- 1987. Explaining the Present: Theoretical Dilemmas in Processual Ethnography. Distinguished Lecture at the annual meeting of the American Ethnological Society, San Antonio.

Moore, W.E. 1963. Social Change. Englewood Cliffs, N.J.: Prentice Hall.

Nisbet, Robert A. 1969. Social Change and History: Aspects of the Western Theory of Development. Oxford: Oxford University Press.

Orlove, Benjamin S. 1977. Alpacas, Sheep, and Men: The Wool Export Economy and Regional Society in Southern Peru. New York: Academic Press.

Ortner Sherry B. 1984. Theory in Anthropology since the Sixties. Comparative Studies in Society and History 26:126-166.

Rosen, Lawrence. 1978. Law and Social Change in the New Nations. Comparative Studies in Society and History 20(1):3-28.

Rostow, W.W. 1960. The Stages of Economic Growth. Cambridge: Cambridge University Press.

Scott, James C. 1976. The Moral Economy of the Peasant: Rebellion and Subsistence in Southeast Asia. New Haven: Yale University Press.

------- 1986. Weapons of the Weak: Everyday Forms of Peasant Resistance. New Haven: Yale University Press.

Seligson, Mitchell A. 1984. The Gap Between Rich and Poor: Contending Perspectives on the Political Economy of Development. Boulder: Westview.

Smelser, Neil J. 1958. Social Change in the Industrial Revolution. London: Routledge & Kegan Paul.

------- 1963. Mechanisms of Change and Adjustment to Change. In: B.F. Hoselitz and W.E. Moore, eds., Industrialization and Society. Pp. 32-54. Paris: Mouton.

Smith, Carol A., ed. 1976. Regional Analysis. Volumes 1 and 2. New York: Academic Press.

------- 1978. Beyond Dependency-Theory: National and Regional Patterns of Underdevelopment in Guatemala. American Ethnologist 5:574-617.

Tambiah, Stanley Jeyaraja. 1985. Culture, Thought, and Social

Action: An Anthropological Perspective. Cambridge: Harvard University Press.

Transmigration Memo. 1986. Adverse Environmental and Socio-Cultural Impacts of World Bank Financed Transmigration under Repelita IV. Memo to World Bank, reprinted in Indonesia Reports 19:2-15.

Wallerstein, Immanuel. 1974. The Modern World System. New York: Academic Press.

Weber, Max. 1958. The Protestant Ethic and the Spirit of Capitalism. Talcott Parsons, trans. New York: Scribner. Originally published 1904-05.

Wittfogel, Karl. 1957. Oriental Despotism. New Haven: Yale University Press.

Wolf, Eric R. 1982. Europe and the People without History. Berkeley: University of California Press.

NOTES ON CONTRIBUTORS

RICHARD N. ADAMS (Ph.D., Yale University, 1951) is Rapoport Centennial Professor of Liberal Arts, Professor of Anthropology, and Director of the Institute of Latin American Studies, at the University of Texas at Austin, He has done fieldwork in Peru and Central America, and has continuing theoretical interests in complex societies and energy theory in social analysis.

ROBERT BATES (Ph.D., Massachusetts Institute of Technology, 1969) is Henry R. Luce Professor of Political Science at Duke University. A political scientist with a deep interest in economics and anthropology, he has published several books on the development of agrarian Africa.

JOHN W. BENNETT (Ph.D., University of Chicago, 1946) is Distinguished Anthropologist in Residence at Washington University in St. Louis. Specializing in ecological and agrarian development problems, Dr. Bennett's long-term research activities have centered on agricultural development, ecology, and social adaptation in the North American West. He has also done research in Japanese society and modernization processes, African pastoralism, and is currently doing research on European settlement of North America. Dr. Bennett has served as President of the American Ethnological Society and of the Society for Applied Anthropology.

SARA S. BERRY (Ph.D., University of Michigan, 1967) is Professor of Economics and History at Boston University. She has done field research in western Nigeria and published books and articles on rural development and economic history in Nigeria and in sub-Saharan Africa.

JOHN R. BOWEN (Ph.D., University of Chicago, 1984) is Assistant Professor of Anthropology at Washington University in St. Louis. He has carried out research in Sumatra and Sulawesi (Indonesia) on social and political history, oral traditions, Islam, and economic change. Currently he is completing a book on changes in poetics, representations of history, and sociopolitical structure in Gayo society of northern Sumatra.

JOHN W. BRUCE (S.J.D., University of Wisconsin, 1976) is Director of the Land Tenure Center at the University of Wisconsin-Madison. A lawyer who has specialized in customary land law and land tenure reform in Africa, he has directed the Center's Africa Program since 1982. He has spent extended periods in Ethiopia with Peace Corps and USAID (1968-74) and in Sudan with the Ford Foundation (1975-80).

C. WALTER COWARD, JR. (Ph.D., Iowa State University, 1969) is

431

Professor of Asian Studies, International Agriculture, and Rural Sociology, Cornell University. For the past decade his research has focused on the organizational and institutional aspects of irrigated agriculture in Asia.

MARY M. CRAIN (Ph.D., University of Texas at Austin, 1987) is affiliated with the Department of Anthropology at the Universitat de Barcelona in Spain. She has conducted research on agrarian class relations in the northern highlands of Ecuador, focusing on peasant politics, ritual, and ideology.

LEO A. DESPRES (Ph.D., The Ohio State University, 1960) is Professor of Anthropology at the University of Notre Dame. He has done extensive research on political economy and ethnicity in Guyana, and has published several articles and books on this topic. In 1984, and again in 1986, he conducted research on the industrialization, culture, and domestic economy of working-class populations in three regions of Brazil.

DAVID M. FREEMAN (PH.D., University of Denver, 1968) is Professor and Chair of Sociology at Colorado State University in Fort Collins. His research has focused on problems of technology assessment, social conflict, natural resources, and irrigation organization, with special emphasis on the Western States and South Asia.

JOHN G. GALATY (Ph.D., University of Chicago, 1977) is Associate Professor of Anthropology and Associate Dean of the Graduate Faculty at McGill University. He is interested in pastoralist societies and development, and since 1974 has carried out research among the Maasai of East Africa.

STEPHEN F. GUIDEMAN (Ph.D.k, Cambridge University, 1970) is Professor and Chair of Anthropology at the University of Minnesota. He has done fieldwork among peasants in Panama and Colombia, with his research interests concentrated on household economies, kinship, and religion.

DON KANEL (Ph.D., University of Wisconsin, 1954) is Professor of Agricultural Economics at the University of Wisconsin-Madison, and is former Director of the Land Tenure Center (1967 and 1976-80). His research interests center in land tenure, economic development of agriculture, and institutional economics.

DOLORES KOENIG (Ph.D., Northwestern University, 1977) is Assistant Professor of Anthropology at The American University. Although her primary interest is in the changing forms of agricultural production in Africa, she has worked on a variety of development projects, ranging from renewable energy to resettlement and women in development.

STEVEN W. LAWRY (Ph.D. candidate, Land Resources, Institute for Environmental Studies, University of Wisconsin) has worked on land management problems in Botswana (1975-79) and the Sudan (1981) and has carried out research on grazing associations in Lesotho (1984-86). He has been associated with the Land Tenure Center since 1980. His research focuses on relations between land tenure and natural resource management in Sub-Saharan Africa.

CONSTANCE M. McCORKLE (Ph.D., Stanford University, 1983) is Research Assistant Professor in the Department of Rural Sociology at the University of Missouri-Columbia. An anthropologist specializing in agricultural development in Africa and Latin America, her research interests and publications focus on farming systems, indigenous knowledge and resource management systems, appropriate technology, policy analysis, and the social sciences' role in international research and development.

EMILIO F. MORAN (Ph.D., University of Florida, 1975) is Professor and Chair of the Department of Anthropology and Professor in the School for Public and Environmental Affairs at Indiana University. Professor Moran is a specialist in ecological anthropology, agricultural development, and tropical agriculture. His books include Developing the Amazon (1981), The Dilemma of Amazonian Development (1983), Human Adaptabililty (1982), and The Ecosystem Concept in Anthropology (1984). He serves on the Advisory Board of the International Union of Biological Sciences' Tropical Soil Biology and Fertility Programme, in charge of incorporating socioeconomic considerations in soil biological and fertility studies at twelve sites worldwide.

EVELYN PINKERTON (Ph.D., Brandeis, 1981) is Research Associate at the School of Community and Regional Planning of the University of British Columbia. She is currently editing a book on fisheries co-management in North America. She is actively involved with British Columbia's fishing communities and with anthropological, biological, and planning specialilsts in an attempt to initiate action research leading to the institution of a fisheries co-management pilot project in British Columbia. Pinkerton is most interested in working with people toward discovering and creating the institutional arrangements most appropriate for both expressing their traditions and allowing them to exercise some control over local resource development within the post-modern industrial state.

JAMES C. RIDDELL (Ph.D., University of Oregon, 1970) is a member of the faculty of the Land Tenure Center and African Studies at the University of Wisconsin-Madison and the Department of Anthropology at the University of Wisconsin-Oshkosh. His research interests and publications have focused on resource control in rural Africa.

SUSAN D. RUSSELL (Ph.D., University of Illinois at Urbana-Champaign, 1983) is Assistant Professor of Anthropology at Northern Illinois University in DeKalb. Her research interests have focused on marketing and political economy in the Luzon highlands of the Philippines. From 1983 to 1985, she was a Rockefeller Foundation Research Fellow and Visiting Professor at the School of Economics, University of the Philippines, Diliman, Quezon City.

RICHARD F. SALISBURY (Ph.D., Australilan National University, 1957) is Dean of the Faculty of Arts and former Director of the Anthropology of Development Program at McGill University. His research on economics in New Guinea and the Caribbean, starting in 1952, has alternated since 1971 with impact assessment and consulting work, in relation to various mining and hydro projects in Northern Canada.

MAHIR SAUL (Ph.D., Indiana University, 1982) is Assistant Professor of Anthropology at the University of Illinois at Urbana-Champaign. He has carried out research in Burkina Faso, among the Mossi and Bisa in 1978-79 and among the Bobo in 1983-84. He also visted the country as a consultant. He has published articles on farm organization, gender relations, trade, and land tenure.

SARA J. SCHERR (Ph.D., Cornell University, 1983) is Agricultural Economist for the International Council for Research in Agroforestry in Nairobi, Kenya. Her research has focused on river basin development in tropical Mexico, agricultural development in petroleum-exporting regions, and agroforestry development in tropical Africa.

HAROLD K. SCHNEIDER (Ph.D., Northwestern University, 1953) was Professor of Anthropology at Indiana University until his death in May 1987. He worked extensively in the field of pastoralist economics. His books include The Wahi Wanyaturu: Economics in African Society (1970), Livestock and Equality in East Africa (1979), The Africans (1981), and, perhaps most widely known, Economic Man (1974). The first President of the Society for Economic Anthropology (1980-1982), Professor Schneider also served as President of the Central States Anthropological Society for 1966 and as Associate Editor of the American Ethnologist from 1980 to 1984.

THAYER SCUDDER (Ph.D., Harvard University, 1960) is Professor of Anthropology at the California Institute of Technology and Director of the Institute for Development Anthropology. He has

434

done intensive fieldwork over the past thirty years in the Middle Zambezi Valley along with surveys in other river basins in Africa, Asia, and the Middle East. His special interests include long-term community studies, land settlement, and river basin development.

J. DAVID STANFIELD (Ph.D., Michigan State University, 1969) is Latin American Program Coordinator for the Land Tenure Center at the University of Wisconsin-Madison. He is a rural sociologist who has conducted research on agrarian land tenure issues in various Latin American and Caribbean countries.

GREGORY F. TRUEX (Ph.D., University of California, Irvine, 1973) is Professor of Anthropology at California State University, Northridge. He has done research on Zapotec Indians of Oaxaca, Mexico, for twenty years. He has also carried out research in Ensenada, Baja California, Mexico. Among his recent research interests has been the impact of property crimes, including fraud and deceit, on rural and urban Mexican household economies.

INDEX OF MAJOR TOPICS BY CHAPTER NUMBER

437